Proclivity to Genocide

Proclivity to Genocide

Northern Nigeria Ethno-Religious Conflict, 1966 to Present

Grace O. Okoye

LEXINGTON BOOKS
Lanham • Boulder • New York • London

Published by Lexington Books
An imprint of The Rowman & Littlefield Publishing Group, Inc.
4501 Forbes Boulevard, Suite 200, Lanham, Maryland 20706
www.rowman.com

16 Carlisle Street, London W1D 3BT, United Kingdom

Copyright © 2014 by Lexington Books

All rights reserved. No part of this book may be reproduced in any form or by any electronic or mechanical means, including information storage and retrieval systems, without written permission from the publisher, except by a reviewer who may quote passages in a review.

British Library Cataloguing in Publication Information Available

Library of Congress Cataloging-in-Publication Data

Okoye, Grace O., author.
 Proclivity to genocide : northern Nigeria ethno-religious conflict, 1966-present / Grace O. Okoye.
  pages cm.
 Includes bibliographical references and index.
 ISBN 978-0-7391-9116-3 (cloth : alk. paper) -- ISBN 978-0-7391-9117-0 (electronic)
 1. Genocide--Social aspects--Nigeria, Northern. 2. Ethnic conflict--Nigeria, Northern. 3. Ethnic conflict--Religious aspects. 4. Nigeria, Northern--Ethnic relations. I. Title.
 DT515.42.O428 2014
 304.66309669--dc23
 2014022572

∞ ™ The paper used in this publication meets the minimum requirements of American National Standard for Information Sciences Permanence of Paper for Printed Library Materials, ANSI/NISO Z39.48-1992.

Printed in the United States of America

Contents

List of Tables	vii
List of Figures	ix
Acknowledgments	xi
Introduction	xiii

Part I: Genocidal Underpinnings and Genesis of Northern Nigeria Ethno-Religious Conflict

1	Historical Background to Northern Nigeria Ethno-Religious Conflict	3
2	Understanding the Conceptual Framework of Genocide	19
3	Theoretical Framework of Nigeria's Ethno-Religious Conflict	71

Part II: Identifying and Establishing Proclivity to Genocide

4	Presenting the Model for Proclivity to Genocide	101
5	Proclivity to Genocide in Northern Nigeria Phase I: 1966 to 1976	115
6	Proclivity to Genocide in Northern Nigeria Phase II: 1976 to 1987	133
7	Proclivity to Genocide in Northern Nigeria Phase III: 1987 to 1996	147
8	Proclivity to Genocide in Northern Nigeria Phase IV: 1996 to 2005	159
9	Proclivity to Genocide in Northern Nigeria Phase V: 2006 to Present	173
10	Bases of Proclivity to Genocide in Northern Nigeria	189
11	Religious Underpinnings in Nigeria's Ethno-Religious Conflict	207

Part III: Resolution Considerations

12	Challenges, Prospects, and Prescriptive Recommendations	223

Appendixes	229

Maps of Nigeria	231
Selected Cases of Religious Crises in Northern Nigeria from 1980 to 2009	239
References	247
Index	261
About the Author	275

List of Tables

Table 4.1	Contexts for the Northern Nigeria Ethno-Religious Conflict	108
Table 4.2	Contexts for (i) Biafra War and (ii) Reprisals in Southern States and/or Extrajudicial Killings**	110
Table 12.1	Selected Cases of Religious Crises in Northern Nigeria from 1980 to 2009.	240

List of Figures

Fig 4.1	Theoretical Model for Proclivity to Genocide	105
Fig 10.1	Schematic Model of the Northern Nigeria Ethno-Religious Conflict	205
Map 1	Nigerian Administrative Borders: Regions in 1966 and States in 2010 to Present	232
Map 2	Twelve States of Nigeria: 1967 to 1976	232
Map 3	Nineteen States of Nigeria: 1976 to 1987	233
Map 4	Twenty One States of Nigeria: 1987 to 1991	234
Map 5	Thirty States of Nigeria: 1991 to 1996	235
Map 6	Sharia Operative States in Northern Nigeria: 1999 to Present	236

Acknowledgments

I owe an immense debt of gratitude to so many, too numerous to mention, whose help in many diverse ways has been crucial to this book. I am particularly grateful to the following people for their contributions to my knowledge and inspiration and other help in creating this book: Jason Campbell, Dustin Berna, Michelle Rice, and Neil Katz. I also acknowledge the following people and organizations for their contributions to this book: Adam Jones, Elizabeth Kendal, Toyin Falola, Eghosa Osaghae, the International Crisis Group, *Newswatch Magazine*, the Christian Solidarity Network, and so many others, whose resources I drew on in completing this book. To my friends and colleagues, T.Y. Okosun, Richard Toumey, Kjell Olsson, Edmund Abaka, and others, who encouraged and spurred me on, as well as to everyone, mentioned or unmentioned, who without their contributions and support this book would not have been written, I personally say, thank you. My biggest gratitude goes to Peter Okoye, my husband, for his unwavering support and encouragement. To him, to my children, Suzylene, Providence, Victory, Confidence, and Faithful, to my mother, Christiana, and above all, to Jehovah-Shalom, the God of peace, I dedicate this book.

Introduction

Nigeria, as a nation-state, has since its 1960 independence been inundated by a myriad of complex problems involving different variables and stakeholders, as a result of which the country has experienced economic downturn, political upheavals, coup d'états and countercoups, civil war, and a deluge of ethno-religious conflicts (Williams, 2011). As a regional giant subsumed by political instability, organized and pervasive crime influences, prodigious corruption, and a climate of entrenched ethno-religious violence, states in the neighboring West Africa region could be affected by the internal religious politics in Nigeria (Chalk, 2004). The country's entrenched sociopolitical, socioeconomic, and socioreligious crises have continued to manifest in an avalanche of exterminations and mass killings involving national, regional, or intergroup ethnic and religious-based conflicts. Most of these conflicts have predominated in northern Nigeria, with the Middle Belt region, primarily Jos in Plateau State (Ostien, 2009), and such other cities as Kano in Kano State (John, Mohammed, Pinto, and Nkanta, 2007), Kaduna in Kaduna State (Aliyu, 2009; Kazah-Toure and Human Rights Monitor, 2003), and Maiduguri in Borno state (Aliyu, 2009), being the major conflict zones where mass killings and exterminations have persisted sporadically for decades, primarily between Muslims and Christians or non-Muslims (Ibrahim, 1989, 1991; Osaghae, 1998a; Ostien, 2009) and Bauchi in Bauchi State, etc., where mass killings and exterminations have also been persisting sporadically for decades, between the two groups.

Accordingly, Nigeria's first ethno-religious conflict occurred in 1953 even prior to independence, with such conflicts recognized to have further occurred in 1966, also in the 1980s in 1980 and 1985, in the 1990s in 1995 and 1999, and in the last decade in 2001 and 2004. More so, the phenomena of ethno-religious conflicts have become a regular feature in the Northern region since 1987 to the present, with such states as Kano, Kaduna, Bauchi, Plateau, and Taraba observed as most offending. Reportedly, thousands of lives were lost from 1987 to 2004, with billions of Naira worth of property destroyed (Ahiante, 2004), and from 1999 to 2006 over 11,000 people died in the region between 1999 and 2006, from ethnic, religious, and political violence (Williams, 2011, p. 44).

These problems have been viewed from different perspectives, with several studies linking the prevalence of these conflicts in northern Nigeria to a myriad of factors including, economic factors such as resource allocation inequity, poverty, retarded development and indigene-settler issues (Harnischfeger, 2004; Osaghae, 1995; Ostien, 2009), while others point to political factors and unbridled power tussles (Ukiwo, 2003). Some of these studies have also identified religious factors and politicization of religion (Ibrahim, 1989, 1991; Osaghae, 1998a; Suberu, 2009; Williams, 2011), as well as ethnicity factors and colonialism's amalgamating of various ethnic groups (Aguwa, 1997) as leading to Nigeria's high ethnocentric politics (Anthony, 2002; Osaghae, 1998a). Still others point to Islamic fundamentalism as undergirding the waves of killings in northern Nigeria (Chalk, 2004; Harnischfeger, 2004). Kukah and Falola (1996) present Islam's political impact in Nigeria, primarily in the north where Islam predominates, which, based on the region's vast Muslim population, the Muslim world perceives Nigeria as a key member, with Islam's politicization impact further compounded by its ideology of non-separation of religion from politics. Harnischfeger (2004) identifies Islamists redefinition of the *demos* entitled to rule with the enforcement of Sharia law which is based on the Muslims' exclusionary ideology in Sharia operational states against non-Muslims (p. 431).

In the article, "Northern Nigeria: Background to the Conflict," the International Crisis Group observes, for instance, that a myriad of complex and interlocking factors undergirds the ethno-religious conflict in northern Nigeria, "including a volatile mix of historical grievances, political manipulation and ethnic and religious rivalries" (2010, p. 1). The International Crisis Group report, though focused on the twelve states of the north that have adopted the Sharia law (see map VI in appendix A) on the basis of their uniqueness in some aspects of the conflict, it also focuses on their similarity in such other aspects as the Muslim Christian tensions or the skirmishes involving land use, which apply to all Nigerian states, and it is thus, applicable to the entire northern states, which is the thrust of this study.

However, while different perspectives—including economic, political, cultural, ethnic, and religious factors, among others—have been, and are being used to explain the conflict, following the Sharia law institution as penal code in twelve out of the nineteen northern states since 1999, more than 50,000 people have been killed in religious violence in northern Nigeria (Christian Solidarity Worldwide [CSW], n.d.). Thus, gruesome killings have continued to take place in northern Nigeria, and according to Ibrahim (1989), an incursion has occurred between Christians and Muslims with extensive loss of life and destruction of property for which researchers have identified several causation factors. And while the Sharia-adopted region may have historically shown ample capacity for peaceful coexistence between its religious and ethnic communities, conflicts between Muslims and Christians have been predominant in the entire northern states. While also both religions' adherents might have generally coexisted peacefully in various areas of the north, there is the aggravation of long-existing tensions, particularly between Islamic groups and Christian groups with the Sharia's reintroduction, as a result of which, hundreds or even thousands were killed as in the Kaduna in February/March 2000 crisis for instance (Angerbrandt, 2011; International Crisis Group, 2010). There are also other dimensions of conflicts between disparate Islamic sects, between Islamic groups that are anti-establishment and security forces or the Nigerian state, and lately, between long-established indigenous communities and settler groups, which, framed by competition for communally based distribution of public resources, are widespread in the country.

Accordingly, while acknowledging such common factors of "political manipulation of religion and ethnicity and disputes between . . . local groups and 'settlers' over distribution of resources . . . failure of the state to assure public order . . . [e]conomic decline and absence of employment opportunities" amidst growing inequality as fueling conflict across Nigeria, the International Crisis Group (2010) observes that, "there is also a specifically northern element. A thread of rejectionist thinking runs through northern Nigerian history, according to which collaboration with secular authorities is illegitimate. [And] . . . calls for an 'Islamic state' in Nigeria . . . demonstrate that many in the far north express political and social dissatisfaction through greater adherence to Islam and increasingly look to the religious canon for solutions to multiple problems in their lives" (p. ii).

Thus, while a confluence of causes ranging from economic, political, religious, cultural, and ethnic, among others, have been identified as undergirding the waves of killings in northern Nigeria, there is no significant understanding of whether there are genocidal inclinations to the killings, nor the extent to which the interplay of religion and ethnicity helps to foment and escalate the conflict, which are the thrusts of this study.

UNDERLYING FACTORS INFLUENCING THE STUDY

The episodic gruesome killings in northern Nigeria have persisted and remained unabated for decades up to the present. The non-abating nature of these atrocious killings has framed my thoughts, namely, that there are other underpinning factors to them. The motivation for this study is rooted in a dire need to raise awareness on the gruesomeness of the ongoing carnages, with an unflinching desire for efforts to be mobilized toward putting an end to such intermittent atrocities. This desire derives from my own family experiences encountered during the 1966 pogrom which was directed primarily against the Igbos in northern Nigeria. Many of my personal relations were killed in the pogrom. My parents, then living in Malumfashi, Katsina State in the North, lost all of their wealth through looting and arson, only narrowly escaping with their lives. The carnages have unfortunately continued unabated since then even while sporadically occurring. Such history of systematically targeting a victim group(s), who more often than not are Christians or non-Muslims, by the perpetrator group(s), who usually are extremist Muslims, continues to be played out in northern Nigeria today (Chalk, 2004; Harnischfeger, 2004; Ibrahim 1989, 1991; Ostien, 2009). These insights have birthed in me the desire to investigate the northern Nigeria conflict, involving an in-depth analysis of such conflict cases in northern Nigeria spanning from the 1966 crisis to the present in order to explore the plausibility of genocidal inclinations to the conflict.

Situated in the sub-Saharan, West African region, Nigeria at independence in 1960 was made up of four regions—Northern, Western, Eastern, and Mid-Western (see map 1 in appendix A)—a structure that was changed in 1967 with the creation of twelve new states which replaced the regions (see map 2 in appendix A). Prior to the 1967 new states creation, northern Nigeria, which is the focus of this study, spanned more than half of the country extending up to the area now known as the Middle Belt including Abuja and Jos, and covering the whole of the former Northern region under the colonial powers (see map 1 delineating the Old Northern region up to its southern part in appendix A). The resulting breakup of the country led to the division of the Northern region into six states out of twelve states nationally in 1967, and these were subsequently further broken up into nineteen northern states out of thirty-six states nationally in 1996.

Nigeria is also politically zoned into six "geo-political zones" which include "the north west; north east; north central; south west; south east; and south south," the grouping of which, while not referring to administrative entities, form the country's geo-political zoning for its federal employment allocation (International Crisis Group, 2010, p. 1). However, the expansion of the country's federal administrative units to thirty-six states by 1996 altered the relationship between majority and minority groupings, particularly fracturing and eroding the major ethnic groups' dominance over minority groups. And while this majority eroding process in the far north did not lead to a shift to the minority overtaking the majority holding in any state, it rather undercut the Hausa-Fulani vision of regional unity, and in Kaduna particularly, it also reduced the power of the Hausa-Fulani dominance over the minority population (International Crisis Group, 2010). Nigeria is, thus, roughly split between a mostly Muslim north and a predominantly Christian south, with a Middle Belt or central region that has a near Christian and Muslim balancing, with each of the regions incorporating some minority traditionalists (Osaghae, 1998a).

This book which is based on my dissertation titled, "Ethno-Religious Conflict in Northern Nigeria: The Latency of Episodic Genocide," completed in my doctoral degree program at Nova Southeastern University, explores the ethnic and religious dimensions of the continuing northern Nigeria gruesome killings to determine whether there are genocidal inclinations to the episodic killings. For instance, "between 1966 and 1970, a genocide-in-part occurred in Nigeria, following the U.N. definition" (Melson 1996, p. 163). As defined by the United Nations Convention on the Prevention and Punishment of Genocide, the crime of genocide constitutes such acts in which patterns of religious, racial, or ethnic massacres have a solid indication of genocidal intent (Hinton, 2002; Jones, 2006). In analyzing the commonalities between the partial genocide that occurred in Bosnia and the Armenian genocide, for instance, the Serbian nationalists just as the Young Turks, and the Croat to some extent, are also imagining a large state which would comprise their people while excluding other national and ethnic groups. Thus, the Bosnian Muslims, like the Armenians as an ethno-religious community with claims to land, are being driven out and massacred by Croatian and Serbian nationalist movements seeking to destroy their culture, to "cleanse" their presence from the area, and to appropriate their lands (Melson, 1996, p. 166). Hence, the Nigerian derivative that is being played out in northern Nigeria today involves *extremist Muslims* intent to "cleanse" the north of *Christians and other non-Muslims* through the "exclusionary ideology" of imposition of the Sharia law (Harnischfeger, 2004) to "force assimilation" or "extermination" (Campbell, 2010, Video Series 30; Harnischfeger, 2004) through massacres and genocidal killings of those who refuse to assimilate or adopt the Muslim ideology (Harnischfeger, 2004; Melson, 1996; Stuijt, 2009).

To contextualize the study within an African setting, I examined data sources from 197 newspaper articles on the ethno-religious conflict in northern Nigeria which were collected from different databases and various newspapers' websites, to explore the plausibility of genocidal inclinations to the conflict. The study period spanning from the 1966 northern Nigeria massacres of thousands of Igbos up to the present, ongoing killings between extremist Muslims and Christians or non-Muslims in the region, is classified into five phases of 1966 to 1976; 1976 to 1987; 1987 to 1996; 1996 to 2005; and 2006 to present, delineated on the basis of operative regional or states creation structure in the country over the period. The approach I adopted in writing this book is to establish similarity of genocidal patterns to the northern Nigeria ethno-religious conflict by examining genocidal occurrences and massacres in history, particularly the twentieth century deluge to contemporary genocides for an understanding of genocide.

I adopted a conceptual framework for my analysis, of identifying genocidal intent in the various manifestations and causes of genocide in specific genocide cases. The study structures a theoretical model for determining proclivity to genocide, and establishes that genocidal inclination or the intent to exterminate the "other" on the basis of religion and/ or ethnicity underlies most of the northern Nigeria episodic but protracted killings. My analysis and approach is grounded in identifiable and provable evidences of specific intent to annihilate the "other" involving *extremist Muslims'* intent to "cleanse" northern Nigeria of *Christians and other non-Muslims* through the "exclusionary ideology" of imposition of the Sharia law, and to "force assimilation" or "extermination" through massacres and genocidal killings of those who refuse to assimilate or adopt the Muslim ideology. The study also suggests that there is latency in the recognition of these genocidal manifestations due to their episodic nature and intermittency of occurrence, and explores measures to forestall and prevent further conflict escalation.

ORGANIZATION OF THE BOOK

The book is delineated into three parts. Part I: Genocidal Underpinnings and Genesis of Northern Nigeria Ethno-Religious Conflict, begins with chapter 1 and explores the historical background to the northern Nigeria ethno-religious conflict in two sections. The first covers the precolonial and colonial northern Nigeria to Independence, and the second outlines the North from independence to present. Chapter 2 examines the conceptual framework for understanding genocide. Chapter 3 examines the theoretical framework of Nigeria's ethno-religious conflict. Part II: Identifying and Establishing Proclivity to Genocide in the Northern Nigeria Ethno-Religious Conflict begins with chapter 4, which presents the *Genocide Proclivity Model* developed in the study. Chapters 5–9 presents the Model's application to each of the study's Phases I–V data, and identity proclivity to genocide in the northern Nigeria ethno-religious conflict in each phase. Chapter 10 presents the bases of proclivity to genocide in northern Nigeria. Chapter 11 establishes the religious underpinnings and antecedents of Nigeria's ethno-religious conflict. In Part III: Resolution Considerations, Chapter 12 outlines challenges and prospects for settlement and proffers recommendations for conflict resolution and measures for genocide prevention and intervention to avert further escalations of the conflict, and the orchestration of a full blown genocide in northern Nigeria.

Part I

Genocidal Underpinnings and Genesis of Northern Nigeria Ethno-Religious Conflict

ONE

Historical Background to Northern Nigeria Ethno-Religious Conflict

To examine the ethno-religious conflict in northern Nigeria, it is necessary to understand the historical background of the region's ethnic and religious societies. It is also essential to understand the North's Sokoto Caliphate center-periphery model, which has profoundly impacted community relations and discussions on religion's position in the politics of the region (International Crisis Group, 2010).

NORTHERN NIGERIA: PRECOLONIAL AND COLONIAL TO INDEPENDENCE

Home to several ethnic and religious communities, northern Nigeria is primarily rural, while also including, historically such key urban centers as Sokoto, Kano, Kaduna, Zaria and Maiduguri, which for centuries have been eminent Islamic world centers of learning (International Crisis Group, 2010). The Hausa, Fulani, and the Kanuri are the predominant groups in the region, all three of which are primarily Muslim, in addition to other smaller groups of about 160 in number, many of which are Christians or animists. There is a Muslim majority in most of the far northern states which in such states as Sokoto and Borno are overwhelming, but also with other states such as Kaduna and Jos being more mixed. The delineations crystallized into majority and minority groupings since the early 1900s British colonization, with its complexity further compounded by the substantial, mainly Christian southern migrants to the region. Other than the northeast, which is dominated by the Kanuri, the Hausa and Fulani predominate across most of the region and are reflective of its political and numerical hegemony (International Crisis Group, 2010). However,

> [n]either the Hausa nor the Fulani is a rigid lineage group—one can become Hausa by adoption or conversion to Islam, although in doing so one enters at the bottom rung of a highly stratified society. As large Islamized ethnic groups closely associated with the nineteenth-century Sokoto Caliphate, the Hausa and Fulani are often seen as dominant in the region and grouped together as a single Hausa-Fulani group. This is encouraged by Nigeria's politics of communal rivalry and to some degree reflects their own political strategies. However, Hausa and Fulani are distinguishable in terms of names and languages and consider themselves distinct. While nearly all Fulani in the region speak Hausa, the region's lingua franca, not all Hausa speak Fulani. (International Crisis Group, 2010, p. 2)

The region's earliest peoples comprised several smaller groupings organized in community-based or autonomous polities, most with state structures which are merely rudimentary with neither imperial rulers nor expansionist ambitions. The Hausa, a self-identifying group formed partly in-situ as well as from migrations, emerged in the twelfth century, and in the absence of forming a unified empire due to internal rivalries, "established seven major city-states and seven other associated-states—collectively now known as Hausaland" which extend into present-day Niger Republic (International Crisis Group, 2010, p. 2). These states had by the thirteenth century gained much control over the region and incorporated different smaller groups into Hausa-speaking multiethnic polities (Falola and Heaton, 2008; International Crisis Group, 2010). By the seventeenth century the Hausa Empire flourished, significantly controlling the trans-Saharan trade in slaves, gold, and salt. The Hausa had in this precolonial era established commercial and social linkages in the presently known northern Nigeria, up to the Senegal valley far west, and as far east as the Arabian Peninsula (Falola and Heaton, 2008).

The Kanuri who originated, on the other hand, from the Kanem Empire emerged in the ninth century in southwest, present-day Chad, and migrated toward Lake Chad, subdued the locals, and by the eleventh century established the Borno Kingdom separate from the Hausa states, becoming in the northeast the largest ethnic group through inter-marriage and assimilation of the locals. The Fulani migrated in the thirteenth century from present-day Senegal through the empires of Mali and Songhai to Hausaland, and in the fifteenth century to Borno mainly as nomadic herdsmen, with their scholars gradually gaining influences with the Hausa nobles through appointments in Hausa royal households as scribes, advisers, tax collectors, and judges (International Crisis Group, 2010). Both the Hausa as well as the Borno kingdoms were equally prominently engaged in the trans-Saharan trade, as people and goods traversed the north-south desert routes, linking societies of sub-Saharan Africa with North Africa as well as Europe, with the fourteenth to the sixteenth centuries observed as the trans-Saharan trade "golden age" during which, slaves and gold were mostly traded (Falola and Heaton, 2008, p. 245). Relationships were established between the Borno and Kannem-Borno kingdoms and the Hausa states, with Borno and the north Africa Maghrib states having long-drawn commercial ties through their trans-Saharan trade engagement, with the back and forth movement of people and goods creating mutual commercial exchanges and relationships. Islam was, thus, brought to both Hausa and Borno states between the eleventh and the fourteenth centuries through these trade routes (Falola and Heaton, 2008, p. 246).

The spread of Islam, commerce, slavery, and war shaped the initial interactions besides the early settlements and migrations, with many states waging wars for expansion of territorial claims and acquiring slaves for export to North Africa or to work the feudal plantations. The major interactions that occurred through the spread of Islam took place in two phases—its peaceful introduction by Arab and North African merchants and clerics through West Africa from the eleventh to the seventeenth century. The Borno Empire rulers converted first in the eleventh century and were followed by the Hausa kings from the fourteenth to the fifteenth centuries through interactions of Mali scholars and traders across the Songhai Empire, with Mali Muslim scholars already occupying key administrative positions in Hausa city-states by the fourteenth century (International Crisis Group, 2010). Islam's second spread phase was the early nineteenth century Shehu Usman dan Fodio, a Fulani preacher's led revivalist revolution jihad to purify the region's Islamic practices and subsequently install righteous leadership. The missionary activities benefited Dan Fodio who drew large discipleship crowds. Criticizing the state, he swayed many toward identifying with his new societal vision by emphasizing the maltreatment of the poor by the Hausa kings who were pagans and lived grandiosely without practicing the Islamic law. Constituting an alternate center of power, Dan Fodio's jihad, which started in 1804, proved successful, with a resultant emergence of a Fulani aristocracy that presided over a caliphate and which was a federation spanning many emirates (Kukah and Falola, 1996). The jihad invaded and subdued the fourteen Hausa city-states from 1804 to 1808, aided by Fulani nomads and Hausa peasants dissatisfied with their kings' corruption and nepotism, and installed Fulani emirs to replace their chiefs. Though partially conquered by the new regime from 1808–1812, only Borno was not fully subdued by the Sokoto Caliphate (International Crisis Group, 2010).

Thus, formed between 1804 and 1808, the Sokoto Caliphate "is a reference point for many in the region . . . [and] a source of great pride" (International Crisis Group, 2010, p. i). Deriving cohesion from Islam, its empire comprised autonomous emirates with separate emirs and administration, and the Sokoto-based caliph at the head doubling up as spiritual guide and political leader. Retaining the feudal pre-jihad system, the caliphate had the Hausa aristocracy replaced with Fulani royal families, with tithes paid to the emirs by the communities and tribute paid to the caliph by the emirs. Islamic practices and values were entrenched in the region by the Fulani rulers (2010), though with the populace's passive resistance at times, in order to foster an ethnicity transcending common culture to hold the caliphate together. Accordingly,

> Sharia was applied "more widely, and in some respects more rigidly ... than anywhere else outside Saudi Arabia," and indigenous religious practices, such as traditional Hausa ceremonies (*Bori*), were suppressed, or at least became less visible. However, the Fulani rulers also assimilated many elements of Hausa culture, thus creating the basis for what some see as a progressively homogeneous Hausa-Fulani identity ... [T]he caliphate also promoted a culture of "knowledge and intellectualism," such that "education became the yardstick for all opportunities in the state and knowledge a ladder for climbing heights of respect and dignity." (International Crisis Group, 2010, p. 3)

Under this *Shari'a* recognition, a relationship developed between the emirs and the sultan. The caliphate in its first formation, however, was not like the jihadists anticipated, being plagued by such disturbing features as slave raiding, unjust practices including the corruption of the judiciary, and power rivalry (Kukah and Falola, 1996). It was, thus, far from ideal as a kingdom as "[r]esistance to Fulani rule, including resistance from Fulani nobles who felt excluded from emerging power structures, and more general insecurity, especially along its periphery, continued throughout the nineteenth century" (International Crisis Group, 2010, p. 3). Hence, while Islam aided the consolidation of political rule, it simultaneously inspired revolts especially among those suffering intensive taxation, with several communities devastated by the nineteenth century, ending by revolts arising from grievances on economic and religious doctrinal differences. Still, haunting relations between the smaller plundered groups and the Fulani are the memories of the emirates warriors' raids and looting of such periphery regions then considered heathen territory, to capture slaves for the caliphate's plantation. The caliphate's late years witnessed rising tensions between the Sufi two major brotherhoods (Tariqa)—the Tijaniyya and the Qadiriyya—which, presenting from the fifteenth century in the region, became the caliphate's dominant/official order. The Tijaniyya, with its bureaucratic and rich traders social base, grew more popular in the nineteenth century and in time was linked with resistance to the region's ruling aristocracies, and in particular, to Sokoto (Loimeier as cited in International Crisis Group, 2010).

With the advent of colonization in the late nineteenth century, the Europeans were recognized to have arbitrarily drawn Nigeria's present-day borders in the 1884/85 Berlin Conference in line with the United

Kingdom mutual agreements with Germany and France, as part of the colonization process for West Africa (Falola and Heaton, 2008). These borders were not linked to any preexisting ecological, geographical, or social boundaries as people, as well as goods, had in the precolonial days freely moved across those borders, forming historical and commercial linkages with other African societies. As the twentieth century approached, however, there had been a decline in the trans-Saharan trade to negligible levels due to the growing Atlantic coast trade with the Europeans which started in the sixteenth century, and which diminished the trans-Saharan route's significance. With colonialism and the delineation of Nigeria's official boundaries, therefore, there was an even greater difficulty in sustaining the trans-Saharan trade which had served to transfer people and goods across Nigerian territories (Falola and Heaton, 2008).

Colonialism ushered in the establishment of the protectorate of Southern Nigeria and the Lagos colony by the British government in the late nineteenth century, and this was followed by a northward extension in 1900 which also established the Northern Nigeria protectorate. Slowly negotiating for the acceptance of colonial rule with the northern emirs, Frederick Lugard, appointed as the Northern Nigeria High Commissioner, got cooperation from most kingdoms with internal dissent having weakened them already with the ending of the profiteering slave trade, while also defeating those that resisted, including Sokoto in 1903 (International Crisis Group, 2010). Thus, "[t]he killing of the fleeing Caliph Attahiru I, in July 1903, marked the end of the caliphate as a sovereign political formation" (2010, p. 4). However, there was a continued prominence of the caliphate in political and religious structures of the region, on which the International Crisis Group observes that,

> [t]he Sokoto Caliphate occupies an important, but ambivalent, position in the consciousness of Muslims in northern Nigeria. Its history is a source of pride, and its legacy gives a sense of community and cohesion . . . It has also left behind a structure of traditional governance, centered on the caliphate emirs and their inheritors . . .
>
> The fact that the caliphate continued to exist under British sovereignty for nearly 60 years has given its heritage much ambivalence. Equally, attitudes to the caliphate and its heritage differ greatly in different locations, following the center-periphery structure of the entity itself. Over the decades, it has become, in the eyes of many, the locus of a northern Muslim "establishment" that is vulnerable to accusations of selling out to non-Muslim outside powers and, more generally, of moral or material corruption. (2010, p. 4)

Thus, while the caliphate was put to an end by Europeans through colonization, with most of it becoming a portion of the colonial Nigeria, the Fulani aristocracy adopted a civil strategy in relating with the British, without adopting their Christian religion, and although some powers of the aristocracy were lost, its Islamic law system remained (Kukah and

Falola, 1996). The British colonial administration governed Nigeria by indirect rule from its 1900 proclamation to the country's 1960 independence, thus controlling the populace and raising revenue using local rulers under supervision of British officials. This involved reorganizing traditional local authorities and creating a local compliant power base to further British interests, while deposing resisting office holders. British indirect rule allowed traditional authorities, mostly the Sultan of Sokoto, to expand, though with such power subject to the British, and while colonial rule aimed to avert disrupting social structures in the region, its religion, and culture, it introduced crucial cultural, judicial, and political changes. The caliph's defeat and the establishment of a new capital for the region in Kaduna diminished the sultan's influence and authority, partially transferring the aristocratic power to an emergent political class, but retaining the sultan's spiritual leadership of the region's Muslims (International Crisis Group, 2010). Shortly prior to independence, fifty years later, concerns were turned toward the reformation of the legal system that would accommodate migrants and the interests of foreign investors, with the power transfer to Nigeria at the end of World War II finally providing the opportunity of using the caliphate's legacy "to build a strong political party based on Islam and ethnicity" (Kukah and Falola, 1996, p. 3).

Hence, although curtailing the emirs' powers through indirect rule, they were in contradistinction, relied on by colonial power for indirect rule, with significant consequences, as it worked effectively in emirates already relatively well established administratively but not in those without effective administrative systems, mainly due to minority group resistance. And, with indirect rule somewhat reinforcing emirate administration, several minority sectors became increasingly subordinate to the power of the emirate with no concern for their distinctive identities. Converting to Christianity was common with the minority or the non-Hausa-Fulani groups, frequently in response to their perception of the emirate administration's power. Thus,

> [t]hese smaller groups expressed fears of domination in a post-colonial Nigeria, but a 1958 commission largely dismissed their concerns. Nevertheless, colonial rule facilitated the domination of Hausa and Fulani elites, especially in areas that minority groups had historically considered their exclusive domains, and sowed the seeds for conflicting claims to political space, economic rights and societal values. (International Crisis Group, 2010, p. 5)

Although the Islamic law that the caliphate established was retained by the British, it was in time restricted to civil cases, while the applications of punishments such as lashings were also restricted, and subsequently, the Sharia's jurisdictional enforcement was scaled down to the native courts at the local level. The colonial period saw an imprecise labor division for Islamic judges, referred to as the *alkalis,* presiding over family matters, and the legal councils of the emirates who applied principles of common law to such issues as commercial property. There was a frequent application of the "Islamic principles of compensation for violence and murder" (International Crisis Group, 2010, p. 5). Sharia content was, however, expunged by the British in 1959, toward the end of colonial rule, on the basis "that some of its provisions were incompatible with the rights of all citizens in a religiously plural society" (p. 5). In the context of the *alkalis'* increasing political role against the emerging pro-independence parties and following the colonial government's mounted up pressure (Bello as cited in International Crisis Group, 2010), the region's government in compromise accepted the Penal Code, which established a Sharia appeal court applying solely to Muslim personal law in its jurisdiction. Several Muslim leaders in the region saw such changes as Christian jurisprudence being elevated over their Islamic legal heritage (Crisis Group Interview, as cited in International Crisis Group, 2010).

Western innovations were largely discouraged by the colonial administration, with Christian missionaries along with their schools only permitted in the defunct caliphate's non-Muslim fringes. By replacing the *ajami* with the Roman script for Hausa language writing, and establishing together with the Islamic system a European system of education, preexisting scholarship was much jeopardized with the cleric's status and that of the English unlettered diminished (Aliyu as cited in International Crisis Group, 2010, p. 5). There was, in time, a further sharpening of existing cleavages between the Hausa-Fulani Muslim and the smaller groups. More so, while most northern parts were shielded from missionary activities, education, and other Western influences by a pact signed between the Laggard administration and the northern emirs, a free rein of these Western influences was allowed in the south, which gave the southerners a head start in education as well as in political development (Osaghae, 1998b).

Furthermore, the demography and economy of the region was also altered by colonial developments. There was an influx of southern migrants in response to the emergent economic opportunities in Zaria, Kaduna, and Kano with the railway lines construction from Lagos to Kano from 1898 to 1912, and the 1914 Southern and Northern Nigeria protectorate's amalgamation. The North's Ibo presence has its origins with their thousands of rail lines workers from the 1910s to 1920s, increasing and becoming more permanent as British activities increased in the North based on "push" and "pull" migration factors (Anthony, 2002, p. 35). Such factors include an unprecedented pressure on the agricultural resource base in Igbo land with the increasing population, the need for cash to cope with the demands of a changing economy and colonial taxation, and the incapacity of the mainly agricultural economy of the Eastern region to absorb the increasing mission-educated Ibos. The culminating effect of these led to the Ibos' migration, initially to Lagos, the country's colonial capital, and in time increasingly to the North with opportunities for skilled employment and trading "pulling" them to Northern Nigeria (Anthony, 2002, p. 35). There was also reluctance by the British to introduce mission schools in the far North's emirates as their structure of Islamic authority worked smoothly with the British indirect rule system, thus occasioning a phenomenal imbalance in western education between the south and the north. Additionally compounding the far North's problem was the imbalance resulting from increasing educated students and teachers in the Northern region coming from the Middle Belt with a limited Islam presence and a large Christian presence that rapidly expanded within the colonial period. These factors, therefore, created the opportunities for public service and private enterprise for southerners' disposition to migrate to the north (Anthony, 2002).

However, though positively contributory in some respects (such as the railway boosting of agriculture, particularly that of cash crops), migration did not entirely produce interethnic integration. Partly undergirding this was the territorial nature of the ruling caliphate era and the originated aristocracies' unwillingness to allow "strangers" within their areas. Also partly undergirding it was the British policy of preserving the Islamic identity of the North to potentially deter intergroup tensions. Hence, the International Crisis Group observes that

> the British discouraged the movement of non-Muslim migrants into the core Muslim areas of some of the region's cities, pushing them instead into the *sabongari* (strangers' quarters). Over time, the distinction between locals ("indigenes") and strangers emerged as a key feature of Nigerian social and political life. (2010, p. 5)

Such multiple communal and overlapping identification mechanisms, referred to as "associational ethnicity," offer particularly important social networks to new immigrants (International Crisis Group, 2010, p. 5). In combination with segregation, however, ethno-religious identities have become sharpened by them, in addition to reinforcing discriminatory practices which have continued to influence the Hausa and Fulani relationships with the other city dwellers. The beginning occurrences of major interethnic violence manifested in the period leading up to the independence, particularly in 1953 when the southern parties' efforts to hold pro-independence rallies resulted in a clash between the Hausas and the Igbo migrants in Kano, with about thirty-six deaths recorded in the riot, out of which twenty-one were Igbos, and over 200 injured. The riot is observed as reflecting the opposition of the northern politicians to independence based on their fear of being dominated by the more advanced south, while also indicative of the resentment felt locally against the economic domination of the Igbos, as in trading, for instance (International Crisis Group, 2010).

Thus, in fear that the southerners' head start educationally and politically would advantageously place them in political dominance after independence, northern nationalists in 1953 objected to self-government. Rather, they capitalized on the preponderance in northern size and population and insisted on countermeasures that would nullify their fears while also paving the way for northern dominance as basic conditions for remaining in the country and agreeing to eventual self-government (Osaghae, 1998b). These measures included the allocation of 50 percent center House of Representatives; the allocation of national revenue resource on the basis of population; the non-granting of the demands of the Yoruba in the northern areas of Ilorin and Kabba to be joined to the Western region; and the introduction of ministerial responsibility only at the instance of the North's readiness for it. There were also the demands for regional autonomy which northern delegates presented in the 1953 Constitutional Conference in London following their threat to pull out from the colonial union, for which the granting of all these demands "conferred political advantages on the Northern region in the federation which emerged, and underlay the problem of Northern domination which was a major source of the country's political problems after independence" (Osaghae, 1998b, p. 6).

Furthermore, religious tensions and conflicts that marked the colonial period include "Madhism," an anticolonial, Muslim-oriented, trans-Saharan movement which posed a major threat to the authorities (International Crisis Group, 2010, p. 6). Professing a doctrine of the return of a messianic Mahdi at each century's turn that would lead to the triumph of justice and strengthening Islam, the movement drew an enormous following, and as an anticolonial influence, instigated clashes with the British officials. Tensions also intensified between the Muslim Tijaniyya and Qadiriyya brotherhoods toward the end of the colonial period, with the Sokoto ruling aristocracy (mainly Qadiriyya) aligning with colonial authorities, increasingly indicted with charges of amassing wealth and power, as well as collaborating with and condoning Western decadent influences. In consequence, the region's different section leaders began aligning with Tijaniyya given its obvious anti-Western and anticolonial posture. Hence, while tensions between the two orders were initially restricted to political elites and scholars, by the early 1940s, under the ruling of prominent Tijaniyya leaders, the order transformed into a mass movement with much influence, possessing extensive economic and political networks as the conflict between them grew into direct confrontation (2010).

Both orders' political importance increased greatly with the election in 1951 and competition for their allegiance by the two northern-based political parties, the Northern Elements Progressive Union (NEPU) and the Northern People's Congress (NPC). In consequence, having religious authority connoted with political implications as both orders' bargaining power grew by the mid-1950s there were several clashes between the two orders in Sokoto with the challenge posed to the Qadiriyya by the Tijaniyya's aggressive presence. The influence of the caliphate, however, remained strong notwithstanding these developments, and by the independence run-up, the primary political party was the NPC, which was a Hausa-Fulani predominantly elite group controlled by the caliphate or Sultan, also called the Sarduana of Sokoto (Alhaji Ahmadu Bello), and an Usman Dan Fodio descendant (International Crisis Group, 2010). While a breakaway of the party's more radical younger elements formed NEPU on the grounds of "seeking to free the *talakawa* (commoners) from the oppressive hold of the *sarauta* (aristocracy)," the region was NPC led at the country's independence in 1960 (2010, p. 6). Thus, while occasioning new economic opportunities, new cities and population movements, colonial rule stimulated new identities and reinforced existing ones, thus setting, in some cases, the stage for violent, long-lasting identity conflicts. There was a strong reinforcement of wider Islamic community links, hence:

> In the far north, with its tradition of religiously informed public authority, there remains a strong feeling that colonial rule was an alien domination that disrupted or eroded the region's legal, political and cultural values.
> ambivalent views among Muslims concerning public authority in the far north—mistrusted in its relations with secular or Christian "others" (external powers, neighbors or compatriots)—continued after independence. (International Croup Group, 2010, p. 6)

And, equally ambivalent and varied was the non-Muslims' experience under colonial rule among both the Christian indigenous groups and the southern immigrants, with some taking advantage of the opportunities for education, to their Muslim counterparts' chagrin on occasions, and others suffering from their perceived Sokoto establishment reinforced powers (International Crisis Group, 2010). Such a state of ambivalence, thus, existed among the North's varied ethno-religious groups up to the country's independence in 1960.

THE NORTH AT INDEPENDENCE TO PRESENT

At independence, the Sarduana Ahmadu Bello-led NPC governed the Northern region out of the country's three regions—the others being Eastern, and Western—and was the power dominating the Nigerian federation-run coalition, with its position nationally reinforced by the fact of the British leaving behind a more populous and larger Northern region than the combination of the two other regions. Intense regional competition and squabbling characterized this first republic (International Crisis Group, 2010). The Northerners had two primary aspirations: "to enhance their influence relative to the more developed south and [to] preserve their religious and cultural identity, inherited from the caliphate era but disrupted by colonial rule" (2010, p. 7). In consequence, the NPC and Sarduana aimed at unifying the northerners as one bloc that would continue to wield dominant power nationally, as well as restoring the region's cultural identity and religious heritage (2010). Hence, the International Crisis Group (2010) observes:

> Proclaiming a principle of "One North, One Destiny," Ahmadu Bello pursued a "northernization" policy favoring northerners (of all religious persuasions) in employment in regional and local administrations. This policy, which dated back to 1954, was informed by fears that migrants from the south, with the advantage of their Western education, would continue to establish themselves in the administration and the economy. (p. 7)

The northernization policy served for the replacement of provincial and regional, non-northern civil service employees with northerners. Observing the goals of the policy as going further than public administration, the Sarduana is stated to have articulated (Kurfi, as cited in International Crisis Group, 2010) that

> the Northernization policy does not only apply to clerks, administrative officers, doctors and others. We do not want to go to Lake Chad and meet strangers [i.e., southern Nigerians] catching our fish in the water, and taking them away to leave us with nothing. We do not want to go to Sokoto and find a carpenter who is a stranger nailing our houses. (p. 7)

In order to realize this goal, crash programs were introduced by the Sarduana to train and equip civil servants of northern origin with adequate qualifications for assumption of greater governmental control at regional as well as federal levels. Aimed at fostering solidarity of all peoples in the region, the policy widely benefited the minority, predominantly Christian groups given their missionary schools and high educational level making them feel belonged. The 1960s is seen by many as an era of much northern unity with minimized religious differences. No major reforms were, however, undertaken administratively by the Sarduana to address the region's minorities' age-old fears and their local autonomy demands to be excised from the rule of the emirate.

The suppression of the minority groups' rallying point opposition parties undermined, to the contrary, the regional unity which the aristocracies and the ruling party sought to sustain. While the efforts to boost the "House of Islam" or the *dar al-Islam* drew strong Muslim majority support, this campaign, in addition to the Sarduana's election in 1963 as the World Muslim League vice president, raised an alarm of Islamic hegemony among the North's non-Muslim minorities and the South's Christian migrants (International Crisis Group, 2010, p. 7). Community relations became affected with such fears, and contributed to the first military coup in January 1966 against the Northern region-led federal government. Furthermore, with the Sarduana and the northern leaders' second priority of promoting Islam "as a unifying instrument," to ensure the preservation of cultural identity of the region, Bello established an umbrella body, "Jama'atu Nasril Islam (JNI, 'Victory for Islam')" in 1962 to unite Muslim sects, propagate Islam, and provide the NPC with an ideological base (International Crisis Group, 2010, p. 7). However, the Sarduana's efforts to forge Muslim unity achieved minimal results, as violent confrontations continued among rival Sufi orders' adherents, while the state-resource-supported campaigns of minority "pagan" groups' conversion to Islam were more successful (2010, p. 7).

Hence, in reaction to the religious and political tension prevailing in the country, the mostly Igbo officers-led coup of January 1966 in which many prominent northern leaders, including Ahmadu Bello and senior military officers, were killed "was partly a revolt against the perceived religious and political agenda of the ruling NPC" (International Crisis Group, 2010, p. 8). However, the initially mixed reactions the coup elicited in the region: 1) to the northern elites, there was a clear setback with the abrupt termination of Sarduana's efforts at forging greater northern cohesion and of restoring the caliphate's heritage in the region, and 2) to the non-Muslims, there was the partial relief of a seeming liberation from the stronghold of the NPC, but which soon turned into outrage with the realization of the killing of their high-ranking military officers as well. The January killings further worsened the perception of northerners of the southern ploy to control the center, with many northern leaders such as Sheikh Abubakar Gumi viewing the coup as having exposed "the deep-seated hostility held by people in the south against the north" (International Crisis Group, 2010, p. 8).

Shortly following the first coup, Ibos in the north witnessed the first onslaught in May 1966 in which hundreds were killed by Hausa mobs (Garrison, 1966d), and this preceded the July 1966 countercoup staged by mainly Hausa-Fulani and some minority northern ethnic groups in "a rare closing of ranks" (International Crisis Group, 2010, p. 8). In this ensuing second coup coming six months after the first, Major General Aguiyi-Ironsi was killed along with over 200 Igbo army officers and men (Garrison, 1968a). In part compromise "to retain the solidarity of the non-Muslim minorities in a united Northern Region," Muslim leaders installed as head of state Lieutenant Colonel Yakubu Gowon, who is from the Middle Belt region of the north and a Christian (International Crisis Group, 2010, p. 8), without unanimity on his accession to office within the military, however (Osaghae, 1998b, p. 61).

After the July countercoup, the spate of Igbo killings in the north intensified with episodes of massacres and pogrom occurring in July and September which were of greater magnitude than the May 1966 killings.

Historical Background to Northern Nigeria Ethno-Religious Conflict 15

The fall of 1966 witnessed the planned killing of about 50,000 civilian Ibos in the Northern region, who were massacred by mobs and troops in the North, which set in motion the flight of about two million Ibos from all parts of the country, to the safety of their region (Garrison, 1968a). Osaghae (1998b) also observes that "[b]etween May and September 1966, an estimated 80–100,000 Easterners were killed and several thousands more wounded in different parts of the North" (p. 63; see also Falola and Heaton, 2008, p. 174). The massacres triggered revenge killings of some northerners living in the Eastern region, even as Ojukwu fearing the non-safety of easterners outside their region urged them to return home, and the non-easterners to leave the region. In reaction to these killings and the returning refugees to the Ibo-dominated Eastern region, the region seceded from Nigeria to declare a sovereign state of Biafra on May 30, 1967, under the leadership of Colonel Ojukwu, "on the grounds that easterners were no longer safe in Nigeria" (Falola and Heaton, 2008, p. 174). This was after the Aburi Ghana accord reached in the negotiations between Ojukwu and Gowon failed (Falola and Heaton, 2008). A three-year civil war ensued from 1967 to 1970 as the Federal Military Government (FMG) moved in to forestall the secession which ended in the collapse of Biafra and surrender on January 12, 1970 (Falola and Heaton, 2008), with about one million lives lost in the war, mainly through starvation (Garrison, 1968b; GlobalSecurity.org., n.d.).

At the start of the war in 1967, the structure of the country became altered by the Nigerian government with the creation of twelve states nationally from the four regions, of which the Northern region had six states (see map 2 in appendix A). Subsequent states creations led to the North's present nineteen states in 1996 out of the country's present 36 states, the process of which has altered the nations' majority-minority relations by fracturing and eroding the regional platform and dominance over minority groupings. This majority eroding process, while undercutting the Hausa-Fulani regional vision of northern unity, particularly in Kaduna, where it reduced the power of the Hausa-Fulani dominance over the minority, resulted in no minority shift and overtaking of majority grouping in the region. However, in some states, new elites emerged from both the minority and majority groupings with the breakup. The north turned to military power as a route to power and influence. The federal government was northern dominated for most of the military rule period, as the North's "historic strength in the army was seen as . . . compensating for their disadvantages in Western education" (International Crisis Group, 2010, p. 8).

However, with mostly Middle Belt soldiers predominating the force in the wake of Gowon's emergence as leader following the July 1966 countercoup, "[t]he Hausa-Fulani oligarchy had to deal with their southern competitors and the upstarts in power, their 'former slaves' from central Nigeria" (Kukah and Falola, 1996, p. 56). The oligarchy, thus, adopted the strategy of focusing on "one north" regardless of religion or ethnicity, so as to defend the Northern region, and some politicians vigorously worked to retain the old unity (1996, p. 57). Islam was once again brought to the fore through the transformation of Jamaatu Nasril Islam (JNI) into "a quasi political association" to work for attaining Northern objectives, and "with all Emirs and powerful Malams as members, the JNI met to discuss politics and how to defend the interests of the North" (1996, p. 57). The use of Islam as a political strategy has, thus, remained basically the same since the First Republic (Kukah and Falola, 1996).

Furthermore, Nigeria experienced a continuous rule by military governments from 1966 through 1999, interlaced by a brief unstable civilian rule between 1979 and 1983, which was cut short by General Buhari's coup. While each of these military governments promised a speedy reversion to democracy, their transitions were on occasions either cut short or thwarted. However, after the dictatorial rule of northern General Sani Abacha from 1993 to 1998, returning to democracy started to be viewed as a way for the north to find political and moral renewal, and more so, for many, the traditional structure had also become tarnished by secular power's corrupting influence (International Crisis Group, 2010).

The return to democracy by the nation in 1999 was celebrated across the country but far less in the north, as "[f]or the first time since 1979 . . . the region had lost control of political power at the center and was faced with the challenge of designing new strategies for regional self-assertion in the federation" (International Crisis Group, 2010, p. 9). It was, thus, in this context, that the Sharia restoration campaign was initiated by the Zamfara State government, and between 1999 and 2002, twelve northern states adopted the Sharia law. While Muslims, as well as some Christians, lost faith in secular leadership and were supportive of a religious government idea, the concept of implementing Sharia exacerbated conflicts between Christians and Muslims in the region, and stimulated democratic debates over law imperatives. The controversy over the constitutionality and compatibility of Sharia with standards of international human rights, as well as Christians' positions in its operative states, became equally intense (International Crisis Group, 2010).

Furthermore, there were other transforming effects of the country's return to democracy in the region with the emergence of the nation's new generation political elites and more commanding substantial financial resources in the region. Thus, with the region's authority figures increasing, although having less allegiance than the religious leaders and traditional rulers did, the political elites had control over funds, which challenged the traditional authorities. With the access to resources conferred by state apparatus, additional tensions were created between religious and ethnic groups as youths increasingly perceived politics as a crucial means for social upward mobility. At the same time, coupled with the unity of the north having been fractured with the states creation in the

1990s, the Hausa-Fulani grouping saw growing, more assertive minorities. Tensions also mounted between the Christians and Muslims amid cynicism created by economic problems, increasing government corruption, social institutions' decline and perversion, and a rise in criminal activity (International Crisis Group, 2010).

A long history of religious and ethnic differences between the Muslim-dominated northerners and Christian-dominated southern immigrants has undergirded the nation since its birth, which, however, has a stronger northern entry on politics given the more substantial number of Nigerian leaders from the north. Violence manifesting mainly as urban riots has, for decades, continued to periodically flare up in northern Nigeria, mostly pitting Muslims against Christians. Tensions in the region have also involved confrontations between different Islamic sects, which have particularly intensified since the *Maitatsine* riots of the 1980s, resulting in a predominance of violent conflicts in the north. More so, since the past decade there have been gruesome killings involving the Boko Haram radical sect in Yobe, Kano, Kaduna, Borno, and Bauchi states to name a few, especially from 2009 up to present, and has been predicative of more violence flaring up any moment (Akaeze, 2009). And, while seen as a "growing Islamic radicalism in the region" by some people in the West, the problem is recognized as being more complex with roots in Nigeria's history, as well as its contemporary politics (International Crisis Group, 2010, p. i). To adequately explore this exterminatory tonation to the conflict, chapter 2 examines the conceptual framework of genocide.

TWO

Understanding the Conceptual Framework of Genocide

To foreground an investigation of the plausibility of genocidal inclinations to the ethno-religious conflict in northern Nigeria, it is essential to understand the contextual meaning of genocide, its conceptual framing and causal factors, as well as the forms and typology of genocide. This involves examining and distinguishing genocidal concepts from other forms of exterminations such as massacres and ethnic cleansing, as well as exploring the underlying and contributory causes of genocide.

DEFINITION AND ORIGINS OF GENOCIDE

Genocide is recognized as one of humanity's most fundamental scourges, "the processes by which hundreds of millions of people met brutal ends," with the understanding and challenging of it seen as a purposeful and needful energy exertion (Jones, 2006, p. xviii). Many scholars understand genocide as a global phenomenon which has been known through history, even where fragmentary (e.g., Jones, 2006; Scherrer, 2002). Tracing genocide's origins and evolutions has involved broaching a historical and legal analytical framework and exploring boundary cases in testing the genocidal framework, as well as examining various genocidal perspectives and cases around the globe (Jones, 2006). Presently, there is the recognition that virtually every identifiable human group which goes by genocide's legal definition, such as religious, racial, ethnic, national, and others, have been genocide victims, and today, are vulnerable in such contexts. Supporting this postulation is the notion that "humanity has always nurtured conceptions of social difference that generate a primordial sense of in-group versus out-group, as well as hierarchies of good and evil, superior and inferior, desirable and undesirable" (Jones, 2006, p. 4).

Conceptually, the coinage of the word *genocide* was by jurist Raphael Lemkin, of Polish-Jewish descent, in 1944, prior to which time genocide as a phenomenon had no name. Lemkin coined the word from a neologism derived from the Greek root word "genos," connoting tribe or race, and Latin root word "cide," connoting killing (Jones, 2006; Scherrer, 2002; Totten and Parsons, 2009). Genocide basically connotes "the intentional destruction of national groups on the basis of their collective identity" (Jones, 2006, p. 10; Lebor, 2006; Totten and Parsons, 2009). In addition to the usage of Lemkin's "new term and new conception for the destruction of nations" in his genocide coinage, he also proposed to incorporate "the whole conception of what is state organized mass murder, terrorism, vandalism and barbarity," as well as detail proposals for the international community's dealing with it (Lemkin as cited in Scherrer, 2002, p. 2). The Nazi occupation and analytical, law breaches work of Lemkin was the first work containing the word *genocide* (Lebor, 2006). Shortly after its coinage, *genocide* became included in the indictments of Nuremberg's Nazi war criminals, and in 1948 it was adopted as an international crime with the General Assembly's "Convention on the Prevention and Punishment of the Crime of Genocide" (CPPCG) (Jones, 2006, p. 12). Hence, Lemkin instrumented the formulation and adoption of the Convention for the Prevention and Punishment of the Crime of Genocide by the United Nations in 1948 (Lemkin as cited in Lebor, 2006; Gellately and Kiernan, 2003; Heidenrich, 2001; Jones, 2006; Sells, 1998; Waller, 2002).

An outline of Articles I to III of the Convention (Gellately and Kiernan, 2003; Heidenrich, 2001; Jones, 2006, p. 12; Totten and Parsons, 2009; Webster, 2007) follows:

> *Article I.* The Contracting Parties confirm that genocide, whether committed in time of peace or war, is a crime under international law which they undertake to prevent or to punish.
> *Article II.* In the present Convention, genocide means any of the following acts committed with intent to destroy, in whole or in part, a national, ethical, or racial or religious group, as such:
> (a) Killing members of the group;
> (b) Causing serious bodily or mental harm to members of the group;
> (c) Deliberately inflicting on the group conditions of life calculated to bring about its physical destruction in whole or in part;
> (d) Imposing measures intended to prevent births within the group;
> (e) Forcibly transferring children of the group to another group.
> *Article III.* The following acts shall be punishable:
> (a) Genocide;
> (b) Conspiracy to commit genocide;
> (c) Direct and public incitement to commit genocide;
> (d) Attempt to commit genocide;
> (e) Complicity in genocide.

Scholarly discourse has since focused on the issue of mass killing defining or not defining genocide and the stressing of national and ethnic groups, such victims of which predominated, as well as preceded, the era of Lemkin's work (Jones, 2006). Political groups have, however, been seen as taking virtually dominant position as destruction targets since the 1940s and the 1950s of the Stalinist era. Hence, the onus of an operation having genocidal inclination lay on whether or not it ensued under policy rubric irrespective of its resulting or not in any or all of the group members' physical destruction (Jones, 2006).

More so, the Convention explicitly defines genocide as "acts committed with the intent to destroy, in whole or in part, a national, ethnic, racial or religious group," with such acts perpetrated "by killing members of the group, causing them serious bodily or mental harm, creating conditions calculated to bring about their physical destruction, preventing births, or forcibly transferring children to another group" (Waller, 2002, pp. xi-xii). The Convention is observed to condemn specifically such measures as "the prevention of births so that a people would die out and forcible transfer of a group's children to another group" (Gellately and Kiernan, 2003, p. 3).

In essence, genocide as a crime fundamentally involves "a wide range of actions [which] . . . are subordinated to the criminal intent to destroy or to cripple permanently a human group," including "deprivation of life," as well as "devices considerably endangering life and health," [and] the acts are directed against groups as such, and individuals are selected for destruction only because they belong to these groups" (Lemkin as cited in Heidenrich, 2001, p. 3). Generally, "genocide does not necessarily mean the immediate destruction of a nation, except when accomplished by mass killings of all members of a nation" (2001, p. 3). However, contrary to Lemkin's definition of the term, genocide is now frequently defined "as the organized extermination of a nation, people, or ethnic group," as in the Rwandan 1994 Tutsis exterminations by Hutu, and the Nazi Holocaust (Lebor, 2006, p. 11).

It is recognized by many scholars (e.g., Heidenrich, 2001, p. 3; Lebor, 2006, p. 11; Totten and Parsons, 2009, p. 3) that, while such mass killings of a nation's entire members or implementing plans of intent for mass killings constitute genocide, Lemkin's definition of genocide has a broader meaning, connoting

> the coordinated plan of different actions aiming at the destruction of essential foundations of the life of national groups with the aim of annihilating the groups themselves. The objectives of such a plan would be the disintegration of the political and social institutions of culture, language, national feelings, religion, economic existence, of national groups and the destruction of the personal security, liberty, health, dignity, and even the lives of the individuals belonging to such groups. Genocide is directed against the national group as an entity,

and the actions involved are directed against individuals, not in their individual capacity, but as members of the national group. (Lemkin as cited in Totten and Parsons, 2009, p. 3)

Hence, "the careful use of the term 'genocide' represents a fragile yet critical strand in the fabric of internationally shared and legally recognized values . . . a term that can be manipulated and misused . . . a name for something that seems to elude naming" (Sells, 1998, p. 10). The Convention's genocide definition is both "extremely broad and extremely narrow" (Totten and Parsons, 2009, p. 3), with many scholars (e.g., Charny, Fein, and Horowitz as cited in Totten and Parsons, 2009) proposing alternative definitions in the absence of a generally accepted definition. Such a definitive dilemma poses serious problems primarily for genocide prevention and intervention measures, as well as for prosecuting genocidal-like cases. It also compounds scholarly works in examining genocide's preconditions, processes, and ramifications (Jonassohn; Charny; Dadrian; Fein; Kuper; and Schabas as cited in Totten and Parsons, 2009). Furthermore, an extensive listing of genocides, as in Diamond's exhaustive list of genocide cases through history to current, stands the risk of expanding the concept's frame to include most or all mass killing occurrences which retrospectively are considered to have been genocides (Webster, 2007).

Additionally, the Convention's legal definition of genocide, which came into effect only in 1948, limited the term to specified actions, events, intentions, and aims, and so, retrospectively designating various mass killing instances as "genocide" loses the specificity of its meaning, primarily as a racial crime. For instance, Webster (2007), citing Morrison's enumeration of "20 'major genocidal acts' committed between 1885 (Belgians victimizing Congolese) and 1994 (Hutu victimizing Tutsi in Rwanda)," observes that the United Nations have retrospectively recognized as genocides nine out of such lists (p. 171). Of paramount importance is the need for clarity on what genocide constitutes without narrowing its legal definition, given that, not having an internationally accepted definitive understanding of what specifically constitutes the crime of genocide poses the risk of using the term for political means, rather than for such humanitarian issues of protection, prevention, and punishment of genocide (Webster, 2007).

Other definitive issues are omitted from the Convention's definition of genocide, such as a totalitarian state's destruction of its "political" opponents (Horowitz and cited in Webster, 2007, p. 172). Also of essence is the importance of recognizing the Convention's implied distinction "between direct (killing) and indirect means (preventing births through sterilization), both aimed at the *biological destruction* of the group," with the first being illegal universally, and the second legal in a number of jurisdictions (Webster, 2007, p. 172). An instance of this is the Nazis' forced sterilization and "euthanasia" programs, which constitute the Nazi genocide integral aspects (Fein as cited in Webster, 2007, p. 172). Subsequent sociological and historical understandings can, therefore, be added to the Convention's legal definition of genocide, and, as argued by Webster, "Genocide is a *process* that involves staged escalation; involves the *biological* destruction of a group (usually, but not always, racially or ethnically defined by the perpetrators); and is nearly always perpetrated by, encouraged or condoned by a *state* (and only the state can prevent it)" (2007, p. 172).

While also recognizing genocide to be legally defined as "the most serious crime . . . considered an 'aggravated' crime against humanity," the Convention requires the perpetrator's proven intent to destroy a people group—"the intent to destroy, in whole or in part, a national, ethnic, racial or religious group, as such" (Gellately and Kiernan, 2003, pp. 14–15). Such proof of intent is not required of "other crimes against humanity and war crimes," other than the mere criminal action of itself, as in the case of mass murder (2003, p. 15). Additionally recognized as genocidal is "the targeting of people for destruction on the basis of what are . . . inherited, perhaps genetic, shared group characteristics that the victims cannot divest . . . irrespective of their intentions or actions" (2003, p. 17). Further establishing a legal distinction between genocide and war, Heidenrich (2001) argues:

> Wars are . . . fought only between armed forces. Genocide is inflicted upon the largely defenseless. In war, to preserve at least some civilized conduct, there is the concept of the *noncombatant:* infants, children, expectant mothers and women generally, the elderly, the infirm, civilians in general, and even some military personnel, including military physicians, medics, and prisoners. International law declares that anyone who wages war must actively try to avoid harm to noncombatants. Genocide, by contrast, is utterly contrary to international law, because its victims—no matter how innocent—are targeted intentionally. War perpetrates killing. Genocide perpetrates murder. (p. 1)

Moreover, a differentiation of ethnic conflict from genocide has been recognized on the basis of two distinctions, each focusing on genocide's definition of the victim target group, the perpetrators, and intentionality. The first distinction is that, in principle, ethnic conflict may sometimes not be more than just a clash of armed ethnic forces, without necessarily being genocidal, and may not target civilians, but often does, however, as in the 1999 Kosovo case (Gellately and Kiernan, 2003). The second distinction is that ethnic conflict presumably entails a popular mass movement with widespread participation or acquiescence. Genocide, on the other hand, may not of necessity entail that, although it may sometimes take the form of mass participation, as in the 1994 Rwandan case (Gellately and Kiernan, 2003). Thus, genocide decision, plan, and order can be carried out, even secretly sometimes, by only a few perpetrators, with genocide, by definition, however, often claiming many victims, a crucial imbalance that is not paramount in ethnic conflict. In resolving genocide's definitional dilemmas by distinguishing it from ethnic conflict, Gellately and Kiernan (2003) argue that "genocide could be considered a subcategory of ethnic conflict, if all we need to define is a specific form that targets civilians for destruction," but not where broadly defined as a social phenomenon, in which case, "genocide, with its essential feature of perpetrator intent, need only be a political operation" (p. 20).

Additionally, "ethnic cleansing" in principle also involves territory "purification" essentially, not of a population, which entails an ethnic group deportation from a territory, and may typically be threatening without necessarily being violent (Gellately and Kiernan, 2003, p. 20). Thus, "[e]thnic cleansing requires either a protected reservation within a state or a free exit for the victims to escape; genocide precludes both protection and exit" (Fein as cited in Gellately and Kierna, 2003, p. 20). Therefore, in practice genocide is usually preceded and/or accompanied by ethnic cleansing though not always, as in the 1975–79 Khmer Rouge case of the Vietnamese minority annihilation in Cambodia; or the LonNol earlier regime's massacres that expelled from Cambodia 300,000 Vietnamese in 1970 (2003, p. 20). Thus, ethnic cleansing could be a mere precedent or a burgeoning genocidal phase, but one which occurs separately (2003).

Moreover, recognizing genocide's coinage as referring to ethnic or national groups murdering, Friedlander (1995) argues that genocide was directed at human groups that "shared racial characteristics" rather than against national groups, as "heredity determined the selection of the victims" (p. xii). There is, therefore, an argument for a redefinition of the Nazi genocide from its understanding "as the mass murder of human beings because they belonged to a biologically defined group" on the basis that the "Jews were not the only biologically selected target" (Friedlander, 1995, p. xii). Thus,

> [a]longside Jews, the Nazis murdered the European Gypsies. Defined as a "darkskinned" racial group, Gypsy men, women, and children could not escape their fate as victims of Nazi genocide. Biology also determined the fate of the handicapped, which, just as Jews and Gypsies, could not change their condition to escape death. The Nazis killed handicapped infants in hospital wards as well as elderly men and women in nursing homes ... the Nazi regime systematically murdered only three groups of human beings: the handicapped, Jews, and Gypsies. (Friedlander, 1995, pp. xii–xiii)

Contemporarily, "the word *genocide* is used so frequently to express hyperbole ... [hence] the word's international legal definition is controversial" (Heidenrich, 2001, p. 2). The Convention's genocide definition as a deliberate destruction primarily involving mass murder of "the targeted groups—national, ethnic, racial, and religious," excludes socioeconomic and political groups, which groups were seen as legally indefinable and imprecise by the various delegate negotiators of the definition in 1948 (2001, p. 2). Hence, "whenever a government has committed mass murder without discriminating according to nationality, ethnicity, race, or religion, that government has not committed 'genocide' as international law defines the crime, even if its victims number in the millions" (2001, p. 2). An instance of this is Cambodian Khmer Rouge Pol Pot followers in 1975–1979 who murdered eyeglasses-wearing people for "political" reasons, with the intent to eliminate the bourgeois intellectuals, on assumption they wore glasses; and in attempt to socially reconstitute the Cambodian society by terrorizing and killing, had about 1.7 million Cambodians murdered out of the country's seven million population. Thus, while Cambodia suffered in per capita terms a most awful mass murder inflicted by a government on its populace, in international legal terms, most of the victims were not "genocide" victims having been killed on purely political rather than racial criteria, with the only exceptions being the Cambodian ethnic minorities (Heidenrich, 2001, p. 2). Therefore, the argument has been made for the inclusion of social and political groups in the genocide definition by various scholars (see Drost; Whitaker; and Totten and Parsons, 2009, p. 3).

The issue of number was inconclusively left open by the Convention delegates with no agreement reached on what number of exterminations constitutes genocide (Heidenrich, 2001). Hence, the killing of a person by a thug gang simply on account of that person's belonging to a specific race, ethnicity, nationality, or religion, such singular murder, legally speaking, constitutes a genocidal act. As a result of the rather restrictive genocide definition by the Convention, some scholars today use the word *politicide* to connote politically based mass murder, and *democide* to connote any deliberately caused mass deaths such as forced labor, direct massacre, avoidable famine, or willful neglect (Heidenrich, 2001, p. 3). Furthermore, genocide implies "actions carried out by a state or ruler with the intention of systematically killing the members of a particular community or social collectivity and thus partially or totally destroying the target group" (Scherrer, 2002, p. 2). This raises the crucial issue of how the victim group is defined, given that any such definition should conform broadly with the Convention's wording even though the Convention omitted some categorizations of victims (Scherrer, 2002).

While in some areas, the Convention goes beyond the current minimal consensus, as in such gray areas of genocide's indirect measures and practices, in others, such as "the killings of members of a particular ethnic or cultural group (ethnocide), a particular political group (politicide), or a particular social group (democide)" they are not adequately covered (Scherrer, 2002, p. 3). Thus, Scherrer (2002) argues:

> Genocide is state organized mass murder and the perpetration of crimes against humanity with the intention of exterminating individuals because of their affiliation to a particular national, ethnic, religious, or "racial" group. It is a premeditated mass crime that has been systematically planned, prepared, and executed. (p. 3)

Two terms—mass murder and genocide—are used by scholars in classifying collective violence, which stems from terrorism that is state directed, and providing a conceptual distinction between them, mass killing is recognized as "killing members of a group without the intention to eliminate the whole group or killing large numbers of people without a precise definition of group membership" (Waller, 2002, p. xi). On the other hand, "collective violence becomes *genocide* when a specific group is systematically and intentionally targeted for destruction" (2002, p. xi). Genocide is also recognized as "the state-sponsored systematic mass murder of innocent and helpless men, women, and children denoted by a particular ethno-religious identity, having the purpose of eradicating this group from a particular territory," thus, recognizing genocide as "mass murder short of eradicating the entire group, but including a significant subset of that group in the killing" (Midlarsky, 2005, p. 10).

Furthermore, anthropologically, genocide can be distinguished through an "othering" process in which an imagined community's boundaries are reshaped with a group "included" previously being recast ideologically and usually, in dehumanizing narrative, as not existing within the community, and as a dangerous and threatening "other" to be annihilated, whether political, economic, racial, ethnic, or religious (Hinton, 2002, p. 6). To establish a distinction between genocide and other violence forms, the definition of violence in its present usage is recognized as the "exercise of physical force so as to inflict injury on, or cause damage to, persons or property," while generally it refers to any form of structural, physical, psychological, or symbolic force exerted against a person, group, or thing (Hinton, 2002, p. 6). Thus, political violence is a violence subset which broadly encompasses covert forms, or "overt state-sponsored or tolerated violence" including "actions taken or not taken by the state or its agents with the express intent of realizing certain social, ethnic, economic, and political goals in the realm of public affairs, especially affairs of the state or even of social life in general" (Nagengast as cited in Hinton, 2002, p. 6).

Accordingly, political violence subsumes conceivably various overlapping phenomena comprising war, ethnic conflict, terrorism, oppression, torture, and genocide (Hinton, 2002). Genocide is distinguished from other political violence forms by the perpetrators' unrelenting and determined effort to destroy a people group. Thus, Fein's "sociological definition of genocide" as "a sustained purposeful action by a perpetrator to physically destroy a collectivity directly or indirectly, through interdiction of the biological and social reproduction of group members, sustained regardless of the surrender or lack of threat offered by the victim," advantageously includes "the sustained destruction of nonviolent political groups and social classes" (Hinton, 2002, p. 64). Hence, definitively,

> while genocide *may* involve terrorism (or acts intended to intimidate or subjugate others by the fear they inspire), ethnic conflict (or violence perpetrated against another ethnic group), torture (or the infliction of severe physical pain and psychological anguish to punish or coerce others), oppression (or the use of authority to forcibly subjugate others), and war (or a state of armed conflict between two or more nations, states, or factions), it differs from them conceptually insofar as genocide is characterized by the intention to annihilate "the other." (Hinton, 2002, p. 6)

While recognizing the blending into each other of the boundaries of such different political violence forms, as a conceptual category, genocide is also undergirded by given presuppositions that are susceptible to discourse and challenge. Hence, delineating "an anthropology of genocide" domain is understood "as encompassing those cases in which a perpetrator group attempts, intentionally and over a sustained period of time, to annihilate another social or political community from the face of the earth" (Hinton, 2002, p. 6).

Moreover, genocide is understood as an organized attempt aimed at systematically destroying an ethnic or politically defined group (Wood, 2001). From a geographic perspective, to comparatively appraise genocidal orchestrations and consequences in its twentieth century recurrence and its international law formulation is undergirded by such geography-linked notions as territorial nationalism, Lebensraum, ethnic cleansing, and forced migration (Wood, 2001). In exploring the Bosnian 1992–95 and the Rwandan 1994 eruptions to understand the genocidal intentions involved, the processes, and the genocides' effects, Wood (2001) observes that genocidal actions involving planned and purposeful targeting of specific areas and groups are implemented methodically through murder and expulsion, and politically interweaved with territorial nationalism aspirations. Accordingly, Wood (2001) argues:

> Genocidal intentions are signaled through rhetoric and actions of political leaders that express an exclusionary and highly territorial form of nationalism. The mechanics of genocide are revealed through patterns of mass murder, destruction, and forced expulsion. The legacy of genocide is most apparent in the accounts of survivors, but is also seen in devastated landscapes and inadequate responses by the international community. (p. 57)

Further on its conceptual explication, genocide constitutes a "dispassionate," controlled, or instrumental violence which serves a political purpose, while massacres which, though based on orders, usually involve "overkill" (Dutton, 2007, p. 22) or excessive violence beyond the military purposes intended, including torture, mutilation, rape, killing of civilians, and infants. However, mixes of genocide and massacre do occur, as in Rwanda where the government's genocidal policy involved sequences of pogroms or massacres representing two methods of political killings. In the case of genocide, sociopolitical reasons may be sufficient in explaining the selection of a target group as well as the group induction to kill. In the case of massacres, however, regardless of the training level, the military actions become violent and cruel, with restraint only of the human imagination. Both massacres and genocide involve complicity of the international community, which involves a deliberate decision to ignore the slaughter and to not regard what is going on (Dutton, 2007).

Further on the definitional debate, genocide basically involves the entire processes through which specific "human beings are both willed and empowered to deprive and deny other human beings, both individually and as part of broader familial and communal groupings, of their basic human dignity" (Levene, 2005a, p. 1). Thus, further exploring the definitions of genocide entails addressing such genocidal issues of *"agents, victims, goals, scale, strategies,* and *intent"* (Jones, 2006, p. 19). On varying perspectives regarding agency, there is a clear focus on state and official authorities, as in Dadrian's "dominant group, vested with formal authority"; Horowitz's "state bureaucratic apparatus"; and Porter's "government or its agents" (Dadrian; Horowitz and cited in Jones, 2006, p. 19). Still, on the issue of agency, however, the state-centric perspective is abjured by some scholars (e.g., Chalk and Jonassohn; Fein as cited in Jones, 2006, p. 19), with the Convention also citing as possible agents "constitutionally responsible rulers, public officials or private individuals" (Article IV). Hence, most scholars of genocide in practice "continue to emphasize the role of the state, while accepting that in some cases—as with settler colonialism . . .—non-state actors may play a prominent or dominant role" (Jones, 2006, p. 19).

On the issue of genocidal intent, legal theorists and most scholars see intent as defining genocide (Jones, 2006). Establishing a distinction between intent and motive, Jones observes that a revolution or conquest which "causes total or partial destruction of a group legally qualifies as intentional and therefore as genocide whatever the goal or motive, so long as the acts of destruction were pursued intentionally" (Gellately and Kiernan as cited in Jones, 2006, p. 21). It is increasingly favored by legal opinion that "regardless of the claimed objective of the actions in question, they are intentional if they are perpetrated with the knowledge *or reasonable expectation* that they will destroy a human group in whole or in part" (Jones, 2006, p. 21). Accordingly, the 1998 Rome Statute of the International Criminal Court is seen as reflecting a reasonably broad meaning of intent such that "a person has intent where . . . in relation to conduct, that person means to cause that consequence *or is aware that it will occur in the ordinary course of events*" (Greenawalt as cited in Jones, 2006, p. 21). Similarly, the Rwandan International Criminal Tribunal in its 1998 Akayesu judgment, declares that "the offender is culpable because he knew or should have known that the act committed would destroy, in whole or in part, a group" (Schabas as cited in Jones, 2006, p. 21).

Hence, the concept of genocidal intent combines the notion of *specific* intent with that of *constructive* intent (Jones, 2006). However, specific intent is being inferred in instances "where actions with predictable results are taken over an extended period of time and the consequences of these actions regularly confirm their outcome" (Jones, 2006, p. 21). Constructive intent, on the other hand, included "cases in which the perpetrators did not intend to harm others but should have realized or known that the behavior made the harm likely . . . [and] clearly results in the destruction of that group of people, even if that result is neither intended nor desired" (Alvarez as cited in Jones, 2006, p. 22). Instances of this include systematic trailing and killing of a group's members, forcible removal of members of a group to reservations while also withholding medication and food, and kidnapping a group's children for enslavement outside of their culture.

Further on genocide's delineation, Schabas (2000) argues that the Armenian Genocide, the Jewish and Gypsy Holocaust, and the Rwandan Genocide are the only real genocides in contemporary history from a legal perspective. Genocide as a term is not to be applied to every atrocious mass killing situation; thus, legally such cases as Stalin's Ukraine carnages, the Holodomor, and Nazi occupied Soviet citizens and Slav killings are not considered genocide (Schabas, 2000). Furthermore, the Bosnian massacres are presented as ethnic cleansing rather than genocide on the basis that the 1970s Cambodian Khmer Rouge did not have an ethnic dimension, and therefore, lacked a port essence of genocide, hence, deploring the United Nations categorizing of ethnic cleansing as genocide. Furthermore in the Darfur atrocities, arguably, genocidal intent is not established even though it involves the non-Arabs' summary execution, and so it does not constitute genocide, according to Schabas (2000).

CAUSES OF GENOCIDE

A multiplicity of factors has been identified by genocide scholars as underlying genocidal orchestrations and processes. For instance, in an extensive investigation of genocidal dynamism involving an in-depth analysis of genocidal intent, dynamism, and the contingency of its processes, the role of imperialism, state-building, social revolution, and war in fueling genocide are identified (Jones, 2006). Furthermore, there is recognition of the need and the process of directly addressing and understanding genocide, deriving from the combinations of widely present actions and influences in today's world (Newbury, 1998). For instance, exploring the Rwandan genocide history identifies such broader issues of the genocide involving the dangers of associating genocide only with the world's remote areas. Thus, in setting out the genocide's background, there is recognition of four conceptual frameworks including ethnicity, gender issues, outside influences, and ecological issues, with an acknowledgment of their importance in understanding genocide, as well as how these issues are illuminated by an understanding of genocide (Newbury, 1998). Accordingly, with the commonality rather than peculiarity of such issues to the Rwandan genocide, the tendency exists of presenting genocide as a remote phenomenon in spite of its widespread occurrence in North America, Asia, Europe, and Africa (Newbury, 1998). Further discourse on genocide causation, while arguing that primarily approaching genocide as a twentieth-century occurrence, fails to grasp genocide's true origins, genocide evolved fundamentally from the Western experiences of modernity and the struggle for the nation-state, which emanated from the Europeanist fifteenth to nineteenth centuries' hemispheric expansion which provided the primary stimulus to genocide's pre-1914 manifestations (Levene, 2005b). This section reviews such diverse views on genocidal causation factors as identified by various scholars.

Imperialism, Colonialism, and Modernity

A theoretical conceptualizing of genocide accounts in history presents an understanding that underlying genocide in the modern world are such broad preconditions and interlinked elements often regarded as the normative underpinnings of "international society," which are, the "rise of the West," "modernity," and "the nation-state" (Levene, 2005a, pp. 10–11). Basically, "the rise of the West" involved "massive expansion of European interference with non-European societies and the forging of wholly new forms of dependency worldwide" (Levene, 2005a, p. 11). Such expansion was done initially through mercantilist outreach and then followed by extensions of overtly capitalist core West European economies into the far-reaching ends of the globe, beginning in the later fifteenth century, and which were accomplished either by conquest or military coercion. This led to extensive or even total disruption, displacement, or destabilization of existing economic and social relationship patterns with their forcible reorientation toward aligning with the metropolitan new "core" hegemonic interests, with previous world empires becoming subservient to the emergent world economy (Levene, 2005a).

While this shift accorded resource base and global market near-monopolization, which advantaged the dominant elites and eventually the core metropolitan masses, it created an inherent process for structural violence for "peripheralized" or "semiperipheralized" societies at the receiving end, while also galvanizing previously independent-of-West societies, or later, imperial-bondage-released societies—to reformulate themselves to be able to compete and possibly evade the dominating dispensation. Hence, Levene (2005a) argues:

> While the rise of the West, was accompanied by no overarching political agenda for the annihilation of foreign peoples, it did create a broader cultural discourse in which such annihilation was considered perfectly conceivable; in which exactly such annihilations sometimes took place, not to mention further multitudinous interactions, tensions and fractures between, and within, extra-Western polities and societies which, in the long run, also carried an almost incalculable potential for extreme, exterminatory violence. (p. 12)

The rise of the West however, intermeshes closely with Western epistemologies and thought systems, or essentially its worldview, which primarily refers to modernity—genocide's underlying second factor. Thus, seen as a principle for organizing for rational awareness and a scientifically informed world, modernity was founded on the Enlightenment's obsession for categorizing and classification. Hence, "in order to respond and ... regulate the planet in the most efficacious and utilitarian manner" (Levene, 2005a, p. 12) "modernity became a quest to 'divide, deploy, schematize, tabulate, index and record everything in sight (and out of sight) and ... make out of every observable detail a generalization and out of every generalization an immutable law'" (2005a, p. 12). Furthermore, modernity posits the knowableness and possibility of all things, as well as the applicableness to humans, of things applicable to things, "thus, just like other living species, human beings too can be 'apprehended, classified and theorized'" (Hinton as cited in Levene, 2005a, pp. 12–13).

Additionally, the use of "the fingerprint as the perfect identifying mark of individual difference" from the nineteenth century British colony, Bengal (Sengoopta as cited in Levene, 2005a, p. 13), was also deployed by the Nazis based on "the same utilitarian premise" for "categorizing and hierarchizing whole groups of Eastern European peoples, on the basis of their 'biosocial attributes'" (Levene, 2005a, p. 13). Hence, describing such tendencies, variously, is understood "as the reifying, essentialising, biologising and manufacturing of difference" (Hinton as cited in Levene, 2005a, p. 13). However, with these tendencies now generally recognized relative to Nazism, as throwing more light on modernity's dark side, such tendencies, paradoxically, are equally founding "those basic self-referential Enlightenment wisdoms by which the world at large is ... made a better, healthier, more productive and ... more efficient place" (Hinton as cited in Levene, 2005a, p. 13). Therefore, progress as the positivist meta-narrative of modernity, which links logically to a Western world order's economic requirements, also implicitly carries the assumptions that non-conforming individuals or groups who, presumably, are unfit or insufficient to the order's demands, are surplus to that ordering's requirements (Levene, 2005a).

Furthermore, modernity aggregates humans into single, static, invariable, and irreducible categories, with people normatively labeled members of particular races, tribes, religions, nations, etc. This shows on one end its complex phenomenal simplification and reduction capability, inclusive of humans, "into a more manageable and schematized form" (Wallerstein as cited in Levene, 2005a, p. 13), as well as its refusal or failure to envision humans' potential for having multilayered loyalties and identities. Hence, as historicized in the Armenian genocide:

> analysis revolving around conflicts over irreducible categories such as race and religion turn history into a field where, instead of human beings interacting, abstract concepts do battle. It is as if hordes of individuals think and act as prescribed by ideologies of nationalism, religion, or race. Terminology then comes to reconfirm the view imposed by the genocide that, ultimately, one need not account for real Armenians leading real lives whose disappearance from their homes and from history must be accounted for; one is comforted by the thought that Armenians can be reduced to a corollary of a concept. (Levene, 2005a, p. 13)

Additionally, indigenous peoples' genocidal and inhumane treatment was frequently framed in modernity metanarratives, especially the conception of "progress" (Hinton, 2002, p. 10). For instance, the Tasmanians' annihilation was legitimized as an endeavor to "bring them to civilization," while the United States westward expansionism was justified by Theodore Roosevelt's argument to not have the land remain "a game preserve for squalid savages" (Maybury-Lewis as cited in Hinton, 2002, p. 10). Also similarly noted is General Roca's ill-famed "Conquest of the Desert" attack on indigenous Indians and his despicable voicing to fellow Argentineans that

> our self-respect as a virile people obliges us to put down as soon as possible, by reason or by force, this handful of savages who destroy our wealth and prevent us from definitively occupying, in the name of law, progress and our own security, the richest and most fertile lands of the Republic. (Hinton, 2002, p. 10)

More so, the massacre of the Herero thousands equally had such similar arguments legitimizing the killings, with an emphasis on the astounding cruelty and greed of the perpetrators, which is often described as "sickening" (Hinton, 2002, p. 10). In this Herero example, the indigenous' land was reason for their displacement and killings, while in other cases it was the need to terrorize them to perform slave labor. Additionally, South American and Congolese rubber-plantation owners, having been exceptionally brutal, were seen as holding hostages of workers' relatives, raping women, torturing and maiming the recalcitrant, and abusing and killing, sometimes for sheer amusement (Hinton, 2002, p. 10). In contemporary times, another modernity's metanarrative imbued with developmental need discourses has become emblematic of the devastation trappings for indigenous peoples. Thus, "the development of Nigeria's oil resources (through the collaboration of the government and multinational companies such as Shell), for example, has led to massive environmental damage and the enormous suffering of the Ogoni who reside in oil-rich areas" (Maybury-Lewis; and Totten, Parsons, and Hitchcock as cited in Hinton, 2002, p. 10). Hence, a summation of contributory factors of indigenous peoples' genocide is plausibly presented as their indigenous' land resources, political weakness and marginality, extreme dehumanization, and modernity's metanarratives, with their plight improving in the globalization era, as nation-states reorganize increasingly on greater pluralist lines (Maybury-Lewis as cited in Hinton, 2002, p. 10).

Furthermore, indigenous peoples' sufferings and death are often depicted by multinational corporations, companies, agencies, and governments as "progress" and "development" or a "necessary by-product" which are manifested in forms of mineral extraction, oil fields, logging, hydroelectric projects, and resource-rich zone land grabs (Hinton, 2002, pp. 11–12). There is thus the resulting displacement, extensive environmental damage, and indigenous peoples' frequent deaths that emanate from such projects, as evidenced in the Ogoni case in Nigeria (Totten, Parsons, and Hitchcock as cited in Hinton, 2002). Accordingly, Hinton (2002) observes that

> the very need for such harmful "development" projects is linked to other dimensions of modernity, the colonial endeavor and the creation of nation states. As European imperialists set out to conquer new territories, they laid claim to large swaths of land throughout the world. Colonial boundaries were "rationally" demarcated in terms of major landmarks and the claims of competing powers. This pattern of "rational planning," establishing territorial borders, and ordering from above is one of the hallmarks of modernity. (p, 12)

Moreover, for creating a centrally manipulated or controlled grid/map, complex phenomena are simplified and reduced by the modern state into a schematized, more manageable form, often with disastrous results, however, especially with disregard to local knowledge (Hinton, 2002). As the colonial powers paid minimal attention to the indigenous understandings of sociopolitical differences in the mapping of new political frontiers, upon their withdrawal, newly emerged independent countries were found controlling minority as well as some majority population groups. These were inclusive of indigenous peoples, some of which clamored for more power, greater autonomy, or the right for outright secession (Hinton, 2002). Furthermore, given the colonial powers' economic exploitative tendencies, trained personnel and basic infrastructure were lacking in many of these nations, while also being poverty plagued with high population growth rates.

Emphasizing colonization as a fundamental cause for the indigenous peoples' destruction, particularly in their "conquest" and "pacification," Hinton (2002), quoting Kuper, observes that "[s]ome of the annihilations of indigenous peoples arose . . . in the course of . . . a genocidal process: massacres, appropriation of land, introduction of diseases, and arduous conditions of labor" (p. 65). Hence, colonialism laid the foundation undergirding most of the suffering and violent conflict plaguing the contemporary world, as exemplified recently in the Rwandan genocide (Hinton, 2002), also on colonialism's effect on the development of intrasocietal violence in Rwanda and Burundi, which framed the Rwandan genocide, Scherrer (2002) argues:

> It was the rapidly increasing strength of ethnicization and polarization fostered by the colonialists and by the postcolonial policies of the ethnopolitical power elites on either side that led to the demonization and dehumanization of the respective opposing group. In both countries there were repeated massacres that made any peaceful political solution difficult and ultimately impossible. (p. 28)

The Nigerian case has seen colonialism's amalgamation of various ethnic groups as instrumenting Nigeria's high ethnocentric politics, which is a fundamental factor undergirding the waves of killings in northern Nigeria (Anyanwu, 1982; Osaghae, 1998b).

The Nation-State

The nation-state is the spatial arena in which such "selective reality" and "tunnel vision tendencies" are manifested (Scott; and Bayly as cited in Levene, 2005a, p. 13). As an element of genocidal orchestration, the nation-state is connected to the political organizational normative framework in the modern age, which notion provides our identities and assures freedom from threat of violence to our persons (Levene, 2005a). Citing Nobert Elias, Levene (2005a) observes that the nation-state proffers the linked, two-fold benefits of reining in human tendencies for aggression through demands for greater self-control and non-violent social encounters, as well as provides legitimized universally recognized authorities monopolistic powers for ensuring social peace and instituting punitive measures against offenders. Accordingly, "the consequent retreat of daily intrusions against our safety . . . powerfully enhanced the potential for a civilizing process" (Elias as cited in Levene, 2005a, p. 14).

While some historical sociologists have observed that in particular states' modernizing trajectories, transition significant break-points have led to periods of extreme violence (Levene, 2005a), such monopolization of violence, which was a primary outcome of the formation process of the nation-state, has only recently been questioned. The nation-state formation process was problematic in itself, except in "those most obvious cases where recognizably anti-democratic and overtly violent groups seized the apparatus" (Levene, 2005a, p. 15). The modern nation-state's general characteristics and broader implications, however, presuppose an absolutely uniform and unmediated authority for its policing, military, legal, administrative, and fiscal functions within its internationally recognized bounded territory and sovereign domain, entailing the entire land and all its appurtenances. This is described as the aspiration of the modern state to make a society "legible" for control and manipulation in its own interests (Scott; and Holquist as cited in Levene, 2005a, p. 15). Hence, applications to cadastral surveys should plausibly apply also to humans through such administrative procedures as birth, marriage, and death registrations, and censuses. However, with some of the procedures preceding the dawn of modernity in some traditional systems of states, the tendency of ascribing equal cross-referencing statistical numbering to every registered individual for purposes of the administrative, fiscal, and military purposes, as well as for ascribing presumably equal uniform responsibilities and rights was essentially unique and revolutionary (Levene, 2005a). The individual citizenship concept that presupposes "an equality before the law," is an extension of the universal suffrage notion which is generally accepted as the human condition's fundamental benefit, as affirmed by the UN's 1948 Declaration of Human Rights (2005a, p. 15).

However, three-fold danger inherency exists in the presumably liberating features of these new political state formulations. First, Levene argues that

> by defining each human being as an individual citizen, the state effectively subordinates all previous, traditional, and often multi-layered loyalties—whether to extended family, clan, tribe, community, sect, estate, or whatever—to itself, repudiating in the process the authority of these bodies to act as meaningful mediators or negotiators vis-à-vis the state, on behalf of those who otherwise might have understood themselves as component elements of exactly such social organisms. (2005a, pp. 15–16)

Levene (2005a) presents that while such bodies are not culturally, economically, or socially rendered redundant, they are politically done so, since only atomized citizens would be subsequently recognized as valid body-politic members, excepting where specific interventions are made for such "group rights" bodies to be allowed by the state itself or other states in an international domain (p. 16). Also significant is that in any temporal contending jurisdiction, while religious authority would be automatically overridden by the primacy of modern nation-states even with the polity's former traditional organization having fundamentally been on religion, the affinity of the nation-state to the "omniscience and omnicompetence" principle of modernity infers that any spiritually emanating challenge to the political authority of the state would be inacceptable technically, such as any emanating from other dissenting voice, ethnic, social, or other voices. Accordingly,

> [w]hile, thus, there is no intrinsic reason why the nation-state has to be a secular one, the general point holds: the modern state's primacy is absolute, regardless of religious authority or sanction, and hence to challenge it, whatever the manner or source of that opposition, is potentially to expose oneself to its monopoly of violence in whatever form the state might choose to respond. (Levene, 2005a, p. 16)

Second, the inevitable drive of the modern state to development bounds and amplifies this situation's inherent dangers, being envisaged through its ongoing venture to achieve a more healthy, productive, and better society, with the modern state assumed as based on an upward continuing trajectory which confirms its fundamental indebtedness to modernity. Even with this as its *raison d'être,* it also carries a plausibly implicit, or even explicit, human, technological, fiscal, and extractive resource organizing mandate for pursuing such terrestrially firmed goals (Levene, 2005a). This does not, however, undermine its basic interest of mobilizing resources, human resources inclusive, for competing with other modernizing nation-states within the universal frame. Hence, Levene (2005a) argues that

> the modern polity provides itself with a totalizing capacity largely undreamt of in the pre-modern world, the resulting options available to its subjects being of a zero-sum nature. As a group, or an individual, one can either be enthusiastic, obeisant or acquiescent in response to the state's mobilizing demands, or, if one dissents or demurs, one ultimately, again, has to reckon with its monopoly of violence. (p. 17)

Third, is the dominant mode of the modern polity, which refers mainly to the "homogeneous state-society" rather than the nation-state as such, given that the modern states have not all automatically maintained a legitimated existence based on the conceptualization of nationhood (Levene, 2005a, p. 17). Thus, ethnic monoculture grounding should not be assumed even where the case has been such. While the United States and Britain and such "avant-garde nation-states" have, in their national features, been notably hybrid, most others that are diversely ethnic, such as Brazil, are virtually color-blind (2005a, p. 17). Thus, in actual genocidal cases, in which conflict issues of race and ethnicity are seemingly turned on, the social coherence premium of the modern state is rather the underlying concern of the modern polities' larger problem of sustainability among other competing nation-states in the international system.

Hence, external as well as internal pressures serve as primary drivers toward the notions of uniformity and unity. There is, however, an unequivocal outcome to this, for which:

> polities intent on long term sustainability in the modern, international political economy are those which, as a matter of necessity, demand that their citizens, or subjects, accommodate and/or assimilate themselves to a set of social, cultural, economic and often linguistic norms, as determined by the state. This usually means . . . recognizing oneself as a member of the national—or some other state defined notion of collective and unified—community. (Levene, 2005a, p. 17)

This recognition will result in the non-further acceptance of living on the state's geographical or emotional borders as a way to avoid compliance, with such tactical means of avoidance becoming more unlikely as the economic imperatives of the modern state ensues (2005a). In such circumstances, those that are unwilling to assimilate voluntarily will likely be encapsulated forcibly, through "national" value inculcation in state schooling universal programs among others, which is another critical underlying indicator of the advent of the modern nation-state (2005a, p. 17). The others that might be claiming exemption for reasons of, say, religious non-conformism will probably find their maneuvering scope profoundly confined. Also, recourse to the status of a minority group, possibly by negotiating with authorities, could be a possible bolt-hole, but such that would only confirm a status of fixity, subordination, and subservience in relation to the state. Accordingly, "any group which thus holds out against these norms is likely to find itself branded as pariahs, outsiders, troublemakers, or where simply individuals are concerned, as insane" (Foucault, as cited in Levene, 2005a, p. 18). Furthermore, even in clearly multi-ethnic states with elitist exclusively manipulative behavior to ensure its own group's ethnic dominance over the other(s), the unified nation's rhetoric provides the most apparent apparatus for marginalizing its competitors (Human Rights Watch as cited in Levene, 2005a).

Additionally, genocidal possibilities are not evidently manifest in all of such situations as can be seen, for instance, where the national state community embarks on the extrusion of a group for reason of its assumed "irreconcilable 'otherness'" or where, being unable to embrace the nation-state's set down existence arrangements for the group, the group actively seeks to secede from the state (Heraclides as cited in Levene, 2005a, p. 18). Rather, "danger from the nation-state's monopoly of violence is implicit in *all* its fundamental arrangements" (Levene, 2005a, p. 18). This does not, however, present any particular thing as leading to genocide *inevitably,* nor that all nation-states are identical, but rather, that genocide occurrence can result only from an assemblage of a milieu of often special ingredients which are contingent mostly under crisis conditions. This also does not present the potentiality of genocide as exempt automatically from some states as a result of their supposedly being more attuned to development. Hence, Levene (2005a) argues:

> Few states, especially liberal democracies, typically or openly exercise their power over their constituency through unmediated violence, though it is always held in reserve. Rather they try to ensure conformity to a set of images that create the illusion of unity, the illusion of consensus about what is and what is not legitimate, what should and should not be suppressed. (p. 18)

Hence, "the refusal of multiplicity, the dread of difference . . . is the very essence of the state" (Clastres quoted by Nagengast as cited in Levene, 2005a, p. 18). In essence, the analytical combination of the emergent nation-state, the rise of the West, and modernity, shows "that the fundamental reconfiguration of human society which these developments inaugurated was the harbinger of *universal* conditions in which genocide, as we understand it, became possible" (Levene, 2005a, p. 18).

Moreover, in examining why genocide, ethnic cleansing, and forced displacement constitute part of the enduring features of the state system, is the exposé that humans accept as morally justifiable, the "systematic mistreatment of other human beings" (Rae, 2002, p. x). Thus, "pathological homogenization," which involves "forced assimilation, expulsion, and genocide," are practiced in the state-building process, with political elites frequently utilizing cultural resources for the redefinition of politically bounded communities as morally exclusive communities, with outsiders to be expelled from that exclusivity (Rae, 2002, p. x). The international state system has through history been "replete with examples of states turning on their own citizens," with no exception for the twentieth century, which rather witnessed an increasing toll on citizens to unprecedented levels as states acquired greater military and bureaucratic capabilities (2002, p. 1). This is notwithstanding the international relation's known scholarship of the state's cardinal responsibility for "providing security for its citizens in an anarchical international environment" with norms of state's legitimate behavior to its citizens developed by the international community since WWII ended (2002, p. 1). Hence, the world has witnessed, in the twentieth century's last decade, an astounding level of brutality and targeting of population segments for expulsions and exterminations.

The Human Agency and Collective Evil

On genocide causation, Waller (2002) observes that people who commit extraordinary evil are ordinary individuals contrary to the common belief that extraordinary human evil perpetrators have historically mostly been extraordinary monsters, psychopaths, and sadists (Waller, 2002). Investigating why ordinary people commit evil extraordinarily, Waller

(2002) presents that most perpetrators of genocide and mass killings, who are extraordinary by their acts rather than by their personalities, which are ordinary and without identification as killers, mentally deranged, or sadists, and in consequence elude demographic categorization. Most extraordinary evil perpetrators are not distinguishable by personality, background, past political affiliation, or behaviors portraying them as men and women who are not likely or unfit to be genocide executioners, such that "a purely evil person is just as much an artificial construct as a person who is purely good" (Waller, 2002, p. 18). Thus, extraordinary evil perpetrators are not to be considered so atavistic or irrational and beyond comprehension, but focus should be in understanding the factors that lead ordinary individuals into committing extraordinary evil. Extraordinary evil is connoted with extra capitalizing of human, with the deliberate harm being perpetrated on one another under social, political, or religious groups' sanctions. Hence, the greatest atrocities are orchestrated with boundary dissolution between criminal conduct and the military; between barbarity and civility; and when social, political, or religious groups embark on collective violence as warfare or progress, toward a vulnerable victim group, such human evil acts are writ large. In essence, "the extraordinary human evil perpetrated in times of collective social unrest, war, mass killings, and genocide . . . the deliberate harm inflicted against a defenseless and helpless group targeted by a legitimating political, social, or religious authority—human evil in extremis" (Waller, 2002, p. 13).

Additionally, the notion of doing evil is understood as the intentionality of inflicting pain on another against the person's will and causing foreseeable and serious harm (Vetlesen, 2005). Investigating the reasons and circumstances underlying such desires, its exploitation, or the manner of its channeling on to collective evildoing, such a form of evildoing that pits entire groups against themselves derives from a fusion of social structure, situation, and character (Vetlesen, 2005). Further analyzing collective evil responses, there is recognition of the varying bystander types, differentiated on the basis of a preexisting relationship with either victim or perpetrator, and the immediacy of the evildoing (Vetlesen, 2005). A bystander who is aware of the atrocities being perpetrated, and has the capability to intervene but fails to do so, becomes the same as a perpetrator. Essentially,

> there is often but a thin line between the stance of bystanders and that of perpetrators: in denying human plurality (Arendt) and hence in denying uniqueness. Perpetrators targeting a "Them" and bystanders deciding to remain indifferent (inactive) in the face of those victimized commit the same destruction of the moral foundation of the other by means of substituting the unique other with reifying categories of the It, making all others appear predictable and alike. (Tester as cited in Vetlesen, 2005, p. 231)

Moreover, reexamining some fundamental studies of conformity, including the notable investigations of Milgram, Zimbardo, and Ash, there is recognition of the factors of emotional development and identity as contributing to genocide (Baum, 2008). Presenting a three personality type model of perpetrators, bystanders, and rescuers, Baum argued that the actions of people during genocide inevitably mirror their everyday behavior in daily living, with perpetrators prone to destruction, and rescuers prone to helping, while bystanders are the onlookers that remain uninvolved, and positioned between both extremes. By analytically combing eyewitness accounts and correlating these personality types with social-psychological factors, similar emotional and mental traits are identified among all three personality types, with the divisions accounted for by conflict between the social and personal identity (Baum, 2008).

Manipulation and Loyalty to Authority

Still on genocide causation factors, undergirding the psychological inclinations motivating such violence extremities as prison riots, lynching, military massacres, and genocide are the issues of the means by which individuals are indoctrinated for military or political reasons into committing ghastly acts by leaders (Dutton, 2007). The group mind deriving from the crowd yearns for obedience and leadership. Such a crowd creates dangerous fanatical leaders with attachment only to self, as well as bounded followers to such leaders as representing an ideal self-type, who are, in turn, bounded to other followers through their idealized leader's common connection—called the "common ego ideal" (Freud, as cited in Dutton, 2007, p. 24). This ideal holds the group together and allows freedom from social anxiety which directs normative rule of everyday life behavior, with such freedom inhibiting in-group aggression. Ensuing from this will be violence regression, referred to as the "primal horde," a notional group depicted as slaying the father figure and erecting totems in its stead (2007, p. 24). Hence, there is an understanding of "the followers as slavishly presenting to the leader" with a yearning to obey which makes the synergy of the leader-follower combination bidirectional and natural (2007, p. 24). Additionally, a stronger motivation for the leader-followership relationship other than social anxiety freedom, which binds self to the group served, provides an emblematic panacea for avoiding the fear of death (Dutton, 2007, p. 24).

Furthermore, by tracing recurrences of massive human violence to determine causal factors for people's willingness to kill others throughout history, politically contrived memory manipulation is fundamental in the unleashing of primal genocidal passions (Hirsch, 1995). Detailing the ways cultural memory becomes created to generate an understanding of the causes and ways mass murder episodes occur, leaders are often invoking or creating past fictitious or real memories of injustices to instigate their cohorts to kill for politics or other motives, with generational accounts of happenings handed over as history. Politics is therefore linked to psychology and culture, and people's view of political systems and politics, as well as their learned manners of interaction with authority, are linked to issues they learned growing up (Hirsch, 2007). In consequence, cultural and political myths learned through the political socialization process present as a framework on which adult worldviews and behaviors are based (Hirsch, 2007). Additionally, obedience reinforcing cues are directed by important culturally, socially, and politically positioned persons, and so where obedience is framed on a national mythology, such a mythological link can be manipulated by leaders to plausibly sway participants' views on the justification for mass destruction. Thus, where leadership spreads dehumanizing symbolizations of other people groups, they convey a justification message of the appropriateness of aggressively acting against such groups, based on the fact that people's hostile impulses are often willingly acted out where reinforced by leadership. Accordingly,

> During the Holocaust, the continued description of Jews as vermin and bacilli was a prime example of dehumanizing symbolization. Anti-Semitism was also reinforced by the lack of opposition to the extermination of the Jews. The fact that political and religious leaders did not object seemed to confirm the legitimacy of the destruction. . . . Leaders, consequently, may prepare a population for genocide in this fashion. (Hirsch, 1995, pp. 131–132)

Moreover, Sells (1998) identified the role of Kosovo mythology manipulation in instigating and justifying the Bosnian atrocities. The Bosnian genocide is observed to have occurred with Western governments' acquiescence in violation of the 1948 Genocide Convention of the UN, as the genocide "has been motivated and justified in large part by religious nationalism, fueled financially and militarily from Serbia and Croatia, and grounded in religious symbols" (Sells, 1998, p. xxi). Thus, the main victims are Bosnian Muslims who have been targeted for destruction as a result of their religion, with the Bosnian genocide being justified by "Balkanism," which connotes a particular historical abuse portending Balkans as fated genetically or historically to kill each other (1998, p. xxii). Furthermore, in examining the recurrences of massive human violence to determine causal factors for people's willingness to kill others throughout history, and Hirsch (1995) presents politically contrived memory manipulation as fundamental in the unleashing of primal genocidal passions. While also exploring recent genocidal developments necessary for understanding the perpetrators, as well as other human behavioral aspects during the Holocaust, the issue of behavior shaping through obedience to authority and role conformity is identified as genocide causation factors (Newman and Erber, 2002).

Additionally, in examining genocidal causation, some genocide experts adopt "a top-down approach," for instance, by examining authoritarian or utopian regimes, in contrast to "a bottom-up" approach to genocide which explores the average person's thought and action frames with an absence or change of rules (Baum, 2008, p. 6). Genocide theorists adopting the top-down approach are recognized as viewing manipulative elites as orchestrating genocide from a "get-go" perspective, a notion that is supported by the apparent leading of genocides by demagogues, both charismatic and uncharismatic, including "Stalin (Russia), Mao/Chiang Kai-shek (China/Taiwan), Tojo (Japan), Agha Mohammed Yahya Khan (East Pakistan now Bangladesh), Pol Pot (Cambodia), Milosevic (Yugoslavia), Hitler (Germany)" (2008, p. 6). With the bottom-up approach, on the other hand, the appearance of a demagogue only serves to echo the minds of the populace. For instance,

> Hitler and his ilk said nothing new, nothing that the *volk* hadn't heard before. For years, people had retained all the social myths about Jews in the back of their minds. Such myths were reflected in fairy tales (the Grimms' *Jew in the Bush*), children's rhymes, state-sponsored statues (such as the Judensau) and church-sanctioned pilgrimage sites that honored sainthood for children martyred by "The Jews." Like a good populist, Hitler echoed what everyone "knew." It was as if God had read their minds. (Baum, 2008, p. 6)

Thus, while there will always be manipulative leaders, they will not succeed without followership support, since without the masses' support, the diatribe of a demagogue will only be regarded as a madman's ranting (Baum, 2008). Hence, "What really matters . . . is that the seductive quality of hate appeals to the average person's irrational fears, their vanities, their greed and their blood lust" (2008, p. 7).

Groupthink, Hate Processes and Dehumanization of "Other"

Moreover, on genocide causation factors, psychological forces have been identified as underlying massacres and atrocious massive killings in narration of dreadful occurrences which marked the twentieth century as eliciting the highest level of systemic human slaughters in history (Dutton, 2007). There is an understanding that such psychological factors undergird the process of Groupthink through which individuals are transformed into committing massive brutal murders with no compunctions. This is identified as the "B process dominance," the mechanism of indoctrinating individuals to habituated brutality with the conviction to commit such hideous acts, which is often initially preceded by tortuous guilt, followed by dehumanization and belief of the target victim's virus-like and unjust status which needs to be destroyed to avoid its destruction of the populace (2007, p. 153). Aspects of "the 'groupthink' drive the military decision outcome inevitably towards annihilation of the target group" (2007, p. 20). Also exploring the human condition in analyzing violence generating situations and people's responses to them is the description of the French revolution, that the revolutionary mobs' behavior is indicative of the "group mind," which is a collective unconscious form all men share, even the civilized (Gustave Le Bon as cited in Dutton, 2007). Thus, in "psychological groups" or crowds with everyone having the same goal, men's behavior descends down the ladder of evolution several steps, to the place of "primitive people" (2007, p. 24). Hence,

> by the very fact that he forms part of an organized group, a man descends several rungs down the ladder of civilization. Isolated, he may be a cultivated individual, in a crowd, he is a barbarian—that is, a creature acting by instinct. In this group situation, the individual gains "a sentiment of invincible power which allows him to yield to instincts, which, had he been alone, he would have kept under constraint. (Le Bon as cited in Dutton, 2007, p. 24)

Moreover, such occurrence results from "anonymity and consequent loss of personal responsibility in crowds," along with a tainting, in which usually proscribed acts are imitated and endorsed (Le Bon as cited in Dutton, 2007, p. 24). The individual's susceptibility in the crowd enables the group mind to control him or her, and is a racial consciousness form, which makes the individual perform acts contrary to his or her moral beliefs. Likened to primeval people, the group mind is presented as unconsciously driven, orchestrating impulsive acts, irritability and changeability, while also longing for obedience and strong leadership, such that, "the crowd . . . acted on 'image-like ideas'—visual impressions lacking reason" (Le Bon as cited in Dutton, 2007, p. 24).

Additionally, examining various notions of hate, such as psychopathology, ideological attraction, and group processes, such prior conditions are inadequate in explaining hate processes (Waller, 2002). Framed on several scholars' works since WWII, Waller presents a four-pronged context model for explaining how people that are ordinary become involved in mass killings. The first two prongs are actor-related factors of "ancestral shadow" involving ethnocentrism, xenophobia, and social dominance need; perpetrators' identities issues of cultural beliefs, moral disengagement, and self-interest; the third is the action's social context or the "culture of cruelty" factors involving socialization, group binding factors, and person/role merger; and the fourth is response to authority based on "social death of victims," including dehumanization, us-them thinking, and victims blaming, which legitimizes them as the enemy (Waller, 2002, p. 20). Hate is also recognized as "one of the most powerful forces . . . underlying mass killings . . . hate that is carefully nurtured and shaped to accomplish ends that are mindfully, planfully, and systematically conceived" (Sternberg, 2003, p. 304). And "hate applies to whatever one calls the killings, from terrorism to massacres, genocides, and ethnic cleansing," many of which are partly instigated by "fires of hatred" (Naimark as cited in Sternberg, 2003, p. 304). In his *Duplex Theory of Hate*, Sternberg's (2003) triangular components of hate—namely, "negation of intimacy, passion, and commitment,"—composed as derivative to his "triangle of love" (Sternberg as cited in Sternberg, 2003, p. 306), were used in combination with propaganda to incite hatred of the Jews. Disgust was whipped up in several ways, for instance, on the basis of which, Sternberg argues:

> The negation of intimacy was fostered by condensing the Jews into a single disgusting entity, as in references to the Jewish bacillus and smelly Jews. Jews were depicted as power crazed, greedy, and so forth, and Germans were depicted as handsome or beautiful, as pure, as saviors of the Aryan race, and even as Godlike. Passion was incited by Hitler's rousing addresses to the masses, by mass demonstrations and parades, by use of films . . . by depictions of Jews in propaganda as defilers and rapists of Aryan women, and by depictions of Jews as evil (e.g., as Christ killers, devils, or purveyors of death). Finally, devaluation and diminution were fomented by youth organizations, control and censorship of the media and cultural artifacts, by demands for active but delimited active participation in persecution, by pressure to turn in Jews, and by the demand from the government for absolute obedience to hate-based government policies, on pain of death (e.g., if one harbored Jews). (2003, p. 307)

Furthermore, hate remains an underlying factor not only in the Rwandan genocide, but also undergirds several of the world's intricate problems. In the Rwandan 1994 genocide, over 500,000 Tutsis and Hutu moderates were killed within a few months (Sternberg and Sternberg, 2008), with a majority of the Hutu population noted to have actively participated in the genocide, basically using such primitive weaponries as machetes, axes, knives, or guns. While humans' capability for such violence predicates the workings of several psychological processes, hatred presents as a major facilitator for such mass killings. According to Sternberg and Sternberg (2008), such hate is not natural, in the sense of an inability of the individuals to act differently; on the contrary, it is "cynically fomented by individuals in power so as to maintain their power or by individuals not in power, so as to gain it" (p. 2). Furthermore, in Rwanda, the radio station's (RTML) broadcasts incited Hutus to slaughter their neighboring Tutsis, a strategy which was ultimately aimed at securing Hutu power in Rwanda. By the same token, just as in Rwanda, the Nazis cultivated hate and exclusionary feelings against the Jews, the Roma or Gypsies, the Communists, and other groups that were marginalized so as to increase and maintain power. Through the education and propaganda ministry established shortly after Hitler took over in March 1933, and the ensuing tight regulation of the media, literature, theater, art, and music, the radio became an essential means of disseminating socialist nationalist slogans that were aimed at manipulating the masses (Diller as cited in Sternberg and Sternberg, 2008).

The Rwandan genocide resonates in several ways with the World War II events of Nazi atrocities against the Jews, Communists, Roma or Gypsies, and other supposedly inferior race groups, who were seen as obstructing the Nazis' establishment of an economically independent nation and an exclusive reign of a seemingly purer race which would be stronger, healthier, and smarter than all other peoples on the globe. In this, too, there was some power struggle with the Nazis aiming "to enlarge their sphere of influence to create the superior living conditions for Aryans at the cost of other people who were 'unfit' for the new nation" (Sternberg and Sternberg, 2008, p. 2). Genocide and massacres are still continuing since the Nazi genocide against the Jews, which are not random killings or a mob's spontaneous irrationality bursts, but are rather "carefully planned and orchestrated killings" with efficiency levels that on occasions nearly paralleled those of the Nazis' death machine (Sternberg and Sternberg, 2008, p. 2).

Furthermore, the intense hatred which accompanied the Rwandan genocide is not considered to be especially uncommon, as it also manifested in the genocide which occurred in west Darfur in Sudan where African groups in Masalit, Fur, and Zaghawa inhabiting the region were being attacked by government forces and the "Janjaweed" Arab militias. The conflict involving "territorial power struggles" intensified in February 2003, with the demand made by two African rebel groups for power-sharing and cessation of economic sidelining and marginalization (Sternberg and Sternberg, 2008, p. 3). Aided by Sudanese soldiers, the Janjaweed burned the African villages, poisoned their wells, raped the women, killed children, women, and men, and forced mass migrations of these African indigenes off the region for the occupation by Arabs (Sternberg and Sternberg, 2008).

Moreover, exploring such issues as stage setting for intergroup violent conflicts caused by difficulties in life conditions and crisis, the genocidal tendency of scapegoating some groups more than others is identified (Newman and Erber, 2002). Arguably, a strong psychological projection element resides in mortals, the basis on which genocidal designs are imputed to perceived enemies with justifying of such designs (Jones, 2006). Hence, identified enemies such as the Jews, Bolsheviks, Croatians, and Tutsis "must be killed because they harbor intentions to kill us," and without preventing/stopping/annihilating them, they will proceed to do so (Jones, 2006, p. 267). Before being killed, they are debased, brutalized, and dehumanized, by which vein they are made to resemble "animals" or "subhumans" to justify their extermination. Additionally, projection also serves to displace blame and guilt from the perpetrators of genocide to their victims (Hatzfeld, as cited in Jones, 2006, p. 267).

Narcissism

Narcissism is also one of the psychological factors motivating génocidaires (Jones, 2006). Humans have a "propensity for hubristic self-love," in account for which Narcissus, the legendary Greek god so enraptured and in love with the pool's reflection of him, without finding consolation died in sorrow by the pool (Freud, as cited in Jones, 2006, p. 262). Accordingly, groups which are seemingly geographically, linguistically, and/or religiously close, such as the Tutsis and Hutus, Croatians and Serbians, and the Protestants and Catholics, accede to vicious intercommunal conflict (Jones, 2006). And, "the communal feeling of groups requires, in order to complete it, hostility towards some extraneous minority" (Freud, as cited in Jones, 2006, p. 262). Hence, "the psychological dynamic by which the 'Self' and the 'We' are defined against the 'Other' is fundamental to genocide" (Jones, 2006, p. 262).

Also recognized is the "malignant or pathological narcissism," which refers to a state of idolized self with others only existing to magnify and fortify the self (Fein as cited in Jones, 2006, p. 262), and is informed by fear that, in absence of others' validation, the self faces being annihilated or undermined, and derives from anxiety, unease, and profound insecurity (Kressel, as cited in Jones, 2006, p. 262). It presents as vanishing however, with malignant narcissism extremities of real psychopathy, and is "a murderous egotism, incapable of empathy with others, that considers human destruction inconsequential where it increases personal power and glory" (2006, p. 262). Thus, psychopathy and malignant narcissism have been identified in contemporary history as a common feature among génocidaires. For example:

> Consider Adolf Hitler, whose stunted, injured ego found transcendence in holocaust. (How Hitler, the failed artist and rootless ex-soldier, must have reveled in the version of the Lord's Prayer devised by the League of German Girls: "Adolf Hitler, you are our great Leader. Thy name makes the enemy tremble. Thy Third Reich comes, thy will alone is law upon earth . . . "!). Consider as well Joseph Stalin and Mao Zedong, "fanatics, poets, paranoiacs, peasants risen to rule empires whose history obsessed them, careless killers of millions" or the Hutu Power extremists of Rwanda, convinced that their crushing of Tutsi "cockroaches" would enshrine their version of manifest destiny. (Jones, 2006, p. 262)

Additionally, "collective pathological narcissism" is also a genocide causal factor, with the diagnostic and analytic level shifting from individual to collective, a state in which a nation's dominant minority or majority of its citizens hold sway to their country's innate superiority, their God's giftedness or destiny, their limitless capability, or their being sole truth bearers (Jones, 2006, pp. 262–263). The conditions underlying narcissist collective pathology include all such factors which occasion cover-ups, antisocial behavior, and large-scale criminal activities, a summation of which includes the group's grandiose feeling and self-importance; obsession with their fantasies of indomitability, omnipotence, power, fame, unequalled brilliance, all-conquering ideals, or all-surpassing political theories with firm conviction of the group's uniqueness; requiring adulation, affirmation, and excessive admiration; wishing to be revered, feared, or seen as notorious; and devoid of empathy, unwilling to accommodate other groups' needs or feelings, exhibiting haughtiness and rage when confronted or frustrated (Vaknin as cited in Jones, 2006, pp. 262–263). Examples of such narcissist countries include Great Britain, which in the nineteenth and twentieth centuries was "the world leader in collective pathological narcissism," as well as "three totalitarian states—Nazi Germany (1933–45), Stalinist Russia (1928–53), and Maoist China (1949–76)—and, since 1945, a democratic one, the United States" in the past century (Jones, 2006, p. 263).

In-group and Out-group Identity

On genocide causation, most people have the capability of visiting gruesome violence on others, particularly in social settings where there is the "us versus them" stratification as defined by their in-group and out-group dichotomy, by which the in-group perceives the out-group as a dangerous threat to their world, requiring extermination (Dutton, 2007). More so, "the drive to kill is fueled by a societal sense of power and destiny—a sense of entitlement called narcissism in an individual but nationalism in a country" (Dutton, 2007, p. x). While there may be individual aggressive differences in various societies, extreme cruelty capability may not be specific to any given culture. Rather, the capability may be stronger in any culture when the conditions for a "perfect storm" descend, entailing a transcultural reasoning that links extreme violence with humans' predator, inherited, and vestigial remnant past of the complex "pain-blood-death" associated with ancient hunting success (Nell, as cited in Dutton, 2007, p. x). Accordingly, "the most powerful human motive by far is the striving for attachment to loved ones in perpetuity. Humans will do anything for this, including blowing themselves (and others) to pieces . . . tribalism is universal" (Dutton, 2007, p. xii). Starting with the human instinct for attachment, and fostered by the in-group/out-group division which establishes "our capability for symbolism," thus, humanity's survival requires our awareness "of humanity as a tribe and of humanity's potential for radical violence" which, if ignored, dooms us to repeating past mistakes with devastating and more powerful weapons (Dutton, 2007, p. xii).

Ideological Influences

Additionally, ideological influences comprising factors such as beliefs and specific cultural values underlie genocide facilitation (Newman and Erber, 2002). Detailing a social psychology of individually absolving meaning frame, there are insights drawn in understanding the formation of human beliefs and behavior shaping which are crucial to an understanding of genocide. For instance, in various contexts that were differentially constrained, the Khmer Rouge aimed at motivating its minions "to kill by invoking ideological discourses that played upon Cambodian cultural models related to revenge, power, patronage, status, face, and honor" (Hinton, 2005, p. 31). Due to cultural knowledge's dialectical duality, however, the understanding and motivational force of such Khmer Rouge-instituted models varied for individual perpetrators. Thus, in varying combinations and differing contexts, the Khmer Rouge cultural models have been a crucial aspect of the genocidal framing for many of the Democratic Kampuchea (DK) perpetrators, effectively motivating the perpetrators to kill. Accordingly, "[c]ultural models theory as inflected by practice theory, then, provides a strong theoretical basis for viewing perpetrators as meaning-making genocidal bricoleurs" (Hinton, 2005, p. 31). Framed in this "distributive view of culture" approach, perpetrator motivation is accounting for the intricate local understandings which influence people's actions, even while such understandings are linked to and are impacted by macro level practices. Hence, by observing perpetrators' motivation to genocidal orchestration:

> in a more complex manner, one that weaves macro level and micro level analysis to comprehend local motivation and the cultural patterning of mass violence. . . . By regarding perpetrators as bricoleurs and not passive ideological automatons, we can gain a better understanding of their motivations for committing genocidal atrocities. Even if perpetrators are highly constrained in some circumstances, they remain active subjects who construct meaning and assert their self-identity through their violent practices. (Hinton, 2005, p. 31)

Furthermore, religious violence resurgence has become prevalent in the post-Cold War era, from Tokyo subways to the Indian mosque ruins, the World Trade Center, the Oklahoma City federal building, and the Israeli prime minister's rally in Jerusalem, with religious militants transgressing civil societal boundaries to pursue their goals (Sells, 1998). Indeed, Bosnians have encountered the most vicious religious violence meted out in the Cold War aftermath, with assaulting forces not of the "age old antagonisms" associated with the Balkans, however, but of "the same myth of the Christ killer that was exploited in the past to instigate attacks on Jews" (Sells, 1998, p. xxiii). In consequence, genocide perpetrators have been rewarded and the victims punished by Western policymakers. There is an acknowledgment of the assault destruction throughout Herzegovina, cultures, and communities that are non-Catholic, particularly in the region of Mostar where the ancient bridge which symbolized the diverse peoples, cultures, and religions in Bosnia through the ages was destroyed.

In essence, Islam and Christendom have been bridged by the Bosnian society's multireligious character, symbolized by the Mostar ancient bridge, now destroyed, with the bridge also practically connoting five centuries of a society's ability to flourish as a culturally pluralistic entity amidst tensions between the diverse religious groups (Sells, 1998). Observing the preservation of the Bosnian society in its multireligious existence as crucially significant to the world at large, "For those who choose a pluralistic society where different religions coexist—whether in Banja Luka, London, or Los Angeles—the struggle to rebuild that bridge is not something occurring over there and far away, but something frighteningly close to home" (Sells, 1998, p. xxiii).

Furthermore, anthropologists are involved as participants and contributors in different genocidal cases, and they have played a vanguard role in forging and deploying the idea of annihilating difference in humans, the basis on which genocide thrives, particularly in contemporary history (Hinton, 2002). With anthropologists' duplicity in failing to utilize their vantage point for making more valuable contributions to genocidal projects is the establishment of genocide's inextricable link with modernity, given modernity's society reordering scope based on goals/rational principles. Thus, by anthropologically exploring genocide's origins, genocide is plausible as in the cases of Rwanda, Burundi, and Cambodia. For instance, focusing on the Cambodian 1975 to 1979 devastation under the Khmer Rouge in exploring the causation for mass murder and perpetrators' motivation to kill, the Cambodian genocidal policies resulted in over 1.7 million deaths out of the country's 7.9 million populace (Kiernan; and Chandler as cited in Hinton, 2002, p. 23) killed through malnutrition, starvation, illness, overwork, and execution (Ebihara as cited in Hinton, 2002, p. 23). Further analyzing the dynamics of this violence are causal factors of manufacturing difference, involving meaning and identity construction, and the combination of emotionally charged cultural knowledge into genocidal ideologies (Hinton, 2002).

In the Armenian genocide, whose primary perpetrators were the central committee and leaders of the "Committee of Union and Progress" (CUP) which was the Ottoman government's ruling faction, "The CUP was formed out of the heterogeneous opposition groups collectively known as the Young Turks that developed in the late nineteenth century" (Bloxham, 2005, p. 4). The orchestrated Armenian murder accepted as a given is, thus, observed as a starting discourse point rather than the end, contrary to the "Armenian" profound historiography which is keen, mainly as a denial response of enforcing the usual interpretation line of the genocide's inadequate debating scope, on the "specific relationship between intention and contingency in the development of the CUP's destruction policy in 1914–15" (Bloxham, 2005, p. 20). However, such debate, while being emblematic of mature historiography, also touches crucial sensitive issues for both Armenians and Turks. Essentially, the Ottoman's 1914–15 policies on the Armenians were significantly shaped by the nationalist activism of the Armenians, also impacting the run-up to the massacres in 1894–96 (Bloxham, 2005, p. 20). Yet, while identifying the policies influencing contingencies without any inexorable determinism in force, the alternative courses available for the Ottoman main actors should constantly be borne in mind, while also remembering the role that prejudice and ideology played in their conclusions, as well as the visceral hatred. Hence, while allowing

> the Marxian caveat that choices are inevitably conditioned by circumstance, that "man" makes history, but not just as "he" would like, Armenians were killed because of choices made by players who were in the strict sense of the word responsible. . . . The Armenian genocide was one ideological response to the very real, related external and internal structural stresses that had accumulated on the Ottoman Empire by 1915. (Bloxham, 2005, p. 21)

Threat and Vulnerability

Further on genocide causation, a comparative analytical study of twentieth-century mass genocides, ethnic cleansings, and politicides show genocide's occurrence and magnitude, focusing on threat and vulnerability which are two vital conditions for genocide to occur (Midlarsky, 2005). Conditions for this causation require a perception of the targeted population as threatening or as having some tenuous connections to external agents that are threatening irrespective of that perception's reality, and there must be the vulnerability of the targeted population to mass murder (Midlarsky, 2005). Similarly, the potential genocide perpetrators must also experience vulnerability for generating fantasized or real images of the civilian population that are threatening. Any threat increasing process to the state, which simultaneously also increases the state's vulnerability, as well as the targeted civilian population's vulnerability, also increases genocide's probability of occurrence (Midlarsky, 2005). Hence, examining two theoretical foci of loss and realpolitik, the state's threat management is recognized as a critical realpolitik function, while loss most often signals the state's vulnerability or probable civilian targets (Midlarsky, 2005).

Fear

Moreover, fear is a powerful psychological factor that motivates genocide, and, "[n]o power so effectively robs the mind of all its powers of acting and reasoning as fear" (Burke quoted by Green in Hinton as cited in Jones, 2006, p. 265). There is a distinction between "mortal terror," which is the "fear of a threat to physical being and integrity," and "existential dread" which "revolves around our sense of personal identity, destiny, and social place," and is evoking or threatening to evoke feelings of humiliation, dishonor, and shame (Jones, 2006, p. 265). Mortal fear, also referred to as "animal fear," which while not easily distinguishable in form from simple reflex, is a commonality across species, and particularly attains an intensity pitch in humans who are presumably the only species able to foresee death (Piven as cited in Jones, 2006, p. 265). Accordingly, such "death anxiety" is acknowledged by some philosophers and scholars as the worm in the psychic apple of humanity and a fundamental genocidal factor (Jones, 2006, p. 265).

Hence, "[d]riven by nameless, overwhelming fears ... men turn to the primitive tools of self-protection, including the belief that they may spare themselves the terrible fate of death by sacrificing another instead of themselves" (Charny, quoted by Kuper, as cited in Jones, 2006, p. 265). This animal fear is seen in predatory animals, with the phenomena recognized as disparately traced from infants' separation anxiety, religious rituals including human sacrifice, and other religious rituals, as well as intercommunal warfare, to prehumans' and primitive humans' terrifying encounters with predator animals (Ehrenreich as cited in Jones, 2006, p. 265). This predator is observed as having been the primary "Other," which transformed into predator out-group as humans gained dominance in the animal kingdom, with this human "Other" then bounding and delineating the in-group, such as ethnic group, tribe, or clan, in which support, sustenance, and communal self-defense can be found (Staub as cited in Jones, 2006, p. 265). In this case, evolutionary psychologists are deploying such connections and arguing that "human behavior in the present is generated by universal reasoning circuits that exist because they solved adaptive problems in the past" (Waller, as cited in Jones, 2006, p. 265).

On the other hand, social psychologists present that people who believe they will be attacked by others respond more aggressively than they would toward targets believed to be benign (Jones, 2006). Presenting such phenomena as intricately linked to genocide and intercommunal violence, Jones (2006) observes:

> Fear of the immediate or more distant future is a pivotal element in a number of approaches to ethnic warfare.... Fear induces people to support even very costly violence, because the choice seems to be between becoming a victim or becoming a participant.... According to this approach, a high degree of affect is expressed when the stakes are large (genocide involves large stakes), and so emotion follows a rational assessment by ordinary people of their situation. The improbability

of genocide is not decisive, for the stakes are too high to chance it. (Horowitz as cited in Jones, 2006, p. 266)

Furthermore, when manipulated and intensified by architects of genocide, mortal terror is a common feature of genocide, with notable examples such as the 1990s Rwandan genocide and the Balkan genocide (Jones, 2006). Likewise, genocidal atrocities perpetrated against the Serbs by the Ustasha fascist regime during WWII, which were part of their prominent historical memories, along with the Ustasha-style symbolism revival and the Croatian nationalist, Franjo Tudjman's, rhetoric, caused deep anxieties that became further heightened when the discrimination against Serb professionals/officials in Croatia started (Jones, 2006). Similarly, the Rwandan 1994 holocaust ensued in the aftermath of the Burundian massive bloodletting in which about 50,000 to 100,000 mainly Hutu civilians were exterminated by a Tutsi-dominant military, following a foiled coup (Jones, 2006, p. 266). As a result, about 350,000 Hutu refugees, on fleeing to Rwanda, brought firsthand reports of the atrocities, among which "were some of the most unrestrained genocidal killers of Tutsis in 1994," as the slaughter only further revived memories of the 1972 even worse Hutu killings involving an "eliticidal" attempt at exterminating virtually all professional or educated Hutus, primarily its adult males (Jones, 2006, p. 266). Along with the 1990 Rwandan invasion by the Tutsi-led rebels, the "image of the Tutsi as the embodiment of a mortal danger ... [was] hauntingly evident" (Lemarchand as cited in Jones, 2006, p. 266). Causing further complexity for the Rwandan Hutu males was their leaders' mortal retribution threat should they fail in participating in the mass murder; indeed, "[m]any Hutu were driven to kill their Tutsi neighbors because they knew they had no other option; refusal to comply meant that they themselves would be killed the next day" (Lemarchand, as cited in Jones, 2006, pp. 266–267).

More so, even in a genocide prototypical case involving an objectively non-threatening and entirely defenseless group, as in the Jewish Holocaust, mortal terror may have also featured presumably in a greatly hystericized form (Jones, 2006). Hence, "the Germans drew a picture of an international Jewry ruling the world and plotting the destruction of Germany and German life" (Hilberg, as cited in Jones, 2006, p. 267). While the depiction of Jewish elderly, women, and children as a "threat" to the Germans may have appeared preposterous, it was easier to present the Jewish adult males in this manner, hence, this demographic group's demonization in both Germany and Eastern Europe's Nazi-occupied territories, in the generated propaganda guide for the genocide, as well as the first directive for physical extermination and incarceration against the group. Furthermore, close linkage of the Jews with Bolsheviks/communists presented a fear-evoking element to the Nazi mindset, with Slavic civilization and Soviet Russia portending as logically threatening to the

German essence. Such notions conveyed in a propaganda handout were circulated to German troops stating:

> Anyone who has ever looked at the face of a red commissar knows what the Bolsheviks are like. Here there is no need for theoretical expressions. We would insult the animals if we described these mostly Jewish men as beasts. They are the embodiment of the Satanic and insane hatred against the whole of noble humanity . . . The masses, whom they have sent to their deaths by making use of all means at their disposal such as ice-cold terror and insane incitement, would have brought an end to all meaningful life, had this eruption not been dammed at the last moment. (Bartov as cited in Jones, 2006, p. 267)

The notions of psychological or physical dispossession and displacement underlie existential dread, and that "desperation . . . runs through a great deal of ethnic violence" with many groups convinced of their impending inundation, control, dispossession, or possibly even extinction by their neighbors (Horowitz as cited in Jones, 2006, pp. 267–268). With the individual's physical annihilation not imminent, existential dread may wrongly be viewed as subordinating mortal terror, but given a group identity's supreme value, many individuals will sacrifice their lives defending it. Also, people will often rather opt for physical death than face existential dishonor, shame, and "respect" or status loss in the presence of one's peers (Des Pres, as cited in Jones, 2006, p. 268), with examples of such respect or honor, including sexual fidelity/female virginity, masculine honor, and warrior-hood time-honored codes.

Demographic Factors, Resource Scarcity, and Greed

Further on genocide causation, demographical factors and resource constraints also contribute to genocide orchestration. The surge in genocide in the twentieth century is attributed to the two underlying factors of exploding population growth and resource scarcity (Waller, 2002). A further psychological factor which motivates génocidaires is greed. Presenting the "Nazi 'Aryanization' of Jewish properties" as an epitome of greed, most Germans saw the dispossession as a "once-in-a-lifetime opportunity, and made the most of it" (Jones, 2006, p. 264). The Nazis encouraged the exploitation of the Jews' plight by the "Aryan" Germans, as well as fully took advantage of it themselves. Even close to the peak of the Holocaust in 1941–42, Hitler was "sanctioning opportunities to extort foreign currency in return for ransoming very rich Jews" (Burleigh as cited in Jones, 2006, p, 264). Furthermore, "in the Nazi death camps, Jews were robbed not only of their few remaining possessions, but of their hair, which was sold for mattress stuffing—and (after death) of the gold fillings in their teeth, melted down for bullion" (Jones, 2006, p. 264).

A dominant subject in human affairs (Marchak as cited in Jones, 2006), greed is a primary motivating factor for genocide perpetrators, as well as bystanders. The opportunity of stripping victims' property and wealth, either by outright looting or desperation-priced purchasing, and occupation of forcefully vacated dwellings, frequent genocidal accounts. Hence, at the climax of Stalin's purges, the Soviets had "frequent house-moving because every execution created a vacant apartment and dacha which were eagerly occupied by survivors and their aspirational Party housewives, ambitious for grander accommodation" (Montefiore as cited in Jones, 2006, p. 264). Similarly, in 1994 Rwanda, opportunity for the land and cows owned by rural Tutsi victims had to be taken over by someone upon death of the owners, serving as significant incentive amid the country's poor and rising overpopulation (Prunier, as cited in Jones, 2006, p. 264).

Presenting greed as exceeding a desiring of material goods over and above survival necessities, there is an understanding of its close connection to the lust for power, prestige, and dominance. Hence, "[m]an does not strive for power only in order to enrich himself economically . . . Power, including economic power, may be valued 'for its own sake.' Very frequently the striving for power is also conditioned by the social 'honor' it entails" (Weber, quoted by Gerth and Mills as cited in Jones, 2006, p. 265). Accordingly, Jewish Holocaust "Functionalist" analysts stressed the underlings' eagerness in implementing the grand plans of Hitler with such dynamo that was tantamount to an independence of direct orders (Burleigh, as cited in Jones, 2006, p. 265). Hence, Simon Sebag Montefiore's notion of "Terror entrepreneurialism" is observed as reigning in Stalinist Russia, with a stream of Stalin's enemies' ambitious torturers only too eager to please and kill for him (as cited in Jones, 2006, p. 265). While such individuals were often marked for execution next, there usually were ambitiously inspiring men and women waiting (Mandelstam as cited in Jones, 2006, p. 265). Furthermore, the génocidaires can be adequately motivated even by a momentary sun, as in the Rwandan genocide's vengeful targeting of Tutsis by "street boys, rag-pickers, [and] car-washers" (Prunier, as cited in Jones, 2006, p. 265). Hence

> [g]reed reflects objective material circumstances, but also, like narcissism, the core strivings of ego. Greed is never satiated; but when it is fed, one feels validated, successful—even omnipotent. Perhaps the only force that can truly match it as a motivator for genocide is fear. (Jones, 2006, p. 265)

Power Politics and Genocide Denial

Still on genocide causation, in examining the origins of the Armenian genocide, its development, and consequences from a broad-based perspective of reappraising all the involved major parties' secondary and primary sources, genocide's underlying causation is attributed to the interplay of power politics (Bloxham, 2005). This power politics interplay involves the Ottoman Empire's interactions within the decades of its final decline, the European imperial power's self-interested policies, and some Armenian nationalists' agenda within the Ottoman territory and beyond. Of special emphasis is the international context's ethnic polarization process which culminated with the 1912–23 massive destruction and particularly the Armenian community obliteration in 1915–16 (Bloxham, 2005). An interconnectedness is, thus, observed in the relationship between the "eastern question" power politics from 1774, the "Armenian question" narrower politics from mid-nineteenth century, and the internal questions of the Ottoman Empire's ethnic and social order reforms which were under intense external pressure (Bloxham, 2005, p. 1).

Furthermore, in an in-depth investigative study on imperial Germany's role in WWI and the genocide, different conclusions emerge from prevailing notions on their complicity (Bloxham, 2005). In examining the Entente wartime and Anglo-French postwar axis to contextually place the various related genocide politics and denial themes into perspective, the interwar phase political interest of America in the Middle East which framed the policy refusing to recognize the genocide is identified. The Armenian question's historical frame is thus undergirded by the genocide's continuing international denial due to several similar relationship concerns that are still underlying interactions between America, Europe, and Turkey as were in operation prior to WWI (Bloxham, 2005). Hence, "great power involvement in Ottoman internal affairs was a key element in exacerbating the Ottoman–Armenian dynamic towards genocide while Turkish sensitivity about external intervention on behalf of the Armenians—whether directed towards reforms before 1914 or independence after 1918—was a vital contributory factor to the emergence of denial" (Bloxham, 2005, p. 5).

Moreover, perpetrators' self-deception and denial of acts committed are genocide-orchestrating factors, the understanding of which is essential for eliciting insights on forestalling and preventing genocide (Newman and Erber, 2002). There is the recognition of various governments' attempts to minimize or cover up genocidal acts with such governments' efforts at rationalizing mass killings exposed, in addition to an observation of the external governments' compromises and excusing of their deterrence to intervene to stop or prevent the perpetration of genocide (Totten and Parsons, 2009). Also, addressing denial is the Holocaust's ongoing cultural hegemony against which contending advocates of other human devastations clamor to present genocide as also applying to their cases, some of which emanated centrally from European power. However, whether the events are occurring in urban or distant peripheries— colonial, post, or neo—the underlying assumption for understanding them lies in using the same reference frame, which has its beginnings rooted in Western development's initial power bases and that power's extrusion into the world at large (Levene, 2005a, p. 4).

The inadequacy of the terms "victims" and "perpetrators" in explaining interactions between state and groups that occasion genocide presents an erroneous notion of the existence of only two absolute human types worldwide—the perpetual wrongdoer and the other perpetually at the receiving end, such notions of which "legitimize and, thus, perpetuate cycles of violence, including genocide" (Levene, 2005, p. 5). Paradoxically, genocidal perpetrators usually claim to be the victims, while similarly, where the actual victimized group has the 'international community' validate its victimhood, such validation status can be used to absolve itself or justify its own heinous acts in generations to come. Thus, Western contemporary culture's accordance of celebrity to "victimhood," and the tendency of valorizing and even making sacred one's own memory of genocide or catastrophe, undermine the ability to break away from such transmissions (Levene, 2005a, p. 6).

Humiliation

Still on genocide causation, the notion of humiliation is a crucial genocidal factor, the fear of which greatly underlies existential dread (Jones, 2006). In world affairs, Thomas Friedman, a columnist with the *New York Times*, observes that "[t]he single most underappreciated force in international relations is humiliation" (Jones, 2006, p. 268). This phenomenon has also been explored at the individual level by others including psychologists. Defined as "the enforced lowering of a person or group, a process of subjugation that damages or strips away their pride, honor or dignity" by Evelin Lindner, humiliation is increasingly acknowledged as a key human behavioral motivating factor, especially violent behavior (Jones, 2006, p. 268). Furthermore, "humiliated fury" plays a crucial role "in escalating conflict between individuals and nations" (Retzinger and Scheff in Lindner as cited in Jones, 2006, p. 268). In addition,

> [h]umiliation involves feelings of shame and disgrace, as well as helplessness in the face of abuse at the hands of a stronger party. These are among the most painful and indelible of human emotions. He who has known extreme shame and humiliation may forever struggle to recover a sense of agency and self-respect. (Lifton as cited in Jones, 2006, p, 268)

In a study of U.S. hardened prisoners, psychologist James Gilligan observed that "the basic psychological motive, or cause, of violent behavior is the wish to ward off or eliminate the feeling of shame and humiliation—a feeling that is painful and can even be intolerable and overwhelming—and replace it with its opposite, the feeling of pride" (Gilligan as cited in Jones, 2006, p. 268). Moreover, humiliation predominantly features in humans' most extreme expressions of aggression such as war, murder, and genocide, and serves as a principal motivating force in virtually every genocidal case in history or contemporary (Horowitz as cited in Jones, 2006, p. 268), for instance, the Armenian genocide, the Young Turkish authorities' humiliation in Constantinople as a result of the 1909–13 military defeats they sustained in northern Africa and the Balkans, as well as by the imperial territories' secessions inclusive of Albania, Bulgaria, and Serbia. Thus,

> [t]hey were humiliated by the presence of a religious and ethnic minority in their midst (Christian Armenians) that included a prosperous "middleman" sector, and was supposedly assisting Russian designs on Turkey at a time of imperial vulnerability (the First World War). (Jones, 2006, p. 268)

Accordingly, this feeling of humiliation is further extended to current Turkish authorities and contemporary commentators, were they to acknowledge the Armenian genocide and proffer apologies. Hence, humiliation is a primary genocide denial underpinning factor (Jones, 2006).

Moreover, the Nazi Germans attained prominence through the exploitation of national humiliation by transforming it into hatred and vengefulness against their perceived tormentors. Stunned by the collapse of their army at the western front in 1918 following four years' fighting in WWI, there was a resultant formation of the extreme right-wing core groups out of the withdrawn, defeated forces astride the Rhine. Proliferating in the early 1920s, one of these groups thrived around Adolf Hitler who had declarations and writings replete with trepidation on the humiliation of Germany (Lifton, as cited in Jones, 2006, p. 269). The penal Versailles 1919 Treaty imposition, having been met with humiliation and outrage, further aggravated revanchist and extremist movements. Thus, seeking a scapegoating outlet for their humiliation, the Nazis presented the Jews as having treacherously delivered a "stab in the back" of Germany, to have them prostrated before Bolshevism, Western Allies, and capitalism. As the country shifted from the 1920s hyperinflation to the end of the decade's Great Depression, privation and economic pressures intensified the humiliation feelings, particularly those of the men, whose "provider" status bounded up their self-image (Jones, 2006, p. 269).

Furthermore, in Belgian-colonized Rwanda, Tutsis were indoctrinated as having descended from the Nile region "civilized" peoples, depicted and in time viewed themselves as educated, powerful, tall, and attractive, while the Hutus were depicted as "unrefined bumpkins" and "humiliating antithesis" (Jones, 2006, p. 269). Established with the revolution of 1959, the Hutus' political dominance portended (for the Hutu masses) a conquering of humiliation on the premise of putting the Tutsis "in their place" (Jones, 2006, p. 269). However, the Hutu dominance was threatened in 1990 with the invasion of an exiled Tutsis (from Rwanda) movement. Furthermore, an economic downturn experienced around the same period meant hundreds of thousands of Hutus facing humiliating unemployment, again especially affecting the male adults, a vast number of which were recruited as genocidal agents. Hence, "that gratuitous and humiliating cruelties are routinely inflicted upon victims" is understandable "given the intense humiliation of the génocidaires" (Jones, 2006, p. 269).

Accordingly, humiliation also strongly features in the "genocides by the oppressed" or subaltern genocide, with virtually every génocidaire considering himself or herself oppressed by the genocide target, for instance, the "Turks by Armenians, Germans by Jews, Khmers by Vietnamese" (Jones, 2006, p. 269). While such framings may usually derive from paranoia and myth, in some cases the convictions may have more objectivity to them, as in the Rwandan Hutus who had experienced humiliation and social subordination by Tutsis. Similarly, the Kosovo extremists, having been motivated by the years of Serb suppression and brutalization, launched a campaign of persecution and plausible genocide against the Serbians in Kosovo (Jones, 2006).

Subaltern genocide also manifests in Islamist terrorism, with its exponents keenly feeling "the humiliation of centuries of conquest and domination by Western 'Crusaders'" (Jones, 2006, p. 270). Hence, Osama bin Laden's proclamation that "[w]hat America is tasting now is only a copy of what we have tasted. . . . Our Islamic nation has been tasting the same for more than 80 years, of humiliation and disgrace" (Stern, quoted by Gilligan as cited in Jones, 2006, p. 270). In fact, commentators have been amazed that Arabs, who are relatively privileged and even those exposed directly to and benefiting from Western cosmopolitanism and affluence, can organize and launch terrorist attacks that could degenerate into genocidal massacre. The key to understanding such phenomenon is humiliation, which is more strongly felt by the privileged, the educated than by the masses. Quoting James Scott, Jones (2006) argues, "The cruelest result of human bondage . . . is that it transforms the assertion of personal dignity into a mortal risk," as well as observed that revolting against that form of bondage by aiming to subdue humiliation in order to reestablish self-respect and dignity can involve vicious and genocidal practices (p. 270).

Race, Racism, and Crime

Additionally on genocide causation factors, a critical examination of the controversies and debates on the issues of race, criminal justice, and crime, focusing on America and Britain, while also taking an international perspective, identify these factors as underpinning genocide (Webster, 2007). Analyzing the United States historical lynching legacy case studies, the Nazi state racist crime, and the Rwandan genocides, a conceptual framework for a better understanding of race, racism, and crime is recognized. Exploring the historical origins of the association of crime with racism, anxieties and fears concerning crime and race are rooted in fast-social-change destabilized places. The primary focus is, thus, in understanding the relationships between and social processes of "'criminalization' and 'racialization' . . . which construct and label certain groups and assign them negative attributes such as 'criminality' or 'inferiority'" (Webster, 2007, p. xi). Lone factors such as ethnicity and race are capable of significantly explaining the divergent ethnic groups' patterns of offending and victimization. Additional insights are drawn from further exploration of race and the system of criminal justice, particularly the issues and evidences of differential treatment of visible minorities by the police and the court system, as well as the crime of a racist state, and genocide primarily—a racist crime that often eludes the attention of criminologists (Webster, 2007).

Moreover, identifying euthanasia as the beginning of the Nazi genocide—which derived from the predicament of Jews with handicaps first targeted for murder, these individuals were murdered purely for racial reasons. Hence, "the killers were motivated by an ideological obsession to create a homogeneous and robust nation based on race . . . to purge the handicapped from the national gene pool" (Freidlander, 1995, pp. xi-xii). Thus, drawing from Germany's increasing eugenics and racist ideologies, the euthanasia of people with handicaps is identified as providing the ideal for mass murder, thus, originating the Holocaust (Freidlander, 1995). Furthermore, an analysis of the African Great Lakes region, focusing on Rwanda, Burundi, and Congo development with emphasis on Rwandan and Burundian ethno-based conflicts, sporadic wars, and genocide, presents the conflicts' negative impacts on the region (Scherrer, 2002). There is recognition of European colonialism and its racism, as well as the region's forty-year postcolonial ideology of genocide derived from the colonial history of German and Belgian's indirect rule and segregation. Exploring the region's pre-independence history highlights the Rwandan and Burundian colonialism experience, ethnicization, and state formation processes which transformed the Tutsi and Hutu, who were initially competing ethnic groups, into irreconcilable opposing castes. Furthermore, there is the contemplation of an escalation into another genocidal round in the region, given the 1994 Rwandan genocide with conceivably one million Tutsis and thousands of Hutu moderates killed, the Burundian civil war, and genocidal killings since 1993, with about 200,000 Burundians killed, and the Congolese extremely internationalized war (Scherrer, 2002).

TYPES OF GENOCIDE

Genocidal orchestrations can be identified with diverse manifestations, presenting the different typologies of genocide. For instance, Fein identified genocide typologies comprising four categories, including developmental, despotic, retributive, and ideological genocides (Hinton, 2002, p. 64). For developmental genocide, the perpetrator harms the victim deliberately with or without deliberation, due to economic exploitation or colonization. Thus, in this typology of genocide, intentional as well as unintentional consequences are addressed, contrary to the United Nations Convention's focus only on intentional consequences. Additionally, for despotic genocide, the perpetrator aims to clear from his or her territory, any form of opposition to his or her reign, whether imagined, potential or real. Also, for retributive genocide, "the perpetrator responds to a challenge to the structure of domination when two peoples, nations, ethnic groups, tribes, or religious collectives are locked into an ethnically stratified order in a plural society" (Fein, as cited in Hinton, 2002, p. 64). And, lastly, the causes of ideological genocide "are the hegemonic myths identifying the victims as outside the sanctioned universe of obligation or myths based on religion [that] exclude the victim from the sanctified universe of salvation and obligation" (Fein, as cited in Hinton, 2002, p. 64).

Additionally, diverse genocidal forms springing from varied roots are observed among indigenous groups. For instance, seeing genocide as developmental and a war product, the destruction of the Brazilian, Paraguayan, and Peruvian Indians was done "out of cold calculation of gain, and, in some cases, sadistic pleasure rather than as the result of a political or economic crisis" (Smith as cited in Hinton, 2002, p. 64). Furthermore, there is a distinction between "domestic genocides," which arise from a society's internal divisions, and genocides occurring in an international warfare context (Kuper as cited in Hinton, 2002, p. 65).

More so, genocidal typologies evolve through different phases or stages of genocide. In examining the Nazi program, for instance, there is an understanding of its evolution from secret extermination of persons with disabilities and handicaps to systematical destruction of Gypsies and Jews. The Nazi genocide's development is trailed with the regime primarily excluding from the general community, the targeted groups' members, through escalating persistent persecution, imbibing more intense exclusionary policies of forced handicapped people's sterilization, gypsies' incarceration, and mandatory emigration of Jews. Ultimately, the regime adopted and implemented a mass murder program for the eradication of the three target groups (Friedlander, 1995). Additionally, insights can be drawn from the forms of genocidal violence, which create the plausibility of genocide always occurring given the multiplicity of symbolic type violence which occurs even in presumably non-genocidal countries such as the United States. Genocide is also recognized as existing along the lines not only of everyday type violence, but also as imperceptible genocides as in the systematic murdering of street-children by the Brazilian police in attempt at street "clean-up" (Hinton, 2002). Further distinction is made in genocide typology between total cum "genocide in whole," and partial cum "genocide in part." For instance, "the Rwandan genocide was a total domestic genocide, what the United Nations would call a "genocide in whole" over a "genocide in part," and as such it was the African version of the Holocaust" (Scherrer, 2002, p. xi).

EXAMPLES OF GENOCIDE

A multiplicity of genocidal examples litters and permeates history up to contemporary times. For instance, many people groups are identified when examining the psychological patterns of the atrocities committed in genocides, which in the twentieth century have tragically claimed lives totaling above 262 million, involving Armenians, Jews, Cambodians, Kosovons, Rwandans, and Darfurians, and many others (Baum, 2008). Further exploring genocide cases of the twentieth century, there is a recognition of historical genocide cases of the Armenians, the Holocaust, Stalin's victims, and that of imperial Japan, as well as more recent genocidal cases and mass murders in Ethiopia, East Timor, Cambodia, former Yugoslavia, Rwanda, and Guatemala (Gellately and Kiernan, 2003). Also, identifying archeology's role in providing historical material foundation for the creation of the Nationalist Socialist Party's notion of a pure German race, as well as anthropologists' involvement in the Jews and other exterminatory campaigns during the Third Reich, the Holocaust is additionally acknowledged among others (Hinton, 2002).

One of the critical outcomes of modernity's turning point is the Vendee destruction during the French Revolution, with the "rise of the West" destabilizing effects on such older empires as the Ottoman, Russian, Chinese, and Austrian, having extensive devastating impacts on such people groups as the East European Jews and the Armenians (Levene, 2005b). Genocide and massive exterminatory deeds perpetrated against indigenous peoples by these four empires in consequence of the half century's hegemonic pressures led up to the 1914 general global catastrophe (Levene, 2005b). Furthermore, with the pathological homogenization factors of expulsion, forced assimilation, and genocide as are practiced in the process of state-building, and with such practices understood as predating the nationalism era, genocidal cases spanning prenationalist as well as nationalist era have been identified, including the fifteenth-century Spanish expulsion of the Jews and the Huguenots persecution, both under Louis XIV, and in the twentieth century, the genocide of the Armenians and former Yugoslavia's ethnic cleansing (Rae, 2002). Such atrocities impelled the development of international norms to define the states' legitimate behavior with sovereignty increasingly streamlined as conditional (Rae, 2002). While also examining the factors that can deter pathological homogenization processes in state-building, the genocidal cases of Macedonia and the Czech Republic are recognized (Rae, 2002).

Moreover, the 1780–1782 Upper Peru region's (of South America) great rebellion is identified in the context of genocide and millennialism, with insights proffered in understanding the rebellion, its paradoxes, heterogeneity, and avoidance of any singular perspective (Robins, 2002). While most genocidal cases with the native peoples have mainly focused on genocide by colonizers, there have been instances in this region where the perpetrators were Indians and the targets were Spaniards. In fact, the discourse focusing on the Indians as victims of varying genocidal forms which evolved over time has obscured "the fact that the native peoples experienced genocide not only as victims, but also as perpetrators" (Robins, 2002, p. 1). However, the rebellion countered such generally held genocidal notions of victims' lack of weaponry and organization in confronting their enemies, as the Indian revolutionaries in the rebellion faced the loyalist army that were more organized and better armed. Furthermore, while a leadership structure that is centralized usually characterizes genocidal policies, the insurgence's leadership was basically confederate in nature and highly fragmented (Robins, 2002). Also, the rebellion's further unusual characteristic of the genocide victims similarly becoming the victors, with the natives—the Indians, Mestizos, Creoles, and the Spaniards—recognizing explicitly its genocidal nature. Accordingly,

> [a]s with almost all genocidal movements, this one was not free of coercion and internal divisions, and as such was riddled by internal contradictions. Not all rebels supported the genocidal cause. . . . Other rebels, while supportive of the goal of eliminating non-Indian culture from the region, were reluctant to embrace genocide. It was at the field level where the genocidal tendencies and conscription were strongest, and those who refused to join or to follow orders were subject to summary execution. In other instances, the rebel leaders tried to deceive people into participating, presenting their goals and actions as the implementation of Spanish royal orders. (Robins, 2002, pp. 3–4)

ALTERNATIVE METHODOLOGICAL APPROACHES IN GENOCIDE STUDIES

Various methodological approaches are used by scholars in genocidal studies. For instance, Dutton (2007) uses the methodology of ethology, mimicking animal behavior naturalistic studies citing Tinbergen, argues for obtaining "an ethology of human aggression . . . from descriptions of violence by perpetrators and eyewitnesses" (p. xi). He provides some descriptions in his review of massacres in several countries including Nanking, Vietnam, El Salvador, and Rwanda. Another approach used involves exploring such underlying themes of modernity, ideology, and genocide's relationship with the body politic; drawing conclusions across case studies; and presenting a multidisciplinary approach to understanding current human atrocities (Gellately and Kiernan, 2003). While also noting that genocide is not a predated twentieth-century notion but a contemporary phenomenon and an inherent human nature product, a functionalist approach is adopted to examine the preceding and accompanying mass murder decision-making processes underlying the directives to kill, thus providing insights that are not revealed by the conventional top-down, leadership directives-focused approach (Gellately and Kiernan, 2003). There is also an examining of genocide at the victim level, going beyond the state decision-making formal dynamics on the premise of espousing full understanding of genocide by taking cognizance of survivors' accounts, thus proffering new avenues for understanding and investigation of genocidal policies. By adopting this approach, such new genocidal forms as rape, which eluded the legalistic 1948 genocide definition, become evident, and hence, deserving of present efforts at prosecution (Gellately and Kiernan, 2003).

Furthermore, an ad hoc explanation of the post-Holocaust sequential, relatively independent aspects that traces the origins of connections to facts of the genocide and exploring their consequences, will enable a challenge of the Holocaust's basic historiographical, theological, philosophical, and moral implications. Underlying the study's approach is the understanding of the provocativeness of speaking about the Holocaust's *interpretations* based on the enormity of the event's systematic genocide, given that "the facts speak for themselves . . . leaving nothing over to interpret, nothing to ponder or contest" (Lang, 2005, p. xi). Thus, the dilemma and tension of the term's evoked evil and sadism sustain its recasting by scholars and survivors in new and differing ways that reconfigure its events and impacts (Lang, 2005). Thus, post-Holocaust reflection analysis, which is focused in different directions, is categorized under the four rubrics of "the Archival, Explanatory, Testimonial, and Representational modes" comprising sets of different reflecting emphasis (Lang, 2005, p. xii). The "Archival works" aim at recording, recovering, or reconstructing physical or empirical evidences of plans, actions, and conditions directed at, or initiated by, anyone involved during the Holocaust, reflecting teleological concerns for understanding the how and why certain outcomes occurred historically in sequence; the "Explanatory design" addresses issues of the relationship between the corporate "mentality" and individual "decision making" or the causes and reasons; the "Testimonial" involves expressive forms that extend from monumental or memorials—whether individual, group, or national—to the testimony; and the "Representational" deals with the descriptive art works of the Holocaust, emphasizing its inception as well as its reception (Lang, 2005, pp. xii–xv).

Further proffering a focused examination of genocide contemporarily in a world history contextual framework, while also broaching genocidal studies' abstraction issues, the study addresses genocide definition-related core problems, and offers conceptual understanding of perpetrators and victims within world historical background (Levene, 2005a). This involves examining the patterns and processes linking up earlier modern genocide up to the present, inclusive of colonial exterminations of the sixteenth through the nineteenth centuries, and the more current genocidal eruptions of the twentieth century (Levene, 2005a). By presenting individual genocides as "part of a whole" rather than in isolation, connecting threads and comparative grounds are identified for the genocides (Levene, 2005a, p. 4). The study, in essence, proffers an understanding of genocide in the modern world, with an analysis of genocide's meaning within a broad-based world historical context. Following up on this is another study setting out genocide's conceptual issues, addressing its fundamental definitional problems, and proffering an understanding of victims' and perpetrators' meaning frames, as well as placing such meaning frames contextually in world history (Levene, 2005b).

Furthermore, analyzing collective evildoing dynamics, generally, a combination of Hannah Arendt's philosophical approach, C. Fred Alford's psychological approach, and Zygmunt Bauman's sociological approach is drawn upon (Arendt; Alford; and Bauman, as cited in Vetlesen, 2005, p. 7). Adopting this hybrid approach, which is employed in examining the former Yugoslavian ethnic cleansing and the Holocaust, is theoretically aimed at a "synthesis between functionalist and intentionalist approaches to collective evil" (Vetlesen, 2005, p. 2). There is an understanding of the closeness of interactions between victims, perpetrators, and bystanders, as well as the manner of recognizing, denying, and projecting of human agency aspects by other agents (Vetlesen, 2005). Additionally, an approach of historical comparative case study is adopted, with an analytical framework that highlights the numerous genocidal underlying factors such as lack of education, past social traumas, deepseated poverty, common historical grievances, economic or political dislocation, colonization, or war (Gellately and Kiernan, 2003). Of paramount importance is the human-agency factor which primarily translates such identified underlying conditions into genocidal episodes, derivative of regimes/political sects, extremist leaders, and criminalist decisions. The analysis offers insights on myriad genocide causal factors, and also proffers challenges for further genocidal investigations and averting future genocides (Gellately and Kiernan, 2003). Also proffering insights on the Holocaust and genocide, social psychological approaches are employed for understanding mass killing episodes with such factors as the genocidal inclined personality, and the adaptation to aggression through violent behavior engagement, identified as genocide causation factors (Newman and Erber, 2002).

Employing a geographical perspective for analyzing genocide and its effects provides a vantage point (Wood, 2001). Over the past century, political geographers have become involved with issues of cultural homelands, ethnic distribution, natural resource-based conflicts, subnational and international political boundaries, and competing state organisms' geopolitical struggles, all of which are pertinent for contextually understanding civil war occurrences (Bowman as cited in Wood, 2001, p. 57). There is a proposition for the mapping of genocidal patterns across the areas affected, involving the specific neighborhoods and villages that are targets of destruction, sites of massacres, particular cultural landmark destruction or defilement, and mandatory displacements from definite areas (Wood, 2001).

GENOCIDE PREVENTION AND INTERVENTION

An examination of genocide prevention and intervention measures calls for an understanding of the Genocide Treaty's primary provisions, which is a continuing area of disagreement and debate (Schabas, 2000). With genocide remaining the international efforts' spur for human rights prevention and punishment, the need for a careful crafting of prospective prosecutions into the Convention is recognized (Schabas, 2000). Thus, tracing the 1948 Genocide Prevention and Punishment Convention's drafting and development, in analyzing contemporary genocides' international tribunals and the United Nations' responses using definitive portions of the Convention, Schabas (2000) examines the treaty reforms and revisions. With recognition of the treaty interpretation norms and foreign policy's interrelationship with international law, and with the incorporation of a genocide legal literature bibliography, there is an understanding of the different Genocide Convention implementation approaches limiting the treaty's impact. Examples of such limitations include several states' omission from genocide definition and various groups' emergent crimes, acts, or incitement (Schabas, 2000). Hence, Schabas recognizes that

> "[t]he fact of genocide is as old as humanity." The law, however, is considerably younger. This dialectic of the ancient fact yet the modern law of genocide follow from the observation that, historically, genocide has gone unpunished. Hitler's famous comment, "who remembers the Armenians?," is often cited in this regard. Yet the Nazis were only among the most recent to rely confidently on the reasonable presumption that an international culture of impunity would effectively shelter the most heinous perpetrators of crimes against humanity.
> The explanation for this is straightforward: genocide was generally, although perhaps not exclusively, committed under the direction or, at the very least, with the benign complicity of the State where it took place. Usually, the crime was executed as a quite overt facet of State policy, particularly within the context of war or colonial conquest. Obviously, therefore, domestic prosecution was virtually unthinkable, even where the perpetrators did not in a technical sense benefit from

some manner of legal immunity. Only in rare cases where the genocidal regime collapsed in its criminal frenzy, as in Germany or Rwanda, could accountability be considered. (2000, p. 1)

The obligation of the international community for genocide prevention and punishment has contradictorily resulted in the unwillingness of the Western authorities to invoke the term. This is due to the fact that genocide recognition presupposes a tenacity of underlying forces that are primordial, and which negate tenets of universal human rights and democratic principles, while also lending enormous emotive power to the genocide concept by its close linkage with the Nazi Holocaust (Schabas, 2000). Through the examination of the Bosnia-Herzegovina ethnic conflict dynamics and the international involvement dilemmas surrounding it, for instance, there is the recognition of the war's causes and its conduct, and the reasons behind the failure of the international efforts to resolve the Bosnian conflict for over three years, as well as why success was finally achieved in late 1995 (Burg and Shoup, 1999). The 1995-produced Dayton accord, with an expectation of its implementation experience after two years occasioning long-term peace for Bosnia, was also reviewed. There is an observation of the warring Bosnian Muslim, the Croatian, and the Serbian communities' goal incompatibility, their disinclination to negotiate in good stead, and the international community's reluctance to indefinitely enforce negotiated settlement, or to incur the cost of ending the fight, hence, presenting the dilemmas of intervention (Burg and Shoup, 1999).

In proffering a detailed analysis of the Bosnia-Herzegovina crisis, there is an insightful understanding of the ethnic conflict dynamics, which also sheds light on the developing of strategies for managing, as well as preventing, ethnic conflicts from disrupting international peace (Burg and Shoup, 1999). Specifically examined are the actions of the crisis' major participants, including the international community as well as the actors in former Yugoslavia, with the study's first part tracing the conflict origins, the war years' major developments including the media role, ethnic cleansing, and genocide, and the second part providing a detailed analytical description of the international community's efforts to resolve the conflict based on the war account background (Burg and Shoup, 1999).

Further on preventing genocide, in the twentieth century there were no external party interventions found in nine genocides until the violence exacerbated itself (Dutton, 2007). Such behaviors of willfully ignoring and remaining disconnected from the occurrences and the obligations to intervene under international law are recognized as political decisions (Dutton, 2007). Exploring ways that policymakers, scholars, the media, and others can contribute toward preventing genocide, the difficulties of preventing genocide are identified along with a genocide prevention guide proffered for policymakers, scholars, and others (Heidenrich, 2001). Limitations of imposing trade sanctions are additionally recognized which usually take upward of two years to become effective, and in some cases may only become effective after a decade, with limitations also on military interventions, covert actions, and the issue of using multinational forces. The need is also recognized for the United Nations' mobilization of its own military force, independent of members' force contributions, to serve as an international volunteer for emergent peacekeeping situations (Heidenrich, 2001).

Moreover, the relationships between the United Nations (UN) Security Council, the Secretariat, and the superpowers, are essential in the understanding of the United Nations in the modern genocide age (Lebor, 2006). Also, the "symbiotic entwining" of the Security Council's relationship with the Secretariat, "has helped shape the United Nations' failures in Bosnia, Rwanda, and Darfur" (Lebor, 2006, p. 7). More so, there is an understanding of the insider details of the behind-the-scenes negotiations and diplomacy which resulted in the Council's 1993 resolutions defining the safe areas and the UN's response limits to attacking them. Observed, for instance, are the tensions within the Secretariat's different departments, particularly between the Zagreb-based UNPROFOR and the Peacekeeping Operations Department (DPKO) in New York which prevented a forceful intervention for the Bosnian genocide, thus providing fresh views and insights on the UN's inner workings (Lebor, 2006, p. 8). While also detailing the Srebrenica catastrophe's causes and consequences, to draw on its contemporary resonance, a template is proffered to help understand why the Darfur genocide has not been stopped by the United Nations. Thus, "the same feeble response mechanisms, inertia, bureaucratic infighting within the Secretariat, and crucial lack of political will by the Security Council to stop the killing remain entrenched" (Lebor, 2006, p.8). Additionally, there are further insights and lessons learned on plausible courses of action to take for preventing genocide (Lebor, 2006).

Still on the possibility of protection against genocide, the problems involved in trying to safeguard against genocide are recognized, such as identified in the military and diplomatic efforts at achieving a humane and just solution to the crisis in Kosovo (Riemer, 2000). Observed as hideously persisting and continuing, the problems highlight the international community's tragic failure in developing a powerful response to genocide's tenacious evil after the Holocaust. While the international community passed the UN's Convention on the Prevention and Punishment of the Crime of Genocide in 1948, after World War II, atrocious genocides have continued to occur in Bosnia, Cambodia, Rwanda, as well as in other parts of the world. The challenge is presently clear for the international community today, after more than fifty years of adopting the UN antigenocide treaty, with the crafting of an effective and judicious response still needed (Riemer, 2000). In response to the challenge of addressing the central question, "Can a Global Human Rights Regime to protect against genocide be put into place—or is this an impossible mission?" four strategic needs are outlined for carrying out such a vital and particularly difficult mission (Riemer, 2000, p. ix). These strategies include the strengthening of actors and institutions of a "Global Human Rights Regime"; articulating a practical prevention philosophy that is cogent; crafting prudently targeted sanctions; and developing of a "just humanitarian intervention" theory and practice that is judicious (Riemer, 2000, p. ix). Further exploring key follow-up questions relating to actors, institutions, policies, principles, problems, and practices of the Global Human Rights Regime, there is recognition of solving the world order problem of genocide by institutions and norms, as well as the existence of tension between mustering the political will for eliminating genocide and transcending the enormous obstacles of genocide prevention (Reimer, 2000).

Also, through analysis of both the Burundian and Congolese developments there is an understanding of the conflicts' intricate roots and seemingly interminable sequences of violence, as well as how to contain and transform such conflicts by employing local cultural mechanisms of dispute resolution systems, particularly the *"gachacha* and *abashingantah"* (Scherrer, 2002, p. xiii). Additionally identified as a dispute resolution mechanism is the international community's role on human rights pursuits, disaster relief, development aid, and peace restoration in order to break the tragic violence cycle (Scherrer, 2002). While outlining strategies for genocide prevention and intervention for averting future genocidal occurrences, the need is also identified "to inform, educate, cajole, prod, and encourage people to break out of their mold of silence, to collectively reach out to the victims and the voiceless, and to demand that such atrocities be halted" (Totten and Parsons, 2009, p. 2). For instance, there is an understanding of politically contrived memory manipulation being fundamental in the unleashing of primal genocidal passions, based on its framing of people's willingness to kill others through history and its resultant recurrences of massive human violence. Hence, understanding the ways cultural memory becomes created enables an understanding of the causes and ways mass murder episodes occur, as well as fosters preventative efforts against their occurrences (Hirsch, 1995).

Furthermore, employing the international community's actions and inactions in the Bosnian and Rwandan genocidal, there is a demonstration of such bystander covert responsibility, with an observation of the purported posture of politicians, the military, and major Western diplomats to the issues of balance and neutrality rather than proffering their authoritative explicit intervention (Vetlesen, 2005). However, the 1994 Rwandan genocide analysis to explore whether the genocide could have been prevented through a rapid military intervention with minimal human and financial outlay to the interveners, had adequate political will been mustered by the international community, is observed as dispelling the conventional notion that the Rwandan genocide and plausibly others could have been averted by a small contingent of about 5000 troops (Kuperman, 2001). Enunciating impeding obstacles that would necessarily have been overcome to forestall the genocide which occurred in such limited timeframe within weeks, there is an outlining of such impeding factors of historical background, as well as cultural and geographical settings. Thus, it would have been virtually impossible, both logistically as well as militarily, to stop the genocide based on the notion of effective intervention involving the airlifting of troops from the U.S. as this would have been constrained by time. Discountenancing this on a personal level, however, the international community's failure to intervene to stop the Rwandan genocide is a dearth of political will and apathy, since any other readily available military contingent could have been deployed, even as an addition to the UNAMIR peacekeeping force of 2500 and other Belgian and French troops in Rwanda at the time, as observed by Kuperman (2001).

Trailing from this forgoing genocide conceptualization, the next chapter explores the theoretical framework of the northern Nigeria ethno-religious conflict.

THREE
Theoretical Framework of Nigeria's Ethno-Religious Conflict

The ethno-religious conflict in Nigeria derives from a variation of sociopolitical, socioeconomic, as well as cultural and religious factors. In particular, the conflict's inherent phenomena of massacres and wanton killings are complex features involving multiple causes, and therefore, also require multiple theoretical approaches to explicate the different facets of the conflict. In this section several theories are accordingly examined to proffer an understanding in the plausible interpretation of the many varied dimensions of the conflict. However, while these theories are discussed singularly as alternate theories, they are essentially complementary, and given the conflict's indistinctiveness from its larger contextual framework, the theories basically provide some insights into the study's assumptions on the conflict parties' behavior and actions as are linked to the conflict. The study's research question is, thus, consequentially grounded from this theoretical construct.

SOCIAL CUBISM THEORY EXPLICATION OF NORTHERN NIGERIA ETHNO-RELIGIOUS CONFLICT

The ethno-religious conflict in northern Nigeria can be examined using the social cubism lens. Social cubism is an analytical framework conceptually designed from a cube's image of six sides, developed by Byrne and Carter (1996), and adopts a holistic method of examining social conflict using a six-dimensional model of interrelated historical, religious, demographical, political, economic, and psycho-cultural factors. These six components of social cubism are seen as working in tandem for a better understanding of the causal factors or social conditions undergirding the conflict. By adopting the social cubism approach in the explication of ethno-territorial conflict, Byrne and Carter (1996) present that an adequate consideration of the combination of all six elements provides an illuminating image that sheds light on emergent societal or intergroup behavior. Hence, the theory captures the multidimensional complexity of any particular social conflict.

The social cubism model can, therefore, adequately explain the northern Nigeria ethno-religious conflict given the multidimensional framing of the conflict. And, by using the six elements of social cubism to analyze the conflict, its multidimensional composition can be seen.

Historical Factors

Social cubism's historical perspective draws on past happenings, traditions, or precedencies that were set in the past. Historically, the northern Nigeria ethno-religious conflict can be traced from the country's colonial past and history of ethnic hostilities. The formation of Nigeria, like most other African nation-states, started with the superimposition of diverse nationalities with the coercive machinery of the state (MacFarlane, 1984). There was no gradual politicization of a nationality to achieve political autonomy and subsequently transform into a nation-state; rather, Nigeria and such other African states were created haphazardly by European imperial powers, and as a result, preexisting independent ethno-political societies were forcibly amalgamated into one state (MacFarlane, 1984). In essence, colonization brought together different ethnic groups inclusive of three majority groups—the Hausas, Ibos and Yoruba—under one nation-state, resulting in Nigeria's characterization by a high degree of ethnic divergence, presently with over 250 ethnic groups (Central Intelligence Agency, 2012). The merging of these different ethnic groups into one national government has continued to frustrate the attempt at creating new political loyalties, as the country's political structure is deeply grounded in ethnic and regional loyalty and makes for unstable governance which, in turn, impacts the ethno-religious conflict in the North. Hence, the prevalence of conflicts in northern Nigeria can be linked to ethnicity factors and colonialism's amalgamating of various ethnic groups leading to Nigeria's high ethnocentric politics as undergirding the waves of killings in northern Nigeria (Anthony, 2002; Osaghae, 1998a).

Furthermore, colonialism brought fundamental changes in Nigeria, primarily in castigating and de-legitimating of traditional religions, which were from then on referred to as "paganism," and the rapid implanting of Christianity (Ibrahim, 1991). This transformative process was so rapid that within a few decades, pagan practitioners' census figures showed a sharp decline from 50 percent in 1931 to 34 percent in 1952, and 18.2 percent in 1963. In contrast, over this same period the census data showed an increase from 44 percent to 47 percent for registered Muslims, and a corresponding increase from 6.25 to 34.6 percent for Christians (Ibrahim, 1991, p. 116). The colonial authorities put in place a system that aimed to virtually remove all "pagans" and all "sects" that had forms of "non-orthodoxy," as these connoted "resistance to existing political authority," a campaign which has remained unabated since independence (Ibrahim, 1991, p. 116). And the justification for imposing Christian and Muslim orthodoxy derives from the strategy to promote unity in Nigeria, based on the notion of their shared philosophical and Abrahamic origins. However, the unity and peaceful national coexistence expected to emerge from the institutionalized religious orthodoxy has yet to materialize, as there is an evolution of conflict and political tension between the proponents of the two rival universal religions of Christianity and Islam in Nigeria. There is the tendency of both religions to delay national integration due to their negative inclinations to generate competing social orders (Ibrahim, 1991).

Additionally, Kukah and Falola (1996), in tracing the history of Islam's emergence in Nigeria "as a political force," acknowledge that "the use of Islam to initiate a large-scale jihad in the North during the 19th century provided a successful case for the establishment of an Islamic state in Nigeria," and argue that "the legacy of this continues to the present day" (pp. 2–3). Thus, Islam penetrated the North in the eleventh century, linking the region with North Africa, Western Sudan, and the Middle East. The social revolution produced by Othman Dan Fodio's jihad caused the creation of an Islamic state in the Northern region (Kukah and Falola, 1996). For instance, the Boko Haram sect, though loose, but with a highly effective terror network, is sustained and driven by a racist and fascist domination ideology. Hence, the mostly Fulani-led quest for the establishment of power in the North to constantly be in dominance over other Nigerians, which follows Ahmadu Bello's envisioning of the country as an Estate bequeathed to the Fulanis, from grandpa Othman Dan Fodio, underlies the country's inability to develop, since 1960, a united, modern, and democratic nation (Adebayo, 2012).

Religious Factors

Religion refers to a people group's article of faith in relation with the supernatural as linked to both the physical and the metaphysical world. Religion helps to preserve and maintain a people's way of life. On the religious dimension, there are two major powerful religions in Nigeria, the Islamic religion and Christianity, but also with some traditionalists following, and while Islam predominates most of the Northern region crossing linguistic and ethnic boundaries as its dominant religion, Christianity predominates across most of the south, including the Igbos of the east and the Yorubas of the west, many of whom view Islam as threatening to secular government (Noble, 1992c). Each of the two religions is, thus, trying to assert its meaning frame, and while one of the religions, Islam, is a political religion that does not divorce religion from the state, the other religion, Christianity, a nonpolitical religion, separates religion from the state. Tracing both religions' different dispositions to violence, for instance, Kukah and Falola observe that

> while Islam's early propagation by prophet Muhammad and his initial followers met with violence, they quickly adopted violence in self-defense waged as jihad which has become institutionalized in Islam. By contrast the propagation of Christianity as preached by Jesus Christ is to be by love and persuasion rather than the sword. However, the quest for political and economic power among those who became Christians in history blurred this injunction for peaceful propagation as the Crusades showed. (1996, p. 195)

Furthermore, religion appeals to millions as an avenue for mobilizing sentiments in choosing their role models and mentors from its rank amid a public that is alienated from the state, as well as for developing an enduring future hope. More so, religion is leaned upon by the elite for engaging in political competition on both an intra- and inter-regional basis, and for the northern ambitious elites, Islam serves as a political tool; as the level of corruption notwithstanding, a politician would "claim the fear of God as a principle of existence" (Kukah and Falola, 1996, p. 2). Thus, Nigeria has had an inundation of religious crisis and conflicts which are often orchestrated by the assertiveness and militancy of the extremist Islamists in the country (Kukah and Falola, 1996). More so, the activities of some Muslim groups, particularly in the northern parts of Nigeria aimed at Islamizing the country, are the cause of the ongoing violence (Haberson and Rothchild, 1991). Hence, the recognition of Islam's revolutionary force, its tendency to shape national as well as international politics (Mazrui; Currey; Rubin; and Pipes as cited in Kukah and Falola, 1996), and its aim to create an Islamic state in Nigeria "is the ultimate evidence of the place of religion in politics" (Kukah and Falola, 1996, p. 2).

Thus, in the final analysis, the effects of this religious politicking are clashes between Muslims and Christians in Nigeria, with religion frequently becoming fertile eruption grounds for political conflicts through manipulation and intrigues of the Nigerian Muslim politicians, with the resultant effect being that the country has, since independence, been in a tug of war concerning its leadership. Religion is an instrumental factor, with Muslims vying to have a Muslim leader and Christians, in the same vein, also vying for a Christian leader. On this perennial power tussle in the country's presidential race, for example,

> [t[he intense debate following the death of President Yar'Adua in May 2010 over the informal "zoning" arrangement, wherein presidential

power is swapped between north and south, shows that ethno-regional politics is alive and well at the national level. The far north is thus still a single unit in the country's power politics. (International Crisis Group, 2010, p. 9)

Thus, each religious group desires to be in control, with the exploitation of religious differences further entrenching the ethnic divide, and greatly intensifying political instability in Nigeria (Haberson and Rothschild, 1991). Hence, religious factors and politicization have been identified among the myriad of causal factors exacerbating the northern Nigeria ethno-religious conflict (Ibrahim, 1989, 1991; Osaghae, 1998a; Suberu, 2009; Williams, 2011).

Demographic Factors

Demographics refer to the number and composition of a population in a given place, as well as such factors as birthrate, gender, age, etc., which affect it. With its north-south dichotomy, Nigeria is unevenly divided into a mainly Muslim north and a predominantly Christian south, with the Middle Belt or central region which has a near balance of Christians and Muslims, straddling the nation. Each of these regions also has some minority traditionalists (International Crisis Group, 2010, p. 1). Northern Nigeria comprises the twelve states of Bauchi, Borno, Gombe, Jigawa, Kaduna, Kano, Katsina, Kebbi, Niger, Sokoto, Yobe, and Zamfara which adopted the Sharia law from 1999–2002 (see map VI in appendix A, showing the Sharia-adopted states in northern Nigeria), as well as the other seven non-Sharia-adopted states of Adamawa, Benue, Kogi, Kwara, Nasarawa, Plateau, and Taraba (see map I in appendix A), in all seven of which there is a large Christian following. Hence, northern Nigeria as presently constituted, covering all nineteen states in the north (see map I in appendix A) spans the far north key conflict zones of Maiduguri, Bauchi, Kano, and Yobe, as well as the perennial Middle Belt conflict zones of Jos, and Kaduna with minority ethnic groupings, and a large Christian following. Hence, demographically, northern Nigeria has a large Muslim majority with a substantial Christian minority who are either northern indigenes or migrants from the south. To the south are the majority ethnic groups of the Yoruba, to the west are minority ethnic groups who are a near equal mix of Christians and Muslims, and to the east are the Ibos, the Ibibios, Efik, and other minority ethnic groups who are mostly Christianized with minority traditionalists (Osaghae, 1998a).

However, ethnicity often does not exist in its pure form, but rather in combination with religion, regionalism, class, race, or "other conflict-generating cleavages" in ways that are mutually reinforcing, as a result of which managing ethnicity problems have tended to be somewhat complex (Osaghae, 1998a, p. 3). Furthermore, Osaghae (1998a) observes that "[e]thnic minorities are usually defined in contradistinction to major groups with whom they coexist in political systems, as groups which experience systemic discrimination and domination because of numerical inferiority and a host of historical and sociological factors," with hegemonic and dominant minority groups such as Nigeria's Fulani ethnic group, however, excluded from such minority grouping (p. 3). Thus, minorities in Nigeria are classified relative to the three major ethnic groups—the Hausa/Fulani, Yoruba, and Ibo. However, while southern minorities in the south are basically ethno-linguistic in form, northern minorities, are additionally and primarily religious minorities and this presents a more complex ethnic setting than the south (Osaghae, 1998a).

Similarly, in the north, three levels of minorities are additionally distinguished, each of which has its political implications as Osaghae delineates:

> At the broadest level, the corporatist, cross-ethnic bond of Islam which is built around the Fulani Sultan of Sokoto who, as Commander of the Faithful, is the head of the Muslim community, has made predominantly Muslim minorities . . . and Muslims from other minority groups politically powerful, having access to political privileges at all levels as protégés of the Hausa/Fulani.
>
> At the next level is the dichotomy between the Sokoto (Hausa/Fulani) "axis" and the Borno (Kanuri) "axis" which is built around the pristine Kanem-Bornu empire-state (and its vassals), and which was and remains a contending center of Islamic civilization and influence. Relations between the Kanuris, who are a political minority and the Sokoto axis have been a mix of separatism . . . , accommodation . . . , and struggles for supremacy.
>
> At the third level are the non-Muslim minority groups which have since the jihad fought and resisted Fulani overlordship and islamisation. These groups are mainly located in the middle-belt, southern Zaria, and Adamawa provinces which were open to Christian and other Westernising influences at a time the Muslim areas were quarantined. (1998a, p. 8)

Consequently, the implication of this development is that Christian groups such as the Zurus of Sokoto, in states like Bauchi that are predominantly Hausa/Fulani Muslims, have become political minorities, with Christianity serving as a primary "minority diacritic" in such states. Furthermore, in attempt to mobilize northern unity against the south through the bonds of Islam, Christianity has become a countermobilization ideology for the Hausa/Fulani elites in the region, but also a rallying point for opponents of their domination (Osaghae, 1998a). Thus, these northern minorities have frontally opposed Sharia's introduction at the federal court of appeal in the 1970s/1990s constitution-making bodies, articulating their interests through the Christian Association of Nigeria (CAN) as their main channel. In consequence, most Hausa/Fulani, minority-involved conflicts in the 1980s/1990s in such areas as Bauchi, Zaria,

Kafanchan, Zangon-Kataf, and Funtua were primarily religious conflicts. These minority groups, though small and isolated, have continuously demanded freedom from Muslim emirates, for increased autonomy and own local government, and for a customary court of appeal for non-Muslims to complement the operative Sharia court of appeal (Osaghae, 1998a).

Additionally, there is the issue of land distribution in Nigeria with the north being arid and more desert-like (the farther north one goes from the south), while the south is grassland and swampy with mangrove forests around the coastal regions, and with the country's vast oil deposits found mainly in the southern parts, primarily in the delta region. The Muslims want to control the petroleum which is in the south where the Christians are. The northern extremist Muslims are destroying the churches, killing the Christians in the north, and encroaching southward on the Christians as a gradual way of gaining control and taking over power in the country. Ultimately, the idea is to turn Nigeria into an Islamic nation (Haberson and Rothchild, 1991; Kukah and Falola, 1996).

Political Factors

Politically, the northern Nigeria ethno-religious conflict can also be explained with political factors entailing processes of control, collective decision making which are not indicative of the individual will, and authoritative resource allocation. There are two very powerful political units in Nigeria, the Muslims and Christians, each struggling for hegemony with conflicts between the two units exacerbating the ethno-religious conflict in northern Nigeria. The experience being played out between these two powerful units is the manipulation of political differences in regional and national politics with manifest instability and political upheavals in the region. Thus, the prevalence of conflicts in northern Nigeria has been linked to political factors and unbridled power tussle as part of the myriad of factors undergirding the conflict (Ukiwo, 2003). Furthermore, according to Haberson and Rothchild (1991), an attempted Christian coup against the Northern Muslim leadership, foiled in 1990, has given rise to fears of the imposition of Islam in Africa and accentuated the differences between countries with Muslim and Christian majorities in Africa. Politically, the spread of Islam has been through jihadist conquests, and as past warriors, extremist Muslims want to continue in that rein of warfare, with Islamic assertiveness seen to have further exacerbated conflicts between Muslims and Christians in Africa, and Nigeria in particular (Haberson and Rothchild, 1991).

More so, Kukah and Falola (1996) identify the political impact of Islam in Nigeria, primarily the Islam-dominated northern Nigeria with its vast Muslim population, the basis on which the Muslim world perceives Nigeria as a key member. Islam's politicization impact is even further compounded by its ideological stance of non-separation of religion from politics, a system which is prevalent and deeply entrenched in the north, as distinct from the Muslims of Western Nigeria who peacefully coexist with Christians. Thus, given Islam's intricate positioning in the nation's political sphere, Kukah and Falola argue that

> Islam is both a religion and a political force in modern Nigeria. Like Christianity, it aims to win more converts. The motive of the Islamic intelligentsia is, however, more ambitious than just number-counting: in the surface, a tiny but powerful Islamic elite wants to turn Nigeria into an Islamic country. (1996, p. 2)

Hence, this Islamization stance of political Islam and some of its adherents continues to significantly undergird and exacerbate the northern Nigeria ethno-religious conflict (Kukah and Falola, 1996).

Economic Factors

Economically, the ethno-religious conflict in northern Nigeria can be traced to a myriad of such factors as resource allocation inequity, indigene-settler issues, unemployment, poverty, etc. The economic factor is seen as playing a crucial role in exacerbating the conflict. For instance, Anthony (2002) observes that "in understanding Northern Nigeria's 1966 riots, the material and the effective are inseparable, just as the inward face of ethnicity is inseparable from its political aspects" (p. 7). The mobilization of fear and anger for generating and sustaining the anti-Igbo violence was primarily "to advance the material interests of Northern elites, and those elites succeeded because ordinary Northerners, driven by their own material concerns, participated" (Anthony, 2002, p. 7).

An economic perspective, therefore, will involve looking at economic differences and resource distribution parameters, which are commonly found to be unevenly spread among groups. Economic inequities breed discontent and tensions which may, in turn, escalate to riots and violent protests. Inequitable resource distribution is a primary conflict causation in the nation, as Nigeria's vast oil and mineral resource is highly politicized, and conflicts often arise from issues of resource allocation. With more than 90 percent of the country's oil sourced from the Niger Delta region in which most of the population are minority groups, incessant conflicts occur in the area with protests against perceived inequities of the federal revenue allocation structure. Furthermore, given that oil presently accounts for over 90 percent of the nation's foreign exchange earnings and most of its tax revenue (*The Economist* as cited in Harnischfeger, 2004; Mitee, 1994), resource distribution involves a lot of power-play and intrigue. This factor coupled with the immunity of Nigerian politicians from accountability and transparency, due to lack of effective probity of public officers but sustained by the enormous inflows of oil revenues for the country, worsens the impoverishment of oil-producing areas through deprivation and marginalization.

Impoverishment has occasioned widespread communal violence and armed rebellion, especially in the Niger Delta region, where incidences of blown up oil pipelines, as well as kidnapped and sometimes murdered oil workers have created a level of anarchy in some parts of the region (Gberie, 2006). Such blatant resource abuse has, by extension, also left in its wake a phenomenal privation of the country as a whole, and in particular the Northern region which is the focus of this study. In the oil-producing south as in the north, blatant economic inequality and corruption fuels the restiveness, with states in the Northern region also noted as the poorest in the country, with more than 70 percent of the region's populace living in abject poverty, as per the United Nations data analysis, with the few rich among them living in mansions with high walls (Nossiter, 2010c).

Psycho-Cultural Factors

Psycho-cultural factors refer to the psychological orientation and dispositions of matters, and involve factors such as emotions and tensions which emerge as a result of conflict and escalate with social change. This dimension involves how people are feeling and how those feelings are translated into their understanding. Thus, the ethno-religious conflict in northern Nigeria can be explained by the psycho-cultural factors undergirding the conflict from a cultural paradigm perspective. There are two distinctive cultures in the conflict, an Islamic culture and a Christian culture, each with strong feelings regarding which should survive or which should be in the center. On the one hand, Muslims believe the Islamic culture will rid Nigeria of corruption, and psychologically, they see an Islamic culture solving the problem of corruption and nepotism in the country. Christians, on the other hand, have strong feelings and believe that the constitution will provide democracy and freedom of expression to all Nigerians—Muslims, Christians, and traditionalists alike—though the Nigerian Constitution being secular is neither Christian nor Muslim. On the state of profligacy for which the Muslims have their bent, Falola observes that

> religious organizations ... rejected the corruption of political (and even religious) leaders. They characterized the society as decadent and excessively materialistic. Electoral malpractices and rivalries among the political parties convinced reformist religious leaders that the secular state was not ideal for the country. Some began to reject the constitution, calling instead for a theocratic state with moral leaders. Colonel Ghaddafi of Libya and the Ayatollah Khomeini of Iran provided alternative models of leadership, both widely believed to be strong, popular, honest, moral, and committed to their people. (1999, pp. 168–169)

80   Chapter 3

Thus, the conflicting perspectives and worldviews of these two religious groups contribute to the tensions that exacerbate the northern Nigeria conflict. More so, Haberson and Rothchild (1991) observe that with the spread of the Arabic language, Islam, and Islamic culture, Islam has become an integral part of African contemporary experience with the result that Islam's significance as a political factor in Nigeria has considerably increased. On the playing out of such cultural divergences between the two religious groups, Falola observes, for instance, that

> [a] major and long-standing source of Christian anger was the belief that Muslims were trying to turn the new capital of Abuja into an Islamic city. Very quickly mosques and Id el Fitr praying ground appeared, a National Mosque was built close to the presidential mansion, and the designs for the city gate and some other places were Islamic. Using the Hausa language and wearing the Hausa garb and cap associated with the president became common as a way to attract notice, while some southern Christian politicians shamelessly converted to Islam for political advantage. In the contest for re-election in 1983, northern politicians demonstrated their commitment to hang on to power and to promote the cause of Islam. (1999, pp. 169–170)

On this control and manipulation of symbols for political advantage, Kukah and Falola (1996) observe, for example, the use of a simple, effective strategy of reminding visitors to Nigeria, as well as citizens, of Islam's dominance with the North's main airports and hotels, for instance, having mosques and prayer grounds attached to them, with a mosque also pronouncingly sited close to the major airport in Lagos. Kukah and Falola, accordingly, further recognize that

> [n]owhere is the use of symbols more effective than at Abuja, the country's new capital city. For long, the Northern oligarchy detested Lagos as the federal capital because it is located among the Yoruba, a rival ethnic group. When Abuja was chosen as a new site in the 1970s, it provided the Northern ruling class the opportunity to realize the dream of shifting the economic and political center to the North. (1996, pp. 60–61)

Given social cubism's conception of a generic worldview presumably, of all things being equal *(a ceteris paribus scenario)*, which is far from the case in the northern Nigeria ethno-religious conflict, the elite theory lens will be next employed to examine the conflict.

ELITE THEORY EXPLICATION OF NORTHERN NIGERIA ETHNO-RELIGIOUS CONFLICT

The elite theory provides insightful understanding of the northern Nigeria ethno-religious conflict. Propounded by C. Wright Mills (1956), elite theory focuses on power relationships in modern society, and argues that a small minority comprising the economic, policy making, or political elites' control power dynamics, which power is distinctive of the democratic electoral processes of the state. The theory's epistemological framework postulates the existence of a clear divide between the brokers and users of power, and those at their disposition. The elite theory's configuration is that the organization and determination of every political and economic system are for the benefit of an elite few. Hence, Mills sees society as constantly organized with the elite few welding overall power over the larger others, and posits that equipping the public with information regarding the nature of societal power distribution will aid the generation of an essential social shift that will greatly alter existing class and other social structural arrangements.

Fundamental causal factors for the intermittent killings in the northern Nigeria ethno-religious conflict is the phenomena of political manipulation and power tussle between the political elites in the north and those in the south that was entrenched into the Nigerian political system from the colonial days. According to Osaghae (1998a), preceding Nigeria's creation of regions, there were neither minority nor majority groupings. Using the Native Authority (NA) system, however, the colonial administration created and ensured the autonomy of the various groups and sub-groups which later became majority groups. Thus, citing Tseayo (1975) and Yahaya (1980), Osaghae (1998a) observes that "the adoption of the administrative machinery of the Fulani-run caliphate and emirates as the NA prototype, and the pact that Lord Lugard made with the emirs, not only kept pre-colonial relations of domination intact, but also led to the imposition of Muslim overlords (appointed by the sultan or emirs) on non-Muslim areas which had successfully resisted Fulani suzerainty before colonization" (p. 4). Although every group constituting an NA unit in the north had enjoyed some autonomy despite this, however, everything changed with the creation of regions. This was due to "power-seeking elites" capitalizing on the new regions' opportunities to unify the various sub-groups, the Yoruba, Igbos, and Hausa/Fulani, which were previously autonomous under the NA, into what then became the majority groups (Osaghae, 1998a, p. 4). Virtually all of Nigeria's heads of states from independence up to Sani Abacha's regime have been Northerners including "Tafawa Balewa, Yakubu Gowon, Murtala Mohammed, Shehu Shagari, Muhammadu Buhari, Ibrahim Babangida, and Sani Abacha," and as each "had the power to distribute power, they did so with their constituency as their paramount consideration," to the chagrin of southerners (Kukah and Falola, 1996, p. 50).

Furthermore, in his seminal work, *The Power Elite*, Mills (1956) presents an analytical structure of society as composed of three distinctive groups—the economic, political, and the military—which completely control the power dynamics. Thus, the society's two major groupings of elites and masses have the elites grouping further broken into competing power brokers of the economic, political, and the military. The northern elites are recognized as "members of the intermingled 'patrimonial aristocracy' (*sarauta*), mercantile capitalists, and politicians" (Lubeck, as cited in Anthony, 2002, p. 20), who broadly constitute the national elite members that are recognized as "a comprador bourgeoisie in power not because of its control of economic resources, but rather over political resources, which it uses to channel state resources through ethnicized channels" (Nnoli, as cited in Anthony, 2002, p. 20).

Furthermore, "the dominant Northern Nigerian political elite manipulates Islam to acquire and consolidate power," and these northern elites are seen by southerners to have "enjoyed a predominant share in the distribution of the national cake (wealth) and federal power" (Kukah and Falola, 1996, pp. 49–50). Thus, the northern Nigeria ethno-religious conflict is being fundamentally sustained because of the economic and political interests of the northern elites that it serves, with such interests being cloaked over by an ostensible fanatical support for religious values. Ezeibe (2009) argues that "behind these seeming passion and love for religious values and dogma shown by religious leaders lies the domination of religious values by religious leaders' selfish economic benefits," and there is the need to educate the masses to "appreciate and identify the voice of a fanatic religious elite who seek to advance his economic interest through religious mask at the masses' perils" (para. 43–44).

Additionally, the elite theory is akin to Marxist humanist perspective of social class, given its focus of aiming to have power structures and political or government setups to connect to society, as harm will be brought to people with these entities' disinterest in the society. In essence, Mills aims to show a disjuncture in relationships among society's different organs. The elites, as well as their subordinates to which privileged status are accorded, seek to utilize and control by manipulating social, economic, and political domains at large. Power contestations are dominated by the elites who, in Nigeria, are characteristically defined as "the rich and the powerful" (Dudley as cited in Osaghae, 1998b, p. 25). Expatiating further on the nature of these sociopolitical entities, Osaghae observes:

> The elite in Nigeria is factionalized mainly along ethnic, regional, religious and institutional lines, being a product of the uneven development and rivalry which British colonial administration fostered among the different segments. It has accordingly built its support constituencies from communal, ethnic, religious and regional groups depending on the level of contestation, and has sought to manipulate and exploit the differences and anxieties arising from unequal size and population to further its interests. At the macro national level, powerful ethno-regional elite blocs have emerged at various times to forge constitutive interests in competition with others. (1998b, p. 25)

For instance, the Kaduna mafia emerged from a group of young intellectuals in northern Nigeria—civil servants, military officers, and business tycoons who were conducting business or residing in the North's former capital city, Kaduna, by the end of the first republic, and who, prodded by the several northern leaders that were lost in the 1966 January coup, rallied round and opposed the new Aguiyi-Ironsi government (Osuntokun, 2012). Though operating mostly underground with speculation on its existence and membership, the Kaduna mafia is solidly politically driven, and manifests as the powers behind the nation's military and civilian rulership (Osaghae, 1998b), with the group having powerful and extensive political connections (Kukah and Falola, 1996). Osaghae (1998b) presents the Kaduna mafia as comprising "core Northern elites, 'old brigade' and 'newbreed' alike—intelligentsia, serving and retired military officers and bureaucrats, and members of the business and political classes—and its objective is believed to be in defence and advocacy of Northern interests, the most important of which is to sustain Northern political domination of the federation" (p. 25). The group is recognized as thriving on power alliances by an elaborate network among government sympathizers and northern aristocrats, who have preference for the Islamic and pro northern bent of the group, and are known for their commitment to Northern Nigeria's sociopolitical interests and traditional values (Osuntokun, 2012). Thus, the North's emergent elites exist alongside the region's traditional power elite without displacing them (Kukah and Falola, 1996), with both elitist groups bringing their machinations to bear on the northern Nigeria ethno-religious conflict.

In the 1987 Muslim-Christian crisis in Kaduna, for instance, General Babangida was observed to have alluded to the instigation of the riots by sinister men, and promising summary justice while speaking against powerful subversives and group interests, as well as threatening not to recognize or spare any sacred cow, in reference to the Kaduna mafia, whose influence had waned since his power seizure in 1985. Babangida's view also collaborated with some northern Christians' view that a horde of uneducated, young Muslims were sponsored by some unidentified conflict seeking barons, to attack them along with their properties (Kotch, 1987).

While recognizing patrimonialism as "getting out of control," the Kaduna mafia is derisively cited as an ill-defined organization formed "to acquire power and wealth by ties with the government officials" starting with the Gowon administration (Falola, 1999, p. 147). The elite theory's explication of the northern Nigeria ethno-religious conflict is manifest in the elitists' main purpose of exploiting human and material resources. For instance, Ezeibe, quoting Nwachukwu, acknowledges that

> [p]olicies are carried by emotional sentiments rooted in ethnicity or religion, politics in Nigeria is characterized by religious cleavages. The

education religious and political elites (class) prey upon the masses and use them as satellite to achieve their socio-political and economic objectives. This is done through orientation, indoctrination or violence using the masses on the already conceived stereotypes against their political and religious opponents. (2009, para. 43)

The elite theory, thus, proffers an understanding of the system of social control processes of elites, which does not include the rest of the society, with the notion that one segment of the society controlling the rest of the populace generates conflict levels, the resolution of which can only occur when such power comptrollers share this resource. Such a form of arrangement may, however, be deemed impossible as social elites see themselves alone as having the sole philosophies and ideologues capable of engendering and sustaining society (Okosun, 2012).

EXCLUSIONARY IDEOLOGY THEORY EXPLICATION OF NORTHERN NIGERIA ETHNO-RELIGIOUS CONFLICT

The ethno-religious conflict in northern Nigeria can also be examined using an exclusive ideological lens. Exclusionary Ideology is recognized as an ideology that is specifically aimed at selecting and justifying the extermination of members of a targeted group (Campbell, 2010, Video Series 18). Exclusionary Ideologues is sometimes a particularly complex set of ideologies that involves phenomenal orchestration, extensive systematization levels, planning, and organization. The system of exclusive ideology is aimed to target. Its whole essence is to select a given population group for whatever differential criteria (physiological, biological, ethnic, or religious) and target such selected people on the preconceived notion that people with such defining criteria "are dangerous and dangerous people should be killed" (Campbell, 2010, Video Series 18). On the basis of such selection and valuation, these people are then targeted for extermination.

In the northern Nigeria ethno-religious conflict, for instance, the adoption of Sharia involves a redefinition of political self-determination in religious terms, based on an exclusionary ideology against the non-Muslim others from participation in determining the central aspects of public legislation (Harnischfeger, 2004). Harnischfeger (2004) argues that with the Sharia law in force, "Muslims redefine the *demos* that is entitled to rule" (p. 431). This exclusion of non-Muslims became apparent in January 2000 with Sharia's first adoption in Zamfara State in the north, with its declaration as "the unanimous wish of the people" (*Hotline Magazine* as cited in Harnischfeger, 2004, p. 431), and other states following later. Presently, twelve out of Nigeria's 36 have adopted the Sharia or Islamic law. While Muslims who are in majority in the north welcome such revival of Islamic traditions, however, some of the twelve Sharia-adopted states have sizeable Christian or non-Muslim minorities. Hence, Christians and some traditionalists in Sharia operative states feel threatened by state-enforced Islamization, and as noted by Harnischfeger (2004), this religious campaign has triggered several clashes with loss of lives of five to ten thousand people (p. 432). Accordingly, Adar (2001) observes,

> At the core of Islamization lie the doctrines of Islamic culture and religion . . . implementation of . . . *Sharia* . . . cannot be brought about in isolation and without the concomitant internal political realities. Islamization . . . is used as a tool for political power and legitimacy . . . *Sharia*, therefore, controls and regulates socio-political and economic life which form the basis of political authority—"reinforced by the dogma of the divine guidance of the community." The incorporation of *Sharia* law in a constitution offers the basis for the promotion of Islamic principles. Islamization is therefore an important vehicle for promoting values associated with Islam and Arabic culture. (pp. 85–86)

However, non-Muslims, primarily Christians, constitute about half the population of Nigeria, and this non-Muslim populace now fears that the secular principles which have prevailed since Nigeria became an independent sovereign state are being eroded. This is notwithstanding the fact that "adopting of any religion as State Religion" is prohibited in Section 10 of the Nigerian constitution (Harnischfeger, 2004, p. 432). Thus, the Sharia law is seen by Christians as state apparatus for political maneuverings, control, and dominance; they (Christians) fear that Sharia will apply to Muslims and non-Muslims alike, in spite of assurances of the Sharia-operating state governments that it will apply strictly to Muslims. Evidently, Sharia's adoption in the predominantly Muslim northern states has heightened the already entrenched hostilities between Muslims and Christians in the country. In the Middle Belt, for instance, the introduction of Sharia has resulted in violent conflicts, as Islamic laws set up claims over territories in which Muslim dictates prevail. Hence, parts of the Middle Belt experience violent conflicts between the mainly Hausa/Fulani migrants from the north, and the indigenous ethnic groups who are mainly Christians and traditionalists (Harnischfeger, 2004).

Thus, looking at the northern Nigeria ethno-religious conflict which is ethno-territorial in nature, it is essential to examine the factors that explain relationship on the basis of exclusionary ideology on each side of the conflict which, as coined exclusivity, leads to alienation, and alienation causes tension between groups. Because of exclusivity, there is mistrust (don't trust that you can do anything for me), suspicion, and distrust (my not allowing you to do anything for me) which is typical of extremist Muslims. There is exclusionary ideology among extremist Muslims because they want to set themselves out among others. Essentially, they want to be separate and distinct from others. Then, on the basis of these exclusionary tendencies, Christians are being discriminated against, targeted, and exterminated in northern Nigeria. Kendal (2004) observes for instance, that

> Islamic zeal is strong in the northern state of Kano. Kano's governor, Ibrahim Shekarau, was elected on a radical, hardline, pro- Sharia platform. Christians suffer intense persecution in Kano, their schools and churches having been closed and burned. It is compulsory for all public-school girls to wear Islamic hijab, and as the Christian schools have been closed Christians don't have much choice. On the night of Shekarau's election (21 May 2003), pastor Chikezie (Sunday) Madumere and his whole family were burned to death in their home in "No Man's Land" Kano city, by Muslim mobs celebrating Shekarau's win. (para. 17)

What are the circumstances that have created exclusionary tendencies among the northerners? And, are there also circumstances that are creating exclusionary tendencies among the southerners? It can be argued that the southerners are not so exclusive because they have gone to the north to work and mix with the northerners. The Christians are not exclusive but are rather creating commerce in the north and other places they reside. But have the northerners themselves accepted the southerners and the Christians into their midst? Is it that the Islamic folks are afraid because the southerners and Christians will Christianize them? What is the population of Muslims, Christians, and others? According to the *World Fact Book* data, religious composition estimates for the country are about 50 percent Muslim, 40 percent Christian, and 10 percent indigenous beliefs (Central Intelligence Agency, 2012). Is that why the extremist Muslims are angry? To answer that question an examination of geography assists by observing the distinction between the North's arid and dry region, and the south with vast oil resources, and the need to control the country's oil wealth as was typified by the Sudan/Darfur conflict (Batruch, 2004) prior to the recent delineation and independence of southern Sudan.

Looking back to 1966, there is no significant change in the population mix, and so there is no need for the extremist Muslims to get agitated over the issue of being overtaken by Christians. Thus, if no proof exists that the population mix is changing adversely for the Muslim population, the exclusion is being created. Why is this exclusion being created? It can be argued, first, that extremist Muslims want to be different. Second, they want to maintain their Islamic tradition. Third, they want to maintain their own Islamic legal system which is the Sharia. And, fourth, they want to be different because they do not want dilution in their religious, social, and political spheres, or the dilution by Christianity from Western education as the Boko Haram professes. They are anti-Western philosophy and Western constitutional law, either of which are part of the secular system. Exclusivity resonates with Islam as defined by Sharia, and extremist Muslims cannot go beyond that while Christian exclusivity resonates with secularism. Tension is, therefore, bred with extremist Muslims in negation of the Christianity that brought in parliament and the secular paradigm.

The question in the ethno-territorial discourse, therefore, is why are these two religious groups excluding themselves from each other? Exclusivity suggests that the end of the road is violence "because I don't want you in my territory, and you are not part of my religion," and this basically is the positioning of extremist Muslims. Thus, in "Victims of Riots: Their Pains, Woes and Regrets," the story remains the same—kidnapping, maiming, and killing, whether in Kano, Kaduna, Bauchi, Plateau, Sokoto, Kebbi, or Taraba, mentioning a few. Such, regrettably, have been the ordinary citizens' lots in northern Nigeria, and Christians have been mostly affected, irrespective of race or ethnicity, with southerners living in the region being meted out even worse plights. Of great import is the chagrin of the inability of even well-trained soldiers to escape the onslaught of the ravaging youths, turned terrorists, even as they gleefully exterminate their neighbors on the ruse of religion (Ahiante, 2004).

What is the position of Christians? Do they also adopt this exclusionary ideological stance? Christians, probably do not. While Christians, as well as Muslims, proselytize for converts, Christians basically are not involved in exclusionary tendencies against Muslims on the parameters of their faith as the extremist Muslims do on grounds of Islam or Sharia practices and implementation. Thus, because the Islamic population did not open themselves to the Christian group, that is why there is this latent genocide emanating from such exclusionism. In addition to this framing of the Islamic religious escapade, there is also the 1966 Nzeogwu assassination of the Sarduana of Sokoto, the anger over which never left the northerners, and exclusivity is further created as a result.

The caveat, however, is that while exclusivity may explain the northern Nigeria conflict in terms of one group excluding the other, postmodernists, on the other hand, may argue that ethno-religious conflict is occurring in the region because the Muslims are living in the historic past, while Christians are bringing education to the north and they are refusing. Thus, the southerners are the postmodernists, but the northerners are refusing to move from their conservative past.

HATE THEORY EXPLICATION OF NORTHERN NIGERIA ETHNO-RELIGIOUS CONFLICT

The ethno-religious conflict in northern Nigeria can further be explicated applying the hate theory. Hate is recognized as a contributing causal factor of numerous genocidal killings and massacres (Sternberg, 2003). Although agreement has as yet to be reached among scholars on the definition of "hate" as a term (Perry as cited in Walters, 2011, p. 315), with laws on hate crime proliferating in the Western world, there has primarily been an increase in legal scholarship on the meaning of hate (Jacobs and Potter as cited in Walters, 2011). Generally, "hate crime" can be committed without the need for an offender to actually "hate" the victim, and thus, for most people, "hate" has been conceptualized to mean "prejudice" (Jacobs and Potter; and Lawrence as cited in Walters, 2011, p. 315), which further raises the onerous task of defining criminally under-girded prejudice. Whereas some prejudices such as antiracist or antifascist are seen as positive, and some as innocuous, for example, dislike of the color green (Jacobs and Potter as cited in Walters, 2011), such other prejudices as homophobia, antireligion, and racism are seen as damaging to societal social cohesiveness and are considered entirely unacceptable (Walters, 2011). Thus, 'ethnic prejudice' is recognized in Gordon Allport's *The Nature of Prejudice,* a seminal contributory work to the conceptualizing of prejudice, "as 'an antipathy based upon a faulty and inflexible generalization. [This] . . . may be felt or expressed. It may be directed towards a group as a whole or towards an individual because he is a member of that group'" (Allport as cited in Walters, 2011, p. 315).

Thus, in the 1966 Igbo massacre, for instance, though the January 1966 coup presented as the anti-Igbo hostility pretext, the actual reasons for the massacres "were more deep rooted and went back several years," with the coup extracting "long held prejudices and negative stereotypes about Igbos" (Siollun, 2009, p. 83). Essentially, there must be the feeling or expression of animosity toward a people group deriving from generalizations made about members of the group, which usually result from stereotyping, with the perpetuation of such negative stereotyping done through communication networks primarily between friends and families (Byers et al. as cited in Walters, 2011), or via the news media and television (Green et al. as cited in Walters, 2011). While resentment and economic competition can influence hate crime, other than having a faulty generalization of a people group (Green et al. as cited in Walters, 2011), "the economic strain and the ensuing resentment felt towards some minority groups may well be based on false generalizations about the perceived economic prosperity and access to state welfare that certain minority groups supposedly receive" (Ray and Smith as cited in Walters, 2011, p. 315).

For instance, while recognizing the economic or material undertone to the northern Nigeria 1966 riots and killings of the Igbos, Anthony acknowledges that

> material interests alone do not explain elites' success in generating and sustaining support. Their appeals succeeded because they could also tap into an established vocabulary of fears and insecurities, emotions that had been imbued over preceding decades with ethnic overtones.

How big a part ethnically framed fears played depended on a range of factors, many of which—particularly media representations—elites could control. Since to "illuminate what is 'our own' darkens the shadow of 'the other,'" the project of vilifying Igbos was accompanied by appeals to Northern virtue (Lonsdale as cited in Anthony, 2002, p. 8).

Accordingly, there is complexity in the way that hate operates, as in Rwanda where a lot of Hutus and Tutsis came to hating one another (Sternberg, 2003). It is essentially challenging for most people, for instance, to not hate a group's members that are systematically exterminating one's own group, including one's family, or are forcing one to be involved in that extermination (Sternberg and Sternberg, 2008). There may, however, be several other contributing factors as "social pressure to act in certain ways, emotional reasoning, fear for one's own life if one disobeys an order from a powerful other, and false beliefs systematically implanted by cynical leaders," and Sternberg and Sternberg (2008) observe that hate cannot be understood in a vacuum (p. 2). Thus, Sternberg (2003) observes that "[n]ot all massacres are perpetrated on the basis of hate" (Browning; Arendt; and Milgram as cited in Sternberg, 2003, p. 305) as "[o]rdinary people can be propelled by unfortunate circumstances into behaviors in which . . . they might [normally] never engage" (p. 305). Hence, in the discourse of hate processes in relation to terrorism, massacres, and genocides, there is the caveat that "[w]ithin a given massacre or genocide, some people may be propelled by hate and others by factors that are quite different, such as the desire to advance their careers or to save their own lives" (Sternberg, 2003, p. 305). Essentially, hate can only be examined in its complex occurring contexts rather than in isolation. On the complexity of this hatred, Onishi (2000) observes, for instance, that the conflict is rooted in the abyss of divisions and real hatreds between the Hausas (Sokoto) and the Igbos (Aba), such divisions and hatreds of which are astoundingly complex, and are fueled by corruption and misrule which has left Nigeria, a top oil-producing country in poverty. The rift is even further exploited and encouraged by rulers in the country, including the British, the military governments, and the American and European oil companies which pump crude oil off the Niger Delta shores, which the federal government has basically abandoned (Onishi, 2000).

Furthermore, the role of propaganda in fomenting mass murders is recognized. Sternberg (2003) links hate to mass killings and observes some hate forms as being more prone to generating such killings than others, and presents propaganda as systematically nurturing hate elements to foment mass murders which, in turn, lead in combination to massacres, terrorism, and genocides. Propaganda is, thus, seen as usually fomenting or reinforcing hate when directed against the target group, or reinforcing love when directed toward the perpetrating group (Sternberg, 2003). In the Rwandan genocide, for instance, a contributing factor to its gravity was the radio propaganda broadcast that incited hatred feelings, insinuating that Hutus killing of remaining Tutsis would significantly advance the formation of a better Rwanda (Des Forges as cited in Sternberg and Sternberg, 2008). Furthermore, the Rwandan genocide is known to have occurred basically in the full glare of the world, as other nations' governments failed to intervene where they could have done so. Similarly, in the northern Nigeria ethno-religious conflict these features are also seen at work in varying situations of the conflict. For instance, propaganda featured prominently in the Nigeria-Biafra war to help draw the attention of foreign collaborators to their side, to the detriment of the opposing side (Osaghae, 1998b). Additionally, while the starvation of the million Biafrans in the war occurred in full glare of the world, the international community watched on as the Nigerian government through economic blockade had these Biafrans starved to death on the basis of deploying starvation as a legitimate weapon of warfare (Emerson, 1970; Garrison, 1968b). Furthermore, the decades of ongoing mass killings in northern Nigeria which is focused mainly on Muslim-Christian conflicts, have also continued to occur with the international community just watching (Ahiante, 2004; CSW, 2008a).

RELATIVE DEPRIVATION THEORY EXPLICATION OF NORTHERN NIGERIA ETHNO-RELIGIOUS CONFLICT

Relative deprivation theory can explain the phenomenon of the ethno-religious conflict in northern Nigeria. Relative deprivation theory posits that actors predispose to conflict as a result of a perceived discrepancy between values expected and values actually derived, with lower value expectations relative to manifest realities of life conditions causing lower predisposition to feelings of discontentment than higher value expectations. Hence, relative deprivation theory focuses on "perceptions of deprivation" (Jeong, 2000, p. 69). Ted Gurr (1971), who is a key proponent of relative deprivation theory, argues in his *Why Men Rebel* that as social beings, humans comparatively evaluate themselves with other groups, as well as with their perceived image of entitlements on the basis of which any gap observed provides grounds for discontent, and conflict. Gurr (1971), adopting this psychological approach in explaining political violence as derivative from collective discontent, argues, however, that it is one's perceived relative deprivation of achieved welfare with respect to those of others that fans discontent, rather than the absolute deprivation positioning, thus, linking frustrations of (or perceptions of) being marginalized with aggressiveness. Thus, "[r]eligious violence is also frequently an expression of frustration with inequities or perceived marginalization, or even of poverty" (Falola, 1998, p. 283).

In the northern Nigeria ethno-religious conflict, for instance, as the spate of killings intensified in the north with reprisals in some southern states following the adoption of the Sharia by some northern states, "[d]efusing the tension is extremely difficult for Obasanjo, a Christian southerner who does not want to offend northern sensibilities after being accused of marginalizing the region that has dominated politics since independence from Britain in 1960" (Tostevin, 2000, para. 9). Thus, the perception of marginalization is undergirded by a sense of a perceived gap between expected and achieved welfare which creates collective discontent. Relative depreciation theory also applies to groups or individuals who find their own welfare to be inferior to those of others with whom they compare themselves, as seen in the 1966 massacres of the Igbos, where the Igbos were perceived as being more educated and dynamic (Garrison, 1968a).

Also, drawing on Walter Runciman's (1972) work which presents a "generalization hypothesis" that a group's relative deprivation derives from the "experiences of personal relative deprivation," recent relative deprivation theorists focus on translating "personal disadvantageous experiences" at the group level (p. 120). Relative deprivation theory provides insight on groups' basis for seeing themselves as marginalized or deprived with such perception precipitating widespread unrest. Thus, socioeconomic factors such as unemployment and lack of education are considered as contributing to or intensifying the perception of deprivation, for instance, with the economic downturn in Nigeria increasing unemployment and producing higher poverty levels, particularly in the north where the educational level among Muslim youths tends to be lower than those of their Christian counterparts. In the Kaduna 1987 attack of Christians and their property by the rabble of uneducated Muslim youths, the country's general state of economic depression and severe unemployment were recognized as the cause of the receptivity to every call to violence by listless hordes of youths (Kotch, 1987).

Furthermore, increases in the general prices of goods and services and lower consumer spending caused by the slowing down of economic growth will bring about rapid societal changes with greater inequitable distribution of wealth occurring. Such inequities increasingly create feelings of relative deprivation among the teeming uneducated youths, or *almajirai* in the north, who mostly roam the streets panhandling (Falola, 1998). Thus, as the economic downturn persists, inflation and poor economic performance heighten poverty levels for marginalized groups, and their feelings of relative deprivation accentuate. Also, relative deprivation theory presents that an individual or a group's perception of entitlements rises faster than the potential for its fulfillment. In essence, the expected ability for the satisfaction of social needs and material benefits increases disproportionately faster than the society's ability to deliver (Gurr, 1971; Runciman, 1972).

Consequently, with the slow economic growth, the potentials of a society for meeting the expectations of its populace reduce, as does the actual delivery of such social needs and benefits. In May 1992, for instance, there were skirmishes in Lagos and some other southern cities involving antigovernment demonstrators against the authorities, which were triggered by an austere economic slump in the country, following which a Muslim-Christian sectarian violence ensued in Kaduna which lasted for ten days with hundreds of people killed. The estimates for the death toll and casualties figures in the violence were put at between 500–800, and hundreds of others wounded. Low oil prices have devastated the nation's export earning-stream, which as a leading African oil exporter, oil accounts for over 95 percent of its export earnings. As the economy floundered, the discontent and frustration grew such that analysts, both Western and African, spoke of discontent's explosion, as threatening the political stability of the country (Noble, 1992c).

Hence, the widening gap between expectations and actual fulfillment of a people's social needs in a period of economic decline and rising general prices, plus the actual increasing poverty levels, provides confirmatory basis for a group's viewing of themselves as marginalized and relatively deprived with such perception precipitating widespread unrest.

SOCIAL IDENTITY THEORY EXPLICATION OF NORTHERN NIGERIA ETHNO-RELIGIOUS CONFLICT

The ethno-religious conflict in northern Nigeria can also be examined applying the framework of social identity theory. Social identity theory is a social psychology theory which posits that an individual does not have one, but multiple selves which correspond to the group membership's widening circles. Social identity theory focuses on self-conception's role in group process, membership, and intergroup relationships (Forsyth, 2010). The key proponents of social identity theory, Henri Tajfel and John Turner (1979), emphasize intergroup differentiation based on cognition and motivation, and present that in different societal contexts, an individual may be triggered to think, feel, or act based on his family or personal, national or self-level. Social identity theorists argue that self-categorization and in-group enhancement is created by group membership in ways favorable to the in-group at the out-group's expense (Forsyth, 2010; Hogg, 2006).

Social identity theorists emphasize the existence of a closer in-group bond at the expense of the out-group. Hence, rather than a perception of deprivation, the in-group's identifying with a super-ordinate group—for instance, a global community—makes individuals more prone to showing increased support for policies beneficial to the larger group even when involving subordinate group sacrifices. For example, Muslim groups by identifying with the larger Muslim body nationally or even globally, will bond in unison to compete dis-favorably against the out-group. Consequently, the in-group's struggle over resources and social benefits will increase against the out-group based on social identity group's favoritism stance. The resource scarcity and increased conflict levels will further exacerbate poverty among the groups, thus, impinging on religious issues more adversely through divisions between the groups.

Furthermore, underlying social identity are two premises of a categorical distinctive organizing of individuals' understanding of their world, such categorization of which minimizes within-group differences and accentuates the intergroup differences. Also, with individuals being members of certain social groupings and not of others, categorization portends with it, the in-group and out-group, or the "us" and "them" classification which, due to social categories' self-relevance, is a superimposed categorical distinction that has emotional and affective significance (Brewer as cited in Senholzi, 2008). Thus, social phenomena has for decades been analyzed using social identity theoretical framework, specifically, with issues such as political violence, intergroup relations, discrimination, prejudice, stereotyping, language use, and negotiation examined through its lens, as in such situations the in-group and out-group categorizations are more often than not made salient (Senholzi, 2008). The conceptualization of such social settings produces a schema of (i) *intergroup accentuation principle,* in which in-group boundaries *assimilation,* and between group contrast, gives the perception of the in-group's greater similarity to the self than are the out-group members; (ii) *in-group favoritism principle,* in which fellow members of the in-group's *positive affect* as trust or like are selectively generalized toward, but not toward members of the out-group; (iii) *social competition principle* in which in-group and out-group *intergroup social comparison* negatively associates their perceived interdependence (Brewer as cited in Senholzi, 2008, pp. 9–10).

In a study of the northern Ireland conflict between the Catholics and Protestants, for instance, centuries-old conflict generated hatred which made it practically impossible for both community groups to trust themselves, and there was in-group favoritism as well as negative, out-group association as social identity theory outlines. And, while solidifying the within group boundaries, there is a further ostracizing of the out-group (Senholzi, 2008). This typifies the northern Nigeria ethno-religious conflict, where the phenomena of the different ethnic groupings are even further compounded by differences of religious affiliations, with the Hausa-Fulani Muslim in-group categorization disfavorably pitted against the out-group, non-Muslim or Christian other ethnic-groupings based on "in-group favoritism and out-group hostility" (Senholzi, 2008, p. 13).

Furthermore, the conflict experience between the two groups is predicative of negative intentions that are accentuated by delineations of in-group identity which underscores a relationship of antagonism with the out-group (Senholzi, 2008). Religious categorizations are evidential along majority and minority groupings, which validate the social identity theory in the northern Nigeria ethno-religious conflict, based on an in-group and out-group dynamics of "us versus them" positioning, which is a core component underlying social identity theory (Senholzi, 2008, p. 14). In consequence, there are ethnic and religious rivalries which undergird the social identity theory found replete in the context of the northern Nigeria ethno-religious conflict, with a resultant polarization and religious divide among the opposing groups.

The conflict is polarized mainly along a Muslim-Christian fault line other than on cases of intraconflicts between different Muslim sects, while also additionally polarized along Muslim north and Christian south lines where both northern, as well as southern Christians are involved on occasions with the Christian Igbos as prime targets ("Muslim Mobs," 2004; Lobel, 2012). In the March 2010 killings in Dogo Na Hawa of Jos, Plateau State axis, the Sunday's killings were observed for instance, as a particularly vicious expression of the protracted hostilities between Muslims and Christians in the nation that is divided, with Jos and its surrounding region observed as lying on the fault line that has the poor, volatile Muslim north meeting the Christian south. Interethnic and interreligious violence is observed to have taken a toll of about 3,000 people killed in the region, in the last decade. The pattern of violence is thus similar and familiar, usually involving a setting of uneasy coexistence which erupts abruptly into killing, and intensified for days through revenge, as occurred in a January 2004 episode, barely two months prior to the Dogo Na Hawa killings (Nossiter, 2010d).

Furthermore, there are segregated areas in some states as in Kano "Sabon Gari" or strangers quarters, where Christians or southerners, notably Igbos live (Ehiabhi, 2012c; Okpi, 2012). Additionally, Kaduna which was once an urban, lively mélange of tribes and faiths, has become a partitioned city with the Kaduna river cutting and delineated it into two distinct areas, Kaduna north and Kaduna south, respectively, for Muslims and Christians who now live apart in their separate quarters (Sengupta, 2003). Additionally, following years of tensions and violence, as well as reprisals and revenge which have continued to escalate the conflict, the city of Jos also became Balkanized, with Christians and Muslims withdrawing to their separate neighborhoods (Polgreen, 2008).

More so, there is stereotyping which is shown by the in-group toward the out-group and usually manifested with discrimination (Senholzi, 2008). As in the northern Nigeria ethno-religious conflict, there is intergroup discrimination against Christians in northern Nigeria, a factor which further undergirds social identity theory (Senholzi, 2008). Such religious discriminatory practices being meted against Christians in the region are in diverse areas, including "discrimination in employment," "discrimination in access to education," "the threat of violence in educational establishments," "discrimination in access to and provisions to services," and "discrimination in construction of churches and the unwarranted seizure of property (CSW, 2008b, pp. 4–8). Accordingly,

> [i]n almost every state in northern and central Nigeria non-Muslims, and particularly Christians, continue to experience discriminatory policies enacted or tacitly sanctioned at state governmental level. These policies appear designed to engineer their social, economic and political marginalization and to severely impair, if not wholly deny, their federally guaranteed right to practice their religion without let or hindrance. (CSW, 2008b, p. 4)

An instance of such discriminatory practices against Christians is in the nonallocation of land to build churches, while also, Christians are being discriminated against in the takeover of their schools and turning them into Muslim schools. A sense of pervasiveness exists among Christians in Nigeria regarding the military authorities' long favoring of Islamic groups in the North, who constitute about fifty percent of the nation's population. This is more so, given that virtually all of the country's leaders have practically emerged from the region, and nearly every one of them has been a Muslim. Of great import, thus, is the fact of the take-over of several Christian schools by the state under the previous military government of Major General Muhammadu Buhari, with permits for building churches being withheld by the state, while the building of mosques was intensified (Noble, 1992c).

SUMMARY

To analyze the underlying causation to the conflict, analytical perspectives of social cubism, elite, exclusionary ideology, hate, relative deprivation, and social identity theories have been employed. The area of focus has been that of exploring the plausibility of genocidal inclination to the ethno-religious conflict in northern Nigeria. The analysis has shown that social cubism theory explains the conflict from a six-dimensional framework of history (religious, demography, psycho-cultural, political, and economic factors), all of which intermeshed have been seen to have undergirded the conflict (Byrne and Carter, 1996). The elite theory has presented the perspective of elitist manipulation, power tussle, and the system of social control processes as generating and sustaining conflict levels in the northern Nigeria ethno-religious conflict (Mills, 1956). The northern elites are seen as manipulating Islam for power acquisition and consolidation, with the conflict basically sustained as a result of the elites' economic and political interests that it serves, even as such interests are being cloaked over by ostensible religiosity (Ezeibe, 2009; Kukah and Falola, 1996).

The exclusionary ideology perspective views the northern Nigeria ethno-religious conflict from an ideological framework that specifically aims to select and justify the extermination of members of a targeted group (Campbell, 2010, Video Series 18). The adoption of Sharia redefines political self-determination in religious terms through an exclusionary ideology against non-Muslims' participation in core public legislative issues (Harnischfeger, 2004). With the implementation of Sharia "at the core of Islamization" (Adar, 2001, p. 85), this exclusivity has left Christians and other non-Muslim minorities in Sharia operative states particularly threatened by state-enforced Islamization through sustained religious campaigns and clashes that have claimed thousands of lives in the conflict (Harnischfeger, 2004).

Hate theory perspective views the ethno-religious conflict in northern Nigeria with the recognition that hate is a contributing causal factor to the numerous genocidal killings and massacres (Sternberg, 2003). Hate is, thus, conceptualized as "prejudice" (Jacobs and Potter; and Lawrence as cited in Walters, 2011, p. 315), while "ethnic prejudice" is seen as an antipathy which derives from a faulty-based generalization that is directed or expressed toward a group or its member(s) (Allport as cited in Walters, 2011, p. 315).

From the relative deprivation theory perspective, the ethno-religious conflict in northern Nigeria is seen as undergirded by poverty relative to the individual or a group's perception of deprivation of social benefits (Gurr, 1971; Runciman, 1972). From the social identity theory perspective, the northern Nigeria ethno-religious conflict has been observed as being framed by intergroup differentiation between Muslims and Christians through cognition and motivation in different societal contexts (Tajfel and Turner, 1979). Thus, while relative deprivation theory focuses on the perceived marginalization of a people group or individuals, social identity theory looking at self-categorization and in-group membership enhancement at the out-group's expense (Forsyth, 2010; Hogg, 2006), emphasizes in-group favoritism against the out-group as providing the analytical basis for the discriminatory practices by the Muslim in-group and their motivation to exterminate the Christian out-group in their midst (Senholzi, 2008).

In conclusion, social cubism, elite, exclusionary ideology, hate, relative deprivation, and social identity theoretical frameworks have been applied in explaining the northern Nigeria ethno-religious conflict. However, given the complexity of the phenomena, involving regional, national, and to some extent international dimensions, an eclectic synthesizing of these theoretical perspectives will provide a more holistic understanding of the underlying causation, its religious overtures, and the plausibility of genocidal undertone to the conflict. Given this theoretical framework, the study's primary focus of investigating proclivity to genocide in the northern Nigeria ethno-religious conflict is examined in Part II.

Part II

Identifying and Establishing Proclivity to Genocide

FOUR
Presenting the Model for Proclivity to Genocide

Gruesome killings have remained ongoing phenomena in the ethno-religious conflict in northern Nigeria in which colossal loss of life and property has continued to occur, albeit in a sporadic and intermittent manner. With the focus of the study being to inquire on the proclivity toward genocide in the conflict, the research questions are constructed specifically to determine: Are there genocidal inclinations to the ethno-religious conflict in northern Nigeria? And furthermore, to what extent does the interplay between ethnicity and religion help to foment and escalate the conflict in northern Nigeria? This study explores the probability of genocidal undertone to the northern Nigeria ethno-religious conflict.

The study involves the thematic analysis of 197 newspaper articles on the conflict cases, spanning from the 1966 pogrom in which thousands of Igbos were massacred in the north up to present, ongoing ethno-religious killings in northern Nigeria. In analyzing the content of these newspaper articles, which are the reported cases of the ethno-religious conflicts in Northern Nigeria, the study focuses on causation and intentionality behind the wanton killings to inquire on the plausibility of genocidal inclinations to the killings. Given the consistency of the emerging patterns (Stake, 1995) over the study phases, the themes from the data have been used to develop a model to explore the plausibility of genocidal inclinations to the northern Nigeria ethno-religious conflict. Figure 4.1 is the *Genocide Proclivity Model* which is developed from the study for identifying proclivity or inclination to genocide. Derived from the Strauss and Corbin (1990) analytic technique, the *model* is a six-part theoretical tool for determining proclivity to genocide in the northern Nigeria ethno-religious conflict.

The model's analytical approach involves examining the phenomenon being studied as the central idea in relation to other categories, with these other categories, including causal conditions which lead to the phenomenon; the contextual framework in which the phenomenon developed; the intervening conditions for the phenomenon; the strategies mapped out for the phenomenon to develop; and the consequences or outcomes of the phenomenon (Strauss and Corbin, 1990). In the northern Nigeria ethnoreligious conflict, these categories have been identified as (1) causal conditions of phenomena relating to genocidal proclivity, which include (i) immediate or trigger factors, (ii) underlying or root causes, (iii) perceived threat of the "otherness," and (iv) exclusive ideological framing; (2) phenomena resulting from trigger factors, underlying causation, perceived threat of the "otherness," and exclusive ideological framing; (3) context in which ethno-religious conflict and genocidal proclivity developed; (4) intervening conditions influencing proclivity to genocide; (5) strategies of attack foreshadowing proclivity to genocide; and (6) consequences or effects of proclivity to genocide.

PRESENTATION OF THE GENOCIDE PROCLIVITY MODEL

1. Causal Conditions of Phenomena Relating to Genocidal Proclivity

Four types of causal conditions which lead ultimately to genocidal proclivity emerged from the data. These causation factors include (i) immediate or trigger factors, (ii) underlying or root causes, (iii) perceived threat of the "otherness," (iv) exclusive ideological framing.

Immediate or trigger factors to the conflict consist of the various issues which may be related or unrelated to the parties in conflict but form the basis from which the killing spree sparks. Trigger factors identified as "catalytic" (Suganami as cited in Williams, 2011, p. 6) "refer to those factors which generate actions . . . that represent the conscious choices of particular actors to engage in . . . violence" (Williams, 2011, p. 6). Such trigger factors identified in the study include, the first coup d'état of January 1966 and the killing of mainly northern army officers in the coup; reprisal mission, revenge or countercoup; massacres of Igbos and returning refugees; secession, and self-determination (Garrison, 1968a, 1968b); insurgency, uprising, or antigovernment riots; anti-U.S.-led Afghanistan air strikes ("Violent," 2001); arrests or persecution of fundamentalist sect members, religious extremism and violence or other fundamentalist activities; election-related and engineered violence; Islam degraded, desecration and/or misinterpretation of Koran (Brooke, 1987a, 1987b), the Danish Cartoon, and the Miss World Publications (Mcveigh, 2002).

The second set of causal conditions comprises underlying or root causes to the conflict which have become entrenched into the relational fabric of the conflict parties. Underlying causes defined as "permissive" (Suganami as cited in Williams, 2011, p. 6) "identify disposition which make organized violence more likely, [but] do not . . . explain why wars [or violence] break out in some cases where these underlying factors are present but not in others" (Williams, 2011, p. 6). Underlying causes are the factors that make a conflict intractable (Hauss, 2003). Such underlying causation identified in the study include historical factors; colonial influences, exploitation and fear of Balkanization; culture of bad governance and corruption or oppressive military rule; Al Qaeda, Afghanistan's Taliban, and Libyan, Iranian links including illegal aliens; and political underpinnings or power struggle. This includes issues of coalition government or federalism versus regionalism disputes (Garrison, 1966a); dynamism and fear of Igbo or southern dominance; infiltration and politicization of religion (Onishi, 2000, 2001b); political divisions and tensions; and political elites or Kaduna mafia perspectives (Kotch, 1987). Underlying causations also include socioeconomic factors, including ethnic groups vying for control of fertile lands, as well as political and economic power ("At Least 21 Are Killed," 2011). Others are indigenes and settlers issues (Polgreen, 2008), and poverty, unemployment, lack of education, and discontent (Nossiter, 2010c).

The third set of causal factors is the perceived threat of the "otherness," and for the ethno-religious conflict in Northern Nigeria this comprises anti-Igbo rioting following the first coup d'état of January 1966 and other anti-Igbo riots in succession particularly in the first phase of the study (Garrison, 1966a, 1966c, 1966g, 1966l, 1968a); ethnic-religious hatreds, rivalries, divisions and animosities ("Africa: Arms Are the Arbiter," 1967; "Africa: Race Hatred," 1967); dynamism and fear of Igbo or Southern dominance (Garrison, 1966a, 1967a, 1968a); North-South split or largely Muslim north and mainly Christian south ("100 Feared Dead," 1992; Polgreen, 2006, 2008; Purefoy, 2010); annihilation attempts by targeting (Abdulkadir, 2012b; Bello, 2012a, 2012b; "Christmas Carnage," 2011; Ehiabhi, 2012c; Kaita, 2011); and/or forceful conversion of Christians to Islam (Brooke, 1987b; "Christian Groups," 2009); and ultimatum to southern Christians living in the North to leave the region (Lobel, 2012; Ohai, 2012; Orude, 2012a, 2012b).

The fourth set of causal conditions involves issues of exclusive ideological framing. Exclusive ideology aims at selecting and justifying the extermination of a targeted member group on the basis of their different worldview, religion, or ethnicity (Campbell, 2010, Video Series 18). For the northern Nigeria ethno-religious conflict, framing of exclusive ideology primarily comprises matters revolving around issues with religious dimensions; anti-Western or ideological differences; fundamentalism and religious fervency; and Sharia or Islamic law institution in northern Nigeria. Ideological framing underlies much of the excessive bloodletting which continues to occur in northern Nigeria, particularly with the introduction of Sharia in some northern states [presently twelve states in Nigeria have established the Sharia as their penal legal code (International Crisis Group, 2010)]; with other Islamic law-related causal factors involving, non-Muslim opposition to Sharia, its constitutionality, and matters regarding the violation of fundamental rights of Christians and non-Muslims in Sharia operative states ("Christian Groups," 2009); gender segregation matters; issues on the strict implementation of Sharia; postures of anti-establishment or rejection of westernized institutions and ideology under Sharia ("700 Die," 2009; "Muslim Sect," 2011); and moves toward imposing Sharia across Nigeria or establishing an Islamic state ("Boko Haram," 2012; Brooke, 1987b; "In Nigeria's North," 2011; Mojeed and Nossiter, 2012).

2. Phenomena Resulting from Trigger Factors, Underlying Causation, Perceived Threat of the "Otherness," and Exclusive Ideological Framing

The study shows that the causal conditions—the trigger factors, underlying causation, perceived threat of "otherness," and exclusive ideological framing in varying situations and contextual settings—resulted in varying forms and degrees of exterminations and killings primarily between extremist Muslims and Christians, as well as other conflict parties which more often than not are divided along ethnic and religious lines. Such subjective phenomena as identified in the study data reveal core categories of attacks and violence unleashed to varying target victims with themes including assault, shoot-out, killings, arson, and looting ("300 Believed Killed," 1982; Fisher, 2006; Garrison, 1966g, 1966i; Jaynes, 1981; Fisher, 2006); and blockade, embargo and civil war (Friendly, 1967a; Garrison, 1968a; "Nigeria: Slow War," 1967). Other phenomenal themes in the study include bloodbath, carnage, pogrom, mayhem, massacres, or barbarism (Brooke, 1987b; Ejembi, 2012; Garrison, 1966b, 1967f; "Hundreds Flee," 2002; Koinange, 2001; "Nigeria Quells," 1992; "Nigerian Death Toll Rises," 2009; "Nigerian Muslims," 2004; Noble, 1992a; Nossiter, 2010b, 2010d, 2010e, 2010f, 2011; Obateru and Mamah, 2004; Onishi, 2001a; Purefoy, 2010); and bombings, suicide bombings, and coordinated gun and bomb attacks (Akau, 2012; "At Least 200 Die," 2008; Ehiabhi, 2012a; Emerson, 1970; Garrison, 1968a; Mgboh, 2012a; "Multiple Explosions," 2011a, 2011b; Ohai, 2012; Onyeose, 2012; Pedro, 2011; Tilley-Gyado, 2012). Additional phenomenal themes include genocide (Emerson, 1970; Friendly 1967a; Garrison, 1968a, 1968b; "Nigerian Muslims," 2004; Nossiter, 2010e; Okoye, 2011). Phenomenal themes identified in the study further include political violence, coups d'état, and political assassinations ("Emergency Declared," 2011; Garrison, 1966a, 1967h, 1968b; "Nigeria Group Threatens," 2011; Ohai, 2012); religious and ethnic violence ("1,000 Are Reported Dead," 1984; "300 Believed Killed,"

Presenting the Model for Proclivity to Genocide   105

Consequences
- Sequential or Complete Victim Annihilation
- Death Toll & Casualties
- Starvation
- Mass Graves & Mass Burials
- Infringing Human Rights

Strategies
- Organization & Planning
- Co-ordinated Attacks - Shootings, Bombings, Maiming, Arson
- Extermination Plot:
  - Mass Murders
  - Starvation/Blockade
  - Ideo-Ethnic Cleansing
  - Forced Migration Exterminations

Context
- Social Space or Lebensraum
- Conceptualized Annihilating Difference
- Perpetrator Traits and Attributes

Intervening Conditions
- Government Censorship and/or Manipulation
- Extrajudicial Killings and Overt Army Policing
- Weak Government, Ineptitude/Lethargy
- Collaborators/Bystanders
  - Foreign and Local

Phenomena
Attacks or Violence
- Targeted, Pre-meditated or Orchestrated Killings and Assaults
- Carnage, Pogrom, Massacres, Bloodbath, Barbarism or Mayhem

Causal Conditions
- Immediate or Trigger Factors
- Remote or Underlying Causes
- Perceived Threat of the "Otherness"
- Exclusive Ideological Framing

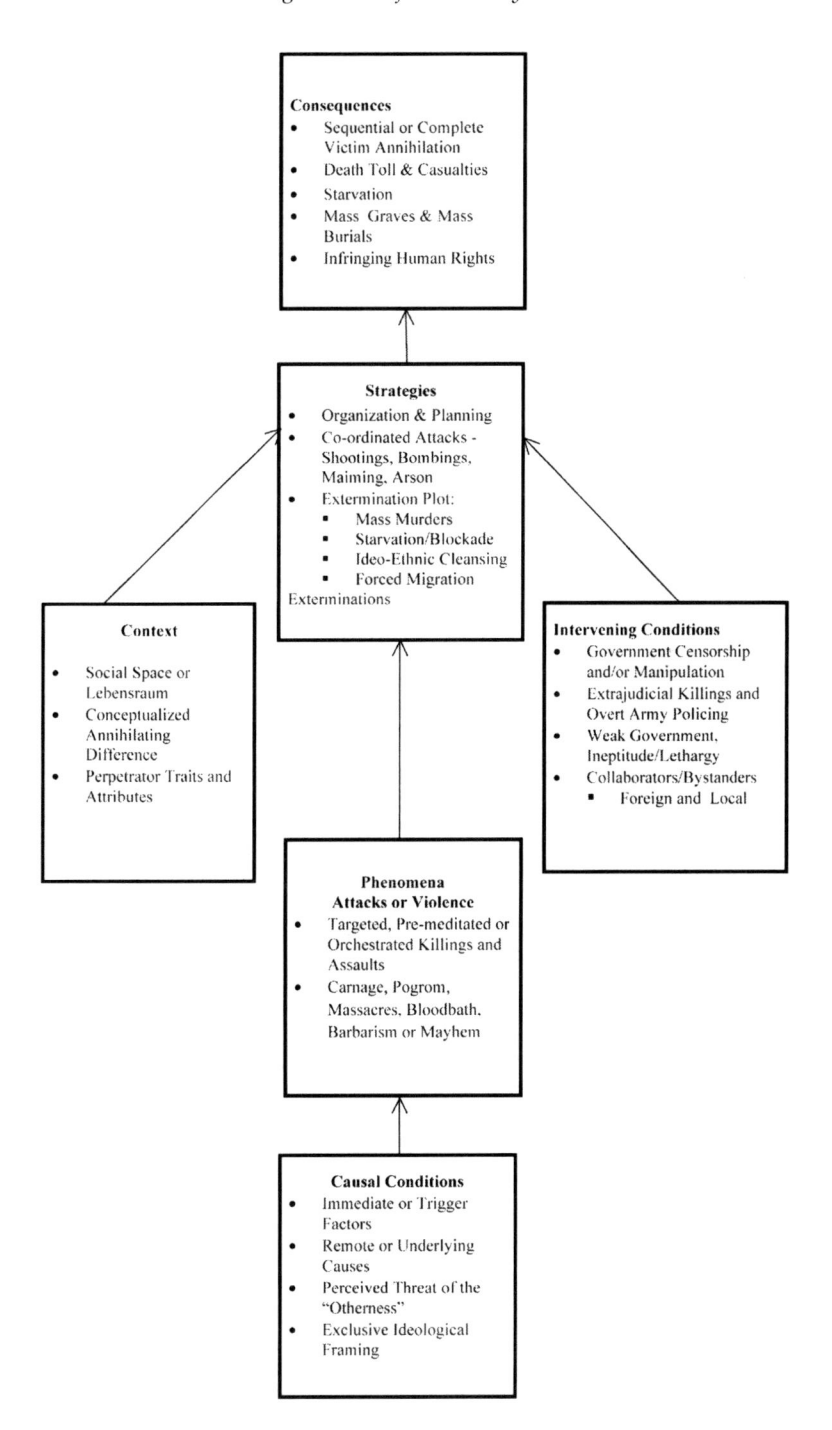

Figure 4.1. Theoretical Model for Proclivity to Genocide

1982; Brooke, 1987b; "Deadly Rioting," 2000; Emerson, 1970; Jaynes, 1981; "Nigeria Quells," 1992; Noble, 1992a, 1992b, 1992c).

The phenomenal themes also include reprisals from southern states (Onishi, 2000; Polgreen, 2006; "Reprisal Attacks," 2006; "Toll Rises," 2006; "Violent," 2001); sectarian violence ("718 Deaths," 1984; Ahiante, 2004; Chidiogo, 2011; Noble, 1992a, 1992c; Ohai, 2012; Sengupta, 2004a); and spiral or escalation of violence ("'Irate Youths' Burn Down," 2006; "Muslim Mobs," 2004; Nossiter, 2011; Sokunbi, 2012). Additionally in the study are the phenomenal themes of targeted, premeditated, or orchestrated killings and assaults (Abdulkadir, 2012b; Agboola, 2011; "Africa: Race Hatred," 1967; Bello, 2012a, 2012b; "Boko Haram," 2012; Brooke 1987b; "Christmas Carnage," 2011; Ehiabhi, 2012c; Emerson, 1970; Garrison, 1966a, 1968a; Kotch 1987; Mshelizza, 2011; Myers, 2006; Nossiter, 2011, 2012; Onishi, 2001a; Pedro, 2011; Sokunbi, 2012; "Suicide Bombing," 2012). Further included as phenomenal themes are terrorist activities (Ahiante, 2004; Akau, 2012; Batty and Mark, 2012; "Christian Groups," 2009; "Christmas Carnage," 2011; "Emergency Declared," 2011; Onah, Shiklam, and Olugbode, 2012); and threats or fears of more attacks, protests, or warnings of full scale war ("Dozens Dead," 2004; Emerson, 1970; Garrison, 1966e, 1967d, 1968a; Mshelizza, 2011; "Nigerian Muslims," 2004; Okpi, 2012; Ola and Orude, 2012; Simmons, 2000; "Violent," 2001). Other phenomenal themes from the study are tit-for-tat killings in northern states ("At Least 200 Die," 2008; "Boko Haram," 2012; Brooke, 1987b; Garrison, 1966i, 1967f; Jaynes, 1981; Lobel, 2012; Nossiter, 2010f; Polgreen, 2006; "Religious and Ethnic Clashes," 2001; Sengupta, 2004a, 2004b).

Further phenomenal themes in the study include uprising, antigovernment rioting, protests, or demonstrations (Brooke, 1987b; Fisher, 2006; Garrison, 1966a, 1966e, 1966h; "Hundreds Die in Religious Riots," 1984; Koinange, 2001; Kotch, 1987; Lacey, 2002; "Miss World," 2002; "Nigerian Police Station," 2010; "Nigerian Quells," 1992; Noble, 1992c; Sengupta, 2003; Sokunbi, 2012). Lastly, the phenomenal themes include violent or deadly clashes, rioting or gun battles ("1,000 Are Reported Dead," 1984; "700 Die," 2009; "718 Deaths," 1984; Brooke, 1987b; Chidiogo, 2011; Cowell, 1982; Dash, 1984; "Dozens Dead," 2004; Garrison, 1966c, 1967h; Jaynes, 1981; Koinange, 2001; "Nigeria Quells," 1992; Noble, 1992c; Nossiter, 2009a, 2009b; Ohai, 2012; Shiaondo, 2011).

The details of each of the phenomenal themes in the varying settings of the northern Nigeria ethno-religious conflict are analyzed and discussed in the different phases of the study. By comparing and contrasting these phenomenal themes and categories, two major categories involving targeted, premeditated, or orchestrated killings and assaults; and bloodbath, carnage, pogrom, mayhem, massacres, or barbarism are identified as being closely associated with the proclivity to genocide.

3. Context in Which Ethno-Religious Conflict and Genocidal Proclivity Developed

Additional themes from the study show the contexts, that is, the social space or lebensraum, which provide a geographic perspective, the framework on which genocide or its proclivity can develop (Wood, 2001). For the ethno-religious conflict in northern Nigeria the contextual settings identified in the study are presented in table 4.1 below. Also presented in table 4.2 are contexts identified in the study with reprisal attacks in some southern states, as well as the State of Biafra, the secession of which led to the 1967–70 civil war. Themes from the study reveal virtually all northern Nigeria states, in addition to Abuja (the federal capital territory) as the various contexts for the northern Nigeria ethno-religious conflict, some cases of which have evidences of inclinations to genocide.

The contextual locations within the various conflict settings identified in the study are presented in table 4.1 below, with reprisals in some southern states or regions presented in table 4.2.

Additionally providing the contextual framework are the thematic categories also identified from the study data which reveal varying conflict parties in the different phenomenal settings for the northern Nigeria ethno-religious conflict. The conflict parties identified include Muslim mobs/gangs, civilian mobs, or sect and Igbos; Muslim mobs or sect, and security forces; Muslim sects and other Muslims or sects (Andersson, 1996); the northern-led federal government and Igbos; Muslim mobs, sect or groups and Christians; Nigeria and Biafra in war; security agents and unidentified civilians; different ethnic groups; northern states government and Christians; and Fulani herdsmen or Hausa-Fulani group and Christian or host communities. The details of each of the conflict parties' themes in the varying settings of the northern Nigeria ethno-religious conflict are analyzed and discussed in the different phases of the study. Such themes for the conflict parties were analyzed by comparison and contrasted with the phenomenal conflict themes and categories and their causal conditions in order to identify conflicts in which there is the plausibility of a conceptualized annihilating difference (Hinton, 2005) that give rise to exterminations involving perpetrator and victim situations, with other conflicts which are devoid of such annihilating difference considered as clashes or fighting between parties without an overt inclination to genocide.

Thematic categories for varying perpetrator-groups identified in the study using the annihilating difference analysis of the conflict parties described above include Muslim mobs, rioters or rampaging Muslim youths; Islamic fundamentalists groups inclusive of the Maitatsine and Boko Haram sect; Fulani herdsmen, Fulani-Hausa group, or gunmen; and rampaging unemployed, or under-aged youths. The perpetrator category also revealed themes for civilian mobs, unidentified attackers or

Table 4.1. Contexts for the Northern Nigeria Ethno-Religious Conflict

Context		Study Phase			
S/N	Northern Region/States	I 1966–76	II 1976–87	III 1987–96	IV 1996–2005
1.	Abuja Jabi Zuba				X
2.	Adamawa State Yola Jimeta Lamurde Mubi	X X			
3.	Bauchi State Bauchi			X X	X
4.	Benue State Makurdi Gbeji; Vaase Zaki Ibiam Dooga; Kpata Lokobi; Ajimaka Ekaae; Giza Yogbo; Mbgawem Gwer West LGA Zongo Akiki Nyijir, Tse Taki, & Agbeke in Guma areas	X			X X X
5.	Borno State Maiduguri Dala Yan'tebura, Bulukuntu Tsallake Zajeri	X	X X		
6.	Gombe State		X		
7.	Jigawa State Dutse				
8.	Kaduna State Kaduna Kafanchan Zaria Zonkwa Zango-Kataf Kufara Ori-Apata	X	X X X X	X X X X	X X X X

9.	Kano State	X	X	X	X
	Kano		X	X	X
	-Sabon-Gari				X
	-Bompai				
10.	Katsina State			X	
	Katsina			X	
11.	Kebbi State				X
12.	Kogi State				
13.	Kwara State				X
	Ilorin				
14.	Nasarawa State				X
	Alago				
	Doma Town				
	Eke & Giza Areas				
	Kadarko				
	Tiv settlements at:				
	Kpata, Donga, Lokobi &				
	Ajimaka				
15.	Niger State				X
	Minna -				
	Angwan Kuje				
	Madalla				
16.	Plateau State	X			X
	Jos	X			X
	Bukuru				X
	Kadyal				X
	Kanam District				X
	Langtang				X
	Yelwa				
	Barkin Ladi				
	Dogon Na Hauwa Kuru				
	Karama Wareng				
	Zot and Ratsat				
17.	Sokoto State				X
18.	Taraba State			X	X
	Jalingo			X	
	Akwana				
19.	Yobe State				
	Damaturu				
	Gadaka				
	Geida				
	Hawan Malka				
	Potiskum				

110   Chapter 4

Table 4.2. Contexts for (i) Biafra War and (ii) Reprisals in Southern States and/or Extrajudicial Killings**

Context		Study Phase			
(i) S/N	Southern Regions (See Map I)	I 1966–76	II 1976–87	III 1987–96	IV 1996–2005
1.	Eastern Region or Biafra (See map I)	X			
2.	Mid-Western Region (See Map I)	X			
(ii) S/N	Southern States				
1.	Abia State Aba				X
2.	Lagos State Lagos				X
3.	Niger Delta State Odi**				X
4.	Anambra State Onitsha Awka Nnobi Nnewi				
5.	Delta State Asaba				
6.	Imo State				
7.	Akwa Ibom Uyo				X

Note. ** Cases of Extrajudicial Killings

gunmen; Christian militia/youths; and security agents, soldiers/army/military, Hausa/Northern troops. Details of involvement of each of these perpetrator groups in the varying settings of the northern Nigeria ethno-religious conflict are analyzed and discussed in the different phases of the study.

Themes from the study also revealed the victim or target groups, which enable the fostering of annihilating difference amid a perpetrator group and social space environment (Wood, 2001) to produce a well-rounded and complete contextual setting for genocidal proclivity to flourish. Target or victim groups for the northern Nigeria ethno-religious conflict include Christians and churches, also involving Christian neighborhoods or mostly Christian villages; civilian targets or innocent citizens; Southerners who are predominantly Christians, and especially Igbos as targets; security agents—police officers, military and government officials; symbols of government authority (including the United Nations offices in Abuja); civilian centers, schools, and school children; media offices and journalists; beer parlors, hotels, banks, and other facilities (structures or institutions with Western connotations); Muslim clerics or mainstream/orthodox Muslims; and Muslims, Hausa-Fulani herders, Muslim sects, Northerners, or mosques. The victimhood of each of these targets is also analyzed and discussed in the different study phases.

4. Intervening Conditions Influencing Proclivity to Genocide

The study also identified themes and categories for intervening conditions in the different contextual settings of the conflict in addition to the context themes. These intervening factors generally involve such broad conditions that influence—increase or diminish—the tendency or proclivity to genocide. For the northern Nigeria conflict, the intervening conditions include press censorship and manipulation or deflation and inflation of casualty figures—this casualty information manipulation facto was used by government parties on occasions to minimize but also sometimes scale-up reprisals or tit-for-tat violence; extrajudicial killings and army involvement in policing; government ineptitude, lethargy or weak central government; and the presence of collaborators or bystanders—foreign collaborators leading to the internationalization of the conflict, and local collaborators or bystanders. The details of the intervening conditions themes in the varying settings of the northern Nigeria ethno-religious conflict are analyzed and discussed in the different phases of the study.

The study further reveals that additionally influencing the tendency to increase or deflate genocidal proclivity are the various intervention measures to control the violence with their implementation. Categories for intervention efforts in the northern Nigeria ethno-religious conflict include: aid and relief support, attempts at dialogue, appeals for intervention or mediation; postwar reunification policy (for the Nigeria Biafra war); rehabilitation efforts or calls for rebuilding of churches; reconciliation attempts; control measures taken (such as curfews and road checks by security agents), investigations and commissions of inquiries utilized; calls to address the constitutionality of Sharia law and security issues; military assault or crackdown of warring factions; mopping-up of rioters or arrests made; warnings and/or calls for action, restraint, justice, or self-defense; and attempts to dialogue, and appeals for intervention or mediation. The details of the intervention measures in the varying settings of the northern Nigeria ethno-religious conflict are analyzed and discussed in the different phases of the study.

5. Strategies of Attack Foreshadowing Proclivity to Genocide

Thematic categories from the study also reveal varying strategies of attack which foreshadowed the tendency toward genocide within the contextual settings and intervening conditions with the resultant phenomena as described above. Strategies foreshadowing inclinations to genocide in the northern Nigeria ethno-religious conflict include organization and planning including weaponry; extermination plots involving mass murders, blockade, and starvation (Biafra war); and ideo-ethnic cleansing (or ideological and ethnic cleansing) involving burning, bombing, or destroying of churches, forceful conversion of Christians to Islam, forced migration, for example refugees and displaced persons, and the ultimatum by Boko Haram fundamentalists sect to southern Christians to leave the north. The strategies also include indoctrination, manipulation, or instigation; and coordinated attacks involving shootings, bombings, maiming, and arson, as well as drive-by or hit-and-run shootings and suicide bombings. The details of the themes of the strategies of attack in the varying settings of the northern Nigeria ethno-religious conflict are analyzed and discussed in the different phases of the study.

6. Consequences or Effects of Proclivity to Genocide

The strategies adopted by perpetrators in the ethno-religious conflict in northern Nigeria have varying effects or consequences in the different conflict scenarios examined. Categories of the consequences identified in the study include death toll and casualties; mutilated bodies or burned corpses; refugees and displaced persons, as well as persons fleeing homes or taking refuge or shelter for safety; starvation; secession and civil war; mass graves or mass burials; churches burned, bombed, or destroyed; mosques burned or destroyed; police stations, and barracks, and government buildings bombed or burned; schools bombed, burned, destroyed, or closed; Christian businesses, homes, hotels, and properties destroyed; destroying, looting, and razing of properties; denial of freedom of worship and desecration of Christian religion; and security threat, apprehension, anxiety, or political and social chaos, including infiltration of police, military, and all areas of government by perpetrator groups. Themes for the consequences category also revealed normalcy or calm returning after episodes of gruesome exterminations, showing an intermittency of occurrence in the killings. The details of the themes for the consequences or effects in the varying settings of the northern Nigeria ethno-religious conflict are analyzed and discussed in the different phases of the study.

END OF MODEL SUMMARY

The study integrates the theoretical approach of Strauss and Corbin (1990) in examining the plausibility of genocidal undertone to the northern Nigeria ethno-religious conflict. Newspaper articles of cases of the ethno-religious conflicts in northern Nigeria were analyzed focusing on causation and intentionality to inquire on the plausibility of genocidal inclinations to the killings. Based on the consistency of the emerging patterns (Stake, 1995) from the analysis, a theoretical model has been developed to explore genocidal tendencies to the conflict. The chapter presents this Genocide Proclivity Model. The next five chapters present the application of the genocide proclivity model to each of the study's five phases.

FIVE
Proclivity to Genocide in Northern Nigeria Phase I

1966 to 1976

This study on the ethno-religious conflict in northern Nigeria spans the period 1966 up to the present, with focus starting from the 1966 pogroms against the Igbos up to ongoing varied, targeted killings in the north. This entire study period—1966 to 2013—is phased into five eras, each era covering about a decade, drawn up on the basis of the changing geographic and structural composition of the country with the creation of additional states in Nigeria over the period of the study. The first phase of the study spans from 1966 to 1976, and sees Nigeria with four regions (see map 1 in appendix A) which were operative from 1963 up to 1967 when twelve states were created to replace the regions (see map 2 in appendix A). This first phase ends in 1976 when seven new states were created increasing the states of Nigeria to nineteen in total (see map 3 in appendix A). The second phase of the study spans from 1976 to 1987 when two additional states were created bringing the total to twenty-one states (see map 4 in appendix A). The third study phase spans from 1987 to 1996 and is inclusive of the years 1987 to 1991 when nine additional states and the Federal Capital Territory (now Abuja) were created bringing the states of Nigeria to thirty in total (see map V in appendix A). This third phase also includes the years 1991 to 1996 when additional states were created, bringing the total to the present thirty-six states of Nigeria (see map 1 in appendix A). The fourth phase of the study spans from 1996 to 2005, and the fifth phase spans from 2006 to present, with both phases having Nigeria's currently operative thirty-six states (see map 1 in appendix A).

PHASE I—1966 TO 1976: SYNOPSIS

Nigeria at independence in 1960 was a federation with three regions—the Northern, Western, and Eastern regions, with a fourth region, the Mid-Western region, created in 1963 (see map 1 in appendix A), and in the same year the country also became a republic. This first republic ended with Nigeria's first military coup of January 1966 by army officers led by Major Kaduna Nzeogwu, with intent to change the status quo of corrupt government officials, election rigging, and nepotism in the country (Garrison, 1966d). Nzeogwu's inspiring words observed in his radio broadcast were:

> Our enemies are the political profiteers, the swindlers, the men in high and low places that seek bribes and demand ten percent, those that seek to keep the country divided permanently so that they can remain in office as ministers and VIPs of waste, the tribalists, the nepotists, those that make the country big for nothing before the international circle, those that have corrupted our society and put the Nigerian calendar backward. We promise that you will no longer be ashamed to say that you are a Nigerian. (Ojiako as cited in Falola, 1999, p. 123)

While the coup succeeded in Kaduna, it failed in its other strategic areas of Lagos, Enugu, and Benin, with Odumegwu Ojukwu, then the battalion commander in Kano, foiling the coup in the northern axis, and Major General Aguyi Ironsi foiling it in the Lagos axis (Falola, 1999). The prime minister of the federation, Sir Abubakar Tafawa Balewa, and the northern premier, Ahmadu Bello, who was then the Sarduana of Sokoto were, however, killed in the coup, in addition to some northern senior officers in the army. These killings, in addition to the fact that most of the army officers involved in the coup were mostly of the Igbo ethnic group, gave the impression of an Igbo plan to control the center. Of this 1966 first coup, Enahoro had this to say of the civilian administration and senior army officers that were killed in the coup: "All of them had one thing in common—they were not Igbos" and for those in like positions that were not killed, "they had one thing in common—they were Igbos" (Enahoro as cited in Mwakikagile, 2001, pp. 192–193). This first coup triggered off anti-Igbo riots in May of 1966 with a resultant massacre of 600 Igbos in the north (Garrison, 1966g).

Furthermore, events following the coup which led to further resentment, as indicated by Enahoro, are that

> [t]he opportunities of January 15 were misused in several ways by the Ironsi regime in the months that followed . . . General Ironsi allowed matters to be taken out of his hands by prominent Ibo leaders in the army, in the public service, and in public life. Affairs in the public service and the armed forces appeared to lend colour to the impression that the coup of January 15 was designed to install Ibos in positions of

power. Out of twenty-one promotions in the Army in April, 1966, for example, eighteen were Ibo officers. General Ironsi drew his principal advisers from the Ibo ethnic group. Ethnic groups tend to be chauvinistic but the Ibos were the most militantly chauvinistic and this naturally created apprehension in the minds of the others. (Mwakikagile, 2001, p. 193)

Contrary to this positioning, however, Siollun (2009), in his book titled *Oil, Politics and Violence: Nigeria's Military Coup Culture (1966–1976)*, observes that other than Aguiyi-Ironsi, the only Igbo member of the Supreme Military Council's (SMC) eleven members was Lt-Colonel Ojukwu, who had automatic membership, as the Eastern region's military governor. Siollun observes:

In an effort to prove that he was not heading an Igbo regime, Aguiyi-Ironsi had with great, even daring courage entrusted his personal security to Northern soldiers. He posted the Principal Staff Officer Lt-Colonel Phillip Effiong out of Supreme Headquarters in Lagos and replaced him with Major T. Y. Danjuma of the northern Jukun ethnic group. He even appointed relatives of the January victims to sensitive positions. On the civilian side he appointed a close relative of the Sarduana (Hamzat Ahmadu) to be his private secretary in replacement of Abdul Kareem Disu. His police Timothy Pam was the younger brother of Lt-Colonel James Pam (who was murdered during the January coup), and most of his bodyguards were Northern. By surrounding himself with Northern soldiers, Aguiyi-Ironsi sealed his own fate. (2009, p. 84)

However, only six months later the January coup was followed by a bloody countercoup in July 1966 which was staged by northern army officers led by Major Murtala Mohammed, in which Major General Aguiyi-Ironsi, the then head of state, was killed. Also killed in the coup were over 200 Igbo officers and men in the army, in retaliation to the January killings (Garrison, 1967d). Yakubu Gowon, who was then a lieutenant-colonel, was by compromise made the new head of state. The July countercoup was then followed by continued bouts of targeting and massacring of Igbos in northern Nigeria in July, September, and October 1966, with over 50,000 Igbo civilians wantonly massacred in the fall of 1966, an episode that set off the displacement of tens of thousands of Igbo refugees (Garrison, 1968a). The perpetrators in each of these carnages were civilian or Muslim mobs—mainly Hausas, and northern troops. In Kano, for instance, where soldiers mutinied to participate in the Igbo killings in 1966:

The troops raided the battalion armory, broke out of the barracks and headed into town to pick up local civilian *yan daba* [thugs] . . . to take them to locations where they could find Igbos . . . Igbos trying to escape were not spared. At Kano airport, the soldiers set upon a crowd of Igbo refugees boarding a flight and killed them. Some were dragged out of

> the plane cabin and shot. Igbo workers at the airport were also hunted down and killed . . . The soldiers also [went to] the railway station where Igbo civilians were waiting to board trains to escape. Many of the Igbo would-be passengers and railway staff were shot dead. . . . This massacre on October 1, 1966 . . . was possibly the worst of the mutiny. The participation of soldiers with firearms greatly increased the kill rate. Several thousand Igbos were killed that day alone in Kano due to the combined efforts of the 5th battalion and civilian mobs. (Siollun, 2009, pp. 134–135)

Consequently, there were thousands of returning Igbo refugees who left the north for their home region in Eastern Nigeria, as well as a mass exodus of about two million Igbos residing all over the Federation who fled to the sanctuary of their home region in the east (Garrison, 1968b). As a result of these episodes of Igbo massacres in the north and the returning Ibo refugees to their homeland, coupled with the failure of subsequent attempts at resolving the conflict, on May 30, 1967, the Eastern region under the leadership of Lieutenant Colonel Odumegwu Ojukwu, seceded from the rest of the country to form a self-declared sovereign state of Biafra (Garrison, 1968a). This declaration was made after unsuccessful calls by Ojukwu to have the country institute a fully regional, rather than a federated system that would accord full autonomy of the four states or regions to ensure the safety of the Igbos as well as avert the perceived northern hegemony in the federal government. The regionalism versus federalism disputes fell through as did the accord of the Aburi meeting in Ghana which was not sustained (Falola, 1999). Shortly after Biafra declared sovereignty, the northern led federal government headed by Gowon passed a military decree on the eve of Biafra's secession (Falola, 1999, p. 122) creating twelve states to replace the four regions then existing (see map 2 in appendix A).

Thus, intent on keeping the unity of the country, the northern-led government of Gowon went to war with Biafra from 1967 to 1970, a war that on the onset was anticipated to be a "police action" but which lingered for thirty months and claimed about a million lives (Falola, 1999, p. 123). The Biafrans, on their part, put up a spirited defense of their right to survival and sovereignty, being enthused by the ordeal of the massacres and refugee crisis they had endured and the quest to survive. Hence, the observation was that, from the viewpoint of the average Biafran, the war was not being fought over such abtract issues as territorial integrity or constitutionality, it was rather the issue of fighting for survival (Garrison, 1968b). The war was, however, lost by Biafra, which was unable to resist a larger fighting force in the face of food shortages, as "the federal side resorted to the strategy of starving the enemy" (Falola, 1999, p. 123).

The preceding presents the contextual framework for the Nigeria-Biafra war of 1967 to 1970, which forms part of the first phase (1966–1976) of analysis of this study.

APPLYING THE GENOCIDE PROCLIVITY MODEL: PHASE I—1966 TO 1976

The application of the themes from study Phase I data to the Genocidal Proclivity Model in figure 4.1 follows.

1. Causal Conditions of Phenomena Relating to Genocidal Proclivity: Phase I— 1966 to 1976

As indicated above, the causal conditions have been classified into four types of contributory factors that could lead ultimately to genocidal proclivity as emerged from the data—namely, immediate or trigger factors, underlying or root causes, perceived threat of the "otherness," and exclusive ideological framing. These causal factors are overlapping rather than static, with a trigger factor in a current conflict, for instance, sometimes becoming in time an underlying or root cause. For the varying times of the conflict in this study phase, themes for the trigger causes identified in the study include the first coup d'état of January 1966 and the killing of mainly northern army officers in the coup; reprisal mission, revenge, or countercoup; massacres of Igbos and returning refugees; secession and self-determination; and insurgency, uprising, or antigovernment riots at varying times of the conflict.

Applying the theoretical model for identifying proclivity to genocide for this study period, the evidences reveal that the initial trigger or immediate cause of the conflict was the first coup, which involved the killing of the prime minister (Sir Tafawa Balewa), the Northern premier (Sarduana of Sokoto), and many senior northern army officers by the mostly Igbo army officers who staged the coup. The North's perception of the coup as an Igbo conception to rid the north of their hitherto hegemonic hold on the central government interests buttressed the long-entertained fear of the dynamism and fear of Igbo or Southern dominance, factors which fed on the perceived threat of the other, as well as served as part of the underlying causation. Investigating this theme of the North's fear of southern dominance, the study data substantiates, for instance, that superficially, the demonstrations seemed merely directed against the newly empowered, post-January coup d'état military government's attempts to centrally impose control, while the problem's actual cause was rooted in the northern Nigeria's traditional fear of being dominated by southerners. These fears have persisted, notwithstanding the sheer force of the North's conservative Hausa Muslim populace of about twenty-nine million then, for which the region presents as a dominant political force in the country, with southerners often being outnumbered by northerners at the polls (Garrison, 1966a).

Hence, as the first coup triggered off anti-Igbo riots and the May 1966 targeting and killing of over 600 Igbo civilians in the north (Garrison,

1966c), a subsequent, additional fodder became Aguiyi-Ironsi's decree dissolving the regions and declaring a Unitary republic which, though aimed at doing away with the regional politics then plaguing the country, was misconstrued and seen as threatening northern interests (Falola, 1999). This subsequent trigger set off the antigovernment riots that paved the way for a bloody second coup in July 1966 (Garrison, 1968a). Additional causal conditions in this phase of the study are the underlying or root causes to the conflict which had become entrenched into the conflict parties' relational framework. In this phase of the study, the themes for underlying conditions include colonial influences, exploitation, and fear of Balkanization; culture of bad governance and corruption or oppressive military rule; political underpinnings or power struggle also involving coalition government or federalism versus regionalism disputes (Garrison, 1967e, 1967f, 1967g) which culminated in the non-adoption of the Aburi accord and precipitated the secession of Biafra and the ensuing civil war (Emerson, 1970; Falola, 1999). Also, politically, there was the factor of politicization of religion (Emerson, 1970; Garrison, 1967h), with other underlying causation involving socioeconomic issues, including poverty, unemployment, lack of education, and discontent, as in the wake of the 1966 anti-Ibo rioting in which civilians, largely unemployed and illiterate Hausa mobs, along with northern troops perpetrated the atrocities against the Igbos, looting, killing, and maiming (Garrison, 1966g, 1966l, 1968b).

Further causal factors in this study phase are the perceived threat of the "otherness," which include dynamism and fear of Igbo or Southern dominance (Garrison, 1966h, 1968a; "Nigeria: Slow War," 1976); and ethnic-religious hatreds, rivalries, divisions, and animosities ("Africa: Arms Are the Arbiter," 1967; "Africa: Race Hatred," 1967; Garrison, 1966f, 1966g). Other perceived threats of the "otherness" include anti-Igbo rioting which followed the first coup d'état of January 1966 and successive anti-Igbo riots which occurred within this phase of the study ("Africa: Race Hatred," 1967; Garrison, 1966a, 1966c, 1966h); and the North-South split or largely Muslim north and mainly Christian south (1968a). This perception of threat being posed is intensified by ethnic, social, and religious divides in the country which its structures defined in terms of the largely Muslim north and the predominantly Christian south, or as in this phase of the study, the mostly Christian Igbos. For instance, tracing the causes of the 1966 massacres of Igbos in the North, the unity of Nigeria has, in the past been strained severely by regional and tribal rivalries, with the root cause of the problem being the North's traditional fear of being dominated by southerners. There is thus, the spontaneity in the violence and assaults on, the close to one million Igbos then living in the region, even as the Hausas have always considered the more educated Igbos among them to be heathen colonizers (Garrison, 1966a).

The final set of causal conditions in this study phase are themes classified under exclusive ideological framing which border primarily on ideological perspectives or worldviews. These include issues with religious dimensions, anti-Western or ideological differences, and fundamentalism and religious fervency. The role played by religious differences in orchestrating most of the Muslim/Christian conflicts in northern Nigeria cannot be overemphasized, and in addition to colonial factors already discussed above, these differences have fundamentally been instrumental to the country's North-South split along religious lines. Accordingly, differences of religion contributed significantly to the country's quick North-South split. At the turn of the twentieth century when the far North was conquered by the British, missionaries have been barred from the region while local rule was by traditional Muslim emirs. The North was thus isolated from change even as Western techniques were being adopted by Southern, mission-educated ethnic groups, who, accepting the prospects for change, soon also demanded change politically (Garrison, 1968a).

2. Phenomena Resulting from Trigger Factors, Underlying Causation, Perceived Threat of the "Otherness" and Exclusive Ideological Framing: Phase I—1966 to 1976

The study Phase I shows that the four-fold causal conditions—the trigger factor, underlying causation, perceived threat of "otherness," and exclusive ideological framing in different contextual settings—resulted in varying forms and degrees of exterminations and killings, primarily between mainly Muslim northerners and troops and Igbos which are divided along ethnic but also religious lines. Such subjective phenomena as identified in the study data reveal core categories of attacks and violence unleashed to the Igbos as the target victims with themes including assault, shoot-out, killings, arson and looting; blockade, embargo, and civil war; bloodbath, carnage, pogrom, mayhem, massacres, or barbarism; bombings and coordinated gun and bomb attacks; and genocide (Emerson, 1970; Friendly 1967a; Garrison, 1968a, 1968b). Additional phenomenal themes also include political violence, coup d'état and political assassinations; religious and ethnic violence; spiral or escalation of violence; targeted, premeditated, or orchestrated killings and assaults ("Africa: Race Hatred," 1967; Emerson, 1970; Garrison, 1966a, 1968a); threats or fears of more attacks, protests or warnings of secession or full-scale war; tit-for-tat killings in northern states; uprising, antigovernment rioting, protests, or demonstrations; and violent or deadly clashes, rioting, or gun battles.

By comparing and contrasting these phenomenal themes and categories, two major categories involving targeted, premeditated, or orchestrated killings and assaults; and bloodbath, carnage, pogrom, mayhem, massacres, or barbarism are identified as being closely associated with the proclivity to genocide. In the September 1966 massacres of Igbos in the north, the bloodbath started the night of September 29, with Nigerian troops opening fire on Igbo refugees as they stood by at the airport. By dawn, the city had been swept through by Northern soldiers who were armed with automatic weapons, as well as civilians armed with machetes, as all in collaboration, ardently burned, looted, and killed (Garrison, 1966b). The extent of the carnage perpetrated spoke of annihilating the Igbos in the then Northern region, such that even the fleeing refugees were sought out by northern troops and civilian mobs and slaughtered. Hence, the observation was that if there had been a plan to purge all Igbos from the North, such a plan had succeeded, as over a million Ibos who were then living in the North as well as in other parts of the country, retreated to the preserve of their home region in Eastern Nigeria (Garrison, 1966b).

Furthermore, this study phase which spans both prewar, the war years, and postwar years up to 1976, also shows blockade, embargo, and civil war as another major phenomenal theme for the period. The study data reveal that the Nigerian federal government, in a bid to crush the secession in the ensuing war, employed strategies of blockade and embargo against Biafra, which turned out to be an instrument of extermination against the Igbos by means of starvation. The blockade led to famine and humanitarian disaster due to a widespread starvation of Igbo civilians, particularly the Biafran children with over a thousand dying daily, subjected to the severe pangs of hunger and malnutrition (Emerson, 1970). There was inertia in the international community—the plausible intervening conditions that would have served to ameliorate the situation. To the contrary, the study themes revealed that collaborators or bystanders, particularly foreign collaborators such as Europe and the United States, were aware of Biafra as one remote African place which had starving children in thousands, who neither whimpered nor blinked as their plights were being recorded in photographs (Emerson, 1970). It was thus, the Biafran wasted children, and the way these children stared, that framed the civil war to numerous people outside Africa, as a rather deeply disturbing, rather inexplicable nightmare (Emerson, 1970). Further affirming the countless Biafran children's ill-fated agony, the study data reveal that Biafra was steadily becoming more of a death trap with every hour that passed, with the death rate from malnutrition said to grow by mathematical progression. Deprivation of protein for the victim occurs with malnutrition setting in, which causes energy to dissipate, even as his skin becomes taut, the hair yellows, and limbs thin out and become matchsticks, at which stage the victim regresses further in the eyes, to the horrifying point or state of no return, especially for a child. At this stage, the victim just stares blankly at you, without any flicker, or trace of recognition, even where candy is dangled before the child, or powdered milk offered in a cup, anything at all, the child merely stares, having become too listless, and indeed, too dehydrated to even relish the taste of food. It is an irony of malnutrition-caused death that in its fading, final hours, the victim at last is freed completely of hunger pangs (Garrison, 1968b).

The deployment of starvation by the Nigerian government as a strategy for winning the war is evident from themes from the study. The study data indicated that the death spiral which was charted for months by a representative of the international Red Cross in Biafra started with a record of 300 deaths a day, increasing gradually in two months to 6,000 a day, and up to 42,000 a week by July 1968 (Garrison, 1968b). Both the relief administrators as well as Biafran officials maintained that, after the halting of the Red Cross flights, child deaths rose 50 percent (Emerson, 1970). The data, however, reveal that, whereas in Europe, observers had believed Nigeria's original intent for the invasion was entirely military, as the starvation death toll mounted, many observers concluded that the Nigerian government as well as the British government, were willingly condoning starvation as a strategy to win the war and preserve Nigeria's unity (Emerson, 1970). The Nigerian government, thus adopted a deliberate extermination policy against Biafrans on the basis of starvation being a legitimate war weapon, and this was even further extended to sectors that were overrun and reoccupied by the federal troops (Garrison, 1968b). Hence, Nigerians banned every Red Cross flight to Biafra as well as to the "liberated," federally controlled Calabar and Enugu sectors, where about one million civilians were starving, six months following their liberation (Garrison, 1968b).

Further evolving from the study are the prewar, identified major categories of targeted, premeditated, or orchestrated killings and assaults; and, bloodbath, carnage, pogrom, mayhem, massacres, or barbarism as phenomenal killings perpetrated against the Igbos in the war. Such categories in this study phase reveal themes showing killings of Igbo civilian targets by Nigerian troops and in places overrun by the Nigerian government as the war progressed, and on occasions, as in the Mid-Western region, in conjunction with Nigerian civilian mobs. The study reveals for instance that in August 1967, as federal troops reoccupied the then Mid-Western state which previously had been seized by the rebels, Biafran troops, an estimate of about 5,000 Igbo civilians were killed ("Africa: Race Hatred," 1967, p. 200). Again in September, as the state capital Benin was retaken by the federal troops, the tally made of Igbo civilians killed was 989. In Warri, about 400 to 500 Igbo civilians were estimated to have been slaughtered by civilian mobs celebrating the Nigerian soldiers' return. A day after Warri was liberated, dead bodies so cluttered the city's main thoroughfare that cars were unable to use it ("Africa: Race Hatred," 1967). Additionally, in Sapele, where federal advance was mostly resisted by Biafran troops, the data reveal civilian casualties to be close to that of

Warri, and along the River Niger west bank, which is an Igbo-speaking predominated area, several thousand Igbo civilians were killed by troops either in the battle, or in the mop-up operations ("Africa: Race Hatred," 1967; Garrison, 1967b).

The evidences from the study data also showed that the Nigerian Air Force, using their MIGs, embarked on a deliberate targeting and bombing of churches, missions, and schools in Biafra, and after one such bombing, involving bombing of the Catholic cathedral in Owerri, the radio station in northern Nigeria made an announcement of the cathedral having been destroyed (Garrison, 1968a). Such deliberate targeting of churches and schools led to the closure of all schools in Biafra. The data indicated that in addition to a Shell refinery, a strategic target, countless air attacks had been made against Biafran front positions, and civilian centers totaling more than 50 had been bombed. Included in the study data is a listing sent to the UN of some of the Biafran civilian centers targeted and bombed by the Nigerian Air Force to support the Biafrans' claim of the war being a genocidal war, each building noted as the only one hit in its area, including, Ituk Mbang' Methodist Hospital; Itu' Mary Slessor Presbyterarian Hospital; Eket' Lutheran Mission Hospital; Umuahia' Holy Ghost Teachers' Training College; Aba' Christ the King Elementary School; Uyo' Lutheran High School; Oruku' Methodist Church; and Itigidi' Eja Memorial Hospital (Garrison, 1968).

Further evidential to these atrocities, in a speech by Lieutenant-colonel Chukwuemeka O. Ojukwu to the Organization of African Unity (OAU) special conference on the Nigerian civil war, Addis Ababa, Ethiopia, on August, 5, 1968, Ojukwu reports that with hostilities against Biafra commenced July 6, 1967, on four fronts on its northern frontiers, Nigeria overran these border towns in the first week of fighting, after which Nigerian atrocities began in these towns:

> Arson, looting, rape and all kinds of torture became the order of the day. Whole villages were remorselesssly burnt to ashes, farms and barns completely looted, churches and shrines outrageously desecrated. Defenseless civilians—men, women and children, fleeing their homes—gave accounts of their experiences of horror and anguish. Mothers told of the wholesale massacre and torture of their sons and of the rape and abduction of their young daughters. Children trekked miles of bush paths in tears, wailing the death at enemy hands of mother and father, sister and brother, aunt and uncle. (Ojukwu as cited in Mwakikagile, 2001, p. 175)

Lastly attesting to the genocidal undertones eminent in this study phase is an editorial by *The Times* of London titled "A Policy of Famine" also with one subheading, "A Deliberate Weapon," in which *The Times* observed: "All the evidence now shows that starvation as an act of war is the effective policy of the Nigerian Government" (*The Times* as cited in

Jacobs, 1987, p. 193). The statement has punctured the British government's propaganda line which it had been successfully propagating for over twelve months. Furthermore, *The Times* in the said editorial reminded its readership of Biafra's one million and half already dead, recalled the facts of a Red Cross relief aircraft that was shot down by the Nigerian forces, the indiscriminate bombings of civilians and hospitals in Biafra, and the successful campaign for cutting off night flights to Biafran's airstrips, and finally concluded:

> When one puts together these pieces of evidence one can be left in no doubt that the Government of Nigeria, whatever intentions it may have had at the beginnig of the war, is now prepared to use blockade and starvation, even at the cost of a further million deaths, rather than agree to secession. Leaving aside the massacre of the Ibos, this has the effect of a policy of genocide.
>
> [Arguing that British influence be used] to moderate and mitigate the evils of this war [and] . . . that we should not cut off the arms supply because that might destroy our influence . . . [i]t is the argument that we should retain our influence on events which seems now the most discredited of all. . . . Mass starvation unites a nation only in death. It is quite simply morally wrong to be the accessory to the slaughter of a million people in order to protect oil supplies and anyone who does not see that it is wrong is a moral imbecile . . .
>
> If one could only see this matter for what it is, the greatest tragedy or crime for which Britain has shared responsibility in this century, the worst since the Irish famine, we should now devote all our diplomatic power, all the influence that remains, all the efforts of the Government to securing effective relief in terms of food for Biafra, at all costs and at once. (Jacobs, 1987, pp. 194–195)

3. Context in Which Ethno-Religious Conflict and Genocidal Proclivity Developed: Phase I—1966 to 1976

In this study period, Nigeria operated a four regional structure—Northern, Western, Eastern, and Mid-Western regions (see map 1 in appendix A) up to 1976 when the structure was altered with the creation of seven states, giving a twelve-state structure (see map 2 in appendix A). Hence, themes for this phase of the study provide contextual themes for the conflict, which include Eastern region or Biafra; Mid-Western region; and Northern region, in Kano, Kaduna, Jos, Bukuru, Maiduguri, and Makurdi (see tables 4.1 and 4.2 for the various contexts, respectively, for the northern Nigeria ethno-religious conflict, and for the Biafra war and/or reprisal attacks in the south). A number of these contexts are identified in the study as some of the notable locations in which the phenomena of targeted, premeditated, or orchestrated killings and assaults; as well as bloodbath, carnage, pogrom, mayhem, massacres, or barbarism took place. The phenomena of blockade, embargo, and civil war and its resultant starvation and famine occurred in Biafra in its secessionist war of 1967 to 1970, while the war year killings of Igbos in re-occupied zones occurred mostly in the then Mid-Western region, notably in Benin, Asaba, Warri, Sapele, and the River Niger axis ("Africa: Race Hatred," 1967). The air raids and targeted bombings of civilians and civilian centers—hospitals, churches, schools, etc.—occurred in various locations in Biafra without protocols observed (Garrison, 1968a).

In addition to the contextual framework of social space in the conflict, this study phase also includes themes and categories showing conflict parties involving Muslim or civilian mobs and Igbos ("Africa: Race Hatred," 1967; Brooke, 1987b; Garrison, 1966b, 1966c, 1966d, 1966e, 1966h, 1968a); and the northern-led federal government and Igbos (Garrison, 1966b, 1966g, 1967a, 1967b, 1967d). Conflict parties for this study phase also include Nigeria and Biafra in the civil war (Friendly, 1967b; Garrison, 1966j; "Nigeria: Slow War," 1967); and different ethnic groups, and/or, different ethnic groups and Igbos (Garrison, 1966b).

By analyzing such conflict-parties themes through comparison and contrast with the causal conditions and conflict phenomenal themes and categories, this study phase identifies the plausibility of a conceptualized annihilating difference between the different perpetrator groups and the Igbos as victims, which gave rise to the various extermination episodes during the period. These episodes as outlined above, involve the 1966 successive massacres or pogrom of Igbos in the north; the war years annihilation of Ibos by starvation, primarily Igbo children; the targeting and mass killings of Igbo civilians in the re-occupied war zones; and the bombings of Ibo civilians and centers in the war, all of which are evidential themes that portend to a proclivity to genocide.

Using the annihilating difference analysis of the conflict parties as described above, this study phase identifies themes and categories for perpetrator-groups involving Muslim mobs, rioters, or rampaging Muslim youths; the army/military, Hausa/Northern troops or the northern-led federal government; and civilian mobs ("Africa: Race Hatred," 1967; Garrison, 1967b, 1968a). In the 1966 Igbo massacres in the north, for instance, themes from the study show the perpetrators of these carnages were Muslim mobs in addition to northern or Hausa troops in the army ("Africa: Race Hatred," 1967; Garrison, 1966b, 1966c, 1966g, 1967a, 1967b, 1967d, 1968a). However, civilian mobs, which might have included Hausa mobs, as well as some of the other non-Hausa ethnic groups in the north, also participated in the Igbo massacres (Garrison, 1966c). Details of the involvement of the perpetrator groups in the different conflict settings of this study phase are analyzed and discussed in the Phase I synopsis above.

This phase of the conflict was, therefore, drawn more along ethnic rather than religious divides, with Igbos and Biafrans at large in the civil war as the object of victimhood or targets. Hence, additional themes and categories from this phase also revealed the victim or target groups which enable the fostering of annihilating difference amid a perpetrator group, and social space environment produces a well-rounded and complete contextual setting for genocidal proclivity to flourish. The identified victim or target groups in this phase are Igbos, or Igbos as Christians, and Biafran civilians, as well as structures such as schools, churches, and other civilian centers also as targets. Details of victimhood of the targets in the different conflict settings of this study phase are also analyzed and discussed in the Phase I synopsis above.

4. Intervening Conditions Influencing Proclivity to Genocide: Phase I—1966 to 1976

In addition to the context themes, this study phase identified intervening conditions in the conflict's various contextual settings, and these involve general or broad conditions with capability to diminutively or incrementally influence the tendency toward developing a proclivity to genocide. This study phase reveals intervening conditions, themes and categories, including government ineptitude, lethargy, or weak central governance, which indicates the ineffectiveness of the government in mitigating the genocidal trend in the conflict. In the 1966 massacres of Igbos in the north, for instance, in which the northern-led federal government forms part of the intervening conditions or factors capable of influencing or ameliorating the conflict, the study data reveal that there was ineptitude of the government in intervening. As the slaughter of Igbos occurred, while the violence was noted to have been deplored by Gowon, he neither extended condolence, nor offered the victims any compensation, being without choice but to remain silent, given that the same soldiers that got him into power were those exact soldiers whose hands reeked the most of Igbo blood, and who had no apologies to tender (Garrison, 1968a).

Furthermore, in the mass killings of the Igbos in the reoccupied war zones in the Mid-Western state, General Gowon is observed as not having emerged as a unifying, charismatic figure. Thus, though generally admired for his sincerity and honesty, missionaries receiving battle field reports and diplomats, however, criticized his inability at enforcing on his soldiers an operative code of conduct. Such a code would have protected civilian men, women, and children from being maltreated, even as its rigid enforcement would have served to convince and reassure Igbos that they were not facing a tribal pogrom of extermination, but rather a restrained effort at ridding them of secessionist dissident leaders. The code vanished almost entirely, other than with the federal propaganda. As the Mid-Western state was being cleared of Biafran forces, in Benin, Sapele, Warri, Asaba, and Agbor, federal troops killed over 5,000 Igbos, or watched in complicity as mobs did the killing. Their underlying explanation was the impossibility of discriminating between combatants and civilians (Friendly, 1968).

Also in this study phase are the intervening conditions themes of press censorship and manipulating or deflating and inflating of casualty figures—which involves understating of toll or casualty figures by the government to deflect publicity and approbation, whether local or international. For instance, the Sabon-Gari area of Kano, where about 30,000 Igbos had lived had become a ghost town, even as other Ibo communities in the Northern region became engulfed with the slayings in the September 1966 Igbo bloodbath, but the federal government conservatively put the region's official toll of Igbo deaths at 7,000 in this killing episode (Garrison, 1966b).

Further intervening conditions in this phase include collaborators or bystanders, involving both local and foreign collaborators leading to the internationalization of the conflict. Of the local bystanders, most stood in quiet complicity to the Igbo massacres in the north, while the few who attempted to appeal to the nation's conscience were either jailed or ostracized. Wole Soyinka's compassionate in acknowledging the traumatic effects of the slaughter of Igbos in northern Nigeria in September 1966, had argued that the nation's only salvaging from its brink of political and moral bankruptcy required a national, massive outpouring of remorse. Contrary to this, and for most of the time, the reaction of the Yorubas to the Igbo's bloodletting took on an ostrichlike withdrawal approach (Garrison, 1967h). As the civil war broke out in 1967 with Soyinka's unsuccessful mediating with the seceeded Biafrans and appeal for cease-fire, he was arrested and jailed for twenty-two months on accusation of conspiracy with Biafrans (Noble, 1989).

On the foreign scene, Britain's initial announcement was to deploy a strict neutrality policy and arms embargo to both sides, with the United States and France following suit. This, however, was until the Russians waded in to supply Nigeria with MIGs, torpedo boats, and more than 200 manned technicians, with ulterior motives of gaining some foothold in the continent in which previous power intrigues continuously produced endless failure chains (Garrison, 1968a). Thus, as its vested traditional interests became threathened by Russia's intervention, Britian quickly scrapped its arms embargo policy and marched fully behind Nigeria. British parliamentarian George Thomson stated in Parliament on August 27, 1968, that

> Nigeria is getting the bulk of her supplies (of weapons) from elsewhere. If Britain stopped supplies, we would lose our capacity to influence the Federal Government. Russia would be only too willing to fill the gap and gain the influence we would lose. (Legum in Thomson as cited in Mwakikagile, 2001, p. 34)

Taking its cue from Russia, Egypt also teamed to support Nigeria on which sentiment was recognized as being a factor, given the country's principal leaders being fellow Muslims, whereas, not only were the Igbos Christians, they had also openly aligned their cause with Israel's struggle for the creation of a homeland. Hence, internationally, the war had gone beyond being a civil war, with the great powers moving in, taking sides, and contributing arms, funding, and tactical support. The lines were thus, drawn along the interests of these collaborators, and as the study data reveal, none of the foreign power involvement with either side had been done purely in an altruistic sense (Garrison, 1968a).

Furthermore, there were intervention measures taken or explored toward resolving the conflict in this study phase, including appeals for mediation (Garrison, 1967c). The study data reveal, for instance, that the internationalization of the Nigeria-Biafra war stifled the chances of resolving the conflict by dialogue and/or any other form of mediation other than militarily; consequently the war became drawn out with a high toll and war casualties of over two million Biafrans, especially through starvation and civilian targeted killings (Emerson, 1970; Garrison, 1967h, 1968a). Foreign involvement tilted the balance both diplomatically and militarily against Biafra, with the prospects for a cease-fire dim. Thus, Ojukwu, in an interview on peace prospects, indicated that unconditional talks and a cease-fire would be welcomed by Biafra at any time, but he observed, however, that the key or road to peace lay with London rather than Lagos, on the premise that the moment Britain stopped its supply of arms to Lagos, peace talks would begin (Garrison, 1968a). More so, in a parliamentary exchange between the then British Minister of State, Foreign Affairs, Mr. Thomas, and that of Labor, Mr. Barnes was questioned on whether the government was allowing the shipments of arms because it hoped to see the war end quickly, or that it might instead drag the conflict for a long time, in which case the best line of action would be for Britain to regain its neutrality. Mr. Thomas, in response, affirmed that they wanted a speedy end to the war, the cause of which, they did not contemplate would be advanced by stopping their supply of arms to Lagos (Garrison, 1968a).

A further analysis of this development and its root causes in the study data observe the conflict as having become profoundly internationalized, with peaceful solution depending on what London, Washington, and Moscow would do, as well as the combatants on their own. Further analyzing the issue to determine what did go wrong, as well as the reason for sudden foreign intervention, the answer is rooted in the West's simple failure in its expectations for Nigeria. Britain and the United States saw the makings of greatness in the independent Nigeria as the most powerful, most populous, most democratic nation in Africa, with the expectation of the country becoming a Western showcase that would serve as a bastion for non-communism, that would also thrive on the basis of free enterprise as well as by extensive influx of foreign aid from the West (Garrison, 1968b). It was, thus, immaterial to foreign collaborators such as Britain and the United States, whether or not the continued war led to the total annihilation of Igbos or Biafrans by the bombing of civilians, mop-up operations, starvation, or whatever device possible, so long as their facade of Nigeria as a Western showcase was maintained to all.

This study phase also reveals that additionally influencing the tendency to increase or deflate genocidal proclivity are the various intervention measures to control the violence. For instance, in the 1966 mutiny of soldiers involved in the Igbo massacres in Kano, although the situation was "beyond police control," the Northern region military governor, Lt-Colonel Katsina, "travelled to Kano to bravely confront the mutineers" (Siollun, 2009, p. 135). Thus, intervention efforts in this phase included aid and relief support; postwar reunification policy for the Nigeria-Biafra war and rehabilitation efforts; reconciliation attempts; control measures taken such as curfews and road checks by security agents; investigations and commissions of inquiries set up; mopping up of rioters or arrests made; warnings or calls for action, restraint, justice, or self-defense; attempts to dialogue, and appeals for intervention or mediation.

5. Strategies Foreshadowing Proclivity to Genocide: Phase I — 1966 to 1976

This phase also reveals strategies which foreshadow the tendency toward genocide in the conflict within the contextual settings and above intervening conditions with the resultant phenomena as described above. The strategies in this study phase include organization, planning, and weaponry, which are essential for achieving an effective, coordinated outcome. For instance, on the northern Nigeria September 1966 Igbo massacres, most of the foreign observers were convinced of the pogrom's planning, given that, as though signaled, the slayings very rapidly spread throughout other Igbo residing communities in the Northern region (Garrison, 1966b).

Strategies in this phase also include weapons of attack or warfare for exterminations, as in the September 1966 Igbo massacres in which the northern soldiers carrying their automatic weapons, and the civilians carrying their machetes, had, by dawn swept through the city, looting, burning, and killing (Garrison, 1966b). Strategies also include extermination plots involving mass murders, as in the above referenced massacres of Igbos in the north and the various slaughters of Igbo civilians in the war years, reoccupied Mid-Western region by Nigerian troops, and further include blockade and starvation strategy as was deployed in the Biafra war (Garrison, 1968b; Emerson, 1970), as well as the strategy of ideo-ethnic cleansing (or ideological and ethnic cleansing), for example, burning or destroying of churches (Garrison, 1966b) or the killing of Igbos as Christians on the basis of their ethnicity as Igbos ("Africa: Arms," 1967;

"Africa: Race Hatred," 1967; Garrison, 1966g, 1968a). Also deployed as strategy in this phase is forced migration of the refugees and displaced Igbos living in northern Nigeria to the sanctuary of their home state in Eastern Nigeria or Biafra. The strategies also include coordinated attacks involving shootings, bombings, maiming, and arson, as well as looting of Igbo-owned shops and businesses (Garrison, 1966b, 1966c, 1966k, 1966m).

6. Consequences or Effects of Proclivity to Genocide: Phase I—1966 to 1976

The strategies adopted by the different perpetrators have varying effects or consequences in this study phase. Consequences identified in this phase include death toll and casualties, mutilated bodies, or burned corpses, as in the several various massacres of Igbos discussed above; refugees and displaced Ibos from the north or Igbos fleeing to the safety of their home state (Garrison, 1966b, 1966); starvation, as has been extensively discussed above (Emerson, 1970; Garrison, 1968b); secession and civil war as the resultant effect of the northern pogroms on Igbos and the refugee crisis (Garrison 1967b, 1968a); and churches burned, bombed, or destroyed (Garrison, 1966b). Other consequences identified in this study phase include Christian/Igbo businesses, homes, hotels, and properties destroyed (Garrison, 1966k; "Nigeria: Slow War," 1967); destroying, as well as looting and razing of properties (Garrison, 1966b, 1966c); and denial of freedom of worship and desecration of the Christian religion, as in Ojukwu's war call to Biafrans, to prepare to die so that their children could live, even as he warned them that federal victory would signify a continuation of genocide for the people, disease, bestiality, poverty, ignorance, anarchy, and the desecration of their religion (Friendly, 1967a).

Further consequences in this phase are security threat, apprehension, anxiety, or political and social chaos (Garrison, 1966e, 1966l, 1967a); and the consequences category also reveals normalcy or calm returning after episodes of gruesome exterminations, showing an intermittency of occurrence in the killings. For instance, after the May/July 1966 episodes of Igbo massacres in the north, and before the even more heinous fratricide of the Igbos in the September/October 1966 eruptions, Garrison (1966k) observes that a peaceful atmosphere returned finally to the vast North, following a week of rioting which took the lives of several hundred last month, with the observation also that, most of these dead were Igbos from southern Nigeria who had become victims of the country's political passions, ingrained in its past.

SIX
Proclivity to Genocide in Northern Nigeria Phase II

1976 to 1987

SYNOPSIS

The second study phase examines the northern Nigeria ethno-religious conflict from 1976 to 1987. This phase saw Nigeria's creation of seven new states in 1976, which increased the number of states for the country to nineteen in total (see map 3 in appendix A), as well as the creation of two additional states in 1987 bringing the total number of states to twenty-one (see map 4 in appendix A). Politically, this phase saw a succession of coups and regimes transiting from military to civil rule and vice versa, beginning with Lieutenant-General Murtala Mohammed, who became head of state following a bloodless coup that overthrew General Yakubu Gowon in January 1975. Following his assassination in an unsuccessful coup in February 1976, Lieutenant-General Olusegun Obasanjo, then his deputy, became the next head of state.

Additionally, in this study phase, Nigeria transited from military to civil rule in October 1979 with Shehu Shagari (1979–1983) elected into office as the president in the Second Republic (1979–1983). Ousted in his second term in office in a palace coup in December 1983, General Muhammadu Buhari (1983–1985) became head of state and chairman of the Supreme Military Council of Nigeria (SMC) which ended the Second Republic. In yet another palace coup that overthrew Buhari in August 1985, General Ibrahim Babangida (1985–1992) came to power as head of state and president of the Armed Forces Ruling Council of Nigeria

(AFRC). The second phase of the study situates in the atmosphere of these successive regimes and structural changes in the country.

In the years following the war, the Igbos who returned to the North had been changed by the 1966 riots and the debilitating effects of having fought and lost the civil war, in which processes ethnicity had functioned "as a carefully directed social and political toxin" (Anthony, 2002, p. 235). The promotion of the Northernization policies of the prewar era had aimed at limiting southerners' ability at gaining political and economic footholds in the north. Threatened with Ironsi's administrative unification policy, however, the region's political elites and power brokers' intent on retaining control over the region was made resoundingly clear by the antiriots, which succeeded in the toppling of Ironsi's government, after which "the violent expulsion of Igbos from the North completed Northerners' assertion of control" (Anthony, 2002, p. 235). Additionally, there was also an economic takeover and change of hands other than the political control as "Igbo property and their niches in local economies found their way into the hands of other Nigerians, often those of local elites" (Anthony, 2002, p. 235). Furthermore, the creation of states enabled the preferential engagement or promotion of each state's own citizens as a result of which the hitherto perceived threat that southerners or Igbos had posed in 1966 became less threatening. More so, Igbos no longer occupied many top positions in the federal government administration then under the headship of Gowon from the Middle Belt, nor were they notable any longer in the parastatals, civil service, or private sector. Essentially, as Anthony (2002) observes, "The monolithic Igbo monster that Northern leaders of the 1950s and 1960s had painted as so fierce had, for all practical purposes, lost its teeth" (p. 235).

Since the 1970s, pressure had been mounting up, primarily, over the issue of religion's role in politics. With the structural changes brought about by the creation of states in Nigeria amid the ensuing regime changes, there was a shift in focus from the hitherto mainly ethnic-fault divide to an intensification of a religious-fault divide. To that end, religious tensions have escalated in northern Nigeria since the civil war, and have remained high with religious issues and constituencies proving more robust than ethnic constituencies in the inherent political fragmentation of smaller states, and its divisions also proving "resistant to the inhabiting effects of military rule" (Anthony, 2002, p. 234). This second phase of the study, therefore, saw the country witnessing another episode in the long annals of northern Nigeria's religious unrest with violence sputtering in the region following the withdrawal of the military from political life in 1979 (Cowell, 1982). Undergirding the phenomena is the crisis posed by the pervasiveness of religion in politics, as a result of which, "[b]eginning with the Shagari administration, religious violence became one of the [nation's] most serious crises of the 1980s and beyond" (Falola, 1999, p. 168).

One such prevalence of religious skirmishes and tensions in the north was the May 1980 crisis in Zaria, involving extensive destruction of mainly Christian property by some Muslims. Soon following this disturbance was a large-scale insurgency which broke out in Kano in 1980, and spreading in the years up to 1985, engulfed a number of major cities in the north. These insurgencies, referred to as "the Maitatsine riots" claimed the lives of thousands, as well as caused extensive property damage (Falola, 2002, p. 168) involving a fundamentalist Islamic sect led by one Mohammad Marwa of Cameroonian descent, previously expelled from the area due to disruptive activities (Jaynes, 1981). Observed as "combining Islam with sorcery" (Falola, 2002, p. 168; see also Falola, 1998), Marwa had by 1980 established a following of about 3,000 to 5,000 in Kano, mostly unemployed youths (Cowell, 1982; Jaynes, 1981), "willing to die for their belief," some of them migrants from neighboring villages, the urban poor, and a number of them foreigners from Cameroon, Chad, and Niger (Falola, 2002, p. 168). Marwa denounced materialism and proffered a compelling substitute to the secular government's modernizing scheme, with his notion of a leader being spiritual, unmaterialistic, and anti-West (Falola, 2002). This December 1980 violence in Kano involved the loss of 4,177 lives, and stands out as the first religious upheaval with a huge death toll and property damage (Akaeze, 2009).

Charging foreign scheming to have allegedly aimed to derail its programs by instigating the riots, the federal government's own investigation tribunal on the violence, however, found "no credible evidence to support the accusation of foreign instigation. . . . Rather, religious violence was a response to internal economic and political decay" (Falola, 2002, p. 168). Marwa was observed to have constantly confronted the police from 1972 until 1982 when he died, as a result of his followers' activities-incited preaching. The sect envisioned their riots to be a jihad and their struggle's end-product, and they were trained and prepared psychologically for war, and had also acquired varied weaponry. The Maitatsine riots targeted security agents and the wider populace, and aiming to checkmate the insurgencies, the government started encroaching on religious matters which involved issuing regulations to control preachers. The government's antagonism only further emboldened and strengthened their resolve to violence. Hostile to nonmembers, they targeted both mainstream Muslims and non-Muslims alike; they were known to harass, kidnap, rape, and kill innocent people (Falola, 1998). Thus, as Marwa, however, also espoused Islamic beliefs that were deviant from traditional Islam (Jaynes, 1981), the Maitatsine movement triggered violent conflicts with Islamic undertones, as his versions of religious dogmas were viewed heretically by mainstream Muslims. Hence, the period witnessed interreligious clashes with other Muslim groups amid the people's steeping in Islam's splintered brand in the country, with adherents of the sect claiming about forty million (Cowell, 1982).

Additionally, others replicated Marwa's example, though with different orientations and motivations, as the worsening economic conditions drove more people into fundamentalist Islamic organizations (Falola, 2002).

Sequel to the heightened religious fervency among other Muslim groups, triggered by the Maitatsine uprisings, young fundamentalists in the Kano metropolis attacked churches and alcohol-serving hotels, sacking or closing them down with a death toll (presumably, of Christians) also recorded (Cowell, 1982). Hence, other than the Maitatsine uprisings which movement was basically intrareligious with its lethal uprisings in the region's Muslim cities against security agents and the populace at large, there were also significant inter-group and intragroup tensions between the Tijanniyya and Quadriyya, who were the major brotherhoods, as well as tensions between them, and within the Muslim Brothers (Shiites) and the Izala who were the more radical or puritanical movements (Osaghae, Suberu, and University of Oxford, 2005, p. 20).

In addition to intrareligious tensions dotting the period, interreligiously, relationships involving Muslim and Christian organizations moved into an era of pronounced tension. In October 1982, eight prominent churches were set on fire by Muslim rioters in Kano, which marked, as Falola (2002) observes, "the beginning of what would become a complicated national problem" (p. 169). The investigating tribunal ordered by the government, as further observed attributed the causation to Christians' growing influence in an Islamic city, in addition to the influence of Iran-originated radical literature with recommendation made, thus, "that caution must be exercised in locating churches among the Muslims" (Falola, 2002, p. 169). This development gave Christians the opportunity to bring to the fore, a multiplicity of "complaints of discrimination in jobs, land allocation, and access to radio broadcasting, and the takeover of their schools" (Falola, 2002, p. 169). Thus commenced the ongoing bitter and drawn out confrontation between Muslims and Christians which has precipitated a fear of the country being engulfed in religious wars (Falola, 2002).

Then, also exacerbating religious tension in the period was the issue of the Babangida administration's registering of Nigeria in 1985 into membership of the Organization of Islamic Conference (OIC), a body which unites Islamic nations on economic and political concerns with funding committal from each member and member borrowing privileges from the organization. Babangida is observed to have pushed the country clandestinely into the OIC, where "previous Nigerian leaders had rejected such a move" (Falola, 1999, pp. 187–188). A prolonged period of tension ensued as a result, as the move was construed by Christians as a move toward turning the country to become an Islamic state. The period, therefore, also witnessed major clashes between Muslims and Christians which occurred primarily in the northern cities of Kano, Bauchi, Zango-Kataf, and

Kaduna, all of which recorded extensive damages of worship centers and a high death toll (Brooke, 1987b; Falola, 1999, p. 188).

Additionally, there have also been fights in the country's Constituent Assembly by Northern delegates over Sharia's inclusion in the judicial system. The National Party of Nigeria (NPN) is observed to have manipulated religion as a strategy in its electioneering campaigns, vigorously seeking the support of emirs and religious leaders, while also using political songs and religious verses (Falola, 2002). Further evidencing the nation's religious divide, as well as this politicization of religion, Osaghae observes:

> Although religious conflicts have roots going back to the foundation of the Nigerian state under colonial rule, and the pragmatic involvement of the state in religious activities, religion became an explosive political issue from the time the Sharia issue divided the Constituent Assembly in 1977/8. The Maitatsine riots and other Muslim uprisings of the 1980s, and allegations of Muslim fundamentalist uprisings of the 1980s, and allegations of Muslim dominance in the Buhari regime were evidence of growing religious tension and politicization. (1998b, p. 249)

Furthermore, in March 1986 Muslims and Christians are recognized to have engaged in a superiority contest that was sparked off in Ilorin by an Easter procession. This was followed in March 1987 by confrontation between the two groups in Kafanchan, a town in Southern Kaduna in which native Kajes and Christians were accused of having destroyed some mosques, and that led to lives being lost and properties destroyed. In a supposed reprisal attack on the same day, Muslims chanted war songs as they marched the streets in Kaduna, Gusau, Katsina, Zaria, and Funtua razing churches and Christian properties, once again recording an extensive death toll in the disturbance (Akaeze, 2009). On the magnitude of this crisis that engulfed parts of the north, Falola observes:

> Very rapidly, the violence spread to other places, where it acquired all the characteristics of the Kafanchan outbreak. But whereas Christians had been strong in Kafanchan, they were to be bested in other places. Many Muslims, mostly youth, organized in small groups to attack Christians in Kaduna, Zaria, Samaru, Wusasa, Kankia, Malumfashi, Katsina, and Funtua, all in Kaduna state. Their targets included churches and residential houses, Christian-owned business and property, and people. By the time the violence abated, 113 churches had been burned to the ground....
>
> The crisis ended in heavy losses to the Christians. Across the region, 152 churches (as compared to five mosques) were burned, most notably in Kafanchan, Zaria, Kaduna, Wusasa, Funtua, and Kaduna. Christians suffered the most damage in Zaria, where the Muslims overpowered and devastated them. (1998, pp. 183, 185)

APPLYING THE GENOCIDE PROCLIVITY MODEL: PHASE II—1976 TO 1987

The application of the themes from study Phase II data to the Genocidal Proclivity Model in figure 4.1 follows.

1. 1. Causal Conditions of Phenomena Relating to Genocidal Proclivity: Phase II—1976 to 1987

This second phase of the study shows causal conditions which led ultimately to genocidal proclivity under the four causation factors outlined above as: immediate or trigger factors; underlying or root causes; perceived threat of the "otherness," and exclusive ideological framing.

The study data for this phase reveal immediate or trigger factors including arrests or persecution of sect members, religious extremism and violence or other fundamentalists' activities. For instance, the data reveal subsequent Maitatsine conflicts as trailing from the sect's 1980 clash in Kano with the military in which Mohammad Marwa (the sect's leader) and 400 died (Cowell, 1982). Other trigger factors include insurgency, uprising, or anti-Government riots, as in the Maitatsine riots or insurgencies, cases of Islam degraded, desecration or misinterpretation of Koran such as the March 1987, Muslim mob attacks of Christians in Kafanchan, in which eleven people were killed and fourteen churches burned as a result of uncomplimentary remarks made by a Christian preacher on the Koran (Brooke, 1987a). Also under trigger factors for this phase was reprisal mission or revenge as in the March 1987 attack on Christians in Zaria which was in retaliation to the Kafanchan clash between the two groups, in the aftermath of which eight Koran teachers were killed by Christian mobs (Brooke, 1987b). Additionally, earlier confrontations of the Maitatsine cult with security agents leading to Marwa's son had triggered retaliatory clashes in which about fifty policemen were killed by the sect in December 1980. Also triggering the clashes was a deadline given by the authorities for the group to leave Kano (Jaynes, 1981). The group targeted the local authorities, and government forces deployed to quell the uprising, ended with the annihilation of the sect, with Marwa and most of his followers killed in December 1980 ("Body of a Nigerian Rebel," 1981; Jaynes, 1981).

Additionally in this study phase are underlying or root causes which include historical factors; culture of bad governance and corruption or oppressive military rule; and Al Qaeda, Afghanistan's Taliban, Libyan, and Iranian links including illegal aliens, as in the December 1980 Maitatsine riots in Kano, which were Libyan backed (Jaynes, 1981). Further underlying causation in this phase are themes for political underpinnings or power struggle, including factors of political elites or Kaduna mafia, a politics larding which is not to be ignored, with allegations of fanning the flames of violence being made by rival political parties (Cowell, 1982).

This phase also includes socio-economic factors involving poverty, unemployment, lack of education, and discontent. The study data reveal, for instance, that the condition of receptivity of the listless hordes of youths, to calls to violence was as a result of the country's general state of economic depression and severe unemployment (Kotch, 1987). Marwa established in 1980 a following of about 3,000 to 5,000 group members in Kano (Jaynes, 1981) which were drawn mainly from unemployed youths (Cowell, 1982).

Furthermore, the Maitatsine exclusive ideological framing had his followers holding him as the true prophet and not Muhammad, while orthodox Muslims view the sect's interpretation of the Koran as heretical (Cowell, 1982). Such perception of differences in, for instance, the Maitatsine sect's exclusive ideological framing vis-à-vis those of the orthodox Muslim groups creates divisions which fan and ignite the embers of intrareligious conflict among the groups involved. The study data further observe that, in northern Nigeria, Islam's strands are diffuse and splintered among social groups and contentious sects, which neither have the prerevolutionary Iran Shiites' cohesion, nor a recognizable leader with an Ayatollah Khomeini authoritativeness. The ferment is there, however, with three foremost sects, within each of which are divisions between the older traditionalists, and the younger fundamentalists with an assertion of their forefathers' corruption of faith and dilution of values (Cowell, 1982). More so, as the study data also reveal, Marwa, whose ideology denounced materialism, also espoused Islamic beliefs which were deviant from traditional Islam (Jaynes, 1981).

Additionally this phase shows perceived threat of the "otherness" as a third set of causal conditions, and these include ethnic-religious hatreds, rivalries, divisions, and animosities. The study data point to rivalries among the country, multiethnic groups as often paralleling religious rivalries, with the conflict in the north in March 1987 involving, primarily, northern Hausa/Fulani Muslims, who basically attacked southern Igbo and Yoruba Christians (Brooke, 1987b). Also under the perceived threat of the "otherness," the data further reveal the theme of annihilation attempts by targeting or forceful conversion of Christians to Islam. For instance, following a March 1987 Muslim and Christian clash in Kafanchan, Muslim mobs went to town in Zaria with chants of "Islam Only," as well as "Allah is Great," and, dousing the city's entire seventy-five churches or more with gasoline and burning them down, including St. Bartholomew Church which is northern Nigeria's oldest church. The mobs also threatened to burn down a Christian community, Wusasa, if it will not accept Islam, and razed the family stead of Yakubu Gowon (Brooke, 1987b).

Also in this phase is the fourth set of causal conditions of exclusive ideological framing including religious dimensions, anti-Western or ideological differences. On the Maitatsine riots, for instance, the study data reveal that the cult, enthused by their ideology of infallibility to guns, staked out against the police for four days until their resistance was broken with a barrage of mortar by security agents. The cult slaughtered and mutilated several ordinary people it regarded as infidels and heretics amid the police moving in to track them down. More so, witnesses from the Bulumkutu suburb where the killings occurred observed that the cult members drank their victims' blood to boost their strength, even as they also covered themselves with charms for the deflection of police bullets (Cowell, 1982).

Other exclusive ideological framing in this study phase include fundamentalism and religious fervency (Cowell, 1982; Dash, 1984; Jaynes, 1981; Kotch, 1987), and Sharia or Islamic law institution in northern Nigeria, involving the theme of imposing Sharia across Nigeria or establishing of an Islamic state (Brooke, 1987b). In the 1987 Kaduna State crisis, a gruesome pogrom was meted on Christians in several cities, with about seventy-five churches in Zaria burned down, even as Christian homes, Christian-owned businesses, and beer-serving hotels were burned by mobs, based on Muslims' intent to have the Islamic Sharia law extended from the Northern region to the whole nation. More so, Christians were outraged when Nigeria was drafted into joining the Organization of Islamic Conference (Brooke, 1987b). As already noted, ideological framing underlie much of the excessive bloodletting which continues to occur in northern Nigeria, especially with the introduction of Sharia in some northern states.

2. Phenomena Resulting from Trigger Factors, Underlying Causation, Perceived Threat of the "Otherness," and Exclusive Ideological Framing: Phase II—1976 to 1987

This study phase also shows that the causal conditions—the trigger factor, underlying causation, perceived threat of "otherness," and exclusive ideological framing in the different conflict situations and contextual settings, resulted in differing degrees and forms of exterminations and killings among different Muslim groups, among Muslims and Christians, and among different ethnic groups with conflict drawn interrelatively along ethnic as well as religious lines. Phenomenal themes as identified in the study data reveal core categories of attacks and violence which are unleashed to target victims, including assault, shoot-out, killings, arson and looting ("300 Believed Killed," 1982; Jaynes, 1981); bloodbath, carnage, pogrom, mayhem, massacres, or barbarism (Brooke, 1987b); religious and ethnic violence ("1,000 Are Reported Dead," 1984; "300 Believed Killed," 1982; Brooke, 1987b; Jaynes, 1981); sectarian violence; and spiral or escalation of violence ("100 Nigeria Policemen," 1982; Brooke, 1987b; Cowell, 1982).

The phenomenal themes for this phase also include targeted, premeditated, or orchestrated killings and assaults (Brooke, 1987b; Kotch, 1987). For instance, in the March 1987 crisis in which Muslim mobs burned the Ahmadu Bello University 2,000-seat, Christian ecumenical chapel in Zaria, the faculty association chairman expressed his association's disgust and horror at the obvious premeditated and organized arson and assaults (Brooke, 1987b). Other phenomenal themes are tit-for-tat killings in northern states; uprising, antigovernment rioting, protests, or demonstrations (Brooke, 1987b; "Hundreds Die in Religious Riots," 1984; Kotch, 1987); and violent or deadly clashes, rioting, or gun battles ("1,000 Are Reported Dead," 1984; "718 Deaths," 1984; Brooke, 1987b; Cowell, 1982; Dash, 1984; Jaynes, 1981). By comparing and contrasting such phenomenal themes and categories, the two major categories of targeted, premeditated or orchestrated killings and assaults, and bloodbath, carnage, pogrom, mayhem, massacres, or barbarism are recognized to be closely associated with the proclivity to genocide.

3. Context in Which Ethno-Religious Conflict and Genocidal Proclivity Developed: Phase II—1976 to 1987

This study phase also shows contextual themes involving the social space or lebensraum, the framework on which genocide or its proclivity can develop (Wood, 2001). The contextual settings identified in the northern Nigeria ethno-religious conflict in the study data in this second phase of the research include the Northern region or states, Adamawa State, in Yola, and Jimeta; Borno State, in Maiduguri; Gombe State; Kaduna State, in Kaduna, Kafanchan, and Zaria; and Kano State, in Kano (see tables 4.1 and 4.2 for the various contexts, respectively for the northern Nigeria ethno-religious conflict, and for the reprisal attacks in the south).

Also providing the contextual framework are the different conflict parties in varying phenomenal settings in this study phase including Muslim mobs or sect and security forces ("100 Nigeria Policemen," 1982; Cowell, 1982; Dash, 1984; Jaynes, 1981); Muslim mobs, sect or groups and Christians ("1,000 Are Reported Dead," 1984; "300 Believed Killed," 1982; Brooke, 1987a; 1987b; Dash, 1984; "Hundreds Die in Religious Riots," 1984; "Nigerian Toll," 1982); Muslim sect and other Muslims or sect ("718 Deaths," 1984; Dash, 1984; "Hundreds Die in Religious Riots," 1984); Muslim sects or civilian mobs or gangs and Igbos; or conflict involving different ethnic groups, for instance, in the March 1987 attack in which Muslim mobs mainly Hausa and Fulani were attacking southerners involving Yoruba and Igbo Christians (Brooke, 1987b). The conflict parties' themes were analyzed by comparison and contrast with the phenomenal conflict themes and categories, and their causal conditions to identify conflicts with the plausibility of a conceptualized annihilating difference (Hinton, 2002) which gave rise to exterminations involving perpetrator and victim situations. Other conflicts devoid of such annihilating difference are considered as clashes or fighting between parties without an overt inclination to genocide.

Additionally, varying perpetrator groups identified in this study phase using the annihilating difference analysis of the conflict parties described above include the Maitatsine fundamentalist group. For instance, battles that erupted in February/March 1984 between the police, soldiers, civilian vigilantes, and the Maitatsine sect in Yola, state capital of then Gongola state, recorded over 1,000 death toll, which had vast swaths of the city laid waste, with more than 500 bodies removed by the authorities off the streets of Yola. This carnage was an aftermath of shoot-outs between sect members and opposing vigilantes, with these religious zealots reported to have overwhelmed the local police as a result of which, troops were deployed to Yola to restore order. As an offshoot of Islam, members of the Maitatsine sect in the riots physically attacked other Muslims, who to them were infidels (Dash, 1984).

Perpetrators in this phase of the study also include Muslim mobs, rioters or rampaging Muslim youths as revealed in the study data. For instance, a March 1987 clash between Muslims and Christians in Kafanchan which ensued from an allegation of misinterpretation of the Koran by a Christian pastor in an evangelist revival meeting, as the conflict escalated and spread to Kaduna, Zaria and some other northern cities, Muslim mobs were noted by the Archbishop of the Roman Catholic church in Kaduna, P. Y. Jatau, to have wreaked an atrocious pogrom in such cities against Christians (Brooke, 1987b). Further remarking on the extent of carnage perpetrated in this episode, Kotch (1987) observes that twenty years following Nigeria's fighting of a bloody civil war to preserve its unity, dozens to hundreds of churches were notably destroyed in attacks on the Christian Minority, which the government said were orchestrated by Muslim mobs.

However, this study phase also identifies perpetrator themes for Christian militia or youths, also involving the March 1987 Muslim/Christian clash, on which the conflict escalated within hours from slaps to beatings, stone-throwing, and three mosques destroyed. This was followed after two days by a Christian mob's laying siege to a Koran itinerant teachers' hostel in Kaduna, with eight teachers dead at the end, seven with slit throats, and one shot by arrow (Brooke, 1987b).

Details of the involvement of the perpetrator groups in the different conflict settings of this study phase are analyzed and discussed in Phase II synopsis above.

This phase also reveals target victims which enable the development of annihilating difference amid a perpetrator group and social space environment to produce a complete and well-rounded contextual setting for proclivity to genocide. Identified target or victim groups for this phase of the study include Christians and churches, also involving Christian neighborhoods or mostly Christian villages; civilian targets; Southerners who are predominantly Christians, and especially Igbos as targets; security agents—police officers, military and government officials; symbols of government authority; media offices and journalists; beer parlors, hotels, banks, and other facilities which represent structures or institutions with Western connotations; Muslim clerics or mainstream/orthodox Muslims; and Muslims, Hausa-Fulani herders, Muslim sect, Northerners, or mosques. Details of the victimhood of the targets in the different conflict settings of this study phase are also analyzed and discussed in Phase II synopsis above.

4. Intervening Conditions Influencing Proclivity to Genocide: Phase II—1976 to 1987

This study phase further identified intervening conditions in the differing contextual settings of the conflict, in addition to the context node involving such general or broad conditions which influence by increasing or diminishing the tendency or proclivity to genocide. Intervening conditions in this study phase include press censorship and manipulation or deflation and inflation of casualty figures—this casualty information manipulation factor was used by government parties on occasions to minimize but also sometimes scaleup reprisals or tit-for-tat violence, as in the October 1982 Maitatsine riots in Maiduguri in which the unofficial estimate of toll is 450, with local estimate put at over 1,000, while the government official figures, however, put the toll of civilians and sect members that died at 133 with 16 police officers, while local estimates indicate that 100 officers were killed (Cowell, 1982). Other intervening conditions include extrajudicial killings and army involvement in policing.

The study data reveal, for instance, that in the December 1980 Maitatsine disturbances, following the sect's attack on the governor's residence, the army deployed to contain the group shelled their base, resulting in a massive slaughter. According to the study data, people were being killed like goats and even as donkeys, which was rather unfortunate, even as they were warned. Thus, the death toll officially put at 1,000, was acknowledged to be at least 10,000, with some witnesses giving a figure of about 7,000 bodies piled up in garbage trucks and buried off in mass graves. In the days following, prisoners were executed summarily, with civilians totaling about 80 (including children) gunned down (Jaynes, 1981).

Additional intervening conditions in this phase include government ineptitude, lethargy, or weak central government, regarding which the study data observed on the Maitatsine killings, for instance, that the army could have more rapidly contained the disturbances before the cultists started their massacring of civilians. Calling for intervention of the army would have connoted, however, a tacit admission of civilian inability at keeping order in Nigeria's House (Cowell, 1982). Intervening conditions in this study phase also include the presence of collaborators or bystanders involving local collaborators, as in the study data on the Maitatsine riots which reveal General Ibrahim Babangida, military president at the time, talking of his government as not going to stand by, to allow an ambitious, power-seeking, mindless group to push the country into another civil war, while also promising summary justice to the instigators of the riots. While not identifying the fomenters of the riots, General Babangida spoke against powerful subversives and "group interest," which was noted in the data as "Kaduna Mafia," or northern political elites, their influence of which had waned since Babangida's seizure of power in 1985 (Kotch, 1987). There is also an indication of foreign collaborators leading to the internationalization of the conflict, and local collaborators or bystanders. For instance, in Lagos, Western diplomats believe that Libya was associated with the crisis problems in the region, if only by financially supporting the cult (Jaynes, 1981).

This study phase also reveals that further influencing the tendency to increase or deflate genocidal proclivity are the various intervention measures to control the violence through their implementation. Intervention efforts in this phase include attempts at dialogue, appeals for intervention or mediation; control measures taken such as curfews and road checks by security agents ("Nigeria Imposes," 1985); investigations and commissions of inquiries set up; and mopping up of rioters or arrests made ("Nigeria City," 1984).

5. Strategies Foreshadowing Proclivity to Genocide: Phase II—1976 to 1987

This study phase further reveals different strategies foreshadowing genocidal tendencies within the contextual settings and intervening conditions which generated the above described resultant phenomena. Such strategies include organization, planning, and weaponry, as in the March 1984 Maitatsine crisis, in which the sect used sophisticated weapons ("Nigeria City," 1984); extermination plots involving mass murders or ideological and ethnic cleansing, such as burning of churches, or the forceful conversion of Christians to Islam. For instance, in the aftermath of the Kafanchan Muslims and Christians clashed in March 1987, which was sparked off by a lady's public slapping of a Christian pastor for allegedly misinterpreting the Koran during a crusade. Muslim mobs invaded all the seventy-five churches or thereabout in Zaria, doused them with gasoline, and burned them, reciting, "Islam Only," as well as, "Allah is Great," while also, threatening to burn down a Christian community, Wusasa, if it did not accept Islam (Brooke, 1987b). Furthermore, the strategies in this phase include indoctrination and manipulation or instigation, as in General Babangida's alluding to "powerful subversives" that were recognized as sinister, instigators of the Kaduna riots in March

1987, by sponsoring a rabble of uneducated young Muslims that attacked Christians along with their property (Kotch, 1987).

6. Consequences or Effects of Proclivity to Genocide: Phase II—1976 to 1987

The strategies adopted by perpetrators in this study phase have various effects or consequences in the different conflict settings examined. Consequences identified in this phase include death toll and casualties, mutilated bodies or burned corpses, for instance, the study data reveal that the Kano Maitatsine riots of 1980 had a death toll of over 1,000 people (Jaynes, 1981), and 452 toll in the Maitatsine October 1982 riots in Maiduguri, with another eighteen toll in Kaduna where the sect moved to as security agents attempted to arrest the sect members ("Nigerian Toll," 1982). Additionally, this Maiduguri uprising had about 100 police officers killed in four days' fighting with the sect ("100 Nigerian Policemen," 1982), with another 1,000 toll reported in Yola in March 1984 also involving the Maitatsine riots ("1,000 Are Reported Dead," 1984). Other consequences include refugees and displaced persons, and/or persons fleeing homes or taking refuge or shelter for safety (Brooke, 1987b); mass graves or mass burials ("1,000 Are Reported Dead," 1984; Jaynes, 1981); churches burned, bombed, or destroyed (Brooke, 1987a, 1987b; Cowell, 1982; Kotch, 1987); mosques burned or destroyed in retaliation by Christians (Brooke, 1987b); police stations and barracks, government buildings bombed or burned (Brooke, 1987a); Christian businesses, homes, hotels and properties destroyed (Brooke, 1987a, 1987b; Cowell, 1982; Kotch, 1987); and destroying, looting, and razing of properties (Brooke, 1987b; "Death Toll Put at 300," 1984; "Hundreds Die in Religious Riots," 1984).

Consequences also include denial of freedom of worship and desecration of Christian religion as in the threat by Muslim mobs to the Wusasa Christians to accept Islam or have their community burned down (Brooke 1987b). Further consequences are security threat, apprehension, anxiety, or political and social chaos (Brooke, 1987b; Dash, 1984; Jaynes, 1981; Kotch, 1987); and the consequences category also reveals normalcy or calm returning after episodes of gruesome killings, evidencing the intermittency of the killing episodes as in the March 1984 Maitatsine riots in which normalcy was reported to have returned in the city of Yola following a week's fighting between the sect and security agents, which left about 1,000 dead, and hundreds fleeing their homes, with most burning, even as bodies littered the streets in Yola ("Hundreds Die in Religious Riots," 1984).

SEVEN

Proclivity to Genocide in Northern Nigeria Phase III

1987 to 1996

SYNOPSIS

The third study phase spans from 1987 to 1996 and is inclusive of the years 1987 up to 1991, when nine additional states and the Federal Capital Territory (now Abuja) were created bringing the states of Nigeria to thirty in total (see map 5 in appendix A). This phase also includes the years 1991 up to 1996 when additional states were created, bringing the total to the present thirty-six states of Nigeria (see map 1 in appendix A). The phase witnessed various regime changes in the political sphere; as with the fall of the second republic in 1983, the country once again entered another prolonged era of military rule. During the Babangida regime, which spanned from 1985 to 1992, there was an unsuccessful coup in April 1990 involving some Middle Belt Christian officers led by Major Gideon Orkar to overthrow Babangida. In 1992 in an attempt to return to civilian rule, Babangida established two political parties, the Social Democratic Party (SDP) and the National Republican Convention (NRC). Thus, Nigeria's third Republic marks the country's unsuccessful attempt at restoring democracy as initiated by the Babangida government during which civilian state governors took office in January 1992 following their elections, but a presidential election won by Moshood K. O. Abiola on June 12, 1993, was, however, annulled by Babangida. In August 1993 amid pressure from the AFRC (Armed Forces Ruling Council), Babangida was forced to step down from office, handing over to Ernest A. O. Shonekan, who assumed power as interim head of state. Shonekan was ousted in a palace coup which brought Defense Minister Sani Abacha into power as head of state, and he established the Provisional Ruling Council of Nigeria in November 1993. In March 1995 the Abacha administration arrested Obasanjo for allegedly supporting a secret coup plot (Falola and Heaton, 2008; Osaghae, 1998b).

This study phase witnessed a period of prolonged tension marked with religious riots and unrest in which thousands of lives were lost with properties and buildings destroyed, and Nigeria was on the verge of a religious war between Christians and Muslims as political leaders opportunely manipulated the nation's diversity problem. More so, economic problems caused by the failure of Babangida's Structural Adjustment Program (SAP), a policy aimed at revamping the down-sliding economy, intensified a general feeling of discontent and the quest for alternative sociopolitical means of survival. Recourse to religion provided the way out for the teeming masses. Accordingly, "[m]illions of people were driven to religion, as both Islam and Christianity accelerated their conversion process, drawing from angry, poor frustrated people" (Falola, 1999, p. 187). The increased religiosity brought about a new wave of fundamentalism in its wake, with radical organizations preaching against secularism and military rule. Recognized to have manifested differently in both religions, Falola (1999) observes that "[a]mong Christians, fundamentalism took the form of evangelism that could be reactionary and conservative in form, among Muslims, the influence of the West, materialism, and secular governments was severely attacked" (p. 187).

Also deriving from the people's discontent with military rule was resurgence among the Muslims of the Mahdi or coming Messiah ideal which would save the nation, as well as reform Islam. Furthermore, Sheikh Ibrahim el-Zakzaky, a preacher who led the Shi'ites (a Muslim group who were also increasing in number), began to demand for the creation of Nigeria's Islamic republic. The Shi'ites engaged in, and clashed severally with the government in different northern cities including Kaduna, Zaria, Kano, Maiduguri, Bauchi, and Katsina, and made demands for a theocratic, God-fearing-led state government (Falola, 1999).

Additionally contributing to the riotous period were mainstream religious groups with media and government access to their leaders. For the Muslims were the Supreme Council for Islamic Affairs (SCIA) and the Jama'tu Nasril Islam (JNI), both of which defended Islamic interests and made politically charged demands, for instance, "replacing Sunday with Friday as a holiday and removing the symbols of the Judeo-Christian tradition in schools and courts" (Falola, 1999, p. 187). For the Christians, there was the Christian Association of Nigeria (CAN) which was their most prominent defender, and it called for a distancing of the government from Islam. These religious organizations began to take on the semblance of political parties, such that in addition to making important demands, their members were on occasions also being mobilized for protest. This inherent politicization of religion derives from the country's drawn-out military rule. Falola (1999) observes that "[m]ilitary rule succeeded in turning religion into a platform from which to organize politics," and argues that "[w]hile the politicians were afraid of being excluded from power or being put in detention, religious leaders were relatively free of harassment" (p. 187).

In April 1991, in the semblance of the Maitatsine sect of the 1980s and the havoc unleashed on the society was the Katsina Shi'ite sect led by one Yahaya Yakubu who staged a bloody protest with his members in the town. Following this was the Bauchi eruption in April 1991 that was noted as the worst religious crisis witnessed in the country since the 1984 Maitatsine episode in which religious fanatics struck, killing about 764 people in Jimeta, Gongola State. Bauchi State was engulfed for four days by religious violence fire, even as thousands of mostly teenage hoodlums went on rampage in a number of cities including Bauchi, the state capital. The terror tale was beyond comprehension with mounting casualty figures even as scores of churches, homes, hotels, and a number of public properties were razed (*Newswatch* report as cited in Akaeze, 2009).

The Bauchi riots, while "not instigated by any particular sect" and "had no leader," were triggered by an incident involving a Muslim and a Christian butcher in the Tafawa Balewa town abattoir which engulfed different parts of Bauchi (Falola, 1998, p. 204). The crisis had about five hundred houses razed down within twenty-four hours, with fifteen hotels burned in the Bayangeri quarter in which most of the city's hotels situate, as well as cars, houses, and a neighborhood Deeper Bible Church that were also burned down (Falola, 1998, p. 207). At the Hospital Road, a Christian-designated zone in which most of the city's churches were situated, the rioters burned all of the twenty churches in the area including "St. John's Catholic Church, the Basara Baptist Church, COCIN Church, Christ Apostolic Church, and St. Paul's Anglican Church" (Falola, 1998, p. 207). Only the ECWA church close to the army barracks escaped the ravaging Muslims, even as they "descended on all the mission houses and destroyed their property, cars, and buses, burning it all," with the Christian Pilgrims Board property, offices, and cars equally destroyed (Falola, 1998, p. 207). Proceeding next to Tudun Wada Street, an area occupied by non-natives, the rioters chanting anti-ethnic and anti-Christian slogans and carrying gasoline and weapons moved against their targets, with the Seyawa, a Christian minority group "selected for destruction" along with other non-native Christians in the area (Falola, 1998, p. 207). On the enormity of venom meted on the victims, most of which were brutally killed, many burned, stoned, or macheted to death, with others decapitated (The Bauchi Massacre as cited in Falola, 1998), and on the magnitude of this killing episode, therefore:

> Casualties were high. Hundreds of homes, churches, and public buildings were burned or destroyed. While official sources initially put the death toll at eighty, mortuary figures had it at five hundred. Thousands more were injured and hundreds hospitalized. Corpses littered the streets of Bauchi City, and the threat of disease from the decomposing bodies forced health authorities to collect these corpses and bury them in mass graves outside the city. People now callous to death stood by as the corpses were piled into trucks. (Death and Destruction as cited in Falola, 1998, p. 208)

Shortly following the Bauchi incident, the religious conflagration train got to Kano, where in October 1991, the Izala sect initially presumed peaceful demonstration to stop an evangelical crusade being organized for Reinhard Bonnke suddenly turned into a violent Muslim-Christian clash, with high death toll and casualty figures, and loss of enormous property (Akaeze, 2009). The sect had earlier been denied the permission of using the venue—the public Race Course for a foreign preacher they had invited—and were enraged by this in addition to CAN's "aggressive publicity" for the crusade (Falola, 1998, p. 211). To avert probable unrest, the state government change of venue which, while not publicized, in addition to CAN's posters already printed, infuriated the Muslims, some militant of whom reckoned they were being challenged by the infidels (Falola, 1998). Even more infuriating was the Christians' use of the public-address system to broadcast Jesus Christ as coming to redeem souls, which to Muslim leaders was a pollution of the city, "raising the name of Jesus over that of Prophet Muhammad" and deemed "that the minority Christian element was acting outside its place" (Falola, 1998, p. 212). The widespread riots claimed lives and had extensive property damage, including forty-two shops, thirty-four houses, hotels, cars, trucks, and many public buildings, even as carnages were wrought in the non-natives' Sabon-Gari neighborhood, and Christians and southerners fled to the police barracks and air force base for safety, abandoning their homes (Falola, 1998). Falola (1998), thus, observes as an unprecedented crisis in the state of Kano where religious violence predominates, "the sole targeting of Christians for destruction on such a massive scale was something new" (p. 212).

Furthermore, in December 1994 Kano once again made headlines when Muslim fundamentalists lynched an Igbo trader, and paraded his head on a spike along Kano streets following his accusation of Koran desecration of inscribing in his Sabon-Gari area shop, words regarded as blasphemous against Muhammad (Akaeze, 2009). A Muslim and Igbo trader fracas escalated the episode into widespread riots in May 1995, and in the ensuing communal violence, churches, shops, and houses were once again razed down with extensive damage and toll before order could be restored (Falola, 1998).

There is thus an increasingly religious tonation to the northern Nigeria ethno-religious conflict. Anthony (2002) observes, for instance, that since the 1980s and 1990s, religion seems to have supplanted ethnicity as the "defining fault line" (p. 234) of the Hausa communities and Kano's Igbo (and by extension Igbos and other Christian ethnic groups in the North). Ethnicity and religion have, thus, long become "intimately entangled" in "the frontier between Hausa Muslims and Igbo Christians" which, with national discourses increasingly turning to issues of religion, have perceptibly shifted intergroup relations in Kano and, by extension in the entire North (Anthony, 2002, pp. 234–235). The relationship between both groups was observed to have remained tense after the 1991 Reinhard Bonnke crusade crisis, as well as the Hausa/Igbo 1995 fracas and ensuing killings, however, with violence occurring in each case "without the explicit manipulation of ethnicity that was present in 1966" on the basis of which each of the disturbances are seen as religious conflict which mostly unfolded between both ethnic groups, as a result of affiliation patterns and circumstances (Anthony, 2002, p. 238). Thus, on the dynamics of this shift from ethno to religious bend in the Igbo-Hausa interactions, Anthony observes:

> The centrality of Islam to Hausa identity and *Kanawa's* often axiomatic association of Christianity with Igbos has meant past grievances, some long dormant, others lingering, were available for both sides to tap into, and almost inevitably surfaced.... While the unresolved baggage was not in and of itself sufficient to lead to open controversy or violence, in moments of anger and tension, it reappeared, and became part of the new moment. Fortunately, unlike the crises of 1966, this happened without the benefit of elite agendas to focus those issues, recruit behind them, or provide rioters with the organizational infrastructure necessary for a massive escalation. (2002, pp. 238–239)

However, the religious crisis was not restricted to Kano as other cities including Jos, Wase, Zangon Kataf, Funtua, Yelwa-Shendam, and Funtua also took their share of the upheavals, sometimes with flimsy quarrels or political differences between the opposing faiths sparking killing sprees which security officials would find challenging to stop. An instance of this was a May 1992 communal feud between Katafs indigenes and Hausas in Kaduna State, which subsequently assumed religious coloration and later spread to other cities in the state, leaving destruction and a huge death toll in its trail (Akaeze, 2009). The Zangon-Kataf crisis, which is "the culmination of an age-old conflict between two groups divided by both ethnicity and religion," broke out on May 14 following altercations of farmlands invasions between the Muslim Hausas and the Christian Katafs (Falola, 1998, p. 213). By May 15, there was a resultant toll of eighty-five to the crisis, and by May 16, the town was destroyed completely with its hundreds of residents killed. Intervention was delayed as the people destroyed themselves while the government and the police did nothing for three days, even as "[o]ver four hundred corpses littered the streets, and most of the houses were burned to the ground ("Massacre in Kaduna" as cited in Falola, 1998, p. 217). Most dead sustained massive machete and dagger wounds, or were shot using poisoned bows and arrows, on occasions shot with guns, or burned in their homes or cars, with all major churches as well as mosques also destroyed (Falola, 1998). The Zangon-Kataf episode is, thus, recognized to have been so destructive and bitter that the Zaria 1987 crisis paled comparatively to it, with every valuable in Zangon-Kataf destroyed completely even as the violence spread to Kaduna. As news of the Zangon-Kataf got to Kaduna and other parts of the north, Hausas in Kaduna launched massive attacks on southern Zarian residents in Kaduna, attacking every neighborhood in which they were concentrated (Falola, 1998, p. 218).

According to Falola (1998), "[a] pogrom similar to the attack on the Igbo in 1966 resulted," and being mostly Christians, the southern Zarians "made an easy target" as they attended church on May 17, oblivious of any plans of ambush (p. 218). Many worshippers and church ministers were gruesomely slaughtered in various churches in Kaduna including the Aminu Road ECWA church where many were killed, the Bardawa Heken church, the Angwar Baptist church, the Rhema church, and the African Baptist church, with these last two also having extensive casualties. Some worshippers fled to the sanctuary of private homes, abandoning their cars, even as roadblocks were mounted by the Hausas to entrap worshippers as they fled, and once again, the police just stood by, observing the rioters (Falola, 1998).

Thus, this study phase also witnessed major clashes between Muslims and Christians which occurred primarily in the northern cities of Kano, Bauchi, Zango-Kataf, and Kaduna, all of which recorded extensive damages of worship centers and high death toll (Falola, 1999, p. 188).

APPLYING THE GENOCIDE PROCLIVITY MODEL: PHASE III—1987 TO 1996

The application of the themes from study Phase III to the Genocidal Proclivity Model in Figure 4.1 follows.

1. Causal Conditions of Phenomena Relating to Genocidal Proclivity: Phase III—1987 to 1996

Phase III of the study also shows the four types of causal conditions of immediate or trigger factors, underlying or root causes, perceived threat of the "otherness," and exclusive ideological framing which led ultimately to genocidal proclivity. In this study phase, the immediate or trigger causes include insurgency, uprising, or antigovernment riots; and arrests or persecution of fundamentalist sect members, religious extremism and violence, or other fundamentalists' activities.

Additionally, this study phase has underlying or root causes as a second set of causal conditions including colonial influences, as in the Zangon-Kataf May 1992 crisis which also engulfed Kaduna, with the violence recognized as having its roots trailed back to the British rule of the country up to 1960, with the conflicts being fueled by religious affiliation and disputes involving land ownership (Noble, 1992c). Other underlying causes in this phase include political underpinnings or power struggles involving political elites or Kaduna mafia, as in the "powerful subversives" that President Babangida alluded to as fomenters of trouble who instigated the May 1987 Kaduna riots in which several churches were destroyed, in attacks orchestrated by Muslim mobs against the Christian Minority (Kotch, 1987). Further underlying causes in this phase are socioeconomic factors including ethnic groups vying for control of fertile lands, and political and economic power, as in the August 1992 ethnic crisis between the Tivs and the Jukuns in Akwana, in which about thirty people were killed in the episode; the crisis ended with the certainty of additional battles in this continuing land dispute between the two ethnic groups. The violence in Akwana as well as in a nearby Jukun village, Kente, typifies scores of such incidences that have persisted in the ruggedly beautiful, thinly populated eastern Nigeria region, since October 1991. While there have been no definitive casualties figures available, Nigerian journalists, Western diplomats, as well as travelers through the key fighting zone, Wukari, in addition to relatives and friends in the area, point to a conservative estimate of 1,000, and plausibly up to a high of 5,000 people who have been killed in the area (Noble, 1992a).

Underlying causes in this phase also include poverty, unemployment, lack of education, and discontent. In the May 1992 Zangon-Kataf crisis that spread to Kaduna, for instance, an intense economic slump triggered the riots, which were antigovernment. Being a leading African oil exporter, the low oil prices have devastated Nigeria, with oil accounting for over 95 percent of its foreign exchange earnings. Hence, a state of exploding discontent has been identified by African as well as Western analysts, as constituting the most threat to General Ibrahim Babangida's military regime's plans for the transition of power to civilian government (Noble, 1992c).

Also included in this phase are the third set of causal factors of the perceived threat of the "otherness," involving ethnic-religious hatreds, rivalries, divisions, and animosities, as in the Taraba State, Tiv-Jukun conflict that emanates from historical animosity between the two ethnic groups, whose intermittent but protracted clashes have left most of the region as a charred-hut war zone (Noble, 1992a). Further causal factor categories of the perceived threat of the "otherness" are themes for

North-South split or largely Muslim north and mainly Christian south; and annihilation attempts by targeting as in the October 1991 Kano crisis, for instance, in which a Christian community was targeted and attacked by Muslim Hausa mobs who set on fire a church, markets, cars, and houses, with over 200 people killed and many more injured (Noble, 1992a).

Lastly in this study phase is the fourth set of causal conditions of exclusive ideological framing which underlie much of the excessive bloodletting that continues to occur in the northern Nigeria ethno-religious conflict. Ideological framing factors in this phase of the study include fundamentalism and religious fervency as in the May 1992 Zangon-Kataf crisis, in respect of which, deadly clashes often erupted between Muslim and Christian activists in the Northern region, with tensions intensified as youths flock to Islamic fundamentalist sect, as well as more people move from the predominant Christian south to the more Muslim north ("100 Feared Dead," 1992). Other ideologically framed causations in this phase involve the institution of Sharia or Islamic law in northern Nigeria as in the 1992 Muslim militants' demonstrations calling for the establishment of Sharia law in Katsina State, in which some people were killed and several others injured ("2 Killed," 1992).

2. Phenomena Resulting from Trigger Factors, Underlying Causation, Perceived Threat of the "Otherness," and Exclusive Ideological Framing: Phase III—1987 to 1996

This study phase also shows that the causal conditions—the trigger factor, underlying causation, perceived threat of "otherness," and exclusive ideological framing in different situations and contextual settings—resulted in varying degrees and forms of exterminations and killings primarily between extremist Muslims and Christians, as well as between other conflict parties which are mostly divided along ethnic and religious lines. Such phenomena as identified in this study phase reveal violence and attacks which are unleashed to different target victims, including assault, shoot-out, killings, arson and looting; and bloodbath, carnage, pogrom, mayhem, massacres, or barbarism. For instance, in the Zangon-Kataf crisis which engulfed other cities in Kaduna State, mutilated corpses overflowed the mortuaries in Kaduna, with people being slaughtered as dogs ("Nigeria Quells," 1992). Further phenomenal themes in this phase include religious and ethnic violence; sectarian violence; spiral or escalation of violence; and targeted, premeditated, or orchestrated killings and assaults. In the May 1991 Kano crisis, for instance, in which "[t]housands of lives were lost and properties valued in millions of Naira were destroyed" in religious rioting (*Newswatch* as cited in Ezeibe, 2009, para. 30), Muslims pursued Christians in their hunt, with most of the violence noted to have been centered in the city's Sabongari neighborhood that has a vast Christian population ("At Least 8 Dead," 1991). Other phenomenal themes in this phase include uprising, antigovernment rioting, protests, or demonstrations; and violent or deadly clashes, rioting, or gun battles. By comparing and contrasting such phenomenal themes, this study phase also shows the two major categories involving targeted, premeditated or orchestrated killings and assaults; and bloodbath, carnage, pogrom, mayhem, massacres, or barbarism, which are identified as being closely associated with the proclivity to genocide.

3. Context in Which Ethno-Religious Conflict and Genocidal Proclivity Developed: Phase III—1987 to 1996

Additionally in this study phase are contextual themes involving social space or lebensraum, which provides the geographic base (Wood, 2001) that enables the fostering of genocidal inclinations. The contexts are in the Northern region or states including Bauchi State, in Bauchi; Kaduna State, in Kaduna, Zonkwa, and Zangon-Kataf; Kano State, in Kano; Katsina State, in Katsina; Nasarawa State; and Taraba State, in Akwana (see tables 4.1 and 4.2 for the various contexts, respectively, for the northern Nigeria ethno-religious conflict, and for the reprisal attacks in the south).

Also providing the contextual framework are different conflict parties in the various phenomenal settings in this study phase including Muslim mobs or sect and security forces; Muslim mobs, sect or groups and Christians; security agents and unidentified civilians; different ethnic groups; and Fulani herdsmen and/or Hausa-Fulani group and Christian or host communities. Such themes for the conflict parties were again analyzed by comparison and contrasted with the phenomenal conflict themes and categories and their causal conditions to identify conflicts with the plausibility of conceptualized annihilating difference (Hinton, 2002) that give rise to exterminations involving perpetrator and victim situations, with other conflicts which are devoid of such annihilating difference considered as clashes or fighting between parties without an overt inclination to genocide.

Additionally, there are varying perpetrator groups identified in this study phase using the annihilating difference analysis of the conflict parties described above including Muslim mobs, rioters, or rampaging Muslim youths; and security agents, soldiers/army/military, Hausa/Northern troops. Details of the involvement of the perpetrator groups in the different conflict settings of this study phase are analyzed and discussed in Phase III synopsis above.

Also included in the study data in this phase are the victim or target groups, which enable the fostering of annihilating difference amid a perpetrator group and social space environment for a well-rounded and complete contextual setting for genocidal proclivity to flourish. Identified in this phase are target victim groups including Christians and churches involving Christian neighborhoods or mostly Christian villages, as in the May 1992 Kaduna crisis in which churches were observed to have been razed, even as two or three pastors were killed in churches in Kaduna ("100 Feared Dead," 1992). Target victim groups also include civilian targets; security agents—police officers, military and government officials; and media offices and journalists. Details of the victimhood of the targets in the different conflict settings of this study phase are also analyzed and discussed in Phase III synopsis above.

4. Intervening Conditions Influencing Proclivity to Genocide: Phase III — 1987 to 1996

In addition to the context themes, this study phase also identified intervening conditions in the different contextual settings of the conflict, involving such broad conditions which influence by increasing or diminishing the proclivity to genocide. Intervening conditions in this study phase include press censorship and manipulation or deflation and inflation of casualty figures, which can be used by government parties on occasions to minimize but also sometimes scale-up reprisals or tit-for-tat violence. For instance, in the October 1991 Kano crisis, while the government reported the death toll as eight people killed in the rioting, an unconfirmed source put the death toll at 300 killed in the crisis ("At Least 8 Dead," 1991). Other intervening conditions in this study phase include government ineptitude, lethargy, or weak central government, as in the Tiv/Jukun 1992 killings at Akwana in which deep concern has been stirred by the assaults being made on unarmed civilians, while also disquieting has been the observation of the inability of the government to forcefully clamp down on either sides, those deemed to be perpetrating such a terror and killing campaign (Noble, 1992a).

This study phase further reveals that additionally influencing the tendency to increase or deflate genocidal proclivity are the various intervention measures to control the violence with their implementation. Intervention efforts in this study phase include control measures taken such as curfews and road checks by security agents as in the May 1992 crisis in Kaduna State, which started in Zangon-Kataf and was put down by troops in helicopters and armored cars, even as the riot in three days claimed over 200 lives of Christians as well as Muslims ("Nigeria Quells," 1992), the sequel to which was the banning of religious, and ethnic-based associations in the country ("Some Groups Banned," 1992). Other intervention themes in this phase include investigations and commissions of inquiries set up, mopping up of rioters or arrests made, attempts to dialogue, appeals for intervention or mediation, and reconciliation attempts as in the Tiv/Jukun protracted conflict in which the two peoples' spiritual traditional leaders were invited to Abuja by the Augustus Aikhomu, Nigera's vice president, in attempt to negotiate a resolution to the conflict. A diplomatic initiative was also started by a delegation led by the Sultan of Sokoto, who is the Nigerian Muslims' leader, acknowledging the conflict's posing a potential threat to the country's survival as a nation. The surge of killings prompted the federal military government's deployment of soldiers to the area, with edgy soldiers manning roadblocks in all Wukari's major thoroughfares, which were continuously patrolled with armored vehicles (Noble, 1992a).

5. Strategies Foreshadowing Proclivity to Genocide: Phase III — 1987 to 1996

The study data also reveal strategies which foreshadowed the tendency toward genocide within the contextual settings and intervening conditions to produce the above described resultant phenomena. Strategies deployed in this phase include organization, planning, and weaponry, as in the August 1992 Akwana killings in which the attackers fell on their victims at dawn, armed with bows and arrows, spears, machetes, and automatic weapons, and firing within point-blank distance, wounding and killing dozens (Noble, 1992a). Other strategies for this phase include an extermination plot involving mass murders as in the May 1992 pogrom of mostly Christian southern Zarian residents in Kaduna by extremist Muslims who gruesomely slaughtered them in their neighborhoods, as well as in various churches while they were worshipping (Falola, 1998, p. 218; Noble, 1992c). Further strategies for this phase include ideo-ethnic cleansing (or ideological and ethnic cleansing), involving burning of churches as in the April 1991 Tafawa Balewa crisis in Bauchi State, in which all twenty churches at the city's Hospital Road area were razed, with the ECWA church only narrowly escaping the perpetrators' ideological cleansing of churches by reason of its close proximity to the army barracks ("Battle in Northern Nigeria," 1991; Falola, 1998, p. 207).

Other strategies in this phase are forced migration, for example, refugees and displaced persons as in the Tiv/Jukun conflict in which many were forcibly displaced with the razing of several homes in the area (Noble, 1992a). Strategies deployed in this phase also include indoctrination, manipulation, or instigation. In the May 1992 Kaduna crisis, for instance, a cabal of proscribed politicians and the military authorities have combined to machinate religious and ethnic hostilities as a strategy to gain power (Noble 1992c), even as the violence was manifested mostly as a result of military authorities' sophisticated scheme to derail the country's transition program to civilian government (Aboubacargumi as cited in Noble, 1992c).

6. Consequences or Effects of Proclivity to Genocide: Phase III—1987 to 1996

The strategies adopted by perpetrators in this study phase have different consequences and effects in the different conflict settings involved. Consequences identified in this phase include death toll and casualties, mutilated bodies, or burned corpses, as in the May 1992 Kaduna killings in which the casualty estimates were varied, with political analysts and some individuals indicating that a minimum of 500, and probably up to 800 people have been exterminated, with some more hundreds wounded (Noble, 1992c). Other consequences in this phase include refugees and displaced persons, involving people fleeing homes or taking refuge or shelter for safety; and churches burned or destroyed as in the May 1992 Kaduna crisis in which numerous Christian churches were reported to have been razed ("100 Feared Dead," 1992; "Toll in Religious," 1992). Consequences in this phase also include destroying, looting, and razing of properties; and security threat, apprehension, anxiety, or social and political chaos. For instance, in the May 1992 Kaduna State killings, in which hundreds were killed or injured in ten days of fighting, the country was observed as sliding toward social and political chaos in the crisis, which is the worst since the military's ascension to power in 1983 (Noble, 1992c).

Additionally, this phase has consequences category for normalcy or calm returning after the intermittent upsurges of the conflict and gruesome killings. For instance, in the Kaduna May 1992 killings, the city was observed as returning to its distinctive normalcy following one week of violence, even as the streets were patrolled by armed legions of soldiers deployed by the federal government in place of the earlier marauding gangs that had held entire neighborhoods under sway. Business was once again booming as bank shutters and traders, storefronts opened, with the earlier evacuated relief international organizations and foreign consulates also back to business (Noble, 1992c).

EIGHT

Proclivity to Genocide in Northern Nigeria Phase IV

1996 to 2005

SYNOPSIS

The fourth study phase spans from 1996 to 2005, and Nigeria's present thirty-six state structure was operative in this phase (see map 1 in appendix A). This phase witnessed Abacha, who was in power from November 1993 and died in office in June 1998, and Abdulsalami Abubakar (1998–1999) became the head of state and chairman of the Provisional Ruling Council of Nigeria. Abubakar's transitional government enabled the registering of political parties and released Obasanjo from prison. Obasanjo (1999–2007) was elected president and sworn into office in May 1999, ushering in the Fourth Republic, and he was reelected May 2003 for a second term in office (Falola and Heaton, 2008, pp. 234–235).

All through the late 1970s up to the early 1980s Nigeria debated the issue of the place of Sharia or Islamic law in the country's judicial system, and as the turn of the new century ushered in a southern Christian as the country's president, the Sharia debate was renewed with it (Anthony, 2002), and throughout Obasanjo's term in office religious tensions were known to have remained high. With the country's return in 1999 to democratic rule, twelve states (see map 6 in appendix A) out of the nineteen northern states instituted Sharia law in their penal code, involving stricter implementation forms such as the punishing of thieves by amputation of a hand, and death sentence by stoning for the crime of adultery, which measures have occasioned national as well as international controversies (Falola and Heaton, 2008). The implementation of such Sharia measures heightened tension in northern Nigeria, with Christians criticizing its harshness and Muslims, on the other hand, arguing that crime rates have significantly reduced as a result of the newly adopted legal codes (Harunah as cited in Falola and Heaton, 2008, p. 238). The issue of Sharia implementation in some northern states has posed a thorny quagmire for the country. In May 2000, for instance, thousands were killed in Kaduna as non-Muslims opposing Sharia's introduction clashed with Muslims demanding its implementation in the state (Adekoya, 2009).

This phase witnessed a recurring spate of religious uprisings interlaced with ethnic clashes, each conflict seemingly bloodier and more ferocious than the preceding (Adekoya, 2009). In Jos, September 2001, for instance, a Muslim-Christian violence that flared up after the Muslim prayers had about 915 people killed in the riots, according to a September 2002 state government panel report on the conflict (Adekoya, 2009; Onishi, 2002). Ethnic tensions had built up before the riots as a result of a federal government appointment of a Muslim politician as local coordinator for its poverty alleviation program in the state. Seen as part of the detrimental political policies that would bar their religious freedom, Christians were disturbed that appointing a Muslim in a community they predominated was an attempt to politically, as well as religiously, dominate them (Minchakpu, 2001). However, the conflict sparked off by a scuffle that started between a Christian woman and some Muslims, as she attempted crossing a street that was barricaded by the Muslims. The fight spread to different areas of the city, in which Muslims spontaneously attacked Christians (Minchakpu, 2001).

In May 2004, a Christian militia attacked an essentially Muslim town of Yelwa with deaths in hundreds—put at 630 (Adekoya, 2009; Reuters; and Agence France-Presse as cited in "Hundreds Die in Attack," 2004) involving the latest break out in a protracted dispute between farmers and herders, of which the farmers were ethnic Tarok Christians, and the herders were Muslims from the Hausa-Fulani ethnic group ("Hundreds Die in Attack," 2004). The Nigeria Red Cross president, who was unable to confirm the number, had also warned "that casualty figures could be inflated by self-interested parties in a strife-torn area," while also the police estimate for the toll was reported at sixty-seven, even as the security agents were unable to enter Yelwa as access into the town was blocked by the attackers (CSW, n.d., pp. 1, 6, 11; "Hundreds Die in Attack," 2004).

Countering this version of the conflict which has "gained International currency," however, non-Muslims in the state who view the incident differently and are exasperated that their version of the episode has not been reported widely. To them the Yelwa attack was not an isolated incident, but rather part of the continuing violence which has plagued the area since 2002, as there had been earlier attacks in February 2004 in which extremist Muslims targeted and killed Christians prior to the May attack. Furthermore, the Yelwa attack, which was reportedly carried out by Christian militia, was refuted by them, on grounds that "there is no such thing as a 'Christian Militia,'" (CSW, n.d., p. 1). The assailants in the attack, on the contrary, involved local non-Muslim farmers who had taken laws into their hands in a retaliatory attack against the violent displacement from their lands amid government ineptitude in dealing with their plight. They argued that, "the term 'Christian Militias' was widely published by the international media, fuelling the perception of a planned conspiracy against Muslims in Plateau State, and rendering Christian leaders vulnerable to prosecution on false grounds" (CSW, n.d., p. 12). Furthermore, they disputed the 630 death toll of the Yelwa attack, "stating that this widely publicized estimate served to heighten Muslim anger, guaranteeing a violent reaction" (CSW, n.d., p. 2). Moreover, on this alarming spate of violence in Plateau State, Kendal observes the conflict as

> escalating, taking on the dimensions of a religious war. The Muslims are recruiting Islamic mercenaries from Chad and Niger, while the "Christian" militia that attacked Yelwa was allegedly armed and supported by retired generals, further escalating the violence. The state government seems to have made little effort to stop the violence. (2004, para. 13)

As the reports of the Yelwa incident in which over 600 Muslims were massacred reached Kano, which is "traditionally a hotbed of religious tensions," a seemingly peaceful protest led by Muslim leaders on May 11, 2004, soon turned violent as "angry Muslims hunted for 'nonbelievers' whom they then killed with machetes before burning the bodies" (Kendal, 2004, para. 21). The Muslim protesters, carrying daggers, clubs, and sickles, searched cars for Christians and animists, and asked that passengers to recite the Muslim prayers. Three young women, "nonbelievers" of Islam wearing Western-styled outfits who were macheted, escaped with bleeding head injuries following some sort of intervention (Kendal, 2004, para. 23). The toll for this Kano episode, in which militants, Muslims, and Christians fought bloody and ferocious street battles, was estimated at about 500 to 600, mostly Christians, killed in the two days of Muslim rioting (Adekoya, 2009). However, putting the death toll for this Kano crisis rather at about 3,000, while decrying "the biased reporting of sections of the international media," Christians saw the Kano events as predictable "given the inaccurate reporting of the Yelwa incident" (CSW, n.d., p. 2).

On the brutality and enormity of this May 2004 killing episode in Kano, the CSW (n.d.) observes that

> Christians and non-indigenes were hacked and battered to death; their homes, churches and properties were set on fire. Others are reported to have been shot dead by policemen.

children appear to have been targeted as . . . mobs descended on schools, separated Muslim children from non-Muslims and killed the non-Muslims. Local sources put the final death toll at over 3000, a fact the Kano State government is at pains to deny . . . "some bodies were burned in wells. Even little children were killed. The bodies of pregnant women were ripped open and their bodies burned" . . . following the violence the State Government ensured that cleaners were on the streets by 5am, and that trucks . . . were being used to gather corpses for a mass burial. (pp. 6–7)

Prior to the Yelwa killings, Zamfara State in the implementation of its "Sharia Phase 2" program, "had ordered the destruction of all churches" in the state (Kendal, 2004, para. 6). Accordingly, there is the possibility of using the Yelwa killings "to justify all manner of repression and persecution being unleashed upon an already besieged Christian minority," given the ripple effect the Yelwa incident had on some northern states (para. 6). In Bauchi State, for instance, security was tightened "after leaflets were found calling on Muslims to avenge the Yelwa killings and on Christians to leave the region," as well as in Kaduna as tensions ran high (para. 6).

Furthermore, violent Muslim-Christian conflicts persisted in northern Nigeria in the period, with the conflicts increasingly linked to events in the international scene. For instance, in 2001 a peaceful demonstration staged by Muslims in Kano in protest of America's Afghanistan campaign turned into a bloody riot with an estimated toll of about 100. Muslim youths trooped out in mass, from poor neighborhoods in which Osama bin Laden posters have largely become popular. As these Muslim mobs invaded and attacked the Christians in their quarter, the Christians resisted them with arms, even as they waved American flag-emblazoned T-shirts, bellowing pro-American slogans, and, in the ensuing three-day riot about 100 people died (Onishi, 2001b). In November 2002 also, following violent protests which involved a death toll of over 200 in Kaduna, the Miss World beauty pageant earlier scheduled in Abuja was relocated to London. The protests had been ignited by an article in a Nigerian newspaper which was suggestive that the Prophet Muhammad might have approved of the beauty pageant, probably choosing a wife among the contestants (Hoge, 2002; "Hundreds Flee," 2002), the riots indicative of the Muslims' frustrations "over the perceived alliance between their government and Western, secular powers" (BBC News as cited in Falola and Heaton, 2008, pp. 238–239). In Kaduna, over 100 people were burned to death, stabbed, or bludgeoned, with another 500 injured (Mcveigh, 2002). Also in the mayhem, eight mosques and a minimum of twenty-two churches were destroyed, ten hotels got damaged, and over 200 people were killed, while hundreds fled Kaduna even as 4,500 were left homeless ("Hundreds Flee," 2002).

These conflicts have been identified as stemming from Islam's rise as a force in politics, and the quick spread of assertive Sharia law in 1999, from one state to the present one-third of the nation's thirty-six states (Onishi, 2001b). The stakes have remained high, as Muslims as well as Christians vie for their greater representation and control at the state as well as federal government levels. Obasanjo, in his eight-year tenure as president, was incapable of defusing these tensions (Falola and Heaton, 2008, p. 239), and since the military power handover in 1999, about 5,000 Nigerians have died in in religious clashes (Onishi, 2001b).

APPLYING THE GENOCIDE PROCLIVITY MODEL: PHASE IV—1996 TO 2005

The application of the themes from study Phase IV to the Genocidal Proclivity Model in figure 4.1 follows.

1. Causal Conditions of Phenomena Relating to Genocidal Proclivity: Phase IV—1996 to 2005

Phase IV of the study also shows the four causal conditions of immediate or trigger factors, underlying or root causes, perceived threat of the "otherness," and exclusive ideological framing which lead ultimately to genocidal proclivity. In this phase, the trigger or immediate causes include insurgency, uprising, or antigovernment riots; arrests or persecution of fundamentalist sect members, religious extremism, and violence or other fundamentalist activities; Islam degraded, desecration, and/or misinterpretation of the Koran; and reprisal mission or revenge, and the massacres of Ibos and returning refugees. For example, in Aba, following the conveying back to Aba, the corpses of the Igbos that were killed in the north, the locals started attacking the Hausas, turning from Muslim-Christian battle in the North to ethnic search for anyone who might be a northerner (Onishi, 2000).

This phase also reveals underlying causation as a second set of causal conditions to the conflict, which include historical factors; colonial influences, exploitation, and fear of Balkanization; culture of bad governance and corruption or oppressive military rule; Al Qaeda, Afghanistan's Taliban, Libyan, and Iranian links, including illegal aliens; and political underpinnings or power struggle, involving issues of infiltration and politicization of religion. In the Jos crisis, for instance

> the Emir of Wase appears to be implicated in fomenting and financing the violence in southern Plateau State . . . as the killing of non-Muslim Tarok got underway in 2002, the Emir . . . refused to direct the military and police forces to quell the violence and informed the Governor of Plateau state that all was well . . . .the Emir . . . used his position as an

Islamic traditional leader to attract mercenaries from Chad and Niger to participate in the violence in the name of Jihad. (CSW, n.d., p. 4)

Additional underlying causal conditions in this study phase include political elites or Kaduna mafia. This phase also showed underlying causal factors involving socioeconomic factors, which include indigenes and settlers' issues; and poverty, unemployment, lack of education, and discontent. In the October 2001 Muslim protests in Kano against the U.S.-led Afghanistan air strikes, for instance, thugs rather than religious tensions were blamed for the crisis, as rioters were observed looting homes and stores shortly following the protests ("Violent," 2001).

Furthermore, this study phase also includes a third set of causal factors of perceived threat of the "otherness," which include ethnic-religious hatreds, rivalries, divisions, and animosities; North-South split or largely Muslim north and mainly Christian south; and annihilation attempts by targeting or forceful conversion of Christians to Islam (Onishi, 2001a). For instance, Kendal observes that

> Islamic zeal is strong in the northern state of Kano. Kano's governor, Ibrahim Shekarau, was elected on a radical, hardline, pro-Sharia platform. Christians suffer intense persecution in Kano, their schools and churches having been closed and burned. It is compulsory for all public-school girls to wear Islamic hijab, and as the Christian schools have been closed Christians don't have much choice. On the night of Shekarau's election . . . pastor Chikezie (Sunday) Madumere and his whole family were burned to death in their home in "No Man's Land" Kano city, by Muslim mobs celebrating Shekarau's win. (2004, p. 17)

This study phase also includes a fourth set of causal conditions involving the thematic category of exclusive ideological framing, comprising religious dimensions; anti-Western or ideological differences; fundamentalism and religious fervency; Sharia or Islamic law institution involving imposing Sharia across Nigeria or establishing of an Islamic state; non-Muslim opposition to Sharia; the unconstitutionality and violation of fundamental rights of Christians; and Sharia implementation, anti-establishment, or anti-Western ideology (Lacey, 2002; Mcveigh, 2002 "Religious Strife," 2001). Kendal observes, for instance, that

> Kano . . . introduced a Mobile Court to monitor and deal with people selling and screening foreign films or videos, and selling or playing foreign audio CDs. The Mobile Court will be guided by Sharia law and is charged to work toward the institutionalization of Islamic norms in all spheres of life. . . .
>
> Sheik Kabo informed Kano's Sharia Enforcement enforcers (HISBA) that the Kano State Sharia Commission would no longer permit any area or any person to be exempt from Sharia. He recommended that anyone who is not willing to adhere to Sharia should leave the state. (2004, para. 18)

2. Phenomena Resulting from Trigger Factors, Underlying Causation, Perceived Threat of the "Otherness," and Exclusive Ideological Framing: Phase IV—1996 to 2005

This study phase further shows that the causal conditions of trigger factors, underlying causation, perceived threat of "otherness," and exclusive ideological framing in the different situations and contextual settings resulted in variant degrees and forms of killings and exterminations mainly between extremist Muslims and Christians, as well as between different ethnic groups which are divided mainly along ethnic and religious lines. Such subjective phenomena as identified in the study data reveal attacks and violence unleashed to different target victims including assault, shoot-out, killings, arson, and looting; bloodbath, carnage, pogrom, mayhem, massacres, or barbarism ("Hundreds Flee," 2002; Koinange, 2001; Obateru and Mamah, 2004; Onishi, 2001a); and genocide ("Nigerian Muslims," 2004). Other phenomenal themes in this phase include political violence, coup d'état, and political assassinations; and religious and ethnic violence ("Deadly Rioting," 2000). Phenomenal themes also include reprisals from southern states (Onishi, 2000; "Violent," 2001); sectarian violence; and spiral or escalation of violence. Kendal (2004) observes, for instance, the escalating cycle of violence in Plateau State, which crisis precipitating event for the May 2004 attack started in February 2004 with the trampling of Tarok crops by Fulani cattle, and in retaliation the Tarok farmers stole and killed Fulani cattle, with crops and cattle respectively both groups' means of livelihood. The Fulani, seeking redress for their loss of cattle, and aided by hired Chadian and Niger Islamic mercenaries, attacked and killed ninety Tarok farmers in Yelwa inclusive of forty-eight axed to death inside a church where they had sought refuge, with the church then razed. A few days after this killing, Christians from the Gerkawa community, in a retaliatory attack, killed some forty Muslim neighbors with cutlasses or swords, and burned their bodies. Following this development, the army moved in to evacuate about 3,000 Muslims from Gerkawa to Yelwa, while Christians feared further attacks and fled Yelwa (Kendal, 2004).

Other phenomenal themes in this study phase include targeted, premeditated, or orchestrated killings and assaults (Onishi, 2001a); terrorist activities; and threats or fears of more attacks, protests, or warnings of full-scale war ("Dozens Dead," 2004; "Nigerian Muslims," 2004; Simmons, 2000; "Violent," 2001). Further phenomenal themes from this phase are tit-for-tat killings in northern states ("Religious and Ethnic Clashes," 2001; Sengupta, 2004a, 2004b). Further phenomenal themes in this study phase are uprising, antigovernment rioting, protests, or demonstrations; and violent or deadly clashes, rioting, or gun battles. By comparing and contrasting of these phenomenal themes and categories, two major categories involving targeted, premeditated, or orchestrated killings and assaults; and bloodbath, carnage, pogrom, mayhem, massacres, or barbarism are identified as being closely associated with the proclivity to genocide.

3. Context in Which Ethno-Religious Conflict and Genocidal Proclivity Developed: Phase IV—1996 to 2005

Additionally included in this study phase is the contextual framework which proffers the geographic dimension of social space or lebensraum for genocide proclivity to foster (Wood, 2001). These contexts are Northern region or states including Abuja; Bauchi State; Benue State, in Gbeji, Vaase, and Zaki-Biam; Kwara State, in Ilorin; Kaduna State, in Kaduna, Kafanchan, and Zaria; Kano State, in Kano—Sabon-Gari; Kebbi State; Nasarawa State; Niger State; Plateau State, in Jos, Kadyal, Kanam District, Langtang, and Yelwa; Sokoto State; Taraba State; and Zamfara State. The study data also showed reprisals or retaliatory killings in Southern states including Abia State, in Aba; Anambra State, in Onitsha; Lagos State, in Lagos; and Niger Delta State in Odi where there occurred extrajudicial killings and the ethnic violence in Lagos. (See tables 4.1 and 4.2 for the various contexts for this phase, respectively, for the northern Nigeria ethno-religious conflict, and for the reprisal attacks in the south.)

Further providing the contextual framework in this study phase are varying conflict parties in the different phenomenal settings for the conflict. The conflict parties identified in this phase include Muslim mobs/gangs, civilian mobs or sect and Igbos ("Deadly Rioting," 2000; Onishi, 2000; Tostevin, 2000). Conflict parties for the phase also include Muslim mobs or sects and security forces (Sengupta, 2004b); Muslim sect and other Muslims or sect; Muslim mobs, sects or groups and Christians; security agents and unidentified civilians; and different ethnic groups as in the Tiv/Jukun long-drawn crisis ("Nigeria: Government," 2001). Other conflict parties in this phase are northern states government and Christians (Ahiante, 2004); and Fulani herdsmen or Hausa-Fulani group and Christian or host communities ("At Least 30 Killed," 2003; "Muslim Mobs," 2004; "Nigerian Muslims," 2004; Sengupta, 2004b). Such conflict parties were analyzed by comparison and contrasted with the phenomenal conflict themes and categories and their causal conditions to identify conflicts with plausibility of a conceptualized annihilating difference (Hinton, 2002), which lead to exterminations involving perpetrator and victim situations, while conflicts devoid of such annihilating difference are considered clashes or fighting between parties without overt genocidal proclivity.

Additionally identified in this study phase are varying perpetrator groups using the annihilating difference analysis of the conflict parties described above, which include Muslim mobs, rioters, or rampaging Muslim youths (Ahiante, 2004; "Dozens Dead," 2004; "Muslim Mobs,"

2004; Onishi, 2001b). Other perpetrator groups include Fulani herdsmen or Fulani-Hausa group or gunmen (Sengupta, 2004b); and also identified under the perpetrator category are Christian militia or youths, which other than the reprisals in the south, primarily involve the Yelwa May 2004 killing of Muslims presumably by Christian militia. However, in this killing episode of Yelwa Muslims reportedly done by Christian militia, Yelwa had witnessed in February 2004 one of the conflict's worst atrocities, when about 100 Christians were killed by Muslim militia, among whom, forty-eight people were killed in a church and later buried ("Nigerian Muslims," 2004). Moreover, while also contesting the allegation of the Yelwa May 2004 killings, Christians counter that employing the term "Christian Militia" gave the connotation of the Church having an armed, trained group who stage attacks against Muslims, where the Church, on the contrary has, to a great extent, discouraged retaliation. More so, local sources have pointed out that the assailants in the May 2004 killings were non-Muslim, local farmers that had violently been displaced from their lands in the past, and who had waited for redress and government protection, in some cases, for several years, and which, when not forthcoming, launched the Yelwa attack in retaliation, thus, taking the law into their hands (CSW, n.d.).

Other perpetrator groups identified in this study phase are security agents, soldiers, the army/military, and Hausa/Northern troops, and these involve extrajudicial killings. For instance, in the May 2004 Kano killings that were supposedly retaliatory to the Yelwa killings of May 2 ("Muslim Mobs," 2004), CAN condemned some Muslim policemen's brutality who were observed "to have intentionally and indiscriminately shot and killed many Christians in Sabon-Gari and other parts of the state" (CSW, n.d., p. 7). Details of the involvement of the perpetrator groups in the different conflict settings of this study phase are analyzed and discussed in Phase IV synopsis above.

Additionally, this study phase reveals target victim groups which foster the developing of annihilating difference amid a perpetrator group and social space environment to produce a complete and well-rounded and contextual setting for the flourishing of a tendency to genocide (Hinton, 2002). Target or victim groups identified in this study phase include Christians and churches (Ahiante, 2004; "Dozens Dead," 2004; Koinange, 2001; Lacey, 2002; Mcveigh, 2002; "Muslim Mobs," 2004; "Nigerian Muslims," 2004; Obateru and Mamah, 2004; "Religious Riots," 2001; Simmons, 2000; "Violent," 2001); and Christian neighborhoods or mostly Christian villages (Sengupta, 2004b). Target victims in this phase also include civilian targets ("13 Nigerians Die," 2001; "At Least 30 Killed," 2003; "Hundreds Flee," 2002; Mcveigh, 2002; "Nigeria: Government," 2001; Onishi, 2001a). Other target victims are Southerners who are predominantly Christians as in the reprisals in Lagos in which Yorubas were the primary target victims ("3rd Day," 2002), and especially Igbos as targets (Ahiante, 2004; "Deadly Rioting," 2000; "Dozens Dead," 2004; "Muslim Mobs," 2004; Onishi, 2000; "Religious Riots," 2001; "Violent," 2001).

Target victims in this phase also include security agents—police officers, military and government officials; media offices and journalists; beer parlors, hotels, banks, and other facilities (structures or institutions with Western connotations). Included also as victims in this phase are Muslims, Hausa-Fulani herders, Muslim sects, Northerners, or mosques as in reprisals in southern states ("Deadly Rioting," 2000; Onishi, 2000; "Youths Besiege," 2000). In the November 2002 Miss World pageant crisis in Kaduna, a soldier and a policeman were charged for having dragged out fifteen Muslims from their homes, killed them, and dumped their bodies into a river, with over a dozen civilians gunned down by soldiers and police officers without provocation ("Hundreds Flee," 2002). Other target victims identified in this phase are Muslims, Hausa-Fulani herders, Muslim sect, Northerners, or mosques, involving mainly the Yelwa May 2004 killings, presumably by Christian militia (CSW, n.d.; "Hundreds Die in Attack," 2004; "Muslim Mobs," 2004; "Nigerian Muslims," 2004). Details of the victimhood of the targets in the different conflict settings of this study phase are also analyzed and discussed in Phase IV synopsis above.

4. Intervening Conditions Influencing Proclivity to Genocide: Phase IV—1996 to 2005

This study phase additionally identified intervening conditions in the different conflict contextual settings in addition to the contexts which are factors generally involving such broad conditions which influence by increasing or diminishing the proclivity to genocide. Intervening conditions in this phase of the study include press censorship and manipulation or deflation and inflation of casualty figures, which are used by government officials on occasions to minimize or scale-up reprisals or tit-for-tat violence tactics. For instance, the toll for the Kano May 2004 killings about 500 to 600, were over 3000 by CAN Kano, who "also alleged that in an effort to hide the true number of casualties, the state government had thrown the bodies of some victims into the Challawa River and given several others a mass burial" (CAN as cited in CSW, n.d., p. 7).

Other intervening conditions in this phase are extrajudicial killings and army involvement in policing as in the May 2004 Kano killings. Intervening conditions in this phase also include government ineptitude, lethargy, or weak central government. For instance, in the Jos Muslim-Christian incessant upheavals in Plateau State, the CSW (n.d.) observes:

> On Sunday 22 February Yamini village was completely destroyed by Fulani herders who claimed to be chasing cattle thieves. Then on 24 February, came the attack on Yelwa during which 41 people were

killed and burnt in a church and 38 murdered outside it. Every church in Yelwa was destroyed save one that was no longer in use, and the Christian population fled the area as it became clear that the state government was unable to protect them. (p. 5)

Other intervening conditions in this study phase are collaborators or bystanders involving both local and foreign collaborators that lead to an internationalization of the conflict. Reportedly, for instance, the Christians in Jos view Muslims as being more aggressive, even as they are getting extensive support from the Arab world, while African Christians by contrast could no longer depend on the backing or support from a secular West (Onishi, 2001b). There is, therefore, an indication of foreign involvement in the persisting Muslim-Christian clashes in Plateau State, with Christians affirming that

the bulk of this violence has been perpetrated by Hausa-Fulanis accompanied by paid fighters from neighboring Republics, and whose victims have overwhelmingly been Christians and traditional believers. They feel the constant presence of foreigners during these attacks indicates the international dimensions of the violence in Plateau State and northern Nigeria, linking the perpetrators of the violence with the global Islamist movement. (CSW, n.d., p. 1)

This phase of the study also reveals that further influencing the tendency to increase or deflate genocidal proclivity are the various intervention measures to control the violence with their implementation. Intervention efforts in this study phase include aid and relief support; rehabilitation efforts or calls for rebuilding of churches; reconciliation attempts; control measures taken such as curfews and road checks by security agents; investigations and commissions of inquiries set up; calls to address the constitutionality of Sharia law and security issues; mopping up of rioters or arrests made; warnings or calls for action, restraint, justice, or self-defense; attempts to dialogue; and appeals for intervention or mediation.

5. Strategies Foreshadowing Proclivity to Genocide: Phase IV — 1996 to 2005

This study phase also reveals different strategies foreshadowing the tendency toward genocide within the contextual settings and intervening conditions with the resultant phenomena as described above including organization, planning, and weaponry; and extermination plot involving mass murders or ideological and ethnic cleansing involving, for instance, burning of churches or forceful conversion of Christians to Islam. For example, following an attack and flight of non-Muslims from Yamini village in Plateau State,

portraits of Osama Bin Laden were hoisted in Yelwa, and the area was declared as part of Zamfara State in a mock celebration marking "the total eradication of the infidels and all that belongs to them." ... The crowd went on to attack Nshar, a settlement of the Gomai people situated close to Yelwa. Churches, buildings and the Yam Market were razed to the ground. This was followed by attacks on the villages of Ajikamai, Lakushim Tumbi, Tukung, Goedo, Mangoro, and Pandam, and official targets in Kwapjur ... 1,500 people were killed during this orgy of violence. (CSW, n.d., p.5).

The strategies identified in this study phase also include indoctrination, manipulation, or instigation. On the Plateau State conflicts, for instance,

> [t]he Emir's appointee as Chairman of the Wase Local Government Area ... was accused of fuelling the violence along with his boss. Not only is he reported to have attempted to incite hatred during the violence in 2002 by falsely claiming to have seen the corpses of 5000 Muslims scattered in the bush ... he also initially refused to pay for the feeding of soldiers stationed around Kadarko, the largest remaining Christian town in Wase. [He] ... commandeered a local government vehicle and sent it ... to gather mercenary reinforcement from Bashar and its surrounding areas. (CSW, n.d., p. 4)

6. *Consequences or Effects of Proclivity to Genocide: Phase IV—1996 to 2005*

The strategies adopted by perpetrators in this study phase have different consequences or effects in the different conflict settings examined. Consequences identified in this phase include death toll and casualties, mutilated bodies, or burned corpses ("3rd Day," 2002; Ahiante, 2004; "Deadly Rioting," 2000; "Dozens Dead," 2004; Koinange, 2001; Lacey, 2002; Mcveigh, 2002; "Miss World," 2002; "Muslim Mobs," 2004; "Nigerian Leader Admits," 2002; "Nigerian Muslims," 2004; Obateru and Mamah, 2004; Onishi, 2001a, 2001b, 2002; "Religious and Ethnic Clashes," 2001; Sengupta, 2003, 2004b). Other consequences include refugees and displaced persons, as well as persons fleeing homes or taking refuge or shelter for safety; mass graves or mass burials ("Nigerian Muslims," 2004; Onishi, 2001a; Simmons, 2000; "Violent," 2001); churches burned, bombed, or destroyed ("13 Nigerians Die," 2001; Ahiante, 2004; "Hundreds Flee," 2002; Koinange, 2001; Lacey, 2002; "Miss World," 2002; Sengupta, 2003, 2004b); and mosques burned or destroyed ("13 Nigerians Die," 2001; "Hundreds Flee," 2002; Lacey, 2002; Onishi, 2000). Consequences in this phase also include Christian businesses, homes, hotels, and properties destroyed (Ahiante, 2004; "Hundreds Flee," 2002; Simmons, 2000); destroying, looting, and razing of properties; and denial of freedom of worship and desecration of Christian religion. In a press conference by northern executives of CAN in Lagos, following the May 2004 crises in Yelwa and Kano, for instance, not only were Christians being denied their freedom of worship, they were also being denied their freedom of association. They observed having been told at the Sharia early introductory stage, that non-Muslims will not be affected, which without any fear of being contradicted, they now avow to be contrary to the case. They reported, for instance, that churches in some of the Sharia operative states have been demolished, with a number of additional churches also earmarked to be demolished in Zamfara State, even as the plight of churches in Kano is the worst (Ahiante, 2004).

Also in this phase are consequences for security threat, apprehension, anxiety, or political and social chaos ("Dozens Dead," 2004; Simmons, 2000; Tostevin, 2000; "Violent," 2001). Consequences also revealed normalcy or calm returning after episodes of gruesome exterminations, showing an intermittency of occurrence in the killings (Sengupta, 2004a).

NINE

Proclivity to Genocide in Northern Nigeria Phase V

2006 to Present

SYNOPSIS

The fifth study phase spans from 2006 to present, with Nigeria's present thirty-six states still operative (see map 1 in appendix A). The preceding and incumbent presidents of the country over this phase of the study include Umaru Yar'Adua who was elected and became president and commander in chief of the federal republic of Nigeria in May 2007. Yar'Adua died in office in May 2010, and his vice president, Goodluck Jonathan, became president from May 2010 and was re-elected May 2011. Jonathan is in Nigeria's incumbent president.

This phase also evidences the increasing direct links between religious tensions in the country and outside happenings in the world, as seen in the February 2006 entire Islamic world demonstrations in response to a Danish newspaper cartoon satirizing the Prophet Muhammad, which turned violent in Nigeria with the riots claiming dozens of lives in Maiduguri, Bauchi, Katsina, and Onitsha (BBC News as cited in Falola and Heaton, 2008, p. 239). On the extent of carnage that was perpetrated in the cartoon riots in Maiduguri,

> [a]t least 65 Christians were killed, 57 churches were destroyed and hundreds of Christian businesses razed to the ground when Muslims rampaged through Maiduguri on 18 February, allegedly in protest at the publication in Denmark the previous year of cartoons depicting the prophet Mohammed. Many victims were burnt alive, often by neighbors they had known for years. The final death toll may be much high-

> er than stated. After the arrival of the mutilated corpses of Igbo victims occasioned retaliatory attacks on Muslims by Igbo youths in southern Nigeria, the Borno State Government refused to immediately release any more bodies for burial, fearing that such a move might provoke further violence. It sought permission to conduct a mass burial for the remaining victims, but the Christian community was loath to agree to this. As a result of this impasse, many corpses remained in the local morgue instead of receiving immediate burial, and the final death toll is still unknown. (CSW, 2008b, p. 10)

The violence began in Maiduguri with the Danish cartoon protests and spread with thirty churches razed to the ground and with eighteen people killed, mostly Christians ("Toll Rises," 2006). It involved a week's rioting by Muslim and Christian mobs, which claimed about 157 lives in Maiduguri (Adekoya, 2009). Further on this crisis, protesting Muslim mobs thronged through Maiduguri carrying machetes, iron rods, and sticks, even as a group of the mobs threw a car tire over a man, doused him with gasoline, and burned him. And, in a rampage of about three hours, fifteen churches were burned by thousands of rioters, with the protesters also attacking and looting shops belonging to Christians, mostly of southern Nigeria origins, amid some toll that included a priest and three children among the victims killed (Fisher, 2006).

Additionally, in Bauchi, 25 were killed as Muslims attacked Christians, as noted by the Red Cross, with the violence fueled by allegation of desecration of the Koran by a Christian teacher. And, in Onitsha there were reprisals in response to the attacks on Christians in the north, with about thirty people (mostly northern Muslims) killed and two mosques burned, even as the violence sparked off with rumors of some northerners having attacked and killed some children in a primary school (Polgreen, 2006; "Toll Rises," 2006).

Furthermore, in November 2008, a disputed election of a local government chairmanship position led to Muslim-Christian gang clashes in which about 400 people were killed in Jos, Plateau state (Adekoya, 2009, para. 9). Countering this positioning on the crisis, however, the CSW observes:

> Several international news agencies have reported that the violence was triggered by the results of a local government election. However, sources in Jos point out that voting passed off peacefully and the violence broke out in the early hours of Friday 28 November before electoral results had even been announced. Moreover, instead of targeting political institutions, rioters armed with guns, spears, machetes and other weapons immediately attacked Christian businesses, churches and the homes of clergymen. A local source informed Christian Solidarity Worldwide: "As usual they took Jos by surprise, and are now hiding behind election results to launch and excuse their mayhem." (CSW, 2008a, para. 2)

Further in this November 2008 conflict in Jos, there was an errant reporting of about 300 Muslims killed by Christians, with the bodies deposited in a mosque. The men were shot as they launched fresh attacks in defiance to the authorities' imposed night curfew, while also staging a large-scale unsuccessful attack on police barracks. According to the CSW, "the men died while obeying orders from a mosque in the Dilimi area, which was using its loudspeakers to instruct all Muslims to defy the authorities, participate in the 'jihad,' loot properties for money and then burn them" (CSW, 2008a, para. 3). Additionally, about sixteen churches were burned down, with the death toll of Christians killed in the attack put at about 100, including four or more pastors shot dead, one of the Church of Christ in Nigeria (COCIN) and another of the Evangelical Church of West Africa (ECWA), and two others (CSW, 2008a).

Furthermore, in January 2010 there were sporadic clashes between Muslims and Christians in Jos, which resulted in a death toll estimate that ranged from 30 to 300 in three days of fighting. The violence was observed to have started when, on Sunday, a church was attacked by Muslim youths and the church members resisted the attackers, resulting in the macheting of several persons most of who were Christians, with more than 100 bodies reportedly seen in Red Cross trucks being carried to the morgue (Nossiter, 2010a).

Moreover, in March 2010 also, in an ethnic, vicious violence in reprisal attacks for the January 2010 crisis in Jos, about 500 people (mostly women and children) were killed in Dogon Na Hauwa near Jos in Plateau State by Hausa-Fulani herders (Nossiter, 2010f). The dead in this killing episode were ethnic group members, who were Christians, and who had feuded with the Muslim, Hausa-Fulani herders that were identified by police officials and witnesses as the attackers. As observed by an investigating Nigerian rights group in the area, the attackers armed with machetes on a Sunday set upon the villages, killing children and women in their homes, while also entrapping the men in animal traps and fishnets as they tried to flee, and slaughtering them, even as some homes were also set ablaze. The victims of this carnage with toll of about 400 were buried in Dogon Na Hauwa in a mass grave, with the violence described as the worst in the area so far, even as some bodies have been mutilated (Nossiter, 2010f).

This phase is equally interlaced with religious upheavals primarily involving a fundamentalist Islamic sect, the Boko Haram group whose Arabic name translated means, "Western education is forbidden or illegal" (Adekoya, 2009), with the mission to institute Sharia in Nigeria ("700 Die," 2009; "Boko Haram," 2012; "Christian Groups," 2009; "Emergency Declared," 2011; "In Nigeria's North," 2011; Lobel, 2012; Mohammed and Idonor, 2012; Mojeed and Nossiter, 2012; "Muslim Sect," 2011; "Thousands Flee," 2009; "Toll Rises," 2006). In 2009 there was the Boko Haram uprising, which was an insurgency by the fundamentalist Islamic group, Boko Haram, against security forces.

Reportedly in July 2009, following the arrest of some Boko Haram members, the sect staged attacks in Bauchi in which over fifty people were killed, with more than 100 arrests made. The violence spread rapidly to Borno, Kano, and Yobe states, with five policemen and sixty others killed, as well as in Potiskum, Yobe State, in which a police station was burned down. As the violence spread further to Maiduguri, Borno State, over 100 were reported killed in an ensuing bloodbath. Furthermore, in an encounter with the Boko Haram group following the deployment of troops to the area, forty-three of the sect members were killed in Hawan Malka in Yobe State, while the leader of the sect, one Mohammed Yusuf earlier arrested in Maiduguri, was shortly killed in custody. Again in Bauchi State, further violence reportedly led to an additional death toll of about eleven with twenty-eight gravely wounded, as well as the razing down of churches, mosques, and several houses (Adekoya, 2009).

The Boko Haram has since this 2009 confrontation with security forces become more proficient and increasingly sophisticated in its attacks, claiming responsibility or being blamed for various attacks on different targets including security agents, symbols of government authority including the United Nations which was bombed in August 2011, and police stations ("Deadly Christian-Muslim Clash," 2011; "Multiple Explosions," 2011a, 2011b; "Nigeria Group Threatens," 2011). The sect has been involved in various instances of violence in the country, several of which involved targeting of Christians, as in the car bomb attack which occurred at the exterior of a Jos Catholic church which left six people dead, in addition to a chain bombing of churches in various cities on Christmas day (Akau, 2012). Thus, the sect has repeatedly mounted attacks on several churches in the north amid worship services (Bello, 2012a, 2012b; Ohai, 2012; Orude, 2012a, 2012b) as in the December 2011, Christmas day bombing of a church in Madalla (Akau, 2012; "Christmas Carnage," 2012; Emewu and Nwosu, 2011a, 2011b). On this onslaught on Christians, the fundamentalist sect Boko Haram was reported to have made good its threat of bombing churches as well as other places all over the country on Christmas day. A suicide bomber smashed a vehicle laden with bombs into a crowd of Christians as they streamed out from an early morning Mass on Christmas day, killing about forty-three people with over seventy-three severely injured, at St. Theresa Catholic Church in Madalla, Niger State. The Madalla bombing which occurred at the outskirts of Abuja caused a great stir as pictures from the incident showing decapitated bodies splashed across international and local media, thus, placing in bold relief, the country's severe security predicament on the global arena (Sokunbi, 2012).

Furthermore, in January 2012, Boko Haram, in a bloody attack wave in Gombe and Mubi, Adamawa State, with the assailants firing into the crowd, killed twenty-eight people and wounding several others in the region. The sect launched a deadly attack on a Deeper Life Christian Church in Nassarawo, Gombe State, during the church's prayer service, with the assailants armed with AK47 rifles and many in number shot through the church windows, killing six worshippers including the pastor's wife, and wounding ten others. This episode was shortly followed by the sect's storming of a meeting venue of Igbos gathered in Mubi, Adamawa state, to plan on transporting a kinsman's body that was shot dead by unidentified assassins and killing all the Igbo mourners at the venue (Ohai, 2012). Both attacks occurred prior to the expiration of Boko Haram's three-day ultimatum to southern Christians living in the north, to leave the Northern region or face calamitous consequences, even as panic spread among southerners living in Mubi (Ohai, 2012) and, indeed, the entire north.

This study period, thus, also evidences a continued deliberate targeting of Christians and southerners, particularly Igbos, during episodes of violence in the northern Nigeria ethno-religious conflict. For instance, while addressing the human rights concerns of the individual's entitlement to state protection against bodily harm and violence under the International Convention on the Elimination of All Forms of Racial Discrimination (CERD), CSW (2008b) observes:

> A feature of the violence in northern Nigeria is the fact that people from the Igbo tribe are targeted, whether or not they profess Christianity. The victimization of Igbos by the Hausa-Fulani regardless of their religious creed may largely stem from historical reasons. However, the regularity of targeted attacks on a specific racial group and the lack of legal consequences for its perpetrators and organizers may amount to a violation, albeit by omission, of Nigeria's obligations under CERD. (p. 13)

Additionally, in March 2012, eleven people were killed and twenty-two injured in a bomb attack on St. Finbarr's Catholic Church in Jos on a Sunday morning (Ehiabhi, 2012a), with the attack being the second attack on churches within a month, following the bomb explosion at the Church of Christ in Nigeria (COCIN), in which three people died, and thirty-eight were injured (Tilley-Gyado, 2012). Moreover, in April 2012 about twenty-five people were killed and thirteen wounded in an Easter Sunday bombing in Kaduna, with the road observed to have been littered with dead bodies following a massive explosion that shattered a nearby church's windows, even as worshippers celebrated Easter in the church (Akau, 2012). On Easter Sunday morning in Kaduna also, a suicide car bomber that was turned away from church premises where it attempted to attack Christians holding Easter services, struck a busy road, killing about thirty-eight people and injuring many others. Pertinently, churches in Nigeria have increasingly been violently targeted on their holy days

("Suicide Bombing," 2012). More so, in April 2012 also, twenty-two people including two professors were killed and several others wounded in a coordinated attack of bomb blasts and gun fire on a Catholic church at the Bayero University, Kano, with the bombers throwing bombs at the worshippers to draw them out, by first laying siege on the churches and ensuring that any worshippers escaping from the bomb blasts, as they fled the theatre, ran into the barrage of the bombers' heavy gunfire (Bello, 2012a, 2012b; "Witness: Gunmen Attack," 2012). Also in April 2012, a bomb was detonated on Sunday in the Sabon-Gari section of Kano which is occupied by mostly Christians and non-indigenes of the state, even as Kano city was rocked earlier in the year by several bomb blasts in which hundreds of people were killed (Ehiabhi, 2012c).

In June 2012, two churches were bombed in Bauchi, killing fifteen people and wounding forty-two others, when a suicide bomber forced his explosive-laden car onto a group of worshippers outside the two churches—Living Faith and Harvest Field—both of which are situate, in the Yelwa Tudu district of Bauchi metropolis (Alli and Tsenzughul). Also in June 2012 three suicide bomb attacks were made on churches in Kaduna state, killing twenty-one people and injuring about 100 others. Two of the bomb blasts had ensued within minutes of the other, targeting churches in Zaria city, killing at least one person in addition to the bomber, and wounding fifty-one others, with a church in Kaduna city being hit next by a third blast which occurred about half hour later, killing ten people and wounding twenty-nine others ("Nigerian Church Blasts," 2012). Again in August 2012 there was mass shooting at Deeper Life Church near Okene, Kogi State, in which 19 people were killed, including the pastor of the church, by three unidentified gunmen ("Nigeria Church Attack," 2012). Such gruesome exterminations and killings have continued unabated in the north, and these attacks, which have been primarily on Christians and churches, have prompted a warning by the Christian Association of Nigeria, that with no other imperatives other than being made mere sitting ducks, Christians might be forced into defending themselves amid government's failure to guarantee their safety (Onah et al., 2012).

APPLYING THE GENOCIDE PROCLIVITY MODEL IN PHASE V—2006 TO PRESENT

The application of themes from study Phase V to the Genocidal Proclivity Model in figure 4.1 follows.

1. Causal Conditions of Phenomena Relating to Genocidal Proclivity: Phase V— 2006 to Present

This phase also shows causal conditions which led ultimately to genocidal proclivity under the four identified causation factors of immediate or trigger factors, underlying or root causes, perceived threat of the "otherness," and exclusive ideological framing. This phase reveals trigger or immediate causal factors including arrests or persecution of fundamentalist sect members, religious extremism, and violence or other fundamentalists' activities; election-related and engineered violence; insurgency, uprising, or antigovernment riots; Islam degraded, desecration and/or misinterpretation of the Koran; the Danish cartoon; and massacres of Igbos and returning refugees, as in the January 2012, in which Boko Haram in Mubi, Adamawa State, stormed a community meeting of Igbos gathered to plan on transporting the body of a kinsman that was shot dead by unidentified assassins (Ohai, 2012). Other trigger factors include reprisal mission or revenge. In the March 2010 killings in Dogo Na Hauwa, for instance, dozens of herdsmen descended on villagers in their sleep, slaughtering hundreds with cutlasses, knives, and machetes in an act of brutal sectarian retribution, with about 500 people reportedly killed in the wee hours of a Sunday morning in three separate villages (Nossiter, 2010d).

This phase also includes a second set of causal conditions comprising underlying or root causes to the conflict involving historical factors among others. For instance, in the said Dogo Na Hauwa, Plateau State vicious killing of over 500 of a Christian ethnic group by the Hausa-Fulani herdsmen, the Middle Belt of Nigeria, a fertile band of land straddling the predominantly Muslim north and the mostly Christian south, has continuously been a religious and ethnic violence hotbed, with Jos the capital of Plateau State bearing the brunt of the atrocities. While most of the original inhabitants of the state are Christians and animists, migrants have, through the centuries been attracted by the area's grazing pasture and farmlands, particularly the Hausa Muslims and Fulani from the largely arid north (Polgreen, 2008).

Other underlying causal factors in this phase include a culture of bad governance and corruption or oppressive military rule (Murray and Nossiter, 2009); and Al Qaeda, Afghanistan's Taliban, Libyan, and Iranian links including illegal aliens ("Nigeria Group Threatens," 2011; "Nigerian Death Toll from Boko Haram," 2012; "Nigerian Death Toll Rises," 2009; Nossiter, 2010d, 2011; "Nigeria: Police Arrest," 2012; "Scores Killed," 2011; Shuaibu, 2012; Smith, 2009; "Unidentified Gunmen," 2011). Further underlying causation in this phase are political underpinnings or power struggle, which include issues infiltration and politicization of religion; and political divisions and tensions (Nossiter, 2010e; Ojo, 2012; Sokunbi, 2012; "Thousands Flee," 2009). Other underlying causation themes in this phase include socioeconomic factors involving ethnic groups vying for control of fertile lands; political and economic power; indigenes and settlers issues; and poverty, unemployment, lack of education, and discontent "At Least 200 Die," 2008; "At Least 21 Are Killed," 2011; ("Attacks Kill 18," 2011; Murray and Nossiter, 2009).

Additionally, this phase comprises the third set of causal factors of perceived threat of the "otherness" including ethnic-religious hatreds, rivalries, divisions and animosities; and North-South split or largely Muslim north and mainly Christian south. Nigeria's religious divide, amid its 250 different ethnic groupings, presents a rather geographical division between a north which, historically, is predominantly Muslim, and a largely Christian and animist south, in addition to the nation's deeply seated political divisions which extend beyond religious confines (Polgreen, 2008). Other perception of "otherness" threat themes are annihilation attempts by targeting ("Africa: Race Hatred," 1967; Chidiogo, 2011; Garrison 1968a; Mgboh, 2012a; Nossiter, 2010f; Orude, 2012a, 2012b) and/or forceful conversion of Christians to Islam (Ahiante, 2004; Brooke, 1987b; "Christian Groups," 2009); and ultimatums to southern Christians living in the North to leave the region (Ohai, 2012; Onah et al., 2012).

This phase also shows themes and categories for the fourth set of causal conditions of exclusive ideological framing, which include issues with religious dimensions, anti-Western or ideological differences ("Nigerian Villages," 2010; Nossiter, 2010c, 2011; Polgreen, 2008); and fundamentalism and religious fervency ("'Irate Youths' Burn Down," 2006; Nossiter, 2010c; Orude, 2012). Other themes for exclusive ideological framing in this phase include Sharia or Islamic law institution in northern Nigeria, involving non-Muslim opposition to Sharia, unconstitutionality and violation of fundamental rights of Christians and other non-Muslims in Sharia operative states (Adekoya, 2009; Fisher, 2006; Lobel, 2012); gender segregation matters (Nossiter, 2010c); Sharia implementation, anti-establishment, or anti-Western ideology ("700 Die," 2009; "Christian Groups," 2009; Mojeed and Nossiter, 2012; Mshelizza, 2011); and moves toward imposing Sharia across Nigeria or establishing an Islamic state ("Boko Haram," 2012; Lobel, 2012; Mohammed and Idonor, 2012; "Nigerian Death Toll from Boko Haram," 2012).

2. Phenomena Resulting from Trigger Factors, Underlying Causation, Perceived Threat of the "Otherness," and Exclusive Ideological Framing: Phase V—2006 to Present

This phase also shows that the causal conditions—the trigger factor, underlying causation, perceived threat of "otherness," and exclusive ideological framing in varying situations and contextual settings—resulted in different degrees and forms of killings and exterminations primarily between extremist Muslims and Christians and other conflict parties, which are divided mostly along ethnic and religious lines. The subjective phenomena identified from the study data in this phase reveal violence unleashed to different target victims including, assault, shootout, killings, arson, and looting; and bloodbath, carnage, pogrom, mayhem, massacres, or barbarism. Of great import, for instance, is the July 2009, Boko Haram crisis in Maiduguri in which 11 Christians were beheaded, among whom were three pastors, with twenty churches also burned in the carnage (Adekoya, 2009; "Christian Groups," 2009; Nossiter, 2010e). Further phenomenal themes in this phase include bombings, coordinated gun and bomb attacks (Elbagir and John, 2012; "Nigeria Attacks," 2011; Ohai, 2012; "Overnight Explosions," 2012; Pedro, 2011; Tilley-Gyado, 2012); as well as phenomenal themes for genocide as in the July 2009 Boko Haram onslaught on Christians in Maiduguri in which the sect was observed to have wielded dangerous weapons, and abducted Christians to their leader, Mohammed Yusuf's enclave in their instance of Sharia implementation in Nigeria. Christians were thus being tortured, and converted forcefully to Islam. More so, eight Christians, and three pastors who resisted the forced conversion, were sacrilegiously beheaded on the Islamic sect leader's order, even as the fundamentalists also burned twenty churches to ashes (Dogo as cited in "Christian Groups," 2009).

Other phenomenal themes in this phase include political violence, coup d'état, and political assassinations; religious and ethnic violence ("Attacks Kill 18," 2011; "Renewed Jos Violence," 2011); reprisals from southern states; sectarian violence; spiral or escalation of violence; and targeted, premeditated, or orchestrated killings and assaults. In the February 2006 Danish cartoons episode, for instance, Christians in Maiduguri were targeted with protesters in the city turning on the minority Christians, and burning down churches as well as shops, even as police officers and troops were deployed to the area to restore order. The victims of this Maiduguri episode were believed to be mostly Christians as they had been attacked inside the churches, with a Roman Catholic priest noted to be among the people killed (Myers, 2006). Further phenomenal themes in this phase include terrorist activities, and threats or fears of more attacks, protests, or warnings of full-scale war (Marama, 2012; "Sectarian Attacks Kill 15," 2012; Sokunbi, 2012; "Violence in Northeast," 2011). Phenomenal themes in this phase also include tit-for-tat killings in northern states ("Boko Haram," 2012); uprising, antigovernment rioting, protests, or demonstrations (Bello, 2011a); and violent or deadly clashes, rioting or gun battles ("700 Die," 2009; "At Least 200 Die," 2008; Chidiogo, 2011; Ohai, 2012). By comparing and contrasting such phenomenal themes and categories, two major categories involving targeted, premeditated, or orchestrated killings and assaults; and bloodbath, carnage, pogrom, mayhem, massacres, or barbarism are identified as being closely associated with the proclivity to genocide.

3. Context in Which Ethno-Religious Conflict and Genocidal Proclivity Developed: Phase V—2006 to Present

The study data for this phase also include the different social space or lebensraum, which provides a geographic framework on which genocide proclivity can develop (Wood, 2001). This involves the Northern region or states including Abuja—Jabi, and Zuba communities; Adamawa State, in Yola, Jimeta, Lamurde, and Mubi; Bauchi State, in Bauchi; Benue State, in Makurdi, Dooga, Kpata, Lokobi, Ajimaka, Ekeae, Giza, Yogbo, and Mbgawem border communities, Gwer West Local Government Area, Zongo Akiki, Nyijir, Tse Taki, and Agbeke in Guma areas; Borno State, in Maiduguri, Dala, Yan'tebura, Bulukuntu Tsallake, and Zajeri; Jigawa State, in Dutse; Gombe State; Kaduna State, in Kaduna, Kafanchan, Kufara, Ori-Apata, Zaria, Zonkwa, and Zango-Kataf; Kano State, in Kano, Bompai, and Sabon-Gari; Katsina State, in Katsina; Nasarawa State, in Alago, Doma Town, Eke and Giza Areas, Kadarko, Tiv settlements at Kpata, Donga, Lokobi, and Ajimaka; Niger State, in Minna—Angwan Kuje, and Madalla; Plateau State, in Jos, Barkin Ladi, Bukuru, Dogon Na Hauwa, Kuru Karama, Wareng, Yelwa, Zot, and Ratsat; Sokoto State; Taraba State, in Jalingo; and Yobe State, in Damaturu, Gadaka, Geidam, Hawan Malka, and Potiskum; Zamfara State. The phase also showed contexts for Southern states where reprisals occurred including Anambra State, in Onitsha, Awka, Nnobi, and Nnewi; Delta State, in Asaba; Imo State; and Niger Delta. (See tables 4.1 and 4.2 for the various contexts, respectively, for the northern Nigeria ethno-religious conflict, and for the reprisal attacks in the south.)

Also providing the contextual framework in this phase are different conflict parties in the different phenomenal settings of the conflict. These include Muslim mobs, sect, civilian mobs or gangs and Igbos; Muslim mobs or sects and security forces (Onyelebocho, Ola, and Mgboh, 2011); Muslim mobs, sects or groups and Christians; security agents and unidentified civilians; different ethnic groups; northern states government and Christians; and Fulani herdsmen or Hausa-Fulani group and Christian or host communities. Such conflict themes were analyzed by comparison and contrasted with the phenomenal conflict themes and categories and their causal conditions to identify conflicts with plausibility of a conceptualized annihilating difference (Hinton, 2002) which lead to exterminations involving perpetrator and victim situations, with other conflicts that are devoid of such annihilating difference considered as clashes or fighting between parties without an overt inclination to genocide.

Additionally, varying perpetrator groups identified in the study using the annihilating difference analysis of the conflict parties described above include Boko Haram Islamic fundamentalist group ("700 Die," 2009; Abdulkadir, 2012b; Akau, 2012; "Boko Haram," 2012; Mgboh, 2012a, 2012b, 2012c; "Muslim Sect Kills," 2011; Ohai, 2012; Onah et al., 2012; Orude, 2012a, 2012b); Fulani herdsmen or Fulani-Hausa group or gunmen (Bello, 2012a; Ebije and Alabelewe, 2011; Ejembi, 2012; Iferi, 2011; Nossiter, 2010b, 2010d, 2010f; Purefoy, 2010; Shiaondo, 2011); and Muslim mobs, rioters, or rampaging Muslim youths (Binniyat, 2012; Chidiogo, 2011; "Deadly Christian-Muslim Clash," 2011; Myers, 2006; Mojeed and Nossiter, 2012; Nossiter, 2010b; Shuaibu, 2012). The perpetrator groups identified also include rampaging or underaged youths and arrested suspects (Connors, 2008; "Deadly Christian-Muslim Clash," 2011; "'Irate Youths' Burn Down," 2006; "Unidentified Gunmen," 2011); and civilian mobs, unidentified attackers, or gunmen ("At Least 200 Die," 2008; "Attacks Kill," 2011; Ola and Orude, 2012; Olatunji, 2012).

Also identified are perpetrator themes for Christian militia or youths, which are mostly reprisal killings, as in the February 2006 Danish cartoons reprisals in Onitsha (Polgreen, 2006); or the August 2011 revenge attack on a Ramadan gathering in Jos for the bomb attacks on Christmas Eve ("Deadly Christian-Muslim Clash," 2011), and other retaliatory killings and reprisals, as in the February 2012 reprisal killing of two Muslims by Christian youths following the bombing of the COCIN church in Jos in which thirty-eight people were killed (Abdulkadir, 2012b). Further perpetrator groups are security agents, soldiers, the army or military, Hausa or Northern troops as in the numerous cases of extrajudicial killings such as the November 2001 massacre of hundreds of civilians in Benue State, in reprisal for the nineteen soldiers killed in the Tiv/Jukun crisis ("Nigeria Defense," 2001), as well as unlawful battering and indiscriminate firing of unarmed citizens by soldiers and police ("700 Die," 2009; Adetunji, 2011; Chidiogo, 2011; Connors, 2008; Nossiter, 2009a, 2009b, 2010b; Okoye, 2011; Tilley-Gyado, 2012). Details of the involvement of the perpetrator groups in the different conflict settings of this study phase are analyzed and discussed in Phase V synopsis above.

Additionally, this phase reveals target victims groups which support the fostering of annihilating difference amid a perpetrator group and social space environment, producing a complete, well-rounded contextual setting for the flourishing of proclivity to genocide. Target victim groups identified in this study phase include Christians and churches, also involving Christian neighborhoods or mostly Christian villages (Akau, 2012; Chidiogo, 2011; Ehiabhi, 2012c; Myers, 2006; Olatunji, 2012; Onah et al., 2012; Purefoy, 2010); civilian targets; Southerners who are predominantly Christians, and especially Igbos as targets ("Boko Haram," 2012; "Christian Groups," 2009; Ebije and Alabelewe, 2011; Ohai, 2012); security agents—police officers, military, and government officials ("700 Die," 2009; Chidiogo, 2011; Ehiabhi, 2012b; Ola and Orude, 2012); symbols of government authority (including the United Nations offices in Abuja) (Adekoya, 2009; Mark, 2012; "Nigerian Death Toll Rises," 2009; "Nigerian Death Toll from Boko Haram," 2011; Pedro, 2011); civilian centers, schools, and school children (Akau, 2012; Nossiter, 2012; Ola and Orude, 2012; Onah et al., 2012); media offices and journalists (International Freedom, 2012; Mohammed and Idonor, 2012; "Nigerian Reporter," 2012; Onyeose, 2012); beer parlors, hotels, banks, and other facilities (structures or institutions with Western connotations); Muslim clerics, mainstream or orthodox Muslims as in the August 2009 Boko Haram bloodbath in which over 700 were killed, including Muslim clerics ("Nigerian Death Toll Rises," 2009); and Muslims, Hausa-Fulani herders, Muslim sect, Northerners or mosques as in reprisals on the postelection violence involving 800 death toll in Kaduna State, where predominantly Christian communities had some Christian mobs killing Muslims, burning their properties as well as mosques in retribution (Chidiogo, 2011). Details of the victimhood of the targets in the different conflict settings of this study phase are also analyzed and discussed in Phase V synopsis above.

4. Intervening Conditions Influencing Proclivity to Genocide: Phase V—2006 to Present

This study phase also identified intervening conditions in the different contextual settings of the conflict in addition to the context themes. Such intervening factors which generally involve broad conditions that influence by increasing or diminishing the proclivity to genocide, and identified in this phase include press censorship and manipulation or deflation and inflation of casualty figures, which is used by government officials on occasions to minimize or scale-up reprisals or tit-for-tat violence; and extrajudicial killings and army involvement in policing (Adetunji, 2011; Chidiogo, 2011; Nossiter, 2009a; "Police Arrested," 2010; Tilley-Gyado, 2012). Other intervention themes in this study phase include government ineptitude, lethargy, or weak central government ("Christian Groups," 2009; Connors, 2008; Okpi, 2012; Onah et al., 2012).

Further intervention themes in this phase are the presence of collaborators or bystanders involving both local and foreign collaborators which internationalizes the conflict. In the January 2012 Kano crisis involving about 185 death toll, for instance, about 80 percent of the 200 attackers arrested were Chadian "mercenaries," with the likelihood of payment having been made to the Chadians to participate in the Boko Haram latest attacks, even as the group has long been suspected by Nigerian security agents of arms smuggling through the northeastern porous border with Niger and Chad into the country. Additionally, according to a UN regional security report, there was evidence which was suggestive of the Boko Haram group having Chadian members that had been trained at Al Qaeda's affiliate in north Africa, even as the African Union counter-terrorism officer warned of the group's effort to expand its activities deeply into Central Africa ("Nigeria: Police Arrest," 2012).

This phase further reveals that also influencing the tendency to increase or deflate genocidal proclivity are the various intervention measures to control the violence with their implementation. Intervention efforts in this phase include aid and relief support ("Christian Groups," 2009; "More Christian Victims," 2012; Orude, 2012a; Shiaondo, 2011); rehabilitation efforts or calls for rebuilding of churches; reconciliation attempts (Polgreen, 2008); control measures taken such as curfews and road checks by security agents (Onah et al., 2012); investigations and commissions of inquiries set up; calls to address the constitutionality of Sharia law and security issues; military assault or crackdown; mopping up of rioters or arrests made; and warnings or calls for action, restraint, justice, or self-defense as in the call in September 2010, made on the Nigerian government by the Human Rights Watch, requesting that Francis Deng, who is the special adviser to the United Nations on genocide prevention, be allowed to visit Plateau, which request was observed to have gone unanswered (Okoye, 2011). Other intervention measures in this phase include attempts to dialogue, appeals for intervention or mediation (Adetunji, 2011; "Christian Groups," 2009; "Nigeria: Police Arrest," 2012).

5. Strategies of Attack Foreshadowing Proclivity to Genocide: Phase V—2006 to Present

This phase also reveals different strategies foreshadowing the tendency toward genocide within the contextual settings and intervening conditions with the resultant phenomena identified above. Strategies foreshadowing inclinations to genocide in this phase include organization and planning including weaponry. For example, in the Jos November 2008 violence,

> [t]here is . . . evidence that the . . . violence may have been planned in advance. So far 500 Muslim rioters have been arrested, some of whom were dressed in fake police and military uniforms. Two hundred are now known to be citizens of the neighboring Republic of Niger, while 300 are from the northern Nigerian states of Kano, Katsina and Sokoto. Some of the rioters informed police that they arrived in Jos three days prior to the violence. "They had weapons, many weapons" . . . "they were ready, very ready." (CSW, 2008b, para. 5)

Also in this phase are the strategies of extermination plot involving mass murders or ideological and ethnic cleansing including, for example, the burning of churches, or the forceful conversion of Christians to Islam as in the Boko Haram's forceful conversion to Islam of Christians they abducted and killing those who refused to convert ("Christian Groups,"

2009). Further strategies include forced migration, for example, refugees and displaced persons, and the ultimatum by Boko Haram fundamentalist sect to southern Christians to leave the north (Lobel, 2012; Ohai, 2012; Onah et al., 2012; Orude, 2012a, 2012b). The strategies for this phase also include coordinated attacks involving shootings, bombings, maiming, and arson, as well as drive-by or hit-and-run shootings and suicide bombings ("Boko Haram," 2012; "Emergency Declared," 2011; Emewu and Nwosu, 2011a, 2011b; Mohammed and Idonor, 2012; "Multiple Explosions," 2011a, 2011b; "Nigerian Death Toll from Boko Haram," 2012).

6. *Consequences or Effects of Proclivity to Genocide: Phase V—2006 to Present*

The strategies adopted by perpetrators in this study phase have different consequences or effects in the different conflict settings examined. Consequences identified in this phase include death toll and casualties, mutilated bodies, or burned corpses ("At Least 200 Die," 2008; Binniyat, 2012; Chidiogo, 2011; Emewu and Nwosu, 2011b; Mgboh, 2012a, 2012b, 2012c; Myers, 2006; Okpi, 2012; Okubenji, 2011; Shuaibu, 2012). Other consequences include refugees and displaced persons, as well as persons fleeing homes or taking refuge or shelter for safety ("At Least 200 Die," 2008; Bello, 2011b; Chidiogo, 2011; "Christian Groups," 2009; Ejembi, 2012; Onah et al., 2011; Polgreen, 2008). Consequence themes also include mass graves or mass burials (Murray and Nossiter, 2009; Nossiter, 2010d, 2010e, 2010f); churches burned, bombed or destroyed (Abdulkadir, 2012b; Akau, 2012; "Boko Haram," 2012; Chidiogo, 2011; "Christian Groups," 2009; Ehiabhi, 2012a; Mgboh, 2012a; Myers, 2006; Polgreen, 2008); and mosques burned or destroyed mostly in retaliation or involving clashes between fundamentalist sect and Christians or security agents (Chidiogo, 2011; Nossiter, 2009a, 2009b; "Thousands Flee," 2009; "Violence in Northeast," 2011). Further consequences in this phase include police stations, barracks, and government buildings bombed, or burned; and schools bombed, burned, destroyed, or closed. In a March 2012 bombing of a school in Maiduguri by the Boko Haram, for instance, the sect now has a new ominous front, which is to wage war on schools, with the dousing of private and public schools with gasoline in the night, and setting them on fire. Homemade crude bombs such as gasoline-filled soda bottles are hurled at concrete, empty classrooms, with eight schools reportedly firebombed by the Islamic Boko Haram group in its deadly war against schools, in conformity to the group's rallying name which connotes Western education as an anathema, with "Boko" in Hausa language signifying, Western learning or book, and "Haram" in Arabic signifying forbidden. In recount, a watchman who reportedly was ordered to lie down at gunpoint, as the sect doused gasoline on the Abbaganaram Primary School at Aruna and set it ablaze, recalled the arsonists' avowal to be Boko Haram, and they would burn down the school (Nossiter, 2012).

Additional consequences in this phase include Christian businesses, homes, hotels, and properties destroyed; destroying, looting, and razing of properties; denial of freedom of worship and desecration of Christian religion. In a Kaduna press conference by CAN following the Boko Haram August 2009 attacks in Maiduguri, in the northern nineteen states and Federal Capital Territory (FCT), the northern governors' attempt at regulating religious preaching in the region by deploying traditional rulers, has been rejected by the Christian Association of Nigeria (CAN), on grounds of its impracticability. CAN was also reported to be holding as responsible the federal government as well as the governments of the five states in which violence erupted in the Boko Haram episode where eleven Christians were beheaded, among whom were three pastors, with twenty churches also burned. The quest to implement Sharia in the entire country constitutes the fundamental motivation that frames the Boko Haram's movement of unleashing terror upon innocent citizens ("Christian Groups," 2009).

Other consequences in this phase are security threat, apprehension, anxiety or political and social chaos, including infiltration of police, military, and all areas of government by perpetrator groups. Consequences category also revealed normalcy or calm returning after episodes of gruesome killings and exterminations, showing intermittency of occurrence (Connors, 2008; Nossiter, 2012).

End of Model Application for Phase V

With genocide proclivity identified in each of the conflict five phases, the next chapter explores the bases of proclivity to genocide in the northern Nigeria ethno-religious conflict.

TEN

Bases of Proclivity to Genocide in Northern Nigeria

SUBSTANTIVE THEORY OF PROCLIVITY TO GENOCIDE

A substantive theory, which is rather particularistic in form (Glaser, 2007), is developed from the study's specific inquiry area of genocidal inclination or proclivity in the northern Nigeria ethno-religious conflict. The theory derives from the analytical technique of Strauss and Corbin's (1990) grounded theory approach which essentially involves "a central phenomenon, causal conditions, strategies, conditions and context, and consequences" (Creswell, 2007, p. 68). The core category or central idea relates with the other categories of causal conditions which lead to the phenomenon, its contextual framework, intervening conditions, strategies deployed for the phenomenon, and its consequences.

In the northern Nigeria ethno-religious conflict, the grounded theory model developed in the study is applied to determine the core phenomenon of genocidal proclivity, which is evidenced as occurring in interplay of its six-part components. As identified in the conflict, the first of these components is causal conditions for genocidal proclivity involving (i) immediate or trigger factors which are catalytic in form and which ignite the killings—for example, the first coup d'état and killing of mainly northern army officers; massacres of Igbos and returning refugees; secession and self-determination (as in the Biafra war); insurgency, uprising, or antigovernment riots; Islamist fundamentalist activities; as well as issues of Islam desecration or misinterpretation of the Koran, and fatwa declared publications such as the Danish cartoon and Miss World publications, etc.; (ii) underlying or root causes which are entrenched into the conflict fabric, including historical and colonial influences on the region, culture of bad governance and political underpinnings, and socioeconomic factors of poverty, unemployment, and lack of education, etc.; (iii) perceived threat of the "otherness," which include ethnic-religious hatreds, rivalries, divisions, and animosities; annihilation attempts by targeting or forceful conversion of Christians to Islam; ultimatum to southern Christians living in the North to leave; anti-Ibo rioting; dynamism and fear of Ibo or southern dominance; and North-South split or largely Muslim North and mainly Christian South, etc.; and (iv) exclusive ideological framing including factors of religious dimensions, anti-Western or ideological differences; fundamentalism and religious fervency; and Sharia law institution, implementation, and moves to impose Sharia across Nigeria and establish an Islamic state, etc.

The second component, which is the phenomena of genocidal orchestration, emanates in interplay of identified causal factors and includes targeted, premeditated, or orchestrated killings and assaults; and carnage, pogrom, massacres, bloodbath, barbarism, or mayhem. The third component of the contextual framework, in which ethno-religious conflict and genocidal proclivity developed comprises the social space, or lebensraum (Wood, 2001); conceptualized annihilating difference; and identified perpetrator. The fourth component involves intervening conditions influencing or mitigating proclivity to genocide, and includes government ineptitude, lethargy, or weak central government; press censorship and manipulation, deflation/inflation of casualty figures to escalate or abet killings/reprisals; extrajudicial killings and army involvement in policing; and collaborators or bystanders which could be local or international with a consequent internationalization of the conflict, etc. The fifth component involves the strategies of attack foreshadowing proclivity to genocide in the conflict, and includes organization, planning, and weaponry; indoctrination, manipulation, or instigation; extermination plot involving blockade and starvation, and mass murders; coordinated attacks of shootings, bombings, maiming, looting, and arson; ideo-ethnic cleansing involving razing, bombing, or destroying of churches; targeting of Christians or forceful conversion of Christians to Islam; forced migrations; and ultimatum to southern Christians to leave the North, etc. The sixth component details the consequences or effects of proclivity to genocide identified in the conflict, including sequential or complete victim annihilation; death toll and casualties, mutilated bodies or burned corpses; mass graves and mass burials; refugees and displaced persons; starvation; churches burned, bombed, or destroyed; infringing human rights; and normalcy returns, etc.

In applying this theoretical framework with evidences focused on intentionality to address the study's core focus of genocidal proclivity or inclination to the northern Nigeria ethno-religious conflict in each of the study's five phases, the study evidences a continuing, though intermittent, perpetration of violence over the period. More so, the study evidences a constancy of the perpetrator groups primarily as Muslim groups against targeted groups which are mainly Christians or non-Muslim groups, on the basis of exclusionary religious ideology that is intentionally genocidal.

The study's substantive theory posits that there is genocidal proclivity to the northern Nigeria ethno-religious conflict resulting from causal factors which trigger and underlie the phenomena amid a perceived threat of "otherness," and exclusive ideological framing. Such perceived threat of "otherness" is evidenced through ethnic-religious hatreds and animosities through annihilation attempts by targeting or forceful conversion of Christians to Islam, and/or ultimatum to southern Christians living in the North to leave the region. The theory posits that the intent to annihilate is framed by exclusive ideological positioning on issues of religious dimensions, anti-Western, anti-establishment, or ideological differences, fundamentalism and religious fervency, and Sharia's institution and implementation amid moves toward imposing Sharia across Nigeria and establishing an Islamic state. The theory argues that such exclusive ideological framing leads to violations of fundamental rights of Christians (mostly southerners) and other non-Muslim minority ethnic groups in the region, particularly the Sharia operative states, are being deprived of their right to existence through intermittent wanton killings. The theory also presents that the genocidal underpinning to the conflict has been episodic in nature, and intermittent in occurrence, as a result of which it has remained unacknowledged for decades, thus, presenting latency for recognition and a delusion as to what is going on in the northern Nigeria ethno-religious conflict.

UNDERSTANDING GENOCIDAL INCLINATION AND SPECIFIC INTENT

Establishing genocidal inclination to the northern Nigeria ethno-religious conflict is pivotal to addressing the fundamental question: Are there genocidal inclinations to the ethno-religious conflict in northern Nigeria? Genocidal inclination borders on intentionality with the intent of the perpetrator group basically defining genocide (Jones, 2006). Thus, "acts of destruction" which cause "total or partial destruction of a group" as in a revolution or conquest, for instance, are legally construed as intentional and hence, genocide, irrespective of the goal or motive where such acts were intentionally pursued (Gellately and Kiernan as cited in Jones, 2006, p. 21). As stated previously, actions are considered intentional where perpetrated with the *reasonable expectation* or knowledge of a resultant partial or whole destruction of a human group, notwithstanding their claimed objective (Jones, 2006, p. 21). As per the 1998 Rome Statute of the International Criminal Court, a person is deemed to have intent vis-à-vis conduct where that consequence is meant by that person to occur, or he or she *"is aware that it will occur in the ordinary course of events"* (Greenawalt as cited in Jones, 2006, p. 21). Intent can be established as in the Rwandan International Criminal Tribunal's 1998 Akayesu judgment that "the offender is culpable because he knew or should have known that the act committed would destroy, in whole or in part, a group" (Schabas as cited in Jones, 2006, p. 21).

Genocide intent is observed as combining the notion of *specific* intent, and *constructive* intent (Jones, 2006), with specific intent inferred "where actions with predictable results are taken over an extended period of time, and the consequences of these actions regularly confirm their outcome" (Reisman and Norchi quoted by Fein as cited in Jones, 2006, p. 21). Constructive intent involves cases where "the perpetrators did not intend to harm others but should have realized or known that the behavior made the harm likely . . . [and] clearly results in the destruction of that group of people, even if that result is neither intended nor desired" (Alvarez as cited in Jones, 2006, p. 22). The notion of specific intent to destroy a racial group is fundamental to genocide (Campbell, 2010, Video Series 11; 2012).

UNDERSTANDING THE TWO PHASED MANIFESTATIONS OF GENOCIDE

There are basically two phased manifestations of genocide, the first involving the destruction of the oppressed group's national patterns, and the second involving the replacement of national pattern through imposition (Lemkin as cited in Campbell, 2010, Video Series 25). The first phase entails destroying the targeted group's cultural practices, their religious beliefs, moral foundation, economic practices, and psychological well-being, all of which constitute their social institutions and collectively constitute their national pattern. In essence, all things, criteria or signifiers which identify the population as such are aimed at by the oppressors in attempt to destroy the oppressed group's identity. This first phase destruction of the targeted group members and the attempt to destroy their national pattern is synonymous with eliminating their identity. The second phase of genocide is to replace that national pattern through imposition, i.e., to impose the national pattern of the oppressor where the national pattern of the targeted group once existed. While in the first phase there is the attempt by the oppressor to destroy the national pattern of the group, in the second phase there is the imposition of the national pattern of the oppressor. Hence, there is destruction and imposition of national patterns (Campbell, 2010, Video Series 25).

Genocide, thus, essentially involves destroying a national group and their patterns of identity and a sort of imposition of the oppressor's own patterns of identity. Hence, there is the imposition of national pattern, for instance, in occupied territories. And, while some national pattern imposition forms are extremely hostile and may result in occupying other people's property, forcing them off their land, exterminations, biological destruction, and destruction of human groups, etc., other forms of imposition of the oppressor's national pattern may not be so hostile, as such imposition basically arises from the notion of "enforced assimilation" (Campbell, 2010, Video Series 25), and entails assimilation which is forced, but rather, depicted as "opportunity" (Lemkin as cited in Campbell, 2010, Video Series 30).

ESTABLISHING PROCLIVITY TO GENOCIDE IN THE NORTHERN NIGERIA ETHNO-RELIGIOUS CONFLICT

From the preceding chapter data analysis, which is elaborated further in this chapter by addressing the study's primary focus of whether there are genocidal inclinations to the ethno-religious conflict in northern Nigeria, there are genocidal inclinations to the conflict on the basis of exclusionary ideology of extremist Muslims and/or imposition of the Sharia, as evidential in all the study five phases as follows:

Study Phase I—1966 to 1976 Evidence

Genocidal undertone killings have intermittently been going on in northern Nigeria since the 1960s beginning with the May to October 1966 massacres of Igbos who are predominantly Christians in northern Nigeria by Muslim mobs and northern troops. Osaghae (1998b) notes, for instance, that the July 1966 "counter-coup resonated in the Northern region in the form of renewed genocidal killings of Igbos and Easterners" (p. 61). The Ibo massacres in the north were followed through in the ensuing three-year Biafra-Nigeria war in which millions of Biafrans lost their lives through the Nigeria government policy of embargo and starvation (Emerson, 1970; Garrison, 1968b), also through killing of Igbo civilians in the enemy recovered territories of the war by Nigerian troops, and through the deliberate targeting and bombing of civilian centers during the war. Thus, Osaghae observes:

> The war was presented as a genocidal one waged by the Muslims of Northern Nigeria who had declared a *jihad* to exterminate the Igbos from the face of the earth (the massacres of Igbos in the North, as well as the strategies of economic blockade and starvation pursued throughout the war, seemed to lend credence to this). (1998b, p. 66)

Thus, genocidal episodes are seen manifesting through the first phase of the study delineated from 1966 to 1976, though with some few years respite after the war.

Study Phase II—1976 to 1987 Evidence

Following a brief lull after the war in the 1970s, the genocidal episodes sparked off once again with the Maitatsine riots of the 1980s in which thousands of lives, this time Christians as well as mainstream Muslims who were considered heretics by the sect; the sect members and security agents were equally killed in the process of trying to subdue the sect. This second phase of the study spanning from 1976 to 1987, thus saw religious extremism and violence or other fundamentalists' activities, insurgency, uprising, or antigovernment riots, as in the Maitatsine riots or insurgencies. For instance, in episodes involving accusations of desecration of Islam or misinterpreted Koran in which Christians and Muslim mobs clashed in Kafanchan in March 1987 with people killed and churches burned, the aftermath of which eight Koran teachers were killed by Christian mobs; Muslim mobs in a supposed reprisal attack on Christians, burned all the churches in Zaria, about seventy-five in number, and threatened to forcefully impose Islam on a Christian community in Wusasa, Zaria (Brooke, 1987b). This phase, thus, evidences exclusionary ideological framing involving ideo-ethnic cleansing or ideological and ethnic cleansing of burning of churches, as well as attempts at forceful conversion of Christians to Islam (Brooke, 1987b). Exclusionary ideology frames genocide orchestration, which is evidentially present in its twosubset, as here again, there is the destruction of the ideology of the targeted group and the attempt at imposition of the ideology of the perpetrator group (Lemkin as cited in Campbell, 2010, Video Series 25). Thus, in this study phase also, genocidal inclinations are evidenced behind the exterminations, mass killings, forced migration, and other core ethnic or ideological purgative tools of genocide.

The target victims or victim groups for this phase of the study include Christians and churches, also involving Christian neighborhoods or mostly Christian villages; civilian targets; Southerners who are predominantly Christians, and especially Igbos as targets; security agents—police officers, military, and government officials; symbols of government authority; and media offices and journalists; beer parlors, hotels, banks, and other facilities which represent structures or institutions with Western connotations, involving the destruction of the national patterns of the targeted group, and imposition of the oppressed groups' national patterns (Lemkin as cited in Campbell, 2010, Video Series 25). Victims identified in this phase, however, also include Muslim clerics or mainstream/orthodox Muslims who were targeted by Islamic fundamentalists for nurturing an opposing ideology to the Maitatsine sect (Dash, 1984). It however also includes Muslims, Hausa-Fulani herders, Muslim sects, Northerners, or mosques, whose exception of victimhood derive from reprisals from Christians as in the March 1987 Kafanchan Koran misinterpretation clash (Brooke, 1987b; Kotch, 1987), and/or counterattacks by security agents, as in the December 1980 Maitatsine clash, in which the authorities sought to annihilate the cult (Jaynes, 1981).

Study Phase III—1987 to 1996 Evidence

The third phase of the study, from 1987 to 1996, witnessed insurgencies, uprisings or antigovernment riots, as well as religious extremism and fundamentalism with the Babangida's administration's registering of Nigeria in 1985 into the OIC which exacerbated religious tension in the period as Christians saw it as a "move to turn Nigeria into an Islamic state" (Falola, 1999, p. 188). There was also extensive display of fundamentalism and religious fervency with Islamic militants calling for the institution of Sharia or Islamic law in northern Nigeria, an ideological framing that underlies much of the excessive bloodletting which continues to occur in northern Nigeria. It was, therefore, a period of prolonged tension marked with religious riots and unrest in which thousands of lives were lost, properties and buildings destroyed, and the country at the verge of a religious war between Christians and Muslims, with political leaders opportunely manipulating the nation's diversity problem. More so, in some northern states, there were also socioeconomic factors of ethnic groups contesting for control of fertile lands, political, and economic power, with poverty, unemployment, and educational lack amid the down-sliding economy intensifying a general feeling of discontent and a quest for alternative sociopolitical means of survival. The discontent led to the recourse to religion, which provided the way out for the masses, resulting in a new wave of fundamentalism due to the increased religiosity. And, further fanning the embers of the conflict were ethnic-religious hatreds, rivalries, divisions, and animosities with most northern cities, other than the Middle Belt zone, delineated in terms of Muslim majority and Christian minority, and nationally, on the basis of the North-South split of largely Muslim north and mainly Christian south.

This phase, thus, also witnessed annihilation attempts by targeting and exterminations or mass killings as in the April 1991 Tafawa Balewa riots in which the Christian ethnic minority "the Seyawa group, were selected for destruction," as were many other Christian non-natives in Bauchi (Falola, 1998, p. 207). Here again, exclusionary ideology, destruction of the oppressed group and their ideology, and the imposition of the ideology of the perpetrator group came to the fore (Lemkin as cited in Campbell, 2010, Video Series 25). Thus, such phenomena identified in this phase involving violence and attacks unleashed to different target victims include targeted, premeditated, or orchestrated killings and assaults, and bloodbath, carnage, pogrom, mayhem, massacres, or barbarism which are identified as being associated with the proclivity to genocide.

Study Phase IV—1996 to 2005 Evidence

The fourth study phase spanning from 1996 to 2005, also witnesses insurgencies, uprisings or antigovernment riots, as well as religious extremism and fundamentalism for varying causal factors, including the desecration of Islam or misinterpretation of Koran, with a recurring spate of religious uprisings interlaced with ethnic clashes, each of which presented as bloodier and more ferocious than the previous (Adekoya, 2009). In essence, the period saw an escalating cycle of violence, notably in Plateau, Kano, Bauchi, and some other northern states, mostly with attacks and counterattacks between ethno-religious groups, each episode taking on a religious tonation with a resultant polarization in the conflict and, more often than not, with extremist Muslims hunting down and killing Christians in different parts of the region, on occasions aided by Islamic mercenaries from neighboring states. An instance of this was the February 2004 episode between Tarok Christian farmers and Muslim Hausa-Fulani herders, the redressing of which the Hausa-Fulani herders, aided by hired Chadian and Niger Islamic mercenaries, attacked and killed ninety Tarok farmers in Yelwa with forty-eight axed to death inside a church where they had sought refuge and with the church razed. In retaliation, Christians from the Gerkawa community attacked and killed some forty Muslim neighbors with cutlasses or swords, and burned their bodies. In response to this development, the army moved in and evacuated about 3,000 Muslims from Gerkawa to Yelwa, while Christians fled Yelwa in fear of further attacks (Kendal, 2004).

There was, however, the May 2004 killings in Yelwa, an essentially Muslim town, which presented as a notable exception to such frequent incidences of Muslims killing Christians, and carried out by a Christian militia with toll of about 630 (Adekoya, 2009; "Hundreds Die in Attack," 2004), and which, once again, was an eruption in a long-drawn dispute between Muslim Hausa-Fulani herders and Tarok Christian farmers in the area ("Hundreds Die in Attack," 2004). Also, there was a likely inflation of the casualty figures "by self-interested parties," as the death toll estimate by the police had been put at sixty-seven rather than 630 (CSW, n.d., pp. 1, 6, 11; "Hundreds Die in Attack," 2004). More so, the idea of "Christian militia" as assailants in the episode did not exist (CSW, n.d., p. 1), on the contrary, it was the local non-Muslim farmers' retaliatory attack against violent displacement from their lands amid government ineptitude in dealing with their plight (CSW, n.d., p. 12).

The phase also witnesses the Sharia implementation program, the launching of which started with the Zamfara State government's ordering of "the destruction of all churches" in the state (Kendal, 2004, para. 6). There was exclusive ideological framing during the period involving issues with religious dimensions, fundamentalism, and religious fervency, and Islamic law institutionalization with aims to impose Sharia across

Nigeria and to establish an Islamic state (Simmons, 2000). Such exclusive ideological framing with the institution of Sharia exacerbated conflict in the period as non-Muslims in opposition, contended the constitutionality of Sharia amid glaring evidences of violation of the fundamental rights of Christians in implementing Sharia's anti-establishment or anti-Western ideals ("Religious Riots," 2001; "Violent," 2001). For instance, in April 2004 Kano State introduced a Sharia-guided mobile court for institutionalizing Islamic norms in every sphere of life, with the Sharia Enforcement agency (HISBA) informed that the state's Sharia Commission would no longer permit the exemption of any person or area from Sharia, with recommendation "that anyone who is not willing to adhere to Sharia should leave the state" (Anthony as cited in Kendal, 2004, para. 19). Thus, once again in this study phase is the wanton destruction of the national patterns of the targeted group and imposition of the oppressed group's national patterns (Lemkin as cited in Campbell, 2010, Video Series 25).

Furthermore, the period witnessed persistent violent Muslim-Christian clashes in the region with events in the international scene increasingly exacerbating the conflict, as in the Kano Muslims' bloody riot in October 2001 in protestation of America's Afghanistan campaign with a high death toll (Koinange, 2001; "Violent," 2001). Other such crises in the period include the November 2002 Kaduna violent protests that had over 200 toll, and churches burned in the Miss World beauty pageant riots, which was ignited by a supposedly blasphemous newspaper article that made suggestive aspersions on Prophet Muhammad ("Hundreds Flee," 2002). These riots are indicative of the Muslims' frustrations over their perception of alliance being forged by the government and the secular Western powers (BBC News as cited in Falola and Heaton, 2008). Thus, such conflicts have emanated from Islam's political rise as a force (Falola and Heaton, 2008), as well as from Sharia's hardline spread from Zamfara State in 1999 to the present thirty-six states (Onishi, 2001b). Esentially, about 5,000 Nigerians have lost their lives in religious clashes between 1999 when the military handed power up to 2001 (Onishi, 2001b), the manifesting of such killings of which, more often than not, involved extremist Muslims targeting and killing Christians and other non-Muslims ("Deadly Rioting," 2000; Koinange, 2001; Onishi, 2000).

The period, however, also saw reprisals in the south, for instance, in Aba where the locals attacked the Hausas following the killings of Igbos in the north as their corpses were brought to Aba (Onishi, 2000). Thus, the data in this study period also evidence the identified two major categories of phenomenal attacks involving targeted, premeditated, or orchestrated killings and assaults; and bloodbath, carnage, pogrom, mayhem, massacres, or barbarism which are identified as closely associated with the proclivity to genocide.

Study Phase V—2006 to Present Evidence

The study's fifth phase from 2006 to present, also evidences increasing killings from Muslim fundamentalism with religious tensions in the country being impacted directly by outside world events (Falola and Heaton, 2008, p. 239). The Danish newspaper cartoons in February 2006, for example, saw week-long violent riots in northern Nigeria which claimed 157 lives in Maiduguri alone (Adekoya, 2009) with mostly Christians killed and thirty churches razed ("Toll Rises," 2006), even as more dozens of lives were lost in other places such as Bauchi, Katsina, and Onitsha (BBC News as cited in Falola and Heaton, 2008, p. 239). As extremist Muslims attacked Christians in Bauchi, twenty-five were killed with the violence fueled by allegation of Koran desecration by a Christian teacher, and in reprisals in Onitsha in the south, responding to the attacks on Christians in the north, thirty mostly northern Muslims were killed and two mosques burned ("Toll Rises," 2006).

This phase also witnessed the killing of about 400 people in Jos, Plateau State, over an election dispute involving Muslim-Christian gang clashes in November 2008. However, in this mayhem launched by armed rioters, churches, Christian businesses, and homes of clergymen were attacked using the electoral results as an excuse (Adekoya, 2009). In this episode also is a wrong media reporting of 300 Muslims being killed by Christians, as the men were shot by security agents when they acted in defiance to an imposed curfew, rather than obeying a "jihad" participation order from the Dilimi area mosque calling all Muslims to loot and burn properties, which ended with about sixteen churches being razed and 100 Christians killed in the crisis, including four or more pastors (CSW, 2008a, para. 3–4). More so, the phase witnessed, in March 2010, the killing of over 500 mostly women and children in an attack by Muslim Fulani machete-wielding hordes on Dogon Na Hauwa, a Christian village ("500 Dead," 2010). This episode, which was a Sunday, over-three-hour orgy, had the victims atrociously entrapped in fishing nets and animal traps and hacked to death as they attempted to flee from their attackers, with the razing of the sleeping victims' straw-thatched mud huts in the wee hours of the morning by the Muslim Fulani assailants first preceding the killing rampage ("500 Dead," 2010).

This last study phase is also equally interlaced with religious upheavals, uprisings, and insurgencies mainly involving the Boko Haram Islamic fundamentalist group which seeks to institutionalize Sharia in Nigeria based on an ideological positioning and an Arabic-translated name that connotes a forbidding or non-acceptance of Western education (Adekoya, 2009). The sect staged attacks in different parts of northern Nigeria beginning with the July 2009 Bauchi attack against security forces who sought to contain them, in which lives were lost even as the violence spread to Borno, Kano, and Yobe states with more lives lost, including some of the sect members and with police stations burned down (Adekoya, 2009). An ensuing bloodbath in Maiduguri, Borno State, saw over 100 people dead (BBC as cited in Adekoya, 2009), with the sect's leader arrested and killed in custody, and in further violence in Bauchi State, churches, mosques, and several houses were razed down with more death toll (Adekoya, 2009). This study period saw the Boko Haram Islamic fundamentalist sect, since this 2009 uprising, becoming more proficient and progressively more sophisticated in confrontation with security forces and attacks on different targets including security agents; symbols of government authority including the United Nations, which was bombed in August 2011, and police stations ("Deadly Christian-Muslim Clash," 2011); Christians and churches (Akau, 2012; Chidiogo, 2011; Ehiabhi, 2012a; Onah et al., 2012; Purefoy, 2010); civilian targets; and schools. For instance, Boko Haram, with its name connoting in the Hausa language a prohibition of Western education, has intensified its attacks, primarily on police and government sites in the region, while also threatening to kill off every Christian living in the North (Mojeed and Nossiter, 2012).

The Boko Haram sect has, particularly in this study phase, repeatedly mounted attacks on churches, including the twenty churches burned down in five northern states in the July 2009 crisis ("Christian Groups," 2009), and the December 2011 Christmas day chain of bombings which struck many churches in various cities (Akau, 2011; "Christmas Carnage," 2011), notably the Christmas day bombing of the Madalla church which had a death toll of forty-three persons and twenty-seven others wounded (Olokor, 2011). There have subsequently been several such bombings and attacks on churches, for example, the January 2012 Boko Haram invasion of a church service of the Deeper Life Christian Church, Nassarawo, Gombe State, killing six and wounding ten others (Ohai, 2012); the February 2012 bombing of the Church of Christ in Nigeria church (COCIN) headquarters in Jos, killing three and wounding thirty-eight others (Abdulkadir, 2012a); the March 2012 bombing of Finbarr's Catholic Church, Jos, killing eleven and wounding twenty-two others (Ehiabhi, 2012a); the Easter Sunday bombing in Kaduna, targeting Christians killing twenty-five people (Akau, 2012); the April 2012 bombing of St. Stephen's Catholic Church in Bayero University, killing fifteen, including two professors (Mgboh, 2012a); and the August 2012 mass shooting at the Deeper Life Church, Okene, Kogi State, by unidentified gunmen, killing nineteen people, including the church pastor ("Nigeria Church Attack," 2012).

Informing the apparent targeting and killing of Christians and razing and/or bombing of churches in the region, is the specific intent to cleanse the north of non-Muslims or *infidels,* and through exclusivity of ideology of destruction of the target victims ideology to be followed by imposition of the ideology of the perpetrator group (Campbell, 2010, Video Series

25), which is equally being played out through exterminations and mass killings. For instance, in the January 2012 Boko Haram attacks on a Christian worship service in Maidiguri in which about fifteen people died, the attacks occurred after the sect had vowed to kill all the Christians that are living in the largely Muslim, northern Nigeria ("Sectarian Attacks Kill 15," 2012). Fundamentalist Muslims, thus, regard Christian presence in the region as a pollution to their *Ummah,* or Islamic community, which essentially requires cleansing or purging by exterminations and mass displacements (Williams, 1997).

Also trailing the motivation to the killings are the identified causal factors which trigger or underlie the phenomena amid a perceived "otherness" threat reflected through ethnic-religious hatreds, rivalries, divisions, and animosities; a North-South split or largely Muslim north and mainly Christian south, that manifests the country's religious divide (Polgreen, 2008); and implemented through annihilation attempts by targeting or forceful conversion of Christians to Islam and ultimatum to southern Christians living in the North to leave the region. While this intent to annihilate is framed from an exclusive ideological positioning on issues with religious dimensions, anti-Western or ideological differences, fundamentalism and religious fervency, and Sharia's institution and implementation, it leads to violations of fundamental rights of Christians and other non-Muslims in the region, particularly the Sharia operative states, as well as to gender segregation abuses. Such violations are further intensified with a bellicose undermining of non-Muslims' opposition and contentions of Sharia's unconstitutionality, amid moves toward imposing Sharia across Nigeria or establishing an Islamic state.

These covert and all-inclusive factors of religious extremism and fundamentalism in manifestations are often, rather, explained away by other wide-ranging causations. Such diverse factors for this study phase include election-related and engineered violence, insurgency, uprising or antigovernment riots, degradation of Islam or misinterpretation and desecration of the Koran, and massacres of Igbos and returning refugees. Also included are reprisal or revenge mission, an instance of which is the Dogon Na Hauwa slaughter of hundreds by Muslim Fulani herdsmen who descended on a sleeping village, macheting and butchering over 500 human lives in a brutal retributory sectarian violence staged against three, mostly Christian, villages (Nossiter, 2010d). Hence, this study phase also identified causal conditions resulting in different degrees and forms of killings and exterminations primarily between extremist Muslims and Christians and other conflict parties which are divided mostly along ethnic and religious lines, with violence unleashed to different target victims in attacks identified among others, in the two major categories involving targeted, premeditated, or orchestrated killings and assaults; and bloodbath, carnage, pogrom, mayhem, massacres, or barbarism are identified as being closely associated with the proclivity to genocide.

SUMMARY

Looking at all these, it is evident that latent genocide is creeping into Nigeria. Rwanda had a similar situation where the latent nature of the genocide was completely missed by the international community. This is a global concern, such instances of which abound as in the genocide in Armenia (Baum, 2008; Levene, 2005b; Rae, 2002), in Lebanon, in Pakistan (Falola, 1998), in the German genocide killing the Jews (Baum, 2008; Gellately and Kiernan, 2003; Hinton, 2002; Levene, 2005b), in Cambodia where Pol Pot aimed to kill off all its educated people (Baum, 2008; Gellately and Kiernan, 2003; Heidenrich, 2001), in the former Yugoslavia's ethnic cleansing—in Bosnia and Kosovo (Falola, 1998; Rae, 2002), and in Rwanda (Baum, 2008; Gellately and Kiernan, 2003; Sternberg and Sternberg, 2008). This latent genocide will destroy the nation and impose Islam as a control mechanism to keep people in bondage which, if Nigeria enters into, will be a replay of the recent Darfurian genocide in Sudan (Sternberg and Sternberg, 2008). Evidentially, the culture of orchestrating vicious genocidal violence as a ploy to push the region's political agenda is an established northern Nigeria practice. Beginning with the Kano riots in 1953, when the Northern People's Congress that was Fulani led, arranged for southerners in Kano to be murdered by hoodlums to clearly convey their message of the non-readiness of the "North" to attain independence by 1957. Next were the massacres of Igbos in 1966, which was aimed to create mayhem and chaos in order to seize back power after Nzeogwu's coup, and also following that were the mass killings of April 2011, accompanied the presidential elections. Thus, Muslim, Fulani-controlled, northern Nigeria has constantly deployed mass organized violence which targets particular religious and ethnic groups to advance its political goals, which practice is scorched earth war (Adebayo, 2012).

Thus, there is a *latent episodic genocide* to the northern Nigeria ethno-religious conflict, a problem where mostly Christians and indeed southerners and other non-Muslim minority ethnic groups in northern Nigeria are being deprived of their right to existence through wanton killings and blatant violations of their fundamental human rights particularly in Sharia operative states. Ultimately the idea is to create an Islamic state. This is a global issue which, if left unchecked, will lead to a manifest open genocide either on the part of the north through a continued attack and killing of Christians and southerners in northern Nigeria while also encroaching southward, or the southerners who would have had enough, may launch a retaliatory offensive to stage off the continued wanton exterminations. If the extremist Muslims succeed, would it be that Nigeria will end? The global community needs to start addressing this latent genocide to avert Rwanda-type genocide in Nigeria.

CONCLUSION

The study has examined the parties to the conflict in the different phases of the conflict and determined its ethno-religious undertones, mainly between ethnic groups along the Muslim and Christian divide. The mechanism that has been employed, as revealed in the strategies adopted in the conflict, as well as investigating the conditions that have led to the conflict. The idea has been to focus on specific intent by examining the motivational factors underlying the killings. Thus, despite the fact that it does not fulfill the generally outlined notion of genocide, it still satisfies the parameters of genocide on the basis of the specific intent of the perpetrators to the killings. The question, thus, is how is it still genocide? While genocide has nothing to do with numbers, the intermittent killings have on occasions involved mass killings with evidences of mass burials and mass graves identified in the conflict. However, proof of genocide is not by numbers but by intentionality, i.e., *dolus specialis*, which is the specific intent to exterminate a people group based on their ethnicity or religion (Campbell, 2012, p. 1; Jones, 2006, p. 21). In the northern Nigeria ethno-religious conflict, there is the specific intent to eliminate Christians and other non-Muslim groups on the basis of religion or ethnicity. And, although the perpetrator groups may and do change from time to time, the underlying motivational factors have remained the same—the intent to eliminate Christians and non-Muslim groups based on an exclusive ideological framing. This genocidal undertone to the conflict has, thus, pitted perpetrator group(s), mostly Islamic fundamentalist sect(s) such as the Maitatsine and the Boko Haram sects, and on occasions Muslim Hausa/Fulani mobs in the north, against varied targeted groups, specifically northern Christians and southerners as the Ibos and Yoruba, as well as other minority non-Muslim ethnic groups in the north.

Thus, beginning with the 1966 pogrom by northern mobs and troops against the Igbos (Osaghae, 1998b), which was also institutionally carried out by the Nigerian government against Biafrans as seen in the one million Biafrans who died of starvation (Garrison, 1968b), and the deliberate targeting and killing of Biafran civilians during the war ("Africa: Race Hatred," 1967; Garrison, 1967b), genocidal episodes have continued unabated in the northern Nigeria ethno-religious conflict up to present (Adebayo, 2012). Furthermore, the region has continued to witness the scourging of churches through bomb attacks and arson, as are evidential in the Boko Haram ongoing scourges of churches in the north, as well as the killings and extermination of Christians and other non-Muslim groups in the region. There has, thus, historically and systematically, been the organizing and killing by perpetrator groups which are mainly Islamic, against victim groups that are Christians or non-Muslims, on the basis of A targeting B with the intent at eliminating B because of their religion and on occasions because of their ethnicity. This is genocide as defined by the United Nations 1948 Genocide Convention on the Prevention and Punishment of the Crime of Genocide (UNGC) (Heidenrich, 2001; Hinton, 2002; Jones, 2006).

Therefore, there are anti-Christian sentiments which are evidential from the motivating factors underlying the killings. Examples of these motivating factors abound, for instance, in the abuses of Islamic Sharia on Christians in northern Nigeria. The appeal of Sharia lends credence to an exclusionary ideology among extremist Muslims that is framed by the ideal to set themselves apart from others by means of an "othering" process, the basis on which genocide can be distinguished (Hinton, 2002, p. 6). In this process, as Hinton observes:

> the boundaries of an imagined community are reshaped in such a manner that a previously "included" group . . . is ideologically recast (almost always in dehumanizing rhetoric) as being outside the community, as a threatening and dangerous "other"—whether racial, political, ethnic, religious, economic, and so on—that must be annihilated. (2002, p. 6)

Thus, in the northern Nigeria ethno-religious conflict, extremist Muslims are seen as wanting to be separate and distinct from others, and on the basis of exclusionary tendencies and Sharia implementation ideals and practices, Christians are being discriminated against, targeted, and exterminated in northern Nigeria, notably by perpetrator, mostly Muslim groups and Islamic fundamentalists (Kendal, 2004). As a result of the primarily religious tonation to the conflict, in addition to the Sharia operative states, the Middle Belt, particularly Jos in Plateau State, which straddles the mostly Muslim north and the predominantly Christian south, has continued to witness escalated killings and attacks. For instance, following the 2004 upsurge of assaults on Christians in the state, Kendal (2004) observes:

> Genuine followers of Jesus Christ are paying a heavy price for this ethnic and religious conflict. Obed Minchakpu reported for Compass Direct on 2 April that the violence in Plateau in late March had resulted in the deaths of 8 pastors and 1,500 Christian believers, and the destruction of 173 churches. Reverend Dr. Alexander Mamdip Lar, President of the Church of Christ in Nigeria (COCIN), reports concerning the Plateau crisis (2 May), "We [COCIN] lost two ordained ministers in Jos and Rim [and] 117 of our churches were destroyed, while six pastors, one ordained minister and hundreds of members were killed in Wase, thus completely obliterating the church there." As he says, the Church in Plateau is "under siege." (para. 26)

However, there are a few instances that might be seen as being in objection to the author's argument that might present as exclusions to this identified pattern of extremist Muslims killing Christians in the region. One such notable exception to the study's identified pattern of Muslim group(s) targeting Christians or non-Muslim group(s) for extermination in the Yelwa massacres of May 2004 where it is reported that Christian militia attacked an essentially Muslim town of Yelwa, killing 630 people (Adekoya, 2009; Reuters; and Agence France-Presse as cited in "Hundreds Die in Attack," 2004).

On this episode, however, the casualty figures were in contestation, with the police estimate put at sixty-seven death toll, and there was warning of the inflating of figures by interested parties ("Hundreds Die in Attack," 2004), even also as "Christians and other non-Muslims insist the death toll is actually sixty-seven or thereabouts and hotly dispute the widely publicized death toll of 630" (CSW, n.d., p. 6). Furthermore, there is also contestation by Christians of the media report of a Christian militia perpetrating the killings on grounds that "there is no such thing as a 'Christian Militia'" (CSW, n.d., p. 1). Thus, on the contrary, the assailants were local, non-Muslim Tarok farmers who, seeking reprieve, had embarked on a retaliatory attack against the violent displacement from their lands by Fulani herders amid government ineptitude in dealing with their plight (CSW, n.d.). Of paramount importance, however, is that reprisal attacks for this Yelwa episode in May 2004 in Kano resulted in about 500 to 600 deaths (put at over 3000 by CAN Kano) even as the state government, aiming to disguise the true number of casualties, gave mass burials to several of the victims, with some thrown into the Challawa River (CAN as cited in CSW, n.d.). More so, local witnesses narrated of truckloads of dead bodies being evacuated, with some of the corpses disposed of by burning them in wells, even as the state government ensured that they were hastily gathered off the streets for mass burial ("The Madness of Kano" as cited in CSW, n.d.).

Furthermore, not every Muslim endorses or supports the violence being perpetrated against Christians in the northern Nigeria ethno-religious conflict, as in the February 2006 cartoon riots in Maiduguri, Borno State, in which

> [s]ources report that a week before the riots rumors were circulating of imminent violence against Christians. Agitators from the Hausa Fulani tribe, who are not indigenous to Borno, were reported to have accused the Kanuri and Shuwa Muslims, who are indigenous to the area, of having been "too quiet" in comparison to Muslims elsewhere who are engaged in a "jihad" against Christianity. Local Christians state that they ignored these rumors, choosing instead to rest on Borno's self-proclaimed reputation as "The Home of Peace" . . .
>
> The violence was organized and systematic. . . . The violence targeted churches, Christians and especially clergymen. The assailants, who were predominantly Hausa Fulani, were said to hail from Kano, Katsina and Sokoto. CSW also heard several reports of indigenous Shuwa and Kanuri Muslims hiding and defending Christians from their attackers. (CSW, 2008b, p. 10)

The study, therefore, mostly demonstrates a constancy of the perpetrator groups as extremist Muslims and the targeted group mainly as non-Muslims or Christians. The periodic nature of the phenomena in the sense that it has been sporadic and episodic has presented latency to the genocidal undertone of the conflict. There is thus evidential proof of genocidal inclination to the northern Nigeria ethno-religious conflict, on the basis of exclusionary ideology, and the determination of specific intent or *'dolus specialis'* to destroy Christians on account of their religious beliefs (Campbell, 2012; Jones, 2006), with the attempt at imposition of the Sharia as the perpetrators' ideology (Campbell, 2010, Video Series 18, 25). Islamization and the institution of Sharia in the region constitute the ideological motivation among the myriad of causal factors to the conflict. Because of the intermittency in the nature of the genocide being perpetuated in the northern Nigeria ethno-religious conflict, however, there has been covertness or latency in recognition of this *episodic genocide,* and this has remained a feature of the conflict for decades. The intermittency and episodic nature of the conflict continues to present a delusion as to what is going on in the region based on a subterfuge presentation of the conflict.

Captured in a schematic form below, figure 10.1 summarizes the conception of the northern Nigeria ethno-religious conflict. This illustrates the vicious circle of attacks and reprisals or counterattacks nature of the conflict which, however, has a covert genocidal undertone that continues to be latent and elusive even to the international community.

With the conceptualization of this latency to the genocidal undertone to the northern Nigeria ethno-religious conflict, the next chapter examines the religious underpinnings in the conflict.

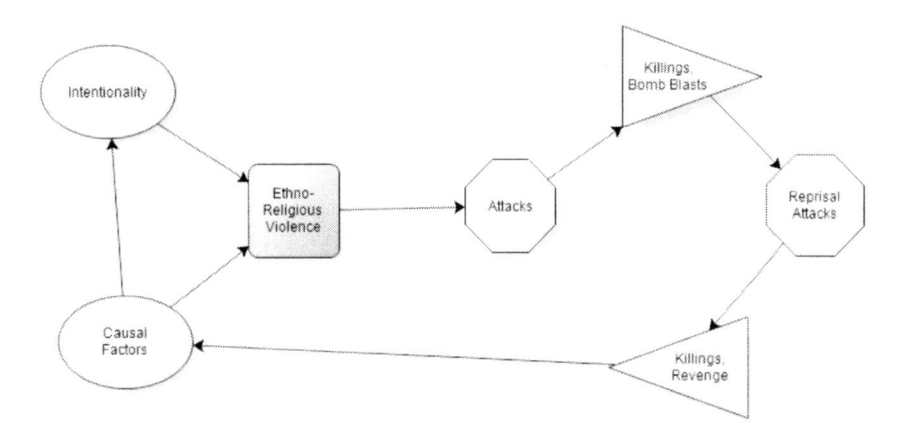

Figure 10.1. Schematic Model of the Northern Nigeria Ethno-Religious Conflict

ELEVEN

Religious Underpinnings in Nigeria's Ethno-Religious Conflict

In addressing the extent to which the interplay between ethnicity and religion helps to foment and escalate the conflict in northern Nigeria, most studies on the issue have taken various perspectives linking the conflict to a mirage of causes. Such multiplicities of conflict causations, however, have remained inexorably and intricately concomitant with the role and underpinnings of religion to the killings. For instance, where ethnicity is identified as the conflict's underlying causation (Osaghae, 1998a), it can be argued that, while ethnocentricity may partially explain the ethno-based dimension to the killings in the north, it does not explain why the perpetrators identify themselves in terms of religion, and kill their victims based on religious identifications. Furthermore, where political factors are seen as orchestrating the conflict (Ukiwo, 2003), the conflict parties in the intermittent killings in the north can be seen, once again, defining themselves on the basis of religion rather than on the basis of the political parties to which they belong, with political motivation also failing to lend credence on why such monstrous killings are not, in turn, experienced in other parts of the country. Establishing the religious undertone to the northern Nigeria ethno-religious conflict, thus, calls for a closer examination of the identified causal and motivational factors to the conflict. Presented in table D1 under appendix D of the study are some over fifty cases of the religious crises in northern Nigeria from 1980 to 2009 (*Newswatch* as cited in Ezeibe, 2009), and reviewing the list, Ezeibe (2009) observes, for instance,

> that most of these conflicts destroyed properties of non-Muslims mainly suggesting that these conflicts want change of property relations between Christians and Muslims where they occurred. Religious conflict became rampant during civilian rule of Obasanjo. Between July

1999 and September 2004 Nigeria recorded 33 different conflicts. (para. 31)

Thus, evidentially, an analysis of the study data has shown causal trigger factors, underlying causation, perceived threat of "otherness," and exclusive ideological framing in different situations and contextual settings, resulting in varying degrees and forms of exterminations and killings primarily between extremist Muslims and Christians, as well as between other conflict parties, but which are mostly divided along ethnic, but also primarily on religious lines, instances of which abound in the study. In the investigation of the November 2008 Jos crisis by Human Rights Watch (HRW), for instance,

> [w]itnesses described . . . how mobs of Muslim youth beat, burned, or bludgeoned to death Christians, in some cases specifically targeting pastors and church officials. One witness from the Yoruba ethnic group said five of his relatives . . . were among 12 Christians burned alive by a mob of Muslims. Other witnesses described how hundreds of Muslim youth besieged and burned churches and homes belonging to Christian families. Church officials reported that seven Christian pastors and church leaders were killed in the violence and that 46 churches were burned. Local community leaders told Human Rights Watch that Muslim mobs burned 133 houses in a predominantly Christian area of the Ali Kazaure neighborhood. (2009, p. 5)

Hence, beginning with the 1966 massacres of Igbos in the north, for instance, which, while fundamentally presenting as ethno-based killings, essentially has religious tonation to the killings with the Igbo victim group basically defined as Christians, their targeting and extermination of which was by mostly Muslim mobs and northern troops (Garrison, 1966c). Further are the Maitatsine religious riots of the 1980s, with over 4,000 people killed in Kano in 1980, and the October 1982 Maiduguri uprising by the sect, with police unofficial toll of 450 deaths, but put at over 1,000 by the locals, while the government official estimate was put at 133 deaths including cult members, civilians, and policemen, although local estimate of officers killed was put at 100 ("100 Nigeria Policemen," 1982; Cowell, 1982; Dash, 1984). The riots culminated with the fanatic February/March 1984 Jimeta, (then) Gongola State uprising in which about 1,000 people were killed (Dash, 1984). Furthermore, in 1985 was the Babangida attempt at enrolling the country into the OIC, for which Christians were reported to have been outraged, even as the period once again saw escalated tensions with the observation of the Muslims' plans to extend the Sharia law in the north to the whole country (Brooke, 1987b). It is thus, evident that Islamic ideological framing underlies much of the excessive bloodletting which continues to occur in northern Nigeria, particularly with the introduction of Sharia in some northern states.

On the characterization of the religious violence in the northern Nigeria ethno-religious conflict, Falola (1998) argues that in

> [t]he heartland of Islam and such traditional cities as Kano and Katsina . . . violence has taken three forms—first, reformists, as in the case of the Shiites in Katsina or the Maitatsine, fighting the state; second, anti-Christian; and third, directed against immigrant Christian settlers, as in Kano. Future conflicts are certain, especially between Muslims and immigrants. [In] Central Nigeria, and cities and towns on the fringes of Hausaland (usually marginalized "pagan" communities in the emirates of the nineteenth century) where violence is both religious and communal, involving confrontations between hegemonic religion (Islam) and ethnicity (Hausa-Fulani) and minority groups defined by ethnicity (Kataf) and minority religion (Christianity). The attempts to assert minority rights, using Christianity as a source of identity, will provoke an Islamic reaction and ensure the continuity of conflict. (p. 280)

Moreover, further towing the argument of religious underpinnings to the conflict, the evidential instances are replete as in the Kafanchan March 1987 Christian-Muslim confrontation. Here again, the triggering event, which supposedly was an erroneous interpretation of the Koran, had an eruption of crisis, the aftermath in which Muslim mobs burned all the churches in Zaria, about seventy-five in number, and threatened to destroy the Wusasa Christian community, if not accepting of Islam (Brooke, 1987a; 1987b). And, as the crisis spread to other cities in the state, a total of 152 churches burned in the region, primarily in Wusasa, Zaria, Kafanchan, Kaduna, and Funtua, relative to five mosques burned (Falola, 1998, p. 185). Additionally, the April 1991 Bauchi State eruption was recognized to have engulfed the state in a religious violence frenzy even as thousands of mainly teenage hoodlums under the cover of religion went on rampage in several cities including Bauchi, with casualty figures mounting, as churches, homes, hotels, and a number of public properties were razed (*Newswatch* as cited in Akaeze, 2009).

Furthermore, there is the instance of the October 1991 Kano killings, where the *Izala* sect initially presumed peaceful demonstration to stop an evangelical crusade being organized for Reinhard Bonnke suddenly turned into a violent Muslim-Christian clash, with a high death toll and casualty figures and loss of enormous property. There was also the beheading of an Ibo trader in December 1994 in Kano with the head paraded on a spike on the streets of Kano after he was accused of Koran desecration (Akaeze, 2009). More so, the study identifies religious riots and upheavals in several other northern cities including Kano, Jos, Wase, Zangon Kataf, Yelwa-Shendam, and Funtua with genocidal killings sometimes with flimsy issues or political difference between opposing faiths sparking off killing orgies as in the communal feud between the Christian, Katafs indigenes, and the Muslim, Hausas in Kaduna State, which assumed religious coloration and spread to other cities in the state

(Akaeze, 2009), with about 500 to 800 people killed in the crisis (Noble, 1992c).

Thus, as Kendal (2004) observes, "Nigeria has seen some radical and devastating retaliatory attacks and rioting by northern Muslims in response to trivial 'Christian' infractions" on occasions, involving accusations of desecration of Islam, the Koran, or the Prophet Muhammad (para. 2). An instance of this is the November 2002 Miss World publication which Muslims saw as disparaging prophet Muhammad, the bloody riot of which "left 200 dead, 1,000 injured, 11,000 homeless and 20 churches destroyed" (para. 2). More so, revenge attacks by the Christian minority groups where they occur are on occasions presented in overwhelming proportions of even more extensive exterminations by Christians, as in the May 2004 Yelwa disputed killings of sixty-seven as against 630 people by "Christian Militia" (CSW, n.d., p. 1). The insidious and escalatory effects of such amplification of casualties on violence-prone hordes and Islamic fundamentalists cannot be overstated. For instance

> [e]ven before the Yelwa massacre, Zamfara state had ordered the destruction of all churches in accordance with its implementation of "Sharia Phase 2." It is possible that the Yelwa massacre will be used to justify all manner of repression and persecution being unleashed upon an already besieged Christian minority. Security has been tightened in the northern city of Bauchi after leaflets were found calling on Muslims to avenge the Yelwa killings and on Christians to leave the region. Security has also been increased in Kaduna as tensions are running high. (Kendal, 2004, para. 6)

Thus, rioting and killings has become a regular feature of northern Nigeria life, and these ensure a state of perpetual, fear-induced submission for the Christian minority in the region (Kendal, 2004).

ANTECEDENTS OF RELIGIOUS UNDERTONES AND RAMIFICATIONS

1. A North-South Split along a Religious, Muslim-Christian Divide

An analysis of the study data reveals a North-South split in Nigeria along a religious fault line of a largely Muslim north with a sizable Christian minority and a predominantly Christian south, each region containing some animist minority. This divide is entrenched and further exacerbated by the country's multiethnic factor and rooted in its history of colonial amalgamation of diverse ethnic groups of different sociocultural, and socioreligious backgrounds into one nation (Aguwa, 1997). Thus, with its over 250 ethnic groupings, the nation's religious divide mirrors geographically a predominantly Christian and few animist south, and a historically mainly Muslim north, in addition to profound political divisions which encompass religious boundaries (Polgreen, 2008).

Hence, there is an in-group/out-group, majority/minority dichotomy based on religious categorization in the country. This dichotomy is evidentially manifest in northern states, particularly in the Sharia operative states where Muslims are in the majority with a government legitimacy that is also Muslim, while Christians are in the minority in such states. The conflict has been most intense in Bauchi, Kano, Kaduna, Sokoto, Taraba, Kebbi, and Plateau states (Ahiante, 2004), as well as in Borno, Zamfara, Katsina, Yobe, Jigawa, Niger, Gombe, and Adamawa (Chidiogo, 2011), all of which are Sharia operative states, excluding Plateau, Adamawa, and Taraba states. The Middle Belt region which straddles the predominantly Christian south and the mostly Muslim north, has continually been a religious and ethnic violence hotbed, with Plateau State, notably Jos, its capital, bearing the brunt (Polgreen, 2008).

Such evidence in the context of the northern Nigeria ethno-religious conflict supports the social identity theory and validates the notion of in-group favoritism and discriminatory feelings against members of the out-group, with both Muslims and Christians projecting negative feelings toward each other. More so, the northern Nigeria ethno-religious conflict resonates negatively nationwide with the conflict being further fed and fueled by such "longstanding mistrust and stereotypes, for example, that the 'Christian south' is pro-West and that the 'Muslim north' is backward and conservative" (Falola, 1998, p. 280). There is, therefore, polarization and religious divide between Christians and Muslims as opposing groups in the region, and by extension in the country.

This evidence has far-reaching implications for the conflict in the sense that tensions involving northern indigenes tend to polarize along a Muslim-Christian fault line other than on cases of intraconflicts between different Muslim sects, while also additionally polarizing along Muslim north and Christian south lines where both northern as well as southern Christians are involved, on occasions, with the Christian Igbos as prime targets. Polarization, thus, accounts for the conflict causation factor of perceived threat of the "otherness" as identified in the study data which manifests in ethnic-religious hatreds, rivalries, divisions, and animosities, as well as a North-South split or largely Muslim north and mainly Christian south, as the data analysis reveal.

2. The Almajiri System in Northern Nigeria

The system of the *almajirai* (plural) known as "catechumens" is practiced in northern Nigeria, and used by "Islamic preachers and leaders . . . for recruitment," involving an established Islamic practice whereby young Muslim boys are attached to Qur'anic teachers with whom they learn Arabic and the Koran, and about Islam (Falola, 1998, p. 148). Such *almajirai,* some of very tender ages, leave their homes sometimes to distant places to learn with the system observed as allowing "for indoctrination into particular beliefs and loyalty to a leader, who became a father figure" (Falola, 1998, p. 148). For instance, Marwa, who led the Maitatsine sect, had many of these *almajiri* (singular) boys, many of age ranges of ten to fourteen, and had a large following which he had to take care of, providing free houses in which they squatted, with their needs being rather small in view of their panhandling. The *almajirai,* in turn, were by law permitted to beg on the roads, at street corners, and in the mosques, keeping part proceeds of alms collected, and surrendering some portion to their leader (Falola, 1998). The tradition is fraught with corruption and abuse as "many preachers exploited young children for money" (Falola, 1998, p. 148), imposing weekly levies on *almajirai* with parents who could pay, while others are sent to beg for alms on the streets and to bring back part proceeds to their preacher-guardians (Falola, 1998). Thus:

> With urbanization, more and more children are sent to schools far from their families, and millions of *Almajiri* children are required to beg for alms (*almajiranchi*) to pay for their upkeep. While this system is ostensibly designed to prepare them for some of the hardships they may encounter later in life, in a context of urbanization and increasing poverty, it is open to abuse and may foster criminality. In cities like Kano and Kaduna, many of the alms-begging street children have graduated into *Yandaba,* adolescent groups that once served to socialize teenagers into adulthood but have now, in many cases, transformed into gangs. In 2005, the National Council for the Welfare of the Destitute estimated there were 7 million *Almajirai* children in northern Nigeria, mostly in the far northern states. (International Crisis Group, 2010, p. 10)

Essentially, the *almajiri* system forms the bedrock of the northern Nigeria ethno-religious conflict as it provides a ready supply of fundamentalists and Muslim mobs that resort to violence and suicide bombing attacks at the flimsiest opportunity. Such violence and mayhem are often played out either by looting for economic reasons as occasioned by their sprawling poverty levels and deprivation, or through elite mobilization of the *almajiri* masses to occasion riots, wanton killings, and destruction in the north, for political agendas. As the study data reveal, significantly contributory to the conflict are the underlying socioeconomic factors of poverty and unemployment. The *almajirai* in the north, facing a lack of education and means to gainful employment, plod the streets and are prone to violence and looting at the slightest opportunity even without provocation, as in the Maitatsine followership, whose ranks swell from the readily available support of unemployed youths (Cowell, 1982). The negating impact of this *almajiri* factor to the conflict cannot be overstated. For instance, following the February/March 1984 Maitatsine riots in which over 1,000 people were killed in Yola, including some members of the sect, since 1980, the sect's ability to replenish its membership from the drove of peasant-youths who are daily flocking to cities in the North has worried Nigerian officials, as has the government's inability at predicting the venue of the next breakout of violence (Dash, 1984).

Furthermore, in the March 1987 Kaduna State crisis that was sparked off by the alleged misinterpretation of the Koran in a Kafanchan Christian crusade, which spread to several cities in the state with over 152 churches razed in Kaduna, Kafanchan, Funtua, Wusasa, and Zaria (Falola, 1998, p. 185), notably, where the city's entire seventy-five churches were burned down, the violence was attributed to small boys whose assimilated strong minds have been influenced by the influx of Iranian ideas into the nation (Brooke, 1987b). In this killing episode, close to 1,000 of the rioters were detained, even as visits to Kaduna and Zaria police headquarters saw hundreds of youths aged between eight and sixteen years squatted in police premises, waiting for their cases to be disposed of (Brooke, 1987b).

More so, the *almajiri* factor in the northern Nigeria ethno-religious conflict is even more compounded by "[t]he presence of Chadian and other 'jihadis' from neighboring countries [which] has been a constant feature during outbreaks of communal violence in several northern and central states since 2000" (CSW, 2008b, p. 10). This foreign jihadist involvement intensifies the suicidal underpinnings of the perpetrators, while plausibly also adding an Al Qaeda dimension to the conflict (Jaynes, 1981; Mshelizza, 2011; Nossiter, 2010d; Shuaibu, 2012). The *almajiri* system, thus, serves as fodder to the inferno of killings in the northern Nigeria ethno-religious conflict, by readily providing violence-prone Muslim mobs and fundamentalists, which has continued to sustain and escalate the conflict.

3. Government Culpability, Complicity/Ineptitude, and Extrajudicial Killings

The playing out of genocidal inclinations to the northern Nigeria ethno-religious conflict do not occur in a vacuum, but rather within a context and ambit of the state(s) and governmental forces in which the exterminations and killings take place. Where not directly the genocide orchestrator as in this northern Nigeria conflict, a state's intervening positioning may either help to abet or escalate conflict through acts of complicity or omissions as extrajudicial killings, government ineptitude, and press censorship or manipulation. Thus, "genocide was generally, although perhaps not exclusively, committed under the direction or . . . with the benign complicity of the State where it took place" (Schabas, 2000, p. 1). The involvement and/or seeming ineptitude of various state governments in which wanton killings have been and are still being carried out in the northern Nigeria ethno-religious conflict tend to support this argument. For instance, in the 1966 Igbo massacres in the north, perpetrators in the carnages were civilian or Muslim mobs—mainly Hausas, and northern troops—as in Kano where soldiers mutinied to participate in the Igbo killings. Siollun (2009) observes that the October 1, 1966, massacre was possibly "the worst of the mutiny," even as "[t]he participation of soldiers with firearms greatly increased the kill rate, and "[s]everal thousand Igbos were killed that day alone in Kano due to the combined efforts of the 5th battalion and civilian mobs" (p. 135). More so, on this 1966 Igbo massacre and the ensuing Biafra war which "was presented as a genocidal one waged by the Muslims of Northern Nigeria who had declared a *jihad* to exterminate the Igbos from the face of the earth," (Osaghae, 1998b) recognizes "the massacres of Igbos in the North, as well as the strategies of economic blockade and starvation pursued throughout the war" as lending credence to the conflict's genocidal underpinnings (Osaghae 1998b, p. 66).

The study also found several incidences of extrajudicial killings in the course of the intermittent northern Nigeria killings, which are deliberate, unlawful killings that are executed by a government's order, or with its acquiescence or complicity, with unlawful killings involving extrajudicial executions in addition to such other killings which result from law enforcement officials' excessive usage of force, all such killings of which violate a country's constitutionally guaranteed right of life (Amnesty International, 2009b). The Nigerian Police Force (NPF) has responsibility for enforced disappearances, varied unlawful killings, and extrajudicial executions of hundreds every year, most cases of which are neither investigated nor punished, with the victims' families often not ably seeking redress nor justice, while public anger at the country's high incidence of crime is exploited by the police for justifying their actions (Amnesty International, 2009b). Between 2000 and 2007, over 8,000 civilians are reported to have been killed by the Nigerian police force (Williams, 2011, p. 44). In the October 2001 extrajudicial killings in Zaki Biam following the death of nineteen soldiers in the Tiv/Jukun crisis, for instance, army officers were observed to have gone to the surrounding area of Zaki Biam in Benue State, searching for those responsible for the killing as well as to recover weapons that had been stolen. These soldiers, who had over the years been stationed in the area to quell the Tiv/Jukun intercommunal violence, have on October 22, fallen upon the civilians, killing more than 130 people in a few days, including women and children, by deliberately shooting and shelling indiscriminately, in reprisal for the nineteen soldiers who had been killed in the area two weeks earlier. Men were reported to have been summarily shot, after assembling them from several villages around the area (Amnesty International, 2002).

The study, thus, identifies other perpetrator groups as security agents, soldiers, the army/military, and Hausa/Northern troops, many of which involve extrajudicial killings, as in the May 2004 Kano killings, which occurred in retaliation to the Yelwa killings of May 2, 2004, in which CAN noted that some Muslim policemen in brutality, "intentionally and indiscriminately shot and killed many Christians in Sabon-Gari and other parts of the state" (CSW, n.d., p. 7). Furthermore, in the November 2009 sectarian clash between Muslims and Christians in Jos, Plateau State, Human Rights Watch also reports that

> deadly clashes between Muslim and Christian mobs and the excessive use of force by security forces left hundreds dead in Jos, Plateau State. [Also] Muslim and Christian authorities . . . collectively documented the deaths of more than 700 people in the two days of violence. In responding to the inter-communal violence, the Nigerian police and military were implicated in more than 130 arbitrary killings, mostly of young Muslim men from the Hausa-Fulani ethnic group. The vast majority of the killings by the police and military came . . . the same day that Plateau State Governor Jonah Jang issued a "shoot-on-sight" order to security forces. (2009, p. 1)

Furthermore, in the May 2011 postelection rioting in which about 800 people were killed in three days, in the twelve northern states of Kano, Kaduna, Borno, Bauchi, Sokoto, Katsina, Zamfara, Yobe, Jigawa, Gombe, Niger, and Adamawa, estimates by Human Rights Watch indicate that about 180 people were killed in Zaria and Kaduna, and the neighboring suburbs. Additionally reported were incidences of unlawful battery of citizens by army officials and the police, in their response to the sectarian violence and riots, with such cases reported in Bauchi, Kaduna, and Gombe, of which eight residents were presumably killed by soldiers and police in Kaduna and Zaria. The Human Rights Watch documented eight incidences of soldiers and police in Kaduna and Zaria allegedly killing unarmed residents unlawfully, with the agency also receiving credible reports of several other incidences (Chidiogo, 2011).

There is, therefore, culpability, complicity, and/or government ineptitude in several northern states with the attendant exacerbating effect such positioning has on the conflict. In the May 2004 retaliatory attacks for the Yelwa killings, the Christian Association of Nigeria (CAN) observes, for instance, that Muslims murdered 1,400 Christians in Kano in two days, while some other thousands were displaced with their homes as well as property looted and destroyed. No one was prosecuted for the killings which were premeditated, with the Kano State governor, Ibrahim Shekarau recognized to have had prior knowledge of the plan to massacre Christians in the state, and even given his approval. According to CAN, the deed is thus, done while the terrorists who perpetrated the killings walk the streets as free men (Ahiante, 2004).

Evidences of government ineptitude abound in the northern Nigeria ethno-religious conflict as the study data reveal. More so, such ineptitude of government is further compounded by the lack of accountability or prosecution of perpetrators of the ongoing heinous killings in the region, while the victims, who are mostly "Christians, rarely, if ever receive compensation for losses sustained during violence" (CSW, 2008b, p.13). Accordingly:

> In northern Nigeria perpetrators and organizers of religious violence are rarely, if ever, brought to justice. This lack of accountability has created a climate of impunity that encourages the continuation of such violence. In addition, the fact that violence erupts regularly and continues unchecked and its perpetrators are never brought to justice in turn causes a buildup of resentment of a kind that eventually fosters retaliation. (CSW, 2008b, p. 13)

4. Problems of Indigenous/Settler Delineations

The evidences in the study also reveal the problems of indigene and settler delineation as also compounding, sustaining, and exacerbating the northern Nigeria ethno-religious conflict. For instance, in Jos, Plateau State, which is in central Nigeria where "1,000 people died in religious riots in 2001, and in 2004 hundreds more were killed in a nearby city of Yelwa," most of the original inhabitants of the state emanated from tribes that are virtually Christians and animists, with the grazing pastures and farmlands attracting migrants over the centuries, particularly, the Muslim Hausas and Fulani from the largely dry north (Polgreen, 2008). The indigene/settler problem in northern Nigeria, particularly in Jos as well as in Taraba State between the Jukuns and the Tivs (Noble, 1992a), has occasioned episodes of attacks and counterattacks as a result of which the conflict has become entrenched and deeprooted. In addition to religious and political divide in the country, there are also other conflicts over political power and land, which are frequently intertwined, due to traditional customs that place indigenous peoples' rights over migrants' rights, with religion usually always serving proxy for such grievances (Polgreen, 2008).

Hence, in the investigation of the November 2008 crisis in which over 700 people were killed in two days of intercommunal violence between Hausa-Fulani Muslims and Christians in Jos, Plateau State, the Human Rights Watch (2009) observes that

> among the root causes of much of the inter-communal violence in Nigeria are government policies that discriminate against "non-indigenes"—people who cannot trace their ancestry to the original inhabitants of an area—essentially relegating millions of Nigerians to the status of second-class citizens. State and local governments throughout Nigeria have enacted policies that deny those designated as non-indigenes access to some of the most important avenues of socio-economic mobility. . . . As poverty and unemployment have both become more widespread and severe in Nigeria, competition for scarce opportunities to secure government jobs, education, and political patronage has intensified dramatically. Religious, political, and ethnic disputes often

serve as mere proxies for the severe economic pressures that lie beneath the surface. (p. 3)

5. The International Media Dimension

The escalatory influence of media reportage on the northern Nigeria ethno-religious conflict, with particular emphasis on some international media, cannot be overemphasized. For instance, in the May 2004 Yelwa killings which were carried out by a Christian militia, " . . . the term 'Christian Militias' was widely published by the international media, fuelling the perception of a planned conspiracy against Muslims in Plateau State, and rendering Christian leaders vulnerable to prosecution on false grounds" (CSW, n.d., p. 12). Furthermore, on the attack's reported death toll of 630 in dispute, "this widely publicized estimate served to heighten Muslim anger, guaranteeing a violent reaction" (CSW, n.d., p. 2). Thus, as reports of the Yelwa incident of over 600 Muslims massacred reached Kano, a notable religious tension hotbed, there was an orgy of killings of Christians by Muslims in a seeming reprisal on the Yelwa incidence as irate Muslims hunted "nonbelievers," killed, and burned them (Kendal, 2004, para. 21). The toll for this Kano episode was estimated at about 500 to 600, mostly Christians killed in two days of Muslim rioting (Adekoya, 2009). However, the death toll estimate for this Kano incidence is put at about 3,000 by Christians, who also decry the reporting bias of some international media on the episode (CSW, n.d.).

Additionally, in the November 2007 killing of about 400 people in Jos, Plateau State, over an election dispute involving Muslim-Christian gang clashes (Adekoya, 2009), the CSW, arguing on Christians' resentment of the international media's inaccurate and biased events reporting, observed that even as the voting ended peacefully, violence started before the results were announced, with armed rioters attacking churches, Christian businesses, and homes of clergymen, launching a mayhem using the electoral results as an excuse (CSW, 2008a). Moreover, in this November 2007 Jos conflict, there was a wrong reporting of about 300 Muslims who were killed by Christians, with their bodies deposited in a mosque. The men were shot as they launched fresh attacks in defiance to the authorities' imposed night curfew, while also staging a large-scale unsuccessful attack on police barracks. Thus, "the men died while obeying orders from a mosque in the Dilimi area, which was using its loudspeakers to instruct all Muslims to defy the authorities, participate in the 'jihad', loot properties for money and then burn them" (CSW, 2008a, para. 3). Additionally, about 16 churches were burned down, with the death toll of Christians killed in the attack put at about 100, including four or more pastors shot dead, one of the Church of Christ in Nigeria (COCIN), another of the Evangelical Church of West Africa (ECWA), and two others (CSW, 2008a).

CONCLUSION

The study has examined the northern Nigeria conflict, focusing on the parties in the different phases of the conflict, and determined its ethno-religious undertones as mainly between ethnic groups along a Muslim/Christian divide. The mechanism that has been employed as revealed in the strategies adopted in the conflict, as well as investigating the conditions that have led to the conflict, have also been examined. The idea has been to focus on specific intent by examining the motivational factors underlying the killings, and while the conflict may not fulfill the generally outlined notion of genocide, it still satisfies the parameters of genocide on the basis of the specific intent of the perpetrators to the killings. While genocide also has nothing to do with numbers, the intermittent killings have on occasions involved mass killings with evidences of mass burials and mass graves identified in the conflict. However, proof of genocide is not by numbers but by intentionality, or the *specific intent* to exterminate a people group based on their ethnicity or religion (Campbell, 2012; Jones, 2006). In the northern Nigeria ethno-religious conflict, there is the specific intent to eliminate Christians and other non-Muslim groups on the basis of religion or ethnicity. And, although the perpetrator groups may and do change from time to time, the underlying motivational factors have remained the same—the intent to eliminate Christians and non-Muslim groups based on an exclusive ideological framing.

Thus, beginning with the 1966 pogrom by northern mobs and troops against the Igbos (Osaghae, 1998b), which was also institutionally carried out by the Nigerian government against Biafrans as in the starvation to death of over one million and the deliberate targeting and killing of Biafran civilians during the war ("Africa: Race Hatred," 1967; Garrison, 1967b, 1968b), and up to the present, genocidal episodes have continued unabated in the northern Nigeria ethno-religious conflict (Adebayo, 2012). Furthermore, the Northern region has continued to witness the scourging of churches through bomb attacks and arson, as are evident in the Boko Haram ongoing scourges of churches in the north, as well as the killings and extermination of Christians and other non-Muslim groups in the region. Thus, the study evidences anti-Christian sentiments which derive from the motivating factors underlying the killings. Examples of these motivating factors abound, for instance, in the abuses of Islamic Sharia on Christians in northern Nigeria. The appeal of Sharia lends credence to an exclusionary ideology among extremist Muslims that is framed by the ideal to set themselves apart from others by means of an "othering" process, the basis on which genocide can be distinguished (Hinton, 2002, p. 6).

Hence, in the northern Nigeria ethno-religious conflict, extremist Muslims want to be separate and distinct from others, and on the basis of exclusionary tendencies and Sharia implementation ideals and practices,

Christians and other non-Muslim groups are being discriminated against, targeted, and exterminated in northern Nigeria, notably by perpetrators that are mostly Muslim groups and/or Islamic fundamentalists (Kendal, 2004). As a result of the primarily religious tonation to the conflict, the Middle Belt, particularly Jos in Plateau State, which straddles the mostly Muslim north and the predominantly Christian south, as well as the Sharia operative states, notably, Bauchi, Borno, Kaduna, Kano, Taraba, and Yobe, has continued to witness escalated killings and attacks on Christians. In essence, there has historically and systematically been the organizing and killing by perpetrator groups which are mainly Islamic, against victim groups that are Christians or non-Muslims, on the basis of A targeting B with the intent at eliminating B because of their religion and on occasions because of their ethnicity. This is genocide as defined by the United Nations 1948 Genocide Convention on the Prevention and Punishment of the Crime of Genocide (UNGC) (Heidenrich, 2001; Hinton, 2002; Jones, 2006).

The genocidal undertone to the conflict has pitted perpetrator group(s), mostly Hausa/Fulani Muslims, as well as Islamic fundamentalists including Maitatsine and Boko Haram sects, against varied targeted groups, specifically northern Christians and southerners as the Ibos and Yoruba, as well as the Tivs and other minority non-Muslim ethnic groups in the north. On the basis of this determination of specific intent to destroy Christians on account of their religious beliefs or ethnicity, there is, thus, proof of genocidal inclination to the northern Nigeria ethno-religious conflict (Campbell, 2012; Jones, 2006). There is also the attempt to impose Sharia as the perpetrators' ideology following the destruction of the targeted Christian group's ideology (Campbell, 2010, Video Series 18, 25). Islamization and the institution of Sharia in the region, thus, constitute the ideological motivation among the myriad conflict causalities.

While there are few exclusions to the study's identified pattern of Muslim group(s) targeting Christians or non-Muslim group(s) for extermination, as in the Yelwa massacres of May 2004 by a Christian militia, which episode the casualty figures and reported perpetrator group were in contestation by a Christians on grounds of the non-existence of a "Christian Militia" in the region (CSW, n.d., p. 1), most other such episodes are more often than not, mainly retaliatory or revenge attacks by Christians groups in the region, as well as reprisal attacks on Hausa/Fulani Muslims in some southern states.

While also, it is not every Muslim who endorses or supports the violence being perpetrated against Christians in the northern Nigeria ethnoreligious conflict, the study mostly, however, demonstrates a constancy of the perpetrator groups as extremist Muslims and the targeted group as non-Muslims or Christians. Thus, there is an *episodic genocide* to the northern Nigeria ethno-religious conflict, a problem where Christians and indeed southerners and other non-Muslim minority ethnic groups in northern Nigeria are being deprived of their right to existence through wanton killings and blatant violations of their fundamental human rights, particularly in Sharia operative states. Ultimately, the idea is to create an Islamic state. The periodic nature of the phenomena in the sense that it has been sporadic and episodic has presented latency to the genocidal undertone of the conflict.

Hence, because of the intermittency in the nature of the genocide being perpetrated in the northern Nigeria ethno-religious conflict, there has been covertness or latency in the recognition of this *episodic genocide*, and that has remained a feature of the conflict for decades. The intermittency and episodic nature of the conflict continues to present a delusion on what is going on in the region based on a subterfuge presentation of the conflict. This is a global issue which, if left unchecked, will lead to a manifest open genocide either on the part of the north as they continue to attack and kill off Christians and southerners in northern Nigeria while also encroaching southward, or southerners who would have had enough may launch a retaliatory offensive to stave off the continued wanton exterminations of Christians and southerners alike. Would Nigeria cease to exist if the extremist Muslims succeed? The global community should begin to address this latent episodic genocide to avert Rwanda-type genocide in Nigeria.

In line with this frame of reference, the next final and chapter proffers some resolution measures to address the northern Nigeria ethno-religious conflict.

Part III

Resolution Considerations

TWELVE
Challenges, Prospects, and Prescriptive Recommendations

Nigeria as a "regional giant," presents the plausibility of affecting states in the neighboring West Africa region by its internal religious politics (Chalk, 2004). The prevalence of this conflict has been in northern Nigeria, where it has persisted for decades between Muslims and Christians (Ibrahim, 1989, 1991; Osaghae, 1998b), primarily in the Middle Belt region, notably Jos, Plateau, and such other northern states as Kano, Bauchi, Kaduna, Katsina, and Borno, notably, Maiduguri, Yobe, and Adamawa State (Falola, 1998; Falola and Heaton, 2008). While the conflict has continued to manifest in sporadic genocidal killings and exterminations, primarily of Christians in these northern states (Falola, 1998), there is the likelihood of a spill-over effect into neighboring states in West Africa.

Nationally, the northern Nigeria ethno-religious conflict has exacerbated the polarization in the country with sociopolitical, socioeconomic, and socioreligious relationships being defined in terms of the mainly Muslim north, and the largely Christian south, with the Christian/Muslim evenly balanced Middle Belt or central region straddling across the north and the south, constituting the battle grounds for Islam's jihadist encroachment southward. The ramifications of this encroachment cannot be gainsaid, considering that since the institution of Sharia by its twelve operative northern states from 1999, over 50,000 lives have been lost (CSW, n.d.). Accordingly, "[f]or many non-Muslims in northern and central Nigeria daily life consists of a veneer of normality that barely conceals an underlying reality of chronic discrimination and tension which periodically erupts into deadly, but organized, violence" (CSW, n.d., para. 1).

Intensifying the nation's polarization further are the policies of "Northernization" in the regional era, and "Islamization" and Sharia implementation in the contemporary period, which has consistently been pursued by the predominantly Muslim north since Nigeria's independence in 1960. These policies align with Sudan's exclusive "Arabization" and "Islamization" policies which Adar (2001) identifies (p. 86; Deng, 2001, para. 3). The complication of Islamization for non-Muslims is their subjugation to Muslim rule, as in the Islamic conquest of the early centuries in which the *jihad* or holy war served under Islamic jurisdiction, as territory conquering and controlling means, even as contemporary Muslim leaders use *jihad* as a propaganda and mobilization tool in the face of external or internal threats (Adar, 2001). Islamization is thus being used by the northern leadership and elites "as a religio-political tool" for promoting unity and a means of survival, and hence constituting for the north "an important rallying point or mobilization tool" as was the case in Sudan (Adar, 2001, p. 105; Deng, 2001).

Islamization policy prohibits conflict resolution, and has indeed been a serious impediment to the forging of religious tolerance and coexistence between Muslims and Christians in northern Nigeria, and by extension between the north and the south, with Christians obviously not accepting of "its implied religious and political superiority and domination" (Adar, 2001, p. 105). While not applicable to all Muslims at large, Islamization, particularly to Muslim fundamentalists embodies divisive, exclusionary ideological traits that involve the destruction of the ideology of the targeted group, and the imposition of the perpetrator group's ideology (Campbell, 2010, Video Series 25). Thus, the country's ethnoreligious divide inhibits the establishment of a national identity, given the exclusionism of Islamization and Sharia, with the North/South divergent perspectives preventing its formation as in southern Sudan, which was persistently rejecting Islamization policy "because it is exclusionary and inherently discriminatory" (Adar, 2001, p. 105). Islamization policy, where pursued whether or not formally institutionalized, negates the essence of national identity in a pluralistic nation such as Nigeria, and according to Adar (2001) "the policy is a fallacy" to the extent "that it renders the process of unity of the north and the south nugatory" (p. 105).

Globally, the northern Nigeria ethno-religious conflict poses its challenges, even as the study's conclusions lend credence to the conception of genocidal proclivity and its covertness in situations of genocidal intermittency. Establishing genocidal inclinations to the northern Nigeria conflict essentially dislodges the latency of such undertones that have persisted as a result of the episodic and intermittent nature of the killings for decades. Genocide, involving the targeted destruction of the *other* on the basis of their religion and on occasions on the basis of their ethnicity, is occurring, the intervention for which is stipulated in the Genocide Convention guiding the conduct of nations. The genocidal undertone to the conflict is thus a global issue that needs to be addressed by the international community, as it might lead to a manifest open genocide on either side—on the part of the north as they continue to attack and kill off Christians and southerners in northern Nigeria while also encroaching southward in their ploy to create an Islamic state, or the southerners who may launch their own offensives to stave off the continued attacks from the north. And, if these northern extremist Muslims succeed, would that portend an end to Nigeria? It is therefore of paramount importance that the global community begins to address this *latent episodic genocide* to avert South Sudan or Rwanda type genocide in Nigeria. The genocidal undertones to the conflict present an element of urgency for intervention in the conflict to prevent further escalation and stem the genocidal killings in northern Nigeria. The international community should thus reconnoiter what is happening in northern Nigeria in the wanton extermination of Christians and non-Muslims which has been episodic and, thus, latent in manifestation, *and* intervene.

CONFLICT RESOLUTION PROSPECTS

It appears that throughout the period over which the northern Nigeria ethno-religious conflict has spanned, the adoption of a military solution has usually been the case, which solution has often not been the best option as can be seen in the repeated incidences of extrajudicial killings in varying instances of the conflict. One such instance which witnessed the starvation and murdering of civilians by the Nigerian army in the Biafra war led to the establishment of the French-based Doctors without Borders or Médecins sans Frontières, a medical humanitarian aid organization, whose deployed volunteer medical personnel realized the blockading Nigerian forces' deliberate tactics of killing everyone, including hospital staff, nurses, and doctors (Bortollotti, 2004). Employing a military solution to the conflict is likely to continue exacerbating rather than ameliorating the killings in the region, even as there is the need to curb the widespread phenomenon of extrajudicial killings by security forces through close investigations of such allegations with due prosecution of the involved security officers. More so, prominent human rights organizations in Nigeria and Amnesty International have called for an urgent cessation of unlawful and arbitrary killings by security officers in Nigeria, such acts of which are carried out under varying situations, and on occasions, in response to the Boko Haram attacks and bombings in the north, even as Amnesty International was acknowledged to have opposed such abhorrent killings by security officers as well as by the Islamic Boko Haram sect (Amnesty International, 2009a, 2009b, 2011).

Essentially, the northern Nigeria ethno-religious conflict is entrenched and protracted involving two powerful groups with two powerful positions maintained between these two groups, amid a myriad of complex underlying causal factors that are historical, sociopolitical, socioeconomic, and sociocultural, all of which are played out in a religious framework. Although there have been the introduction of collaborative efforts in some areas in attempt at conflict resolution, the conflict has continued unabated as a result of the two powerful positioning of these two groups. In Jos Plateau State, for instance, following the 2001 riots, interfaith commissions were set up with aims at relationship building between the different faiths, as well as between ethnic groups, with its years of community bridge-building continuously being threatened by further eruptions of violence, as observed in the November 2008 crisis in the area (Polgreen, 2009).

Thus, any attempt at conflict resolution would be one that aims at dislodging the entrenched underlying and delineating factors which feed on nonacceptance and intolerance between the two groups. There is the need for tolerance and acceptance in diversity in a multiethnic, multicultural, as well as multi-religious society such as Nigeria, and the north particularly, for such dislodgement of the entrenched divisive perception of differences to be achieved. Tolerance and acceptance in diversity is an ideal that can be fostered through dialogue and collaboration between the two groups as represented by their national bodies, such as the Jama'tu Nasril Islam (JNI) for the Muslims and the Christian Association of Nigeria (CAN) for Christians.

PRESCRIPTIVE RECOMMENDATIONS

Specific peace resolution efforts that would help engender the collaboration of the ideals of negotiation and dialogue to resolve the conflict would include the following:

International and Local Effort

This will be a collaborative effort that would involve the convening of a national and international group of interested individuals everywhere to meet in Nigeria to explore the prospects of resolving the conflict. The plan would be to dialogue with these contending extremist groups to practically ask them, "What is it that you want?" and to see if there is a way to answer and redress their demands or grievances in order to put an end to the wanton killings. In the event of ensuing difficulty, the interested group could serve as an advisory body to reconnoiter and proffer recommendations for policy formulations that will serve to eliminate the problem of religious intolerance in the region, and put an end to the killings.

Nigerian-Led International Effort

This will be a Nigerian-led effort that would also involve the convening of various peace-loving individuals, nationally and internationally to meet in a neutral place outside Nigeria, for instance, in China, France, or South Africa, to specifically inquire from the orchestrating conflict parties, to again ask, "What is it that you want?" "What do you want to happen to stem the killings?" And, following their dialoguing and plausible negotiations with such warring parties, the intermediary group would then take back their recommendations to Nigeria for implementation.

Dialogue in Economic Advancement with Religious Extremists

Inequities and the perception of marginalization amid perverse corruptive tendencies in Nigeria has also been one of the pivotal factors that breeds discontent and fuels the looting, killing, and maiming in the region, with property worth billions of Naira continuously being razed down by religious fundamentalists. A dialogue process on economic advancement should be put in place by the Nigerian government to economically educate these extremists through looking at examples like Saudi Arabia, which is so economically stabilized, notwithstanding its Islamic disposition. Also aligning with this recommendation is the need to streamline the prodigious corruption and the attendant marginalization in Nigeria, given that curbing corruption will reduce the widespread discontent as well as plausibly stem the killings. Further linked to the economic consideration is the necessity to address the problems of settler/non-indigene discriminatory practices as existing in Kaduna, Plateau, Taraba, and such other applicable states through legislation by the national government with a nationwide coverage.

Plausible State Breakup

In the event that these wanton killings continue, the United Nations can carve out a portion of the country and give the extremist fundamentalist Muslims in the region a state of their own, to satiate their demands for an Islamic state, as well as stem the killings. While the idea of state breakup may be hard for Nigerians who have lived all their lives in the north, it would be a tenable option if nothing else succeeds in putting a halt to the exterminations. However, only a small portion (say about a quarter to one-third) of the country would be carved out for them since it is only the extremist Muslims who are vying for an Islamic state that would have their own state, while all others who sanction and advocate coexistence and religious pluralism can remain in Nigeria as they so elect. The new state so carved out would, however, be placed under genocide watch, and if the killings continue, the rest of the country can go to war with them and subdue them.

Adoption of Genocide Prevention and Intervention Measures

In the final analysis, most essential, is the need for the urgent adoption of genocide prevention and intervention measures in the northern Nigeria ethno-religious conflict to curb its genocidal manifestations and halt the killings. The adoption of such measures will be preemptive, given the international community's prerogative for human rights prevention and punishment. A clarion call for intervention is thus being made on the global community to stop the *latent episodic genocide* in the northern Nigeria ethno-religious conflict to avert South Sudan or Rwanda type genocide in Nigeria.

Appendixes

Appendix A
Maps of Nigeria

Map 1: Nigerian Administrative Borders: Regions in 1966 and States in 2010 to Present. Nigerian Administrative Borders: Regions in 1966 and States in 2010 to Present (International Crisis Group, 2010, p. 29). Reprinted with the permission of International Crisis Group.

Maps of Nigeria

States of Nigeria
1967 - 1976

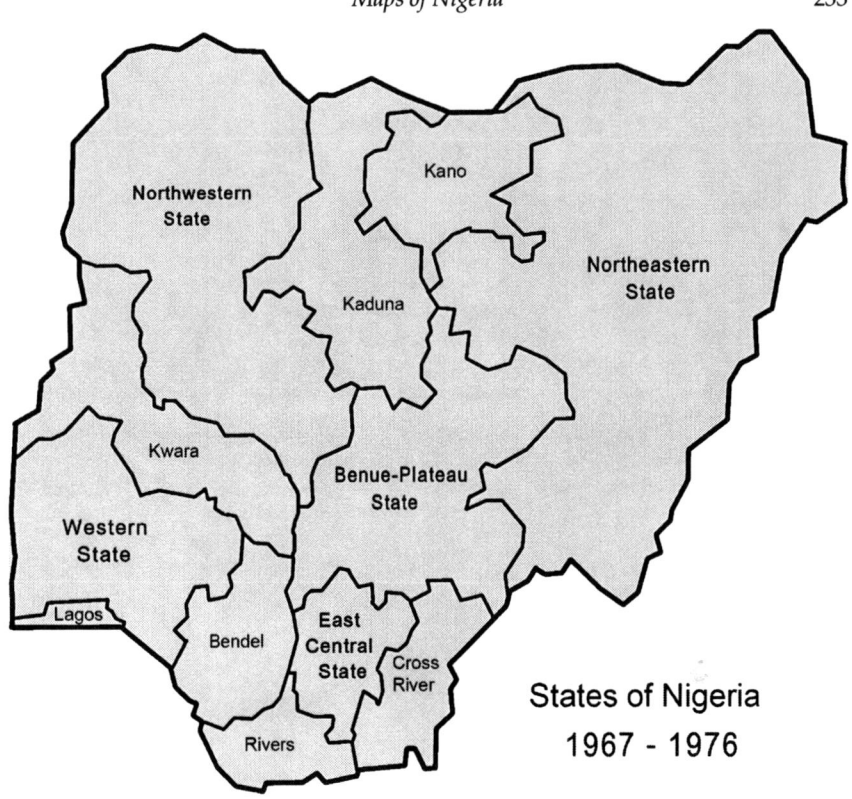

Map 2: Twelve States of Nigeria: 1967 to 1976. Source: Wikipedia, "Nigeria States 1967–1976." http://en.wikipedia.org/wiki/File:Nigeria_states-1967-1976.png.

234 Maps of Nigeria

States of Nigeria
1976 - 23 Sep. 1987

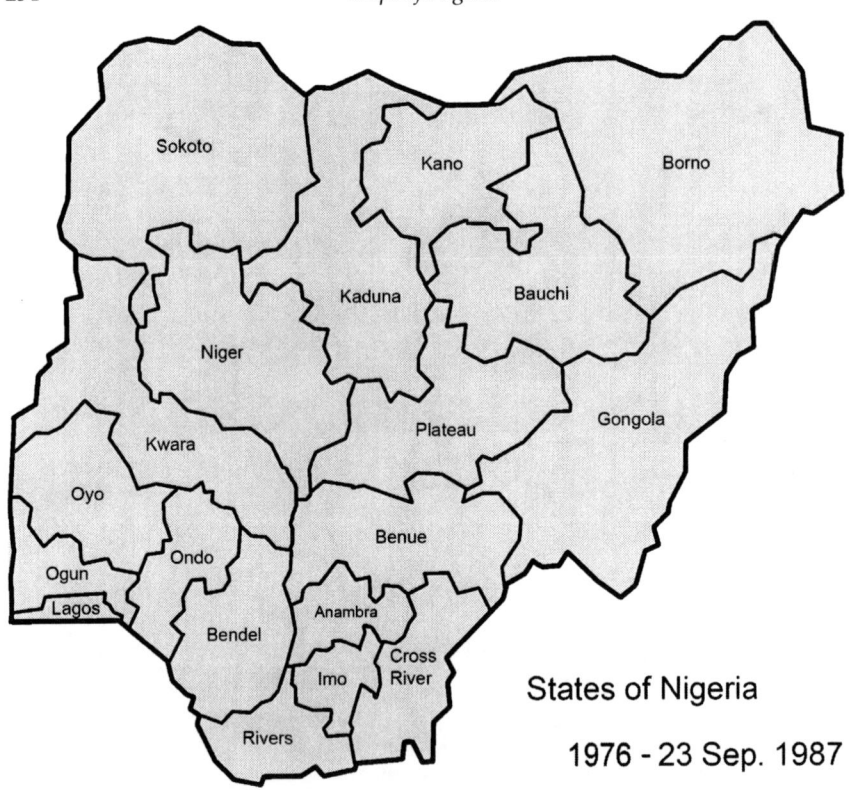

Map 3: Nineteen States of Nigeria: 1976 to 1987. Source: Wikipedia, "Nigeria States 1976–1987." http://en.wikipedia.org/wiki/File:Nigeria_states-1976-1987.png.

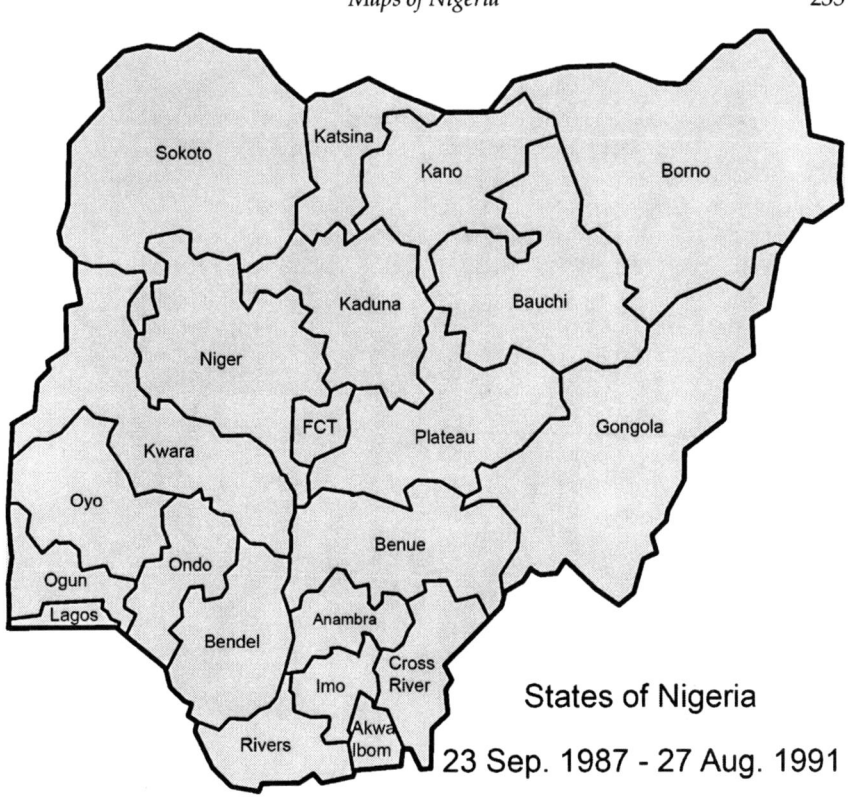

Map 4: Twenty One States of Nigeria: 1987 to1991. Source: Wikipedia, "Nigeria states 1987–1991." http://en.wikipedia.org/wiki/File:Nigeria_states_1987-1991.png.

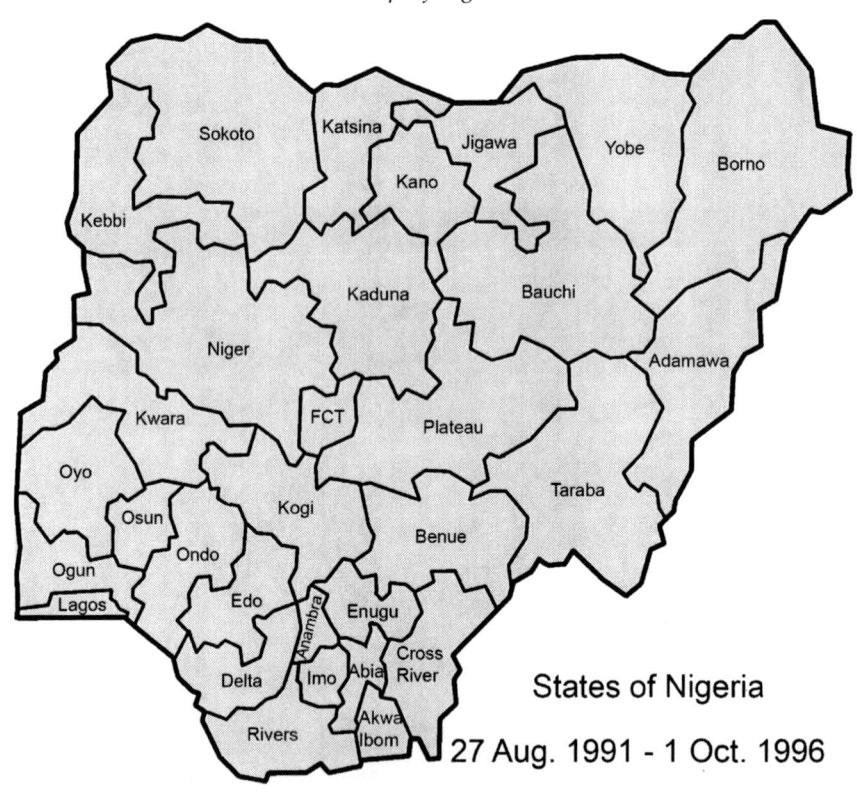

Map 5: Thirty States of Nigeria: 1991 to 1996. Source: Wikipedia, "Nigeria states 1991–1996." http://en.wikipedia.org/wiki/File:Nigeria_1991-1996.png.

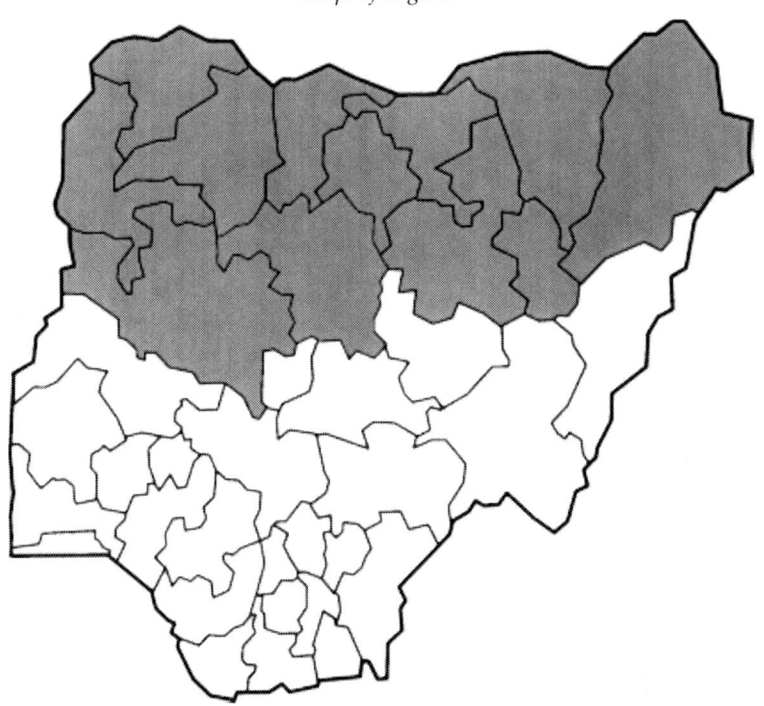

Map 6: Sharia Operative States in Northern Nigeria: 1999 to Present. Source: Wikipedia, "NG-Sharia." http://commons.wikimedia.org/wiki/File:NG-Sharia.png.

Appendix B

Selected Cases of Religious Crises in Northern Nigeria from 1980 to 2009

Table 12.1. Selected Cases of Religious Crises in Northern Nigeria from 1980 to 2009.

S/N	Date	Location	Principal Actors
1.	Thursday, May 1, 1980	Zaria (Kaduna State)	Disturbances in Zaria during which property belonging to mainly Christians were destroyed.
2.	December, 18–29 1980	Yan-Awaki Ward in Kano (Kano State)	Riots by *Maitatsine* sects. 118 people died. Extensive damage to property.
3.	October 29–30, 1982	Bullumkutu, Maiduguri (Borno State)	*Kala-Kato* and *Maitatisine* sects. 118 people died. Extensive damage to property.
4.	October 29–30, 1982	Kano (Kano State)	Muslim demonstrators burned down churches.
5.	February 27–March 5, 1984	Dobeli Ward	*Maitatsine* sect. 568 died. Wanton destruction of property.
6.	April 26–28, 1985	Pantami Ward, Combe (Bauchi State)	*Maitatsine* sect. 105 died. Wanton destruction of property.
7.	March 1986	Ilorin (Kwara State)	Muslims and Christians clashed during a Christian procession at Easter.
8.	March 1987	Kafanchan (Kaduna State)	Clash between Muslims and Christians at the College of Education, Kafanchan. Loss of some lives and the burning of some mosques by Christians and native Kajes.
9.	March 1987	Katsina, Funtua, Zaria, Gusau, and Kaduna (Kaduna State)	Wave of religious riots in which Muslims burned down numerous church buildings, and damaged properties belonging to Christians. Many lives were lost.
10.	February 1988	Kaduna, Kaduna Polytechnic (Kaduna State)	Religious riots, ostensibly among students, destroyed the foundation walls of the Christian chapel.
11.	April 1991	Katsina (Katsina State)	Religious violence spearheaded by Malam Yahaya Yakubu, leader of the fundamentalist Shiite sect in Katsina. It was a protest over a blasphemous publication, *Fidi Times*. Several lives were lost and property destroyed.

Selected Cases of Religious Crises in Northern Nigeria from 1980 to 2009 241

12.	April 1991	Tafawa Balewa (Bauchi State)	Started as a quarrel between a Fulani man and a Sayawa meat seller in Tafawa Balewa. Escalated into full-blown violence and later took the colouring of a religious war in Bauchi. Several lives were lost and property valued over hundreds of million Naira was destroyed.
13.	October 1991	Kano (Kano State)	A peaceful procession initiated by the *Izala* sect to halt Rev. Reinhard Bonnke from having a crusade in Kano later degenerated into a very violent and bloody religious confrontation. Thousands of lives were lost and properties valued in millions of Naira were destroyed.
14.	May 1992	Zangon Kataf, (Kaduna State)	A communal feud between the Katafs and the Hausas later took the dimension of an interreligious war between Muslims and Christians in other major cities of Kaduna State. Several lives were lost and properties were destroyed.
15.	January 1993	Funtua (Katsina State)	The *Kalakato* religious sect assaulted the village head and burned down the police vehicle. Lives and property were also lost.
16.	December 1994	Kano (Kano State)	Communal violence triggered by the beheading of a Christian who had allegedly desecrated the Koran.
17.	May 1995	Kano (Kano State)	Communal violence triggered by quarrel between Hausa and Ibo led to the burning of houses, churches, and shops and killing of innocent people.
18.	Thursday, July 22, 1999	Kano Reprisal Killing (Kano State)	Hausa/Fulani youth took vengeance on the killing of their Kith and Kin in Sagamu. Their target was the Yoruba community.
19.	February 28, 2000	Kaduna Mayhem (Kaduna State)	Kaduna city exploded in violence as Muslim and Christian extremists and other hoodlums clashed over the proposal to introduce Sharia.

242 *Selected Cases of Religious Crises in Northern Nigeria from 1980 to 2009*

20.	Friday, April 14, 2000	Agyragu Crisis (Nasarawa State)	Communal clash that started with a protest against the location of Local Government Headquarters. The militant youth group started the riot and later took to the streets, killing and destroying.
21.	July 2000	Tsagari Crisis (Kwara State)	Clash between Tsagari and Share communities of Kwara State, which claimed several lives.
22.	September 8, 2000	Kaltungo Religious (Combe State)	A religious violence that was sparked off by the presence of the state's Sharia implementation committee.
23.	October 17, 2000	OPC-Hausa/ Fulani (Kwara)	A faceoff between the militant members of OPC and Hausa/Funlani community over supremacy of Emirate system in the state.
24.	Saturday, October 27, 2000	Minna reprisal (Niger)	Violent ethnic crisis erupted after the OPC assaults in Kwara and Lagos states.
25.	Saturday, December 2, 2000	Hadejia Crisis (Jigawa)	A sectarian disturbance that was caused by a debate between Muslims and Christians in Hadeja (Jigawa). There was wanton destruction of worship places.
26.	Thursday, June 28, 2001	Azara Crisis (Nasarawa)	An ethnic conflict between the Tiv and the Azara indigences. It started with the gruesome killing of an Azara traditional leader, and later spread to the Tiv village, with the Tiv community on the defense.
27.	Friday, September 7, 2001	Jos Crisis	A violent ethnic/religious crisis between the Muslim/Hausa-Fulani and Christian/ Indigences. The subject of discord between the Jasawa Development Association and Plateau Youth Council was over political appointment in Jos North.
28.	October 12, 2001	Kano Riot	A peaceful anti-American protest over the bombing of Afghanistan turned violent, taking ethnic and religious dimension; it degenerated into uncontrollable violence which claimed lives and damaged properties and places of worship.
29.	Monday, October 29, 2003	Tiv-Jukun/Fulani Conflict	An ethnic clash between Tivs and Jukun/ Fulani which was an extension of the May 2001 clash and could be linked to the protracted dispute between both sides. *Newswatch* reported that 16 soldiers were killed which later led to the gruesome revenge on the Tivs by the Nigerian army.

Selected Cases of Religious Crises in Northern Nigeria from 1980 to 2009 243

30.	Friday, November 2, 2001	Gwantu Crisis	A clash that started on political grounds (over the relocation of LG Headquarters) later took on ethno-religious dimension in which places of worship were destroyed.
31.	Sunday, December 30, 2001	Vwang Crisis	A violent communal conflict in Vwang district between the indigenes and non-indigenes exploded in the backdrop of the September 7 Jos crisis. It started when an illegal group of 40 men attacked the district head of Vwang. It also had religious coloring.
32.	January 18, 2002	Awe Crisis	A renewed communal clash between two indigenous communities in Awe Local Government of Nasarawa State. The cause was not certain but two people were killed and several others injured.
33.	May 2, 2000	Jos Mayhem	Another mayhem that followed PDP congress but later took an ethno-religious color.
34.	May 2, 2002	Fulani-Irigwe Crisis	An ethnic clash between the Hausa/Fulani and the Irigwe indigenes in Basa, Plateau, which was said to be a reprisal attack.
35.	Saturday, June 1, 2002	Yelwa-Shendam Mayhem (Plateau)	A religious-cum-ethnic fracas between the native people (predominantly Christians) and Hausa settlers (predominantly Muslims). This violence extended to about four Local Government councils in Southern Plateau.
36.	Monday, July 1, 2002	Wase (Plateau)	The Yelwa-Shendam riots spilled over to Wase.
37.	Tuesday, July 1, 2003	Edo/Kogi	Communal clashes between border communities in Edo and Kogi states Ekepedo and Ogori over land ownerships.
38.	Thursday, January 1, 2004	Ganye, Adamawa	Clash between Fulani herdsmen and farmers over grazing lands.
39.	Thursday, January 1, 2004	Yobe	Militant Islamic group operating under the name of *Muhajiran* launched a Taliban-like attack on police. Men of the Nigerian Army killed five and arrested several others.
40.	Sunday, February 1, 2004	Wase/Kanam (Plateau)	Violent clash between Mavo and Taroh communities, which claimed II lives. Suspected Taroh youth were alleged to have raided Mavo villages.
41.	Saturday, February 1, 2004	Wase/Kanam (Plateau)	Communal clash over land ownership between Minda and Kparev groups. Several lives were lost.

42.	Saturday, April 3, 2004	Makarfi, Kaduna	Religious protest in Makarfi town over the desecration of the Kran by a Christian teenager.
43.	Sunday, April 11, 2004	Lantang South, Plateau	Continued clashes that led to the sacking of Taroh villages in Lantang South LGC by suspected Hausa-Fulani insurgents.
44.	Monday, April 26, 2004	Bakin Chiyawa Plateau	Renewed hostilities launched by suspected displaced Fulani herdsmen. The conflict was believed to be a spillover of the ethno-religious crisis that has been bedevilling southern Plateau Local Government of Langtang South and North, Wase, Kanam and Shendam.
45.	Saturday, May 1, 2004	Yelwa Shendam, Plateau State	A fresh ethno-religious mayhem that claimed over 650 lives and over 250 women abducted by suspected Taroh militia.
46.	Wednesday, May 12, 2004	Kano	Kano mayhem following the Yelwa Shendam ethno-religious crisis in Plateau. Non-Muslims were attacked in reprisal of the Plateau crisis. Over 200 lives were lost and the traditional ruler of the area deposed.
47.	Saturday, June 8, 2008	Konshisha Gwer, Benue	Boundary disputes between neighbouring Konshisha and Gwer communities. Thirteen lives were lost.
48.	Tuesday, June 8, 2004	Numan, Adamawa	Ethno-religious crisis in Numan over the contruction of a mosque minaret over the Humma Bachamas palace. Over 50 people were feared killed and the traditional ruler of the area deposed.
49.	Tuesday, August 3, 2004	Quanpam, Plateau	Fresh outbreak of violence in Lankaka village. Suspected armed milita from neighboring state allegedly stormed the village community killing two and razing twenty houses.
50.	Monday, September 27, 2004	Limankara, Borno	A self-styled Taliban group hiding on the Goza hills and Madara mountains on the north-eastern border with Cameroon raid police station killing officers and stealing ammunition.

Source: *Newswatch Magazine,* November 2, 2009 (as cited in Ezeibe, 2009, para. 29). Reprinted with the permission of *Newswatch Magazine.*

References

13 Nigerians die in Christian-Muslim fighting. (2001, October 15). *The New York Times*. Retrieved from http://www.nytimes.com

100 feared dead as Christians battle Muslims in Nigerian city. (1992, May 19). *Reuters-Associated Press in The Toronto Star*. Retrieved from http://www.lexisnexis.com

100 Nigeria policemen said to be riot victims. (1982, October 31). *Associated Press in The New York Times*. Retrieved from http://www.nytimes.com

1,000 are reported dead in north Nigeria clashes. (1984, March 5). *Reuters in The New York Times*. Retrieved from http://www.nytimes.com

2 killed in northern Nigeria in a clash over Islamic law. (1992, January 8). *The New York Times*. Retrieved from http://www.nytimes.com

3rd day of ethnic violence in streets of Lagos. (2002, February 5). *The New York Times*. Retrieved from http://www.nytimes.com

300 believed killed in religious rioting in Nigeria. (1982, October, 30). *Reuters in The New York Times*. Retrieved from http://www.nytimes.com

500 dead in Nigeria religious attacks. (2010, March 8). *Times Live*. Retrieved from http://www.timeslive.co.za

700 die in fighting in northern Nigeria. (2009, August 2). *CNN*. Retrieved from http://www.cnn.com

718 deaths cited in Nigeria riots. (1984, March 11). *Associated Press in The New York Times*. Retrieved from http://www.nytimes.com

Abdulkadir, A. (2012a, January 21). Multiple blasts rock Kano. *Daily Times of Nigeria*. Retrieved from http://dailytimes.com.ng

Abdulkadir, A. (2012b, February 26). Bomb explodes in Jos church. *Daily Times of Nigeria*. Retrieved from http://www.dailytimes.com.ng

Adar, K. G. (2001). Ethno-religious nationalism in Sudan: The enduring constraint on the policy of national identity. In S. Bekker, M. Dodds, & M. Khosa (Eds.), *Shifting African identities* (pp. 81–113). Pretoria: Human Sciences Research Council.

Adebayo, A. (2012, February 7). Nigeria: Beware of Boko Haram apologists. *Vanguard in AllAfrica.com*. Retrieved from http://allafrica.com/stories/201202070534.html

Adekoya, A. (2009, August 1). Orgy of violence: Deadly bolts from Boko Haram. *Vanguard (Nigeria)*. Retrieved from http://www.vanguardngr.com

Adetunji, J. (2011, June 26). Bomb attack kills at least 25 in northern Nigeria. *The Guardian*. Retrieved from http://www.guardiannews.com/

Africa: Arms are the arbiter. (1967, July 16). *The New York Times*, p. 132. Retrieved from ProQuest Historical Newspapers: The New York Times (1851–2009) database.

Africa: Race hatred in Nigeria. (1967, October 22). *The New York Times*, p. 200. Retrieved from ProQuest Historical Newspapers: The New York Times (1851–2009) database.

Agboola, M. A. (2011, December 26). Policeman killed as bombers invade church in Jos. *Sun News Online*. Retrieved from http://www.sunnewsonline.com

Aguwa, J. C. (1997). Religious conflict in Nigeria: Impact on nation building. *Dialectical Anthropology, 22*(3/4), 335–351.

Ahiante, A. (2004, June 7). Victims of riots: Their pains, woes and regrets. *This Day (Nigeria)*. Retrieved from http://infoweb.newsbank.com

Akaeze, A. (2009, October 29). From Maitatsine to Boko Haram. *Newswatch Magazine*. Retrieved from http://www.newswatchngr.com

References

Akau, S. (2012, April 8). 25 killed in Easter Sunday bombing in northern Nigeria. *CNN*. Retrieved from http://cnn.com

Alli, Y., & Tsenzughul, A. (2012, April 6). Bombs kill 15 in Bauchi churches. *The Nation*. Retrieved from http://www.thenationonlineng.net/2011/index.php/news/48949-bombs-kill-15-in-bauchi-churches.html

Aliyu, S. (2009). *Religious-based violence and national security in Nigeria: Case studies of Kaduna State and the Taliban activities in Borno State* (Master's thesis). Available from Google Scholar. (Accession No. ADA501810)

Amnesty International. (2002, May 28). *Amnesty International Report 2002—Nigeria*. Retrieved from http://www.unhcr.org/refworld/docid/3cf4bc0330.html

Amnesty International. (2009a, May 28). *Amnesty International Report 2009—Nigeria*. Retrieved from http://www.unhcr.org/refworld/docid/4a1fadcf2.html

Amnesty International. (2009b, December 9). Killing at will: Extrajudicial executions and other unlawful killings by the police in Nigeria. Retrieved from http://www.amnesty.org/en/library/info/AFR44/038/2009

Amnesty International. (2011, July 14). Killings by security forces in north Nigeria must stop. Retrieved from http://www.unhcr.org/refworld/docid/4e4ca02b2.html

Andersson, H. (1996, October 11). 2 branches of Islam clashing in Nigeria. *The New York Times International*, p. A9. Retrieved from ProQuest Newsstand: New York Times (1923–Current file) database.

Angerbrandt, H. (2011, January 01). Political decentralisation and conflict: The Sharia crisis in Kaduna, Nigeria. *Journal of Contemporary African Studies, 29*(1), 15–31.

Anthony, D. A. (2002). *Poison and medicine: Ethnicity, power, and violence in a Nigerian city, 1966 to 1986*. Portsmouth, NH: Heinemann.

Anyanwu, K. C. (1982, September). The bases of political instability in Nigeria. *Journal of Black Studies, 13*(1), 101–117.

At least 8 dead in Nigerian city as Muslim-Christian riots go on. (1991, October 17). *The New York Times*. Retrieved from http://www.nytimes.com

At least 21 are killed as Christian-Muslim clashes continue in central Nigerian city. (2011, September 11). *Associated Press in The New York Times*. Retrieved from http://www.nytimes.com

At least 200 die in Nigeria clashes. (2008, November 29). *Associated Press in The New York Times*. Retrieved from http://www.nytimes.com

At least 30 killed in clashes in central Nigeria. (2003, March 13). *The New York Times*. Retrieved from http://www.nytimes.com

Attacks kill 18 in Plateau. (2011, January 12). *Reuters in Daily Times of Nigeria*. Retrieved from http://dailytimes.com.ng

Batruch, C. (2004) Oil and conflict: Lundin petroleum's experience in Sudan. In A. J. K. Bailes & I. Frommelt (Eds.), *Business and security: Public-private sector relationships in a new security environment* (pp. 148–160). Stockholm: SIPRI.

Battle in northern Nigeria. (1991, April 24). *Associated Press in The New York Times*. Retrieved from http://www.nytimes.com

Batty, D., & Mark, M. (2012, January 21). Scores killed in terrorist attacks in Nigeria. *The Guardian*. Retrieved from http://www.guardiannews.com/

Baum, S. K. (2008). *The psychology of genocide: Perpetrators, bystanders, and rescuers*. Cambridge: Cambridge University Press.

Bello, I. (2011a, November 4). Riot breaks out in Kaduna. *The Daily Times of Nigeria*. Retrieved from http://www.dailytimes.com.ng

Bello, I. (2011b, November 9). Residents flee Damaturu. *The Daily Times of Nigeria*. Retrieved from http://dailytimes.com.ng

Bello, I. (2012a, April 29). Bomb blasts in Kano University. *Daily Times of Nigeria*. Retrieved from http://dailytimes.com.ng

Bello, I. (2012b, April 30). BUK confirms death of 2 dons in blasts. *Daily Times of Nigeria*. Retrieved from http://dailytimes.com.ng/article/buk-confirms-death-2-dons-blasts

References

Binniyat, L. (2012, April 9). Easter tragedies: 58 die in bomb blast, church collapse. *Vanguard (Nigeria)*. Retrieved from http://www.vanguardngr.com

Bloxham, D. (2005). *Great game of genocide: Imperialism, nationalism, and the destruction of the Ottoman Armenians*. New York: Oxford University Press, Inc.

Body of a Nigerian rebel Moslem reported found in shallow grave. (1981, January 1). *Associated Press in The New York Times*. Retrieved from http://www.nytimes.com

Boko Haram: Why we're attacking Christians. (2012, January 11). *This Day Live*. Retrieved from http://www.thisdaylive.com

Bortolotti, D. (2004). *Hope in hell: Inside the world of Doctors without Borders*. Richmond Hill, ON: Firefly Books.

Brooke, J. (1987a, March 13). Moslem mobs in Nigeria said to kill 11 in North. *Special to The New York Times*. Retrieved http://www.nytimes.com

Brooke, J. (1987b, March 22). Nigeria torn with rioting over religion. *Special to The New York Times*. Retrieved from http://www.nytimes.com

Byrne, S., & Carter, N. (1996). Social cubism: Six social forces of ethnoterritorial politics in Northern Ireland and Québec. *Peace and Conflict Studies*, 3(2), 52–71.

Burg, S. L., & Shoup, P. (1999). *War in Bosnia-Herzegovina: Ethnic conflict and international intervention*. Armonk, NY: M. E. Sharpe, Inc.

Campbell, J. J. (2010). Video series [Class lectures]. *Foundations of genocide*. Fall term 2010, Department of Conflict Analysis and Resolution, Nova Southeastern University.

Campbell, J. J. (2012). *On the nature of genocidal intent*. Lanham, MD: Lexington Books.

Central Intelligence Agency. (2012). Nigeria. In *The World Factbook*. Retrieved from https://www.cia.gov/library/publications/the-world-factbook/geos/ni.html

Chalk, P. (2004). Islam in West Africa: The case of Nigeria. In A. M. Rabasa, C. Benard, P. Chalk, C. C. Fair, T. Karasik, R. Lal, I. Lesser, and D. Thaler (Eds.), *The Muslim world after 9/11* (pp. 413–432). Santa Monica, CA: RAND Corporation.

Chidiogo, E. (2011, May 16). 800 people killed in post-election violence. *Daily Times of Nigeria*. Retrieved from http://dailytimes.com.ng

Christian groups reject attempt to regulate preaching. (2009, August 8). *AAGM in Vanguard (Nigeria)*. Retrieved from http://infoweb.newsbank.com

Christian Solidarity Worldwide. (2008a, December 1). "Inaccurate reporting" causes resentment among Christian community. Retrieved from http://dynamic.csw.org.uk/article.asp?t=press&id=805&search=

Christian Solidarity Worldwide (CSW). (2008b, August). Briefing, Nigeria: Current Human Rights Concerns. Retrieved from http://lib.ohchr.org/HRBodies/UPR/Documents/Session4/NG/ CSW_NGA_UPR_S4_2009_anx_FullReport.pdf

Christian Solidarity Worldwide. (n.d.). Recent religious violence in central and northern Nigeria, pp. 1–13. Retrieved from http://cswng.org/fact-findings/

Christmas carnage in Nigeria; 5 churches bombed. (2011, December 25). *CNN*. Retrieved from http://cnn.com

Church attack foiled in northern Nigeria. (2011, February 16). *Daily Times of Nigeria*. Retrieved from http://www.dailytimes.com.ng

Connors, W. (2008, December 1). Counting the bodies in the aftermath of clashes in Nigeria. *The New York Times*. Retrieved from http://www.nytimes.com

Cowell, A. (1982, November 16). An outburst of cult strife tests Nigeria's civil rule. *Special to The New York Times*. Retrieved from http://www.nytimes.com

Creswell, J. W. (2007). *Qualitative inquiry and research design: Choosing among five approaches* (2nd ed.). Thousand Oaks, CA: Sage Publications, Inc.

Dash, L. (1984, March 6). Religious strife said to kill hundreds in Nigeria. *The Washington Post*. Retrieved from http://www.lexisnexis.com

Deadly Christian-Muslim clash in Nigeria. (2011, August 30). *Al Jazeera*. Retrieved from http://www.aljazeera.com

Deadly rioting spreads in Nigeria. (2000, February 29). *Reuters in Times Colonist*. Retrieved from http://www.lexisnexis.com

Death toll put at 300 in Nigerian violence. (1984, March 4). *Reuters in The New York Times*. Retrieved from http://www.nytimes.com

Death toll rises to 63 in riot in Nigeria. (1984, February 29). *Reuters in The New York Times*. Retrieved from http://www.nytimes.com

Deng, F. M. (2001, Winter). Sudan—civil war and genocide: Disappearing Christians of the Middle East. *Middle East Quarterly, 8*(1), 13–21. Retrieved from http://www.meforum.org/22/sudan-civil-war-and-genocide

Dozens dead in Nigeria religious riots. (2004, May 13). *Reuters in Al Jazeera*. Retrieved from http://www.aljazeera.com

Dutton, D. G. (2007). *Psychology of genocide, massacres, and extreme violence: Why "normal" people come to commit atrocities*. Westport, CT: Praeger Security International.

Ebije, N., & Alabelewe, A. (2011, December 8). Explosion rocks Kaduna. *Sun News Online*. Retrieved from http://www.sunnewsonline.com

Ehiabhi, V. (2012a, March 11). 11 dead, 22 injured in Jos blast. *Daily Times of Nigeria*. Retrieved from http://dailytimes.com.ng

Ehiabhi, V. (2012b, April 27). Boko Haram kills 12 in police station attack. *Daily Times of Nigeria*. Retrieved from http://dailytimes.com.ng/article/boko-haram-kills-12-police-station-attack-0

Ehiabhi, V. (2012c, April 16). Bomb explodes in Kano. *Daily Times of Nigeria*. Retrieved from: http://dailytimes.com.ng/article/bomb-explodes-kano

Ejembi, R. (2012, March 8). Fulani invasion: Death toll rises to 43. *Sun News Online*. Retrieved from http://www.sunnewsonline.com

Elbagir, N., & John, H. (2012, January 21). Scores dead as assailants target northern Nigerian city: Boko Haram. *CNN*. Retrieved from http://cnn.com

Emergency declared in 4 Nigerian states. (2011, December 31). *Associated Press in The New York Times*. Retrieved from http://www.nytimes.com

Emerson, G. (1970, January 12). Story of secessionist Biafra: Tribal hatreds, civil war and starvation; obduracy at home, bitterness abroad. *The New York Times*, p. 12. Retrieved from ProQuest Historical Newspapers: The New York Times (1851–2009) database.

Emewu, I., & Nwosu, I. (2011a, December 27). Madalla: Suicide bomber did it—church security officer. *Sun News Online*. Retrieved from http://www.sunnewsonline.com

Emewu, I., & Nwosu, I. (2011b, December 26). Reporter's diary: Death in the holy place on Christmas. *Sun News Online*. Retrieved from http://www.sunnewsonline.com

Ezeibe, C. C. (2009). Inter-religious conflicts and crisis of development in Nigeria: Who benefits? *International Journal of Research in Arts and Social Sciences, 1*. Retrieved from http://www.academicexcellencesociety.com/inter_religious_conflicts.html

Falola, T. (1998). *Violence in Nigeria: The crisis of religious politics and secular ideologies*. Rochester, NY: University of Rochester Press.

Falola, T. (1999). *The history of Nigeria*. Westport, CT: Greenwood Press.

Falola, T. (2002). *Nigeria in the twentieth century*. Durham, NC: Carolina Academic Press.

Falola, T., & Heaton, M. M. (2008). *A history of Nigeria*. New York: Cambridge University Press.

Fisher, I. (2006, February 19). Italian quits over cartoons; 15 die in Nigeria. *The New York Times*. Retrieved from http://www.nytimes.com

Forsyth, D. R. (2010). *Group dynamics* (5th ed.). Belmont, CA: Wadsworth Cengage Learning.

Friedlander, H. (1995). *The origins of Nazi genocide: From euthanasia to the final solution*. Chapel Hill, NC: University of North Carolina Press.

Friendly, A., Jr. (1967a, October 1). Leader exhorts Nigerian rebels: Ojukwu urges defense of capital—exodus reported. *The New York Times*, p. 8. Retrieved from ProQuest Historical Newspapers: The New York Times (1851–2009) database.

Friendly, A., Jr. (1967b, August 16). Nigeria moves to curb attacks on Ibo tribesmen. *The New York Times*, p. 10. Retrieved from ProQuest Historical Newspapers: The New York Times (1851–2009) database.

Friendly, A., Jr. (1968, January 18). Pressure rising in Nigeria to end civil war as military standoff continues. *The New York Times*, p. 14. Retrieved from ProQuest Historical Newspapers: The New York Times (1851–2009) database.

Garba, I. (2012, August 21). Nigerian government enters talks with Boko Haram. *The Christian Science Monitor*. Retrieved from http://www.csmonitor.com

Garrison, L. (1966a, June 1). The crisis in Nigeria: Regional riots put nation to biggest test thus far. *The New York Times*, p. A8. Retrieved from ProQuest Historical Newspapers: The New York Times (1851–2009) database.

Garrison, L. (1966b, December 13). Ibo quarter of city is deserted 2 months after Nigeria killings. *The New York Times*, p. 7. Retrieved from ProQuest Historical Newspapers: The New York Times (1851–2009) database.

Garrison, L. (1966c, October 14). Injured refugees stun Nigeria city: Ibos from north return to eastern region homeland. *The New York Times*, p. 8. Retrieved from ProQuest Historical Newspapers: The New York Times (1851–2009) database.

Garrison, L. (1966d, September 6). Suspense mounting in Nigeria on regional pressure to divide. *The New York Times*, p. 19. Retrieved from ProQuest Historical Newspapers: The New York Times (1851–2009) database.

Garrison, L. (1966e, October 12). Nigeria's eastern chief fights to bar secession: Killings of region's people in north inflame populace. *The New York Times*, p. 14. Retrieved from ProQuest Historical Newspapers: The New York Times (1851–2009) database.

Garrison, L. (1966f, November 20). 55 still in jail in Nigerian plot: Detained for role in coup, they are political pawns. *The New York Times*, p. 27. Retrieved from ProQuest Historical Newspapers: The New York Times (1851–2009) database.

Garrison, L. (1966g, October 3). 300 Ibo tribesmen killed by troops and Nigerian mob: Refugees trying to board plane in North are shot—week's toll near 1,000. *The New York Times*, p. 1. Retrieved from ProQuest Historical Newspapers: The New York Times (1851–2009) database.

Garrison, L. (1966h, May 29). Anti-Ironsi demonstrations sweep north Nigeria. *The New York Times*, p. 7. Retrieved from ProQuest Historical Newspapers: The New York Times (1851–2009) database.

Garrison, L. (1966i, August 31). Day of mourning splits Nigerians: East's action denounced by supreme commander. *The New York Times*, p. 13. Retrieved from ProQuest Historical Newspapers: The New York Times (1851–2009) database.

Garrison, L. (1966j, August 4). Nigeria outwardly placid but killings increase: Unity apparently shattered in Hausa take-over—Ironsi reported to be dead. *The New York Times*, p. 10. Retrieved from ProQuest Historical Newspapers: The New York Times (1851–2009) database.

Garrison, L. (1966k, July 23). Nigeria peaceful in wake of strife: North, rent by tribal riots, calmed by Ironsi. *The New York Times*, p. 3. Retrieved from ProQuest Historical Newspapers: The New York Times (1851–2009) database.

Garrison, L. (1966l, October 9). Nigeria totters on the brink. *The New York Times*, p. E3. Retrieved from ProQuest Historical Newspapers: The New York Times (1851–2009) database.

Garrison, L. (1966m, December 14). Refugees helped in Nigeria's east: Region attempts to resettle million who fled killings. *The New York Times*, p. 13. Retrieved from ProQuest Historical Newspapers: The New York Times (1851–2009) database.

Garrison, L. (1967a, March 19). A Time Bomb Ticks in Nigeria. *The New York Times*, p. E7. Retrieved from ProQuest Historical Newspapers: The New York Times (1851–2009) database.

Garrison, L. (1967b, July 21). Civilians accuse Nigerian troops: Killings in eastern region appear to be mounting. *The New York Times*, p. 5. Retrieved from ProQuest Historical Newspapers: The New York Times (1851–2009) database.

Garrison, L. (1967c, April 12). East Nigeria urges mediation; Sees breakup if Lagos balks: Military governor appeals for action by leading African heads of state. *The New York Times*, p. 19. Retrieved from ProQuest Historical Newspapers: The New York Times (1851–2009) database.

Garrison, L. (1967d, March 11). East Nigerian leader pessimistic on future of nation's unity. *The New York Times*, p. 4. Retrieved from ProQuest Historical Newspapers: The New York Times (1851–2009) database.

Garrison, L. (1967e, April 6). East Nigerians urged to leave the country's "Enemy" regions: Those on the federal police force are especially asked to return at once. *The New York Times*, p. 17. Retrieved from ProQuest Historical Newspapers: The New York Times (1851–2009) database.

Garrison, L. (1967f, June 10). Eastern Nigeria awaiting attack: Secessionist troops expect blow from Lagos regime. *The New York Times*, p. 5. Retrieved from ProQuest Historical Newspapers: The New York Times (1851–2009) database.

Garrison, L. (1967g, May 27). Head of eastern Nigeria calls for independence: Asks assembly of region for mandate to declare it to be only course left. *The New York Times*, p. 11. Retrieved from ProQuest Historical Newspapers: The New York Times (1851–2009) database.

Garrison, L. (1967h, June 11). The Ibos go it alone. *The New York Times*, pp. 30, 32–34. Retrieved from ProQuest Historical Newspapers: The New York Times (1851–2009) database.

Garrison, L. (1968a, March 31). Biafra vs. Nigeria: The other dirty little war Biafra vs. Nigeria. *The New York Times*, pp. SM36–41, 47, 50–52. Retrieved from ProQuest Historical Newspapers: The New York Times (1851–2009) database.

Garrison, L. (1968b, September 8). The "point of no return" for the Biafrans. *The New York Times*, pp. SM29, 84–94. Retrieved from ProQuest Historical Newspapers: The New York Times (1851–2009) database.

Gberie, L. (2006, May 19). Nigeria: Checking a dictatorial bid. *Africa Analysis*, 493(15).

Gellately, R., & Kiernan, B. (Eds.). (2003). *The specter of genocide: Mass murder in historical perspective*. New York: Cambridge University Press.

Glaser, B. G. (2007). *Doing formal grounded theory: A proposal*. Mill Valley, CA: Sociology Press.

GlobalSecurity.org. (n.d.) Biafra War. Retrieved from http://www.globalsecurity.org

Golafshani, N. (2003, December). Understanding reliability and validity in qualitative research. *The Qualitative Report*, 8(4), 597–607.

Gurr, T. R. (1971). *Why men rebel*. Princeton, NJ: Princeton University Press.

Haberson, J. W., & Rothchild, D. (Eds.). (1991). *Africa in world politics: The African state system in flux*. Boulder, CO: Westview Press.

Harnischfeger, J. (2004, July). Sharia and control over territory: Conflicts between "settlers" and "indigenes" in Nigeria. *African Affairs*, 103(412), 431–452.

Hauss, C. (2003, July). Addressing underlying causes of conflict. *Beyond intractability*. Retrieved from http://www.beyondintractability.org/bi-essay/addressing-underlying-causes

Heidenrich, J. G. (2001). *How to prevent genocide: A guide for policymakers, scholars, and the concerned citizen*. Westport, CT: Praeger.

Hinton, A. L. (2002). *Annihilating difference: The anthropology of genocide*. Berkeley, CA: University of California Press.

Hinton, A. L. (2005). *Why did they kill?: Cambodia in the shadow of genocide*. Berkeley, CA: University of California Press.

Hirsch, H. (1995). *Genocide and the politics of memory: Studying death to preserve life*. Chapel Hill, NC: University of North Carolina Press.

Hoge, W. (2002, December 8). World pageant goes ahead over protests; A Turk wins. *The New York Times*. Retrieved from http://www.nytimes.com

Hogg, M. A. (2006). Social identity theory. In P. J. Burke. (Ed.), *Contemporary social psychological theories* (pp. 111–136). Stanford, CA: Stanford University Press.

References

Human Rights Watch. (2009, July). *Arbitrary killings by security forces: Submission to the investigative bodies on the November 28–29, 2008 violence in Jos, Plateau State, Nigeria.* Retrieved from http://www.hrw.org/reports/2009/07/20/arbitrary-killings-security-forces-0

Hundreds die in attack on Nigerian village. (2004, May 7). *The New York Times.* Retrieved from http://www.nytimes.com

Hundreds flee Nigerian city swept by riots. (2002, November 25). *The New York Times.* Retrieved from http://www.nytimes.com

Hundreds die in religious riots. (1984, March 4). *Facts on File World News Digest.* Retrieved from http://www.lexisnexis.com

Ibrahim, J. (1989). The politics of religion in Nigeria: The parameters of the 1987 crisis in Kaduna State. *Review of African Political Economy, 16*(45/46), 65–82.

Ibrahim, J. (1991, March). Religion and political turbulence in Nigeria. *The Journal of Modern African Studies, 29*(1), 15–136.

Iferi, B. (2011, November 10). Fresh violence reported in Kaduna. *Daily Times of Nigeria.* Retrieved from http://dailytimes.com.ng

In Nigeria's north, deadly clashes with an Islamist group. (2011, December 24). *Reuters in The New York Times.* Retrieved from http://www.nytimes.com

International Crisis Group. (2010, December 20). Northern Nigeria: Background to conflict. Africa Report No. 168. Retrieved from http://www.unhcr.org/refworld/docid/4d104b7c2.html

International Freedom of Expression Exchange Clearing House [IFEX]. (2012, January 25). Journalist killed while covering terrorist bombings. Retrieved from http://www.ifex.org/nigeria/2012/01/25/akogwu_killed/

"Irate youths" burn down 10 worship centres in northern Nigeria. (2006, September 21). *BBC Monitoring Africa.* Retrieved from www.lexisnexis.com

Jacobs, D. (1987). *The brutality of nations.* New York: Alfred A. Knopf.

Jaynes, G. (1981, January 12). At least 1,000 people are killed as Nigeria crushes Islamic sect. *The New York Times,* p. A1. Retrieved from ProQuest Historical Newspapers: The New York Times (1851–2009) database.

Jeong, H. (2000). *Peace and conflict studies: An introduction.* Burlington, VT: Ashgate Publishing Company.

John, I. A., Mohammed, A. Z., Pinto, A. D., & Nkanta, C. A. (2007, January). Gun violence in Nigeria: A focus on ethno-religious conflict in Kano. *Journal of Public Health Policy, 28*(4), 420–431.

Jones, A. (2006). *Genocide: A comprehensive introduction.* New York: Routledge.

Kaita, I. (2011, March 20). Breaking: Bomb blast in Jos. *Daily Times of Nigeria.* Retrieved from http://dailytimes.com.ng

Kazah-Toure, T., & Human Rights Monitor (Nigeria). (2003). *Ethno-religious conflicts in Kaduna State.* Kaduna, Nigeria: Human Rights Monitor.

Kendal, E. (2004, May 5). Nigeria: Turmoil in Plateau and Zamfara states. *World Evangelical Alliance Religious Liberty Commission (WEA RLC) in Assist News Service* (ANS). Retrieved from www.assistnews.net

Koinange, J. (2001, October 14). Anti-U.S. rampage kills hundreds. *CNN.* Retrieved from http://cnn.com

Kotch, N. (1987, March 18). "Sinister men" promised summary justice for Nigerian riots. *Reuters in The Globe and Mail* (Canada). Retrieved from http://www.lexisnexis.com

Kukah, M. H., & Falola, T. (1996). *Religious militancy and self-assertion: Islam and politics in Nigeria.* Aldershot, Hants, England: Avebury.

Kuperman, A. J. (2001). *The limits of humanitarian intervention: Genocide in Rwanda.* Washington, DC: Brookings Institution Press.

Lacey, M. (2002, November 29). Fiery zealotry leaves Nigeria in ashes again. *The New York Times.* Retrieved from: http://www.nytimes.com

Lang, B. (2005). *Post-Holocaust: Interpretation, misinterpretation, and the claims of history.* Bloomington, IN: Indiana University Press.

Lebor, A. (2006). *"Complicity with evil": The United Nations in the age of modern genocide.* New Haven, CT: Yale University Press.

Levene, M. (2005a). *Genocide in the age of the nation-state: Volume I, The meaning of genocide.* New York: I. B. Tauris & Co. Ltd.

Levene, M. (2005b). *Genocide in the age of the nation-state: Volume II, The rise of the West and the coming of genocide.* New York: I. B. Tauris & Co. Ltd.

Lobel, M. (2012, March 15). Nigeria attacks: "Boko Haram bombed my church." *BBC News.* Retrieved from http://www.bbc.co.uk/news/world-africa-17369800

MacFarlane, S. N. (1984, Spring). Africa's decaying security system and the rise of intervention. *International Security, 8*(4), 127–151.

Marama, N. (2012, January 22). Nigeria: Why we attacked Kano—Boko Haram. *Vanguard (Nigeria).* Retrieved from http://www.vanguardngr.com

Mark, M. (2012, January 21). Scores dead in northern Nigeria as Islamist militants terrorize the country. *The Observer.* Retrieved from http://www.guardian.co.uk/world/2012/jan/21/scores-dead-nigeria-islamist-militants

Mcveigh, K. (2002, November 23). Miss world and a deadly clash of cultures. *The Scotsman.* Retrieved from http://www.lexisnexis.com

Melson, R. (1996). Paradigms of Genocide: The Holocaust, the Armenian Genocide, and Contemporary Mass Destructions. In F. H. Little (Ed.), *The Holocaust: Remembering for the future* (pp. 156–168). Thousand Oaks, CA: Sage.

Mgboh, D. (2012a, April 30). As Boko Haram attacks BUK worship centres: Two profs, 13 others killed. *Sun News Online.* Retrieved from http://www.sunnewsonline.com

Mgboh, D. (2012b, January 22). Corpses litter Kano. *Sun News Online.* Retrieved from http://www.sunnewsonline.com/

Mgboh, D. (2012c, January 21). Multiple bombs rock Kano. *Sun News Online.* Retrieved from http://www.sunnewsonline.com

Midlarsky, M. I. (2005). *Killing trap: Genocide in the twentieth century.* New York: Cambridge University Press.

Mills, C. W. (1956). *The power elite.* New York: Oxford University Press.

Minchakpu, O. (2001). Religious riots in Nigeria leave hundreds dead: Leaders condemn the use of religion as a tool for violence. *Christianity Today.* Retrieved from http://www.christianitytoday.com/ct/2001/octoberweb-only/10-1-23.0.html

Miss world article sets off deadly riot. (2002, November 22). The *New York Times.* Retrieved from http://www.nytimes.com

Mitee, L. (1994, January—March). Changing the formula. *Constitutional Rights Journal, 3*(9), p. 13.

Mohammed, A., & Idonor, D. (2012, January 12). Nigeria: Kano bombings claim 162 lives—more attacks coming—Boko Haram spokesman. *Vanguard* in AllAfrica.com. Retrieved from http://allafrica.com/stories/201201220041.html

Mojeed, M., & Nossiter, A. (2012, January 22). Dozens killed by radical Islamic group in Nigeria. *The New York Times.* Retrieved from http://www.nytimes.com/

'More Christian victims in Boko Haram attacks'—Kwankwaso. (2012, February 19). *Daily Times of Nigeria.* Retrieved from http://dailytimes.com.ng

Mshelizza, I. (2011, February 3). Boko Haram threatens uprising. *Daily Times of Nigeria.* Retrieved from http://dailytimes.com.ng

Multiple explosions hit Nigerian cities. (2011a, November 5). *Al Jazeera.* Retrieved from http://www.aljazeera.com

Multiple explosions hit Nigerian city. (2011b, November 27). *Al Jazeera.* Retrieved from http://www.aljazeera.com

Murray, S., & Nossiter, A. (2009, August 3). In Nigeria, an insurgency leaves a heavy toll. *The New York Times.* Retrieved from http://www.nytimes.com

Muslim mobs, seeking vengeance, attack Christians in Nigeria. (2004, May 13). *Associated Press in The New York Times.* Retrieved from http://www.nytimes.com

Muslim sect kills more than 100 in attacks on north-east Nigeria. (2011, November 6). *Associated Press in The Guardian.* Retrieved from http://www.guardiannews.com/

Mwakikagile, G. (2001). *Ethnic politics in Kenya and Nigeria*. Huntington, NY: Nova Science Publishers, Inc.
Myers, S. L. (2006, February 21). 2nd Russian paper shut in cartoon furor. *The New York Times*. Retrieved from http://www.nytimes.com.
Newbury, D. S. (1998, April). Understanding genocide. *African Studies Review, 41*(1), 73–97.
Newman, L. S., & Erber, R. (Eds.). (2002). *Understanding genocide: The social psychology of the Holocaust*. New York: Oxford University Press, Inc.
NG-sharia. (2006). In *Wikipedia*. Retrieved from http://commons.wikimedia.org/wiki/File:NG-Sharia.png
Nigeria 1991–1996. (2007). In *Wikipedia*. Retrieved from http://commons.wikimedia.org/wiki/File:Nigeria_1991–1996.png
Nigeria attacks kill 67; Sect claims responsibility. (2011, November 5). *Associated Press in The New York Times*. Retrieved from http://www.nytimes.com
Nigeria church attack in Kogi state "kills 19." (2012, August 7). *BBC News*. Retrieved from http://www.bbc.co.uk
Nigeria city summons army to quell renewal of rioting. (1984, March 3). *Reuters in The New York Times*. Retrieved from http://www.nytimes.com
Nigeria defense minister denies massacre role. (2001, November 6). *The New York Times*. Retrieved from http://www.nytimes.com
Nigeria: Government sets up inquiry into ethnic clashes in northern states. (2001, November 27). *The Guardian*. Retrieved from http://infoweb.newsbank.com
Nigeria group threatens more deadly attacks. (2011, November 6). *Al Jazeera*. Retrieved from http://www.aljazeera.com
Nigeria imposes curfew to end religious riots. (1985, April 29). *Reuters in The New York Times*. Retrieved from http://www.nytimes.com
Nigeria: Police arrest 200 after attacks. (2012, January 26). *Radio Netherlands Worldwide in AllAfrica.com*. Retrieved from http://allafrica.com/stories/201201261032.html
Nigeria quells religious riots; 200 dead. (1992, May 20). *The New York Times*. Retrieved from http://www.nytimes.com
Nigeria: Slow war in the elephant grass. (1967, July 23). *The New York Times*, p. 132. Retrieved from ProQuest Historical Newspapers: The New York Times (1851–2009) database.
Nigeria states 1967–1976. (2010). In *Wikipedia*. Retrieved from http://commons.wikimedia.org/wiki/File:Nigeria_states-1967–1976.png
Nigeria states 1976–1987. (2010). In *Wikipedia*. Retrieved from http://commons.wikimedia.org/wiki/File:Nigeria_states-1976–1987.png
Nigeria states 1987–1991. (2007). In *Wikipedia*. Retrieved from http://commons.wikimedia.org/wiki/File:Nigeria_states_1987–1991.png
Nigerian church blasts kill 21 in Kaduna state. (2012, June 17). *Associated Press in The Guardian*. Retrieved from http://www.guardiannews.com/
Nigerian death toll from Boko Haram attacks "nears 1,000." (2012, January 24). *Reuters in The Guardian*. Retrieved from http://www.guardiannews.com/
Nigerian death toll rises to 700. (2009, August 2). *Associated Press in The New York Times*. Retrieved from http://www.nytimes.com
Nigerian leader admits he deployed army. (2002, September 12). *The New York Times*. Retrieved from http://www.nytimes.com
Nigerian Muslims speak of horror. (2004, May 8). *Al Jazeera*. Retrieved from http://www.aljazeera.com
Nigerian police station torched. (2010, October 12). *Al Jazeera*. Retrieved from http://www.aljazeera.com
Nigerian reporter murdered while covering bombings. (2012, January 20). *Committee to Protect Journalists*. Retrieved from http://www.cpj.org/
Nigerian toll put at 452 in religious riots. (1982, November 1). *Reuters in The New York Times*. Retrieved from http://www.nytimes.com

Nigerian villages and churches are struck in deadly attacks. (2010, December 25). *Reuters in The New York Times*. Retrieved from http://www.nytimes.com

Noble, K. B. (1989, March 5). Islamic militants threaten Nigerian Nobel winner. *Special to The New York Times*. Retrieved from http://www.nytimes.com

Noble, K. B. (1992a, August 5). Akwana Journal; Dawn brings death: One more day of ethnic war. *The New York Times*. Retrieved from http://www.nytimes.com

Noble, K. B. (1992b, May 26). Nigeria plans new force to deal with unrest. *The New York Times*. Retrieved from http://www.nytimes.com

Noble, K. B. (1992c, May 23). Nigerians brace for fallout of civil strife. *The New York Times*. Retrieved from http://www.nytimes.com

Nossiter, A. (2009a, July 26). Clashes between militants and the police in Nigeria. *The New York Times*. Retrieved from http://www.nytimes.com

Nossiter, A. (2009b, July 27). Scores die as fighters battle Nigerian police. *The New York Times*. Retrieved from http://www.nytimes.com

Nossiter, A. (2010a, January 19). Christian-Muslim mayhem in Nigeria kills dozens. *The New York Times*. Retrieved from http://www.nytimes.com

Nossiter, A. (2010b, March 7). Clashes kill dozens in central Nigeria. *The New York Times*. Retrieved from http://www.nytimes.com

Nossiter, A. (2010c, October 18). Killings in Nigeria are linked to Islamic sect. *The New York Times*. Retrieved from http://www.nytimes.com

Nossiter, A. (2010d, March 10). Nigerians recount night of their bloody revenge. *The New York Times*. Retrieved from http://www.nytimes.com

Nossiter, A. (2010e, March 9). Ravaged Nigerian village is haunted by latest massacre. *The New York Times*. Retrieved from http://www.nytimes.com

Nossiter, A. (2010f, March 8). Toll from religious and ethnic violence in Nigeria rises to 500. *The New York Times*. Retrieved from http://www.nytimes.com

Nossiter, A. (2011, December 25). Nigerian group escalates violence with church attacks. *The New York Times*. Retrieved from http://www.nytimes.com

Nossiter, A. (2012, March 25). Wielding fire, Islamists target Nigeria schools. *The New York Times*. Retrieved from http://www.nytimes.com

Obateru, T., & Eyoboka, S. (2012, March 13). Tension in Jos as death toll rises to 19. *Vanguard (Nigeria)*. Retrieved from http://www.vanguardngr.com

Obateru, T., & Mamah, E. (2004, May 14). Obasanjo spits fire, calls CAN boss "idiot." *Vanguard (Nigeria)*. Retrieved from http://infoweb.newsbank.com

Ohai, C. (2012, January 7). Boko Haram attacks Christians in Gombe, Adamawa, kills 28. *Punch*. Retrieved from http://www.punchng.com

Ojo, Y. (2012, May 1). Taraba: Bombers explore new targets, new territories. *The Daily Times of Nigeria*. Retrieved from http://dailytimes.com.ng

Okosun, T. Y. (2012). *When two elephants fight: A historical-critical examination of the 2010–2011 presidential election conflict in Cote d'Ivoire, its implication to governance, power, and social justice*. (Doctoral dissertation). Nova Southeastern University, Fort Lauderdale-Davie, FL.

Okoye, C. (2011, January 28). Clashes have killed 200 in past month-group. *Reuters in Daily Times of Nigeria*. Retrieved from http://dailytimes.com.ng

Okpi, A. (2012, January 22). Death toll rises to 162. *Punch*. Retrieved from http://www.punchng.com

Okubenji, E. (2011, May 30). Bomb blast kills 12. *Daily Times of Nigeria*. Retrieved from http://www.dailytimes.com.ng

Ola, T., & Orude, P. (2012, February 29). Boko Haram attacks another school. *Sun News Online*. Retrieved from http://www.sunnewsonline.com

Olatunji, S. (2012, March 17). Gunmen kill 10, injure five in southern Kaduna community. *Punch*. Retrieved from http://www.punchng.com

Olokor, F. (2011, December 30). Madalla explosion: Death toll hits 43. *Punch*. Retrieved from http://www.punchng.com

Omeje, K. (2004, January). The state, conflict & evolving politics in the Niger Delta, Nigeria. *Review of African Political Economy, 31*(101), 425–440.

Onah, M., Shiklam, J., & Olugbode, M. (2012, January 8). 20 killed in fresh attacks in Adamawa, Yobe, Borno. *This Day Live*. Retrieved from http://www.thisdaylive.com/

Onishi, N. (2000, March 26). Deep political and religious rifts disrupt the harmony of Nigerian towns. *The New York Times*, p. 22. Retrieved from ProQuest Historical Newspapers: The New York Times (1851–2009) database.

Onishi, N. (2001a, October 30). Nigeria army said to massacre hundreds of civilians. *The New York Times*. Retrieved from http://www.nytimes.com

Onishi, N. (2001b, November 1). Rising Muslim power in Africa causes unrest in Nigeria and elsewhere. *The New York Times*. Retrieved from http://www.nytimes.com

Onishi, N. (2002, September 19). Nigeria—a higher Christian-Muslim toll. *The New York Times*, p. A12. Retrieved from ProQuest Historical Newspapers: The New York Times (1851–2009) database.

Onyelebocho, A., Ola, T., & Mgboh, D. (2011, December 24). Massacre continues in Yobe, Borno. *Sun News Online*. Retrieved from http://www.sunnewsonline.com

Onyeose, C. (2012, April 26). Bomb blasts hit media houses. *Daily Times of Nigeria*. Retrieved from http://dailytimes.com.ng/article/bomb-blasts-hit-media-houses

Orude, P. (2012a, January 7). Bloody day: 8 killed in Gombe church. *Sun News Online*. Retrieved from http://www.sunnewsonline.com

Orude, P. (2012b, January 8). How Boko Haram attacked Deeper Life Church in Gombe. *Sun News Online*. Retrieved from http://www.sunnewsonline.com

Osaghae, E. E. (1995). The Ogoni uprising: Oil politics, minority agitation and the future of the Nigerian State. *African Affairs*, 94(376), 325–344.

Osaghae, E. E. (1998a, March). Managing multiple minority problems in a divided society: The Nigerian experience. *The Journal of Modern African Studies*, 36(1), 1–24.

Osaghae, E. E. (1998b). *Crippled giant: Nigeria since independence*. Bloomington, IN: Indiana University Press.

Osaghae, E. E., Suberu, R. T., & University of Oxford. (2005). *A history of identities, violence and stability in Nigeria*. Oxford: Centre for Research on Inequality, Human Security and Ethnicity, University of Oxford.

Osuntokun, A. (2012, May 24). Ode to the Kaduna mafia. *Premium Times*. Retrieved from http://premiumtimesng.com

Ostien, P. (2009, August). Jonah Jang and the Jasawa: Ethno-religious conflict in Jos, Nigeria. *Muslim-Christian Relations in Africa*. Available from www.sharia-in-africa.net/pages/publications.php

Overnight explosions heard in Nigeria's Kano. (2012, January 24). *Al Jazeera*. Retrieved from http://www.aljazeera.com

Pedro, E. (2011, June 6). Bomb explodes at police headquarters Abuja. *Daily Times of Nigeria*. Retrieved from http://dailytimes.com.ng/article/bomb-explodes-police-headquarters-abuja

Polgreen, L. (2006, February 24). Nigeria counts 100 deaths over Danish caricatures. *The New York Times*. Retrieved from http://www.nytimes.com

Polgreen, L. (2008, November 30). Deadly Nigeria clashes subside. *The New York Times*. Retrieved from http://www.nytimes.com

Police arrested in Nigeria killings. (2010, February 28). *Al Jazeera*. Retrieved from http://www.aljazeera.com/news/africa/2010/02/201022820193376744.html

Purefoy, C. (2010, March 17). 11 dead in fresh Muslim-Christian violence in Nigeria. *CNN*. Retrieved from http://cnn.com

Rae, H. (2002). *State identities and the homogenization of peoples*. New York: Cambridge University Press.

Religious and ethnic clashes in Nigeria spread, killing at least 165. (2001, September 12). *The New York Times*. Retrieved from http://www.nytimes.com

Religious riots leave 18 dead in Nigeria; Muslims protest U.S.-led strikes. (2001, October 15). *Associated Press in Hamilton Spectator* (Ontario, Canada). Retrieved from http://www.lexisnexis.com

Religious strife in Nigeria leaves bodies in the streets. (2001, September 10). *The New York Times*. Retrieved from http://www.nytimes.com

Renewed Jos violence claims 22. (2011, September 2). *The Daily Times of Nigeria*. Retrieved from http://dailytimes.com.ng

Reprisal attacks on Muslims spread in southeast, government urges calm. (2006, February 23). *The Guardian*. Retrieved from http://infoweb.newsbank.com

Riemer, N. (2000). *Protection against genocide: Mission impossible?* Westport, CT: Praeger.

Robins, N. A. (2002). *Genocide and millennialism in Upper Peru: The great rebellion of 1780–1782*. Westport, CT: Praeger.

Runciman, W. G. (1972). *Relative deprivation and social justice: A study of attitudes to social inequality in twentieth-century England*. Harmondsworth: Penguin.

Schabas, W. (2000). *Genocide in international law: The crimes of crimes*. New York: Cambridge University Press.

Scherrer, C. P. (2002). *Genocide and crisis in central Africa: Conflict roots, mass violence, and regional war*. Westport, CT: Praeger.

Scores killed in Nigeria clashes. (2011, December 25). *Al Jazeera*. Retrieved from http://www.aljazeera.com/news/africa/2011/12/20111224124241652788.html

Sectarian attacks kill 15 in Nigeria. (2012, January 7). *Associated Press in The New York Times*. Retrieved from http://www.nytimes.com

Sells, M. A. (1998). *The bridge betrayed: Religion and genocide in Bosnia*. Berkeley, CA: University of California Press.

Sengupta, S. (2003, February 21). Kaduna Journal; Piety and politics sunder a riot-torn Nigerian city. *The New York Times*. Retrieved from http://www.nytimes.com

Sengupta, S. (2004a, May 19). Nigerian declares emergency in restive region. *The New York Times*. Retrieved from http://www.nytimes.com

Sengupta, S. (2004b, May 24). Violence jolts the still fragile democracy in Nigeria. *The New York Times*. Retrieved from http://www.nytimes.com

Senholzi, K. B. (2008). *Conflict in northern Ireland: Through the lens of social identity theory and social dominance theory* (Masters thesis). Retrieved from http://www.lib.unc.edu/digitalprojects.html

Shiaondo, J. (2011, December 2). Nigeria: 79 killed as Fulani, Tiv clash again in Benue, Nasarawa. *The Moment (London) in AllAfrica.com*. Retrieved December 2, 2011 from http://allafrica.com/stories/201112020225.html

Shuaibu, I. (2012, January 22). Horror, anger in Kano as death toll reaches 200. *This Day Live*. Retrieved from http://www.thisdaylive.com

Simmons, A. M. (2000, February 25). Editorial. *The Vancouver Sun* (British Columbia). Retrieved from http://www.lexisnexis.com

Siollun, M. (2009). *Oil, politics and violence: Nigeria's military coup culture (1966–1976)*. New York: Algora Publishing.

Smith, D., & Associated Press. (2009, July 30). Nigerian forces storm militant Islamist mosque. *The Guardian*. Retrieved from http://www.guardiannews.com/

Sokunbi, W. (2012, January 2). The Christmas massacre and security in 2012. *Sun News Online*. Retrieved from http://www.sunnewsonline.com

Some groups banned by Nigeria after riots. (1992, May 21). *The New York Times*. Retrieved from http://www.nytimes.com

Stake, R. (1995). *The art of case research*. Thousand Oaks, CA: Sage Publications.

Sternberg, R. J. (2003). A duplex theory of hate: Development and application to terrorism, massacres, and genocide. *Review of General Psychology, 7*(3), 299–328.

Sternberg, R. J., & Sternberg, K. (2008). *The nature of hate*. New York: Cambridge University Press.

Strauss, A., & Corbin, J. (1990). *Basics of qualitative research: Grounded theory procedures and techniques*. Newbury Park, CA: Sage Publications, Inc.

Stuijt, A. (2009, March 16). Oil-rich Nigeria will become Islamic soon, warn Dutch MPs. *Reformatorisch Dagblad*. Retrieved from http://www.digitaljournal.com/article/269323

Suberu, R. T. (2009). Religion and institutions: Federalism and the management of conflicts over Sharia in Nigeria. *Journal of International Development, 21*(4), 547–560. doi:10.1002/jid.1572

Suicide bombing kills dozens in Nigeria. (2012, April 8). *Associated Press in The New York Times.* Retrieved from http://www.nytimes.com

Tajfel, H., & Turner, J. C. (1979). An integrative theory of intergroup conflict. In W. G. Austin & S. Worchel (Eds.), *The social psychology of intergroup relations* (pp. 33–47). Monterey, CA: Brooks-Cole.

Thousands flee Nigeria violence. (2009, July 30). *Al Jazeera.* Retrieved from http://www.aljazeera.com

Tilley-Gyado, T. (2012, March 11). Bomb blast rocks Jos church, casualities reported. *Daily Times of Nigeria.* Retrieved from http://dailytimes.com.ng

Toll in religious riots in Nigeria is put at 24. (1992, May 19). *The New York Times.* Retrieved from http://www.nytimes.com

Toll rises in Nigeria sectarian riots. (2006, February 22). *Al Jazeera.* Retrieved from http://www.aljazeera.com

Tostevin, M. (2000, February 29). Riots over Islamic law spread in Nigeria. *Reuters in The Philadelphia Inquirer.* Retrieved from http://www.lexisnexis.com

Totten, S., & Parsons, W. S. (Eds.). (2009). *Century of genocide: Critical essays and eyewitness accounts* (3rd ed.). New York, NY: Routledge.

Ukiwo, U. (2003). Politics, ethno-religious conflicts and democratic consolidation in Nigeria. *The Journal of Modern African Studies, 41*(1), 115–138. http://dx.doi.org/10.1017/S0022278X02004172

Unidentified gunmen said kill 18 people in Nigeria's Plateau state. (2011, January 11). *The Guardian.* Retrieved from http://infoweb.newsbank.com

Vetlesen, A. J. (2005). *Evil and human agency: Understanding collective evildoing.* New York: Cambridge University Press.

Violence in northeast Nigeria sparks fears. (2011, July 12). *Al Jazeera.* Retrieved from http://www.aljazeera.com

Violent weekend in Nigeria. (2001, October 15). *Associated Press in The Leader Post.* Retrieved from www.lexisnexis.com

Walker, I., & Smith, H. J. (2010). *Relative deprivation: Specification, development, and integration.* New York: Cambridge University Press.

Waller, J. (2002). *Becoming evil: How ordinary people commit genocide and mass killing.* New York: Oxford University Press.

Walters, M. A. (2011). A general theories of hate crime? Strain, doing difference and self control. *Critical Criminology, 19*(4), 313–330. doi:10.1007/s10612–010–9128–2

Webster, C. (2007). *Understanding race and crime.* New York, NY: The McGraw-Hill Companies.

Williams, P. D. (2011). *War and conflict in Africa.* Cambridge, UK: Polity Press.

Williams, P. A. T. (1997). Religion, violence and displacement in Nigeria. *Journal of Asian and African Studies, 32*(1–2), 33–49.

Witness: Gunmen attack Nigeria university campus. (2012, April 29). *CNN.* Retrieved from http://cnn.com

Wood, W. B. (2001). Geographic aspects of genocide: A comparison of Bosnia and Rwanda. *Transactions of the Institute of British Geographers, 26*(1), 57–75.

Youths besiege Uyo, torch properties. (2000, March 1). *The Guardian.* Retrieved from http://infoweb.newsbank.com

Index

Abacha, Sani, 16, 81, 148, 159
abductions. *See* kidnappings
Abiola, Moshood K.O., 147
Abubakar Abdulsalami, 159
Abuja, 80, 107, 111, 115, 147, 156, 162, 166, 176, 182, 183
Aburi accord, 15, 118, 120
Adamawa, 75, 76; violence in, 176–177, 179, 211, 215
Aguiyi-Ironsi, Johnson. *See* Ironsi, Aguiyi
Ahmadu, Hamzat, 117
Aikhomu, Augustus, 156
ajami, 9
Akayesu judgment, 29, 192
aliens, illegal, 103, 138, 179
Alford, C. Fred, 64
Allport, Gordon, 88
almajiri system, 211–213
alms-begging, 212
Al Qaeda, 103, 138, 163, 213
ambush, 152
Amnesty International, 225
animist groups, 3, 180
annihilating difference analysis, 107, 126, 142, 155, 166, 182
anti-Western ideology, 11, 86, 103, 121, 139, 164, 180, 190, 191, 197, 200
archaeology, and genocide, 61
Arendt, Hannah, 64
Argentina, 32
Armed Forces Ruling Council (AFRC) of Nigeria, 133, 147
Armenian genocide, 29, 32, 49–50, 55, 57, 61, 201
Armenians, 58, 61
arson, 112, 121, 122, 124, 131, 140, 141, 145, 154, 165, 181, 186, 190, 218. *See also* churches and chapels, destruction of

Ash experiments, 40
assassinations, 121, 181
assault, 141, 154, 165, 166, 180, 181, 190, 195, 197, 200
Attahiru I (Caliph of Sokoto), 7
authority, loyalty to, 40–42

Babangida, Ibrahim, 81, 83, 133, 136, 144, 147, 148, 153, 195, 208
Balewa, Tafawa, 81, 116, 119, 149, 157, 195
Balkan genocide, 52, 57. *See also* Armenian genocide; Bosnia; Kosovo
Balkanization, 94, 103, 120, 163
Bangladesh, 42
barbarism, 106, 121, 123, 125, 141, 154, 155, 165, 181, 190, 195, 197, 200
Bauchi, violence in, 17, 87, 149–150, 152, 155, 157, 162, 166, 173, 174, 176, 178, 195, 196, 198, 198–199, 209, 210, 211, 215, 219
Bauman, Zygmunt, 64
beheadings, 181
Belgian victimization of Congolese, 22
Bello, Alhaji Ahmadu, 12, 13, 14, 73, 116
Berlin Conference, 7
Biafra, 15, 107; secession of, 112, 118. *See also* Biafra Nigeria War; blockade; embargo
Biafra Nigeria War, 15, 110, 112, 118, 122–125, 193, 202, 214, 218, 225; internationalization of, 128–129. *See also* civil war
Biafrans, as victims, 126, 127
bin Laden, Osama, 58
blasphemy, 150, 197
blockade, 112, 121, 122, 125, 130, 190, 214, 225

261

bloodbath, 106, 121, 123, 125, 141, 154, 155, 180, 181, 183, 190, 195, 197, 200
bodies mutilated or burned, 112, 131, 145, 154, 158, 170, 175, 186, 190, 196
Boko Haram, 17, 73, 86, 107, 112, 175–177, 180–181, 182, 183, 185, 187
bombs and bombings, 112, 121, 126, 131, 145, 176, 178, 180–181, 185, 186, 190, 199, 202, 218; car bombs, 176, 177; suicide bombings, 104, 112, 176, 177, 178, 185, 212
Bonnke, Reinhard, 150, 151, 209
Borno Kingdom, 4–5, 76; violence in, 17, 176, 198–199, 204, 211, 215, 219. *See also* Maiduguri
Bosnia, 27, 29, 41, 48–49, 67, 68, 201
Bosnia-Herzegovina, 66. *See also* Bosnia; Herzegovina
B process dominance, 42
Brazilian street children, 60
Britain: ethnic diversity in, 36; government of, 7, 8; narcissism in, 47; response to Biafra Nigeria War, 124–125, 128, 129
Buhari, Muhammadu, 16, 81, 95, 133, 137
Burundi, 49, 52, 59, 68

Calabar, 123
Caliphate of Sokoto, 4, 5–6, 7, 12, 13, 14, 76, 87, 116, 119, 156. *See also* Sokoto Caliphate
Cambodia, 24, 25, 29, 42, 48, 49, 61. *See also* Khmer Rouge
car bombs, 176, 177
carnage, 106, 121, 123, 125, 141, 154, 155, 165, 166, 181, 190, 195, 197, 200
cartoon riots. *See* Danish newspaper cartoon
casualty figure deflation/inflation, 128, 156, 158, 168, 190, 204, 210
censorship of press, 111, 128, 143, 168, 190
chaos : as intent of massacres, 201; political, 112, 158, 171; social, 112, 131, 145, 158, 171, 187
Chiang, Kai-shek, 42
children: maltreatment of, 127; as target of ethno-religious conflict, 111; as victims, 126, 143, 174, 175, 183, 214; as victims in Biafra Nigeria War, 122, 123
China, 42, 47
Christian Association of Nigeria (CAN), 76, 148, 150, 178, 187, 215
Christian evangelism, 148
Christianity: association with Igbos, 73, 75, 76, 81, 94, 151; in Bosnia, 49; conversion to, 8; desecration of, 170; in Nigeria, 72–73, 73–74, 75. *See also* Christian militia; Christian missionaries; Christians
Christian militia, 142, 160, 161, 167, 183, 196, 204, 210, 217, 219
Christian missionaries, 9, 121, 127. *See also* missionary schools
Christians : critical of Sharia law, 76–77, 85, 104, 160, 164, 180, 200; discrimination against, 85, 94–95, 136, 167, 203, 216, 218; ethnic groups, 151; forced conversion of, 103, 112, 139, 164, 169, 180, 181, 185, 190, 194, 200; forced expulsion of, 103, 112, 180, 190, 200; fundamentalists, 148; involvement, in ethno-religious conflict 107; as migrants, 13–14; as minorities, 3, 57, 75, 85, 142, 149, 150, 153, 162, 181, 195, 209, 210, 211; in Nigeria, 76, 77, 79; as out-group, 93; as perpetrators of violence, 138, 145, 155, 160, 163, 175, 184, 217; persecution of, 164; political involvement of, 148–149; as "pollution", 200; Seyawa, 149, 195; in Southern Nigeria, 75, 110, 120, 142, 164, 167, 183, 194, 200, 203, 211, 219, 223; as targets and victims of violence, 91, 110–111, 127, 135, 138, 140, 142, 144, 145, 149–150, 151–152, 155, 160, 160–163, 163, 165, 167, 168–169, 173–174, 174–175, 176–178, 180–181, 183, 187, 190, 191, 194, 196, 197, 198, 199, 199–200, 200, 201, 202, 203, 203–205, 208, 215, 217, 218, 218–219, 220, 225; Tarok, 160, 163, 165, 196, 204; view of Muslims by, 83; Wusasa, 139, 144, 194, 209, 213; Zuru, 76. *See also* Christian militia;

Christian missionaries; Christianity; missionary schools; Muslim-Christian hostilities

churches and chapels: destruction of, 124, 136, 138, 140, 141, 142, 149, 150, 152, 155, 157, 158, 162, 167, 168–169, 169, 170, 170–171, 175, 176, 176–177, 177, 178, 180, 181, 183–184, 185, 186, 190, 194, 196, 197, 198, 199, 202, 208, 209, 210, 217, 218; non-allocation of land for, 95; as target in ethno-religious conflict, 110, 112, 126, 130, 131

civilian mobs, 107, 123, 141, 183; violence by, 126. *See also* civilians

civilians: maltreatment of, 127; as target of ethno-religious conflict, 110–111, 199; as victims, 27, 123, 126, 127, 156, 167, 183, 194; violence against, 124. *See also* civilian mobs

civil war, 112, 121, 123, 126, 128. *See also* Biafra Nigeria War

collaborators, 90, 111, 122, 128, 129, 143, 144, 169, 184, 190

colonial influences, 103, 120, 153, 163

colonialism, 30–34, 72, 81

common ego deal, 40

Communists, Nazi atrocities against, 44–45

conflict resolution: adoption of genocide prevention and intervention measures, 228; dialogue in economic advancement with religious extremists, 227; international and local effort, 226; Nigerian-led international effort, 227; prescriptive recommendations, 226–228; prospects, 225–226; plausible state break-up, 227–228

conflict, Muslim-Christian. *See* Muslim-Christian hostilities

Congo, 59, 68

Congolese, Belgian victimization of, 22

Constituent Assembly, debate over Sharia law in, 137, 159–160

Constitutional Conference (London, 1953), 11

Convention on the Prevention and Punishment of the Crime of Genocide (1948) (UNGC), 20, 21, 22–23, 24–25, 41, 65, 67, 203, 219, 224

corpses. *See* bodies

coup d'état (in Nigeria): attempted by Christians, 10, 17, 77; first military coup, 14, 83, 88, 102–103, 116, 119, 120, 189; riots following, 103; in Rwanda, 10, 52; second military coup (counter-coup), 14, 15–16, 102, 117, 120; as theme of episodic genocide, 102, 104, 121, 124, 165, 181

Croatia, 66

Czech Republic genocide, 62

Dan Fodio, Shehu Usman, 5, 12, 73

Danish newspaper cartoon, 102, 173, 181, 189, 198, 204

Danjuma, T. Y., 117

Darfur, 29, 45, 61, 67, 201

dehumanization, 33, 34, 42, 43

democide, 25, 26

Democratic Kampuchea (DK), 48. *See also* Cambodia; Khmer Rouge

demographics: colonial developments' effect on, 9; as factor in genocide causation, 53; in Nigeria, 75–77

Deng, Francis, 185

displaced persons. *See* refugees

Disu, Abdul Kareem, 117

Doctors Without Borders (Médicins Sans Frontières), 225

Dogon Na Hauwa slaughter, 175, 198, 200

drive-by shootings, 112, 185

Eastern Europe, German murders in, 52

East Pakistan, 42

East Timor, 61

economic blockade. *See* blockade

economic destabilization, 30

economics, colonial developments' effect on, 9

education: in the British north, 10; European/Western system of, 9, 13, 15; in Southern Nigeria, 11

Effiong, Phillip, 117

Efik, 75

Egypt, response to Biafra Nigeria War, 129
El Salvador, 62
elite theory, 80–84
elites : as cause of ethno-religious conflict, 95, 96; ethno-regional, 82; Hausa-Fulani, 8, 12, 76; Islamic, 78, 82; in Nigeria, 15, 30, 42, 81, 82, 84, 88–89, 151; northern, 14, 74, 78, 82, 83, 95, 144, 224; political, 11, 16, 34, 38, 74, 81, 82, 84, 103, 134, 138, 144, 153, 164; social, 84
el-Zakzaky, Ibrahim, 148
embargo, 121, 122, 123, 193
Enugu, 123
ethnic cleansing, 24, 27, 29, 38, 50, 112, 144, 169, 185, 194; in former Yugoslavia, 61, 64, 201. *See also* genocide
ethnic conflict. *See* northern Nigeria ethno-religious conflict
ethnic groups, in Nigeria, 72, 75, 75–77. *See also* Fulanis; Hausa-Fulani Muslims; Hausas; Igbos; Muslims
ethnic monoculture grounding, 36
ethnic prejudice, 88, 96
ethnicity, 134; autoassociational, 10; and religion, 151, 207
ethnocentrism, 43
ethnocide, 25
ethno-religious conflict. *See* Northern Nigeria ethno-religious conflict
euthanasia programs, 23
evil: analysis of, 64; collective, 38–40
exclusionary ideology theory, 84–87
exclusive/exclusionary ideological framing, 103, 152, 154, 163, 164, 165, 190, 194, 195, 196
exclusive/exclusionary ideology, 95, 96, 102, 103, 191
extermination plots, 112

famine, 125
fatwa, 189
Federal Capital territory (Abuja), 80, 107, 111, 115, 147, 156, 162, 166, 176, 182, 183
fingerprinting, 31
forced assimilation, 38

forced displacement, 38
forced migration, 27, 60, 130, 157, 185, 190, 194
forced sterilization, 23, 60
foreign collaborators, 90, 111, 122, 128, 129, 144, 169, 184
France, response to Biafra Nigeria War, 128
freedom of association, denial of, 170–171
freedom of worship, denial of, 170
French Revolution, 43, 61
Fulanis, 3–4, 4, 73, 216; Fulani aristocracy, 5, 6, 7–8, 8; Fulani herdsmen, 107, 155, 166, 167, 168, 182; Fulani language, 4; Fulani rulers, 6. *See also* Hausa-Fulani Muslims
Fulani-Tarok hostilities, 165
fundamentalism, 164, 166. *See also* Islamic fundamentalists
fundamentalist sect members, arrest and persecution of, 102, 152, 163, 179
Funtua, violence in, 77, 137, 151, 209, 213

genocidal proclivity in Northern Nigerian ethno-religious conflict, 101; major categories identified, 106, 121. *See also Genocidal Proclivity* model; genocide causation; genocide in Northern Nigeria
Genocidal Proclivity model, 101–102, 105, 113; causal conditions, 102–104, 119–121, 138–140, 152–154, 179–180, 189–190; consequences or effects, 112, 131, 145, 158, 186–187, 189, 190; context for development, 107–111, 108, 110, 125–127, 141–143, 155–156, 182–184, 189, 190; intervening conditions, 111, 127–130, 156–157, 184–185, 189, 190; results of trigger factors, underlying causation, perceived threat and exclusivity, 104–106, 121–125, 140–141, 154–155, 180–181, 189–190; strategies of attack, 112, 130–131, 144, 157, 185, 189, 190

Index   265

genocide, 121, 165, 181; causes of, 29–30; defined by UN Convention, 20, 21, 22–23, 24–25; definition of, 19–23; determining features of, 203; as differs from ethnic cleansing, 24; as differs from ethnic conflict, 23; as differs from massacres/mass killings, 21, 27; as differs from war, 23; episodic, 219–220, 228; examples of, 61–62; geographic perspective, 107; government complicity in, 213–216; human agency and, 38–40, 64; inclination and intent, 28–29, 29, 191–192, 218; intentionality of, 202; intervention attempts, 65–69, 144, 156, 185, 228; latent episodic, 201, 205, 228; mass genocide, 50; and the nation state, 37–38; origins of, 30; "othering" as factor in, 26; prevention of, 65–69, 228; role of state in, 28, 42; social and political groups included in, 25; starvation in Biafra as, 125; two-phased manifestations of, 192–193; types of, 59–61. *See also* genocide causation; genocide in Northern Nigeria; genocide studies methodology

genocide causation, 29–30, 64; demographic factors, 53; denial themes, 55–56; fear, 50–53; greed, 53–54; Groupthink, hate processes and dehumanization, 42–45; human agency and collective evil, 38–40; humiliation, 56–58; ideological influences, 48–50; imperialism, colonialism, and modernity, 30–34; in-group vs. out-group identity, 47, 51; manipulation and loyalty to authority, 40–42; narcissism, 46–47; the nation-state, 34–38; power politics, 54–55; race, racism, and crime, 58–59; threat and vulnerability, 50

Genocide Convention of the UN. *See* Convention on the Prevention and Punishment of the Crime of Genocide

genocide in Northern Nigeria: attempts at intervention or mediation, 111; causal conditions, 102–104, 119–121, 138–140, 152–154, 179–180, 189–190; consequences or effects of, 112, 131, 145, 158, 186–187, 190; context for development of, 107–111, 108, 110, 125–127, 141–143, 155–156, 182–184, 190; events foreshadowing, 112; intervening conditions, 111, 127–130, 156–157, 184–185, 190; perpetrators of,. *See also* violence, perpetrators of 107–111; results of trigger factors, underlying causation, perceived threat and exclusivity, 104–106, 121–125, 140–141, 154–155, 180–181, 189–190; strategies of attack, 112, 130–131, 144, 157, 185, 190; victim or target groups, 110–111

genocide studies methodology: ethology, 62; geographical perspective, 64; hybrid approach, 64; ideology, 63; modernity, 62–63; post-Holocaust reflective analysis, 63; relationship with body politic, 63

Genocide Treaty, 65
Germans, 58, 201; extermination of Jews by, 52. *See also* Nazis
Germany, 42, 47
Ghaddafi, Muammar al-, 79
Gilligan, James, 56, 58
Global Human Rights Regime, 68
Gombe, violence in, 176–177, 199, 211, 215
government : ineptitude or weakness of, 111, 127, 143, 156, 161, 168, 184, 190, 196, 204, 213, 215. *See also* Nigerian republics
Gowon, Yakubu, 14, 81, 117, 118, 127, 133, 134, 139
Great Britain. *See* Britain
Groupthink, 42
Guatemala, 61
Gumi, Abubakar, 14
gun battles, 106, 121, 141, 155, 165, 181
Gurr, Ted, 90
Gypsies, 24, 29, 44, 45

handicapped people, 24, 60
hate: complex nature of, 89; triangular components of, 44
hate crime, 88
hate theory, 87–90, 95, 96
Hausa-Fulani Muslims, 9, 11, 17, 76, 81, 139, 141, 155, 169, 182, 204, 209, 219; Hausa-Fulani oligarchy, 15–16; as in-group, 93; involvement in counter-coup, 14; involvement in ethno-religious conflict, 107. *See also* Fulanis; Hausas; Hausa-Fulani herders
Hausa-Fulani herders, 143, 160, 175, 179, 194, 196; as victims, 111, 168
Hausa-Fulani mobs, 202
Hausa-Northern troops, 155, 167, 183, 213, 214
Hausaland, 4, 209
Hausas, 3–4, 72, 89, 163, 197, 209, 216; aristocracy, 6; clashes with indigenes, 151–152; Empire, 4–5; identity with Islam, 151; language, 4, 9; mobs, 154; Muslims, 119, 120; tensions with Igbo, 117, 151; troops, 126. *See also* elites, Hausa-Fulani; Hausa-Fulani Muslims; Hausa-Northern troops
Herero people, 32
heresy and heretics, 135, 139, 194
Herzegovina, 49. *See also* Bosnia; Herzegovina
hit and run shootings, 112, 185
Hitler, Adolf, 42, 44, 46, 53, 57
Holocaust, 21, 23, 41, 45, 52, 53, 54, 59, 61, 66, 67; interpretation of, 63. *See also* Nazis
Holodomor, 29
hospitals as targets, 124, 126
House of Islam, 13. *See also* Islam; Muslims
Huguenot persecution, 61
human agency: and evil, 38–40; and genocide, 38–40, 64
Human Rights Watch, 185, 208, 215, 216
Hutu people, 21, 22, 44, 46, 52, 57, 58, 59, 88, 90

Ibibios, 75
Ibos. *See* Igbos (Ibos)
ideo-ethnic cleansing, 112, 130, 157, 190
ideological cleansing, 112, 144, 157, 169, 185, 194
ideological framing: exclusive/exclusionary, 103, 152, 154, 163, 164, 165, 190, 194, 195, 196; Maitatsine, 139
ideology: anti-Western, 11, 86, 103, 121, 139, 148, 164, 180, 190, 191, 197, 200; exclusive, 95, 96, 102, 103, 191
identity: destruction of, 192; in-group vs. out-group, 19, 40, 47, 51, 92–94, 211; Islamic, 10; social, 92–93; social vs. personal, 40
Igbos (Ibos) : attacked by Hausas and Fulanis, 141; chauvinistic nature of, 117; and colonization, 72, 81; continuing massacres of, 117; fear of, 103, 120; forced expulsion of, 134; killed in counter-coup, 117; killing of by Hausa, 14, 125, 139, 197; killed by Nigerian troops, 127, 128; involvement in January 1966 coup, 14, 116, 119; loss of influence by, 134; massacre of, 88–89, 101, 102, 116, 117–118, 121–122, 126, 127, 130, 131, 193, 200, 201, 208, 213–214; as members of Christian minority, 73, 75, 76, 81, 94, 151; migration of, 9–10; as refugees, 15; as target of ethno-religious conflict, 107, 110–111; tensions with Hausas, 89, 151; as victims of violence, 123, 126–127, 141, 142, 150, 167, 177, 179, 183, 194, 202, 211, 218, 219
illegal aliens, 103, 138, 179
Ilorin, 11
immigrants, southern, 9–10, 12, 17
imperialism, 29–30, 72
indigenous peoples, 32, 33, 45, 78, 103, 151, 179, 209, 216–217
indoctrination, 84, 112, 144, 157, 170, 190, 212
inequities, 90
infants, killing of, 27
infiltration, 103, 112, 163, 179, 187

in-group vs. out-group identity, 19, 40, 47, 51, 92–94, 211
instigation, 83, 112, 135, 144, 157, 170, 190
insurgencies, 138, 152, 163, 179, 189, 195, 196, 200
integration, interethnic, 10
interfaith commission, 226
international community: and the Biafra Nigeria War, 122; obligation to prevent and punish, 66; response of, 27; response to Nigerian situation, 201, 225; response to Rwanda, 201; as witness to mass killings, 90
International Convention on the Elimination of All Forms of Racial Discrimination (CERD), 177
Iran, 103, 138
Ironsi, Aguiyi, 14, 116, 116–117, 117, 119, 134
Islam: in Africa, 80; in Bosnia, 49; degradation of, 102, 163, 196, 200, 210; forceful conversion to, 103, 112, 139, 164, 169, 180, 181, 185, 190, 194, 200; and the Hausa identity, 151; importation of, 5; in Nigeria, 73, 73–74, 75, 76, 77, 77–78, 79; as political strategy, 16, 95, 148–149; and power in Nigeria, 82; revolutionary force of, 74. *See also* Islamic fundamentalists; Muslims
Islamic centers of learning, 3
Islamic fundamentalists, 101, 136, 150, 186, 189, 194, 198, 202, 203, 210, 213, 219, 224. *See also* Boko Haram; Maitatsine riots
Islamic judges (*alkalis*), 8
Islamic law. *See* Sharia law
Islamist terrorism, 58. *See also* terrorist activity
Islamization, 78, 85, 96, 205, 219, 223–224
Izala Islamic sect, 150, 209

Jama'atu Nasril Islam (JNI; 'Victory for Islam'), 14, 148
Jang, Jonah, 215
Janjaweed militia, 45
Japan, 61
Jatau, P. Y., 142
Jews, 58, 61, 201; demonization of, 52; expulsion from Spain, 61; Nazi genocide against, 24, 29, 42, 44, 44–45, 52, 54
Jigawa, violence in, 211, 215
jihad, 135, 163, 217, 223, 224; against the Igbos, 193; led by Dan Fodio, 5; and the Nigerian Islamic state, 73, 74
jihadis, foreign, 213
Jonathan, Goodluck, 173
Jos, 3; violence in, 94, 160, 163, 168–169, 174–175, 176, 177, 179, 181, 183, 185, 198, 199, 203, 208, 209, 211, 215, 216, 217, 218
journalists as victims, 111, 143, 156, 168, 183, 194
Jukun, 117

Kabba, 11
Kaduna, 3, 8, 11, 15; separate quarters for Muslims and Christians in, 94; success of coup in, 116; violence in, 83, 91, 92, 137, 140, 142, 144, 145, 148, 151–152, 153, 154, 155, 156, 157, 158, 160, 162, 168, 177, 178, 183, 197, 199, 209, 210, 211, 213, 215, 219. *See also* Kaduna mafia
Kaduna mafia, 83, 103, 138, 143, 153, 164
Kafanchan, violence in, 76, 137, 138, 139, 141, 142, 144, 166, 182, 194, 209, 213
Kannem-Borno Kingdom, 5
Kano, 3; violence in, 87, 117–118, 125, 128, 130, 135–136, 138, 145, 148, 150, 151, 152, 153, 154, 156, 161–162, 164, 166, 167, 168, 170–171, 176, 178, 182, 184, 185, 196, 197, 198, 201, 204, 208, 209, 211, 212, 213–214, 215, 217, 219
Kanuri, 3, 4, 76
Katafs, 209
Katsina, Lt.-Colonel, 130
Katsina, violence in, 137, 148, 154, 173, 185, 198, 209, 211, 215
Katsina Shi'ite sect, 149
Kebbi, violence in, 87, 211

Khan, Agha Mohanmmed Yahya, 42
Khmer Rouge, 24, 25, 29, 48, 49, 58. *See also* Khmer Rouge
Khomeini, Ayatollah, 79
kidnappings, 87, 135, 181, 185
killings : by Boko Haram, 17; as causal condition, 154, 165, 180, 181; of civilians and infants, 27; extrajudicial, 80, 110, 167, 184, 190, 213–216; gruesome/brutal, 150, 152, 157, 161–162, 171; of Igbos, 14, 14–15, 120; mass, 194, 195, 201; of military officers, 14; after second coup, 14; shoot-out, 121, 140, 154, 165, 180. *See also* mass murders; massacres; Muslim-Christian hostilities; reprisal killings; retaliation; retribution; violence
Koran, alleged desecration or misinterpretation of, 102, 138, 139, 142, 144, 150, 174, 179, 189, 194, 195, 196, 200, 209, 210, 213
Kosovo, 23, 41, 61, 201

Lagos: as capital, 10, 80, 129, 144; under colonialism, 7; violence in, 166, 167, 170
land ownership disputes, 153
latent episodic genocide, 201, 205, 228
Lebanon, 201
lebensraum, 27, 107, 141, 155, 166, 182, 190
Lemkin, Raphael, 20, 21
Libya, 103, 138, 143
Lindner, Evelin, 56
Lon Nol, 24
looting, 120, 121, 122, 124, 131, 140, 145, 154, 158, 164, 165, 166, 170, 174, 180, 187, 190, 217
Lugard, Frederick, 7
lynchings, 40, 58, 150

Macedonia, 61
Maghrib states, 5
Mahdi/Mahdism, 11, 148
Maiduguri, 3, 75, 125; violence in, 143, 145, 148, 173–174, 176, 180–181, 186–187, 198, 199, 204, 208. *See also* Danish cartoon; Maitatsine riots

maiming, 86, 87, 112, 120, 131, 185, 190
Maitatsine fundamentalist group, 107, 142, 149, 202, 209, 212; ideological framing of, 139; riots by, 135–136, 137, 138, 139–140, 143, 144, 145, 194, 195, 208, 212
Mali Muslim scholars, 5
malnutrition, 122. *See also* starvation
mandatory emigration. *See* forced migration
manipulation, 35, 40–41, 68, 74, 80, 81, 95, 111, 112, 143, 144, 156, 157, 168, 170, 184, 190, 213
Mao Zedong, 42, 46
marginalization, 45, 79, 90, 91, 95, 96, 227
Marwa, Mohammad, 135–136, 138, 139, 212. *See also* Maitatsine fundamentalist group
Marxist humanist perspective, 82
mass burials/graves, 112, 145, 150, 168, 170, 174, 175, 186, 190, 204
mass genocide, 50
mass killings, 194, 195, 201
mass migration, 45. *See also* forced displacement; forced migration
mass murders, 25, 26, 50, 89, 112, 190
massacres, 27, 89, 106, 118, 121, 123, 125, 141, 154, 155, 165, 181, 195, 197, 200; of Igbos, 88–89, 101, 102, 116, 117–118, 121–122, 126, 127, 130, 131, 193, 200, 201, 208, 213–214
mayhem, 106, 121, 123, 125, 141, 154, 155, 165, 181, 190, 195, 197, 200, 201, 212
media: censorship of, 111, 128, 143, 168, 190; international, 217. *See also* journalists; press; radio
mercenaries, 161, 164, 165, 184, 196
Middle Belt Region, 14, 15, 75, 76, 85, 134, 147, 179, 195, 203, 211, 219, 223
migration factors, 9–10. *See also* forced migration
Milgram experiments, 40
military coups. *See* coup d'état
Mills, C. Wright, 80, 81
Milosevic, Slobodan, 42
minorities: Christian, 3, 57, 75, 85, 142, 149, 150, 153, 162, 181, 195, 209, 210,

211; colonial and postcolonial, 3, 8, 13–14, 14, 15; ethnic and religious, 75–76, 209; non-Muslim, 14, 76, 77, 191, 202, 219
Miss World beauty pageant riots, 102, 189, 197, 210
missionaries, 9, 121, 127
missionary schools, 10, 13
modernity, 30, 31, 31–32, 33, 61
Mohammed, Murtala, 81, 117, 133
mosques, 80, 175; as target of ethno-religious conflict, 111, 112; destruction of, 143, 145, 152, 168, 170, 176, 183, 184, 194, 209
Muslim-Christian hostilities, 11, 16, 17, 77, 86, 87, 90, 92–95, 104–106, 136, 137, 138, 140, 142, 144, 148, 149–150, 152, 153, 153–154, 154, 160–163, 163, 164, 168–169, 174–175, 195, 196, 197, 200, 207–208, 209, 217
Muslim fundamentalists. *See* Islamic fundamentalists
Muslim groups, 3
Muslim mobs, 107, 126, 138, 141, 142, 153, 154, 155, 166, 174, 182, 193, 194, 213
Muslim personal law, 9
Muslims: anti-West sentiment among, 11, 86, 103, 121, 139, 148, 164, 180, 190, 191, 197, 200; Bosnian, 41, 66; hiding and defending Christians, 204; as in-group, 93; killed by Christians, 175, 184, 196; as majority, 3; in Nigeria, 73, 73–74, 75, 76–78, 79, 93–94; and non-Muslims, 84; as perpetrators of violence, 91, 94, 183, 190–191, 197, 201, 203–204, 208; Shi'ite (Shiite), 148, 149, 209; Sufi tensions between brotherhoods, 6; as target of ethno-religious conflict, 111; unity among, 14; as victims of Islamic fundamentalists, 194; as victims of violence, 111, 168, 183, 196, 217. *See also* Hausa-Fulani Muslims; Islam; Muslim-Christian hostilities; Muslim youths
Muslim sects, 107. *See also* Boko Haram; Islamic fundamentalists; Maitatsine riots
Muslim youths, 107, 126, 139, 142, 155, 166, 175, 183, 208
mutilation, 27, 112, 131, 140, 145, 154, 158, 170
mutiny, 117, 130, 214

Nanking, 62
narcissism, as cause of genocide, 46–47
National Council for the Welfare of the Destitute, 212
National Party of Nigeria (NPN), 137
National Republican Convention (NRC), 147
nation-states, 30, 32–38, 33
Native Authority (NA) system, 81
The Nature of Prejudice (Allport), 88
Nazi Holocaust. *See* Holocaust
Nazis: and classification of people by biosocial attributes, 31; extermination of Jews by, 52, 53, 57; genocidal atrocities committed by, 24, 29, 42, 44, 44–45, 52, 54, 60; hate campaigns of, 44; killing of Soviet citizens and Slavs by, 29; quest for pure Aryan race, 44, 45, 54; and racist crime, 58. *See also* Holocaust
Niger (state), violence in, 176, 211, 215
Nigeria: conflicting cultures in, 79–80, 148; creation of additional states in, 15, 133, 147; environmental damage in, 33; ethnic and religious diversity in, 72, 75, 210–211; factors inimical to unity in, 72–73; foreign exchange in, 78; geographical framework, 86, 125–126, 155, 166, 182, 190; history of, 72–73; income inequity in, 78–79; at independence, 116; as Islamic nation, 76, 77, 78, 80, 85, 136, 140, 148, 180, 190, 195, 197, 200, 201, 220; Islamization of, 78, 85, 96, 205, 219, 223–224; land distribution in, 77; North/South ideological split in, 75, 121, 153–154, 164, 180, 195, 200, 210–211; oil and mineral resources in, 77, 78–79; polarization in, 223–224; political instability in, 75; present borders of, 7; regionalism vs. federalism disputes in, 118, 120;

religion in, 72–75, 76; tax revenue in, 78; traditional religions in, 72, 73, 75. *See also* coup d'état (in Nigeria); Nigerian republics; Northern Nigeria

Nigerian Constitution, 79

Nigerian Police Force (NPF) : inactivity of, 152, 163, 214; as perpetrators of violence, 141, 161, 167, 183, 214–215; rioters masquerading as, 185; as targets of violence, 111, 142, 168, 183, 186, 194, 199, 218; as victims of violence, 112, 138, 143, 145, 156, 176, 208

Nigerian republics: First Republic, 12, 16, 83, 116; Second Republic, 133, 147; Third Republic, 147; Fourth Republic, 159; return to democracy in, 16; Unitary republic, 119–120

non-Muslims: as minorities, 14, 76, 77, 191, 202, 219; and Muslims, 84; in Northern Nigeria, 12, 13, 14; as out-group, 93; opposition to Sharia by, 76–77, 85, 104, 160, 164, 180, 200; as victims, 85, 95, 96, 104, 135, 160, 162, 169, 171, 180, 197, 199–200, 202, 204, 205, 207, 219, 223, 224, 225

Northern Elements Progressive Union (NEPU), 11–12

northern Ireland, 93

Northern Nigeria: *almajiri* system in, 211–213; colonial, 7–12; early settlers to, 4; efforts at unity in, 16; pre-colonial, 3–7; protectorate established in, 7; since independence, 12–17. *See also* Nigeria; Northern Nigeria ethno-religious conflict

Northern Nigeria ethno-religious conflict, 38, 120, 153, 160; participants by region/state, 108; participants in, 107–111; phase one, 116–118; phase two, 133–137; phase three, 147–152; phase four, 159–163; phase five, 173–178; prescriptive recommendations, 226–228; prospects for resolution, 225–226; victim or target groups, 110–111. *See also Genocidal Proclivity* model; genocidal proclivity in Northern Nigerian ethno-religious conflict; genocide in Northern Nigeria; Northern Nigeria ethno-religious conflict as genocide; Northern Nigeria ethno-religious conflict history; Northern Nigeria ethno-religious conflict theoretical framework

Northern Nigeria ethno-religious conflict as genocide, 218–220, 224–225; phase 1, 193; phase 2, 194–195; phase 3, 195; phase 4, 196–197; phase 5, 198–200; summary, 201–205, 205

Northern Nigeria ethno-religious conflict history: colonial, 7–12; historic underpinnings, 225–226; pre-colonial, 3–7; since independence, 12–17

Northern Nigeria ethno-religious conflict theoretical framework : demographic factors, 75–77; economic factors, 78–79; elite theory analysis, 80–84; exclusionary ideology theory analysis, 84–87; hate theory analysis, 87–90; historical factors, 72–73; political factors, 77–78; psycho-cultural factors, 79–80; relative deprivation theory analysis, 90–92; religious factors, 73–75; social cubism analysis, 71–80; Social Identity Theory analysis, 92–95; summary, 95–96

Northern People's Congress (NPC), 11–12, 12, 13, 201

"northernization" policy, 13, 134, 223

Nzeogwu, Kaduna, 116, 201

Obasanjo, Olusegun, 133, 148, 159, 163

Ogoni people, 33

Oil, Politics and Violence: Nigeria's Military Coup Culture (1966-1976) (Siollun), 117

oil resources, 77, 78–79

Ojukwu, Chukwuemeka Odumegwu, 116, 117, 118, 124, 129, 131

Onitsha, violence in, 166, 173, 174, 183, 198
oppression, 26–27
Organization of African Unity (OAU), 124
Organization of Islamic Conference (OIC), 136, 140, 195
Orkar, Gideon, 147
"other," dehumanization of, 42
"othering," as factor in genocide, 26, 46, 51, 203, 218
"otherness," perceived threat of, 102, 103, 120, 139, 140, 152, 153, 154, 163, 164, 165, 180, 200, 203

paganism, 72–73
Pakistan, 201
Pam, James, 117
Pam, Timothy, 117
Peacekeeping Operations Department (DPKO), 67
Plateau state, violence in, 161, 165, 166, 169, 170, 174, 175, 179, 185, 196, 203, 211, 215, 216, 217, 219
pogroms, 101, 106, 121, 125, 131, 140, 141, 152, 154, 155, 157, 165, 181, 190, 195, 197, 200, 202
police. *See* Nigerian Police Force (NPF)
politicide, 25, 50
politics, link to psychology and culture, 41
Pol Pot, 25, 42, 201
post-modernism, 87
poverty, 78, 79, 90, 103, 120, 139, 153, 179, 190, 195, 212, 216
power : concentration of, 81, 82, 83; manipulation of Islam for, 16, 95, 148–149; power relationships, 80–81; power struggles, 138, 153, 179; social class and, 81–84
prejudice, 50, 88, 93, 96
press: censorship of, 111, 128, 143, 168, 190; international, 217
primal horde, 40
propaganda, 89
property damage and destruction, 26, 91, 135, 137, 144, 145, 149, 150, 158, 170, 176, 183, 187, 194, 195, 209, 215, 227

property seizure, 95
Protestant-Catholic hostilities, 93
protests, 121; against US campaign in Afghanistan, 102, 162, 164, 197. *See also* riots and rioting
Provisional Ruling Council of Nigeria, 148, 159
psychological groups, 43

Qadiriyya brotherhood, 6, 11, 12, 136
Qur'an. *See* Koran

racism, relationship with crime, 58–59
radio, used for manipulation, 44–45
railway construction, 9
rape, 28, 45, 63, 124, 135
Red Cross, 123, 125, 160, 174, 175
refineries, violence against, 124
refugees, 112, 118, 130, 131, 145, 157, 170, 185, 186, 190, 200
relative deprivation theory, 90–92, 95, 96
religion: in Nigeria, 72–75, 151; politicization of, 75, 77, 103, 120, 134, 137, 149, 163, 179; relationship with ethnicity, 151, 207; traditional, 72, 73, 75. *See also* animist groups; Christianity; Christians; Islam; Muslims; paganism; traditionalists
religious extremism, 102, 138, 152, 163, 179, 195, 200
religious fervency, 140, 164
religious fundamentalism, 121, 138, 140, 180, 190, 195, 200
reprisal killings: by Christians, 194, 219; as context for proclivity to genocide, 111, 119, 138, 141, 143, 155, 156, 163, 165, 166, 168, 181, 182, 183, 184, 190, 205; in the coup d'état, 102; in Jos, 94, 175, 179, 200; in Kano, 204, 217; by military, 214; by Muslims, 137, 194; in Onitsha, 174, 183, 198; for post election violence, 183; in southern states, 91, 106, 107, 110, 125, 141, 155, 165, 166, 167, 168, 181, 182, 183, 197, 198
resources : distribution of, 78–79; exploitation of, 83; oil and mineral resources, 77, 78–79

retaliation, 181, 182, 183, 184, 186, 190, 200, 210; cattle theft as, 165; in the counter-coup, 117; destruction of mosques as, 145, 186; discouraged by Christian church, 167; for the Kafanchan violence, 138; for religious violence, 216; for Yelwa killings, 167, 196, 214. *See also* reprisal killings; retribution

retribution : destruction of mosques as, 184; sectarian, 179; threat of, 52. *See also* reprisal killings; retaliation

riots and rioting, 121, 126, 150, 212; anti-government, 102, 106, 120, 121, 134, 138, 152, 153, 154, 163, 179, 181, 189, 194, 195, 196, 200; anti-Igbo, 116, 119, 120; in protest of beauty pageant, 102, 189, 197, 210; in protest of U.S. action in Afghanistan, 102, 162, 164, 197; religious, 148, 154, 195; in response to Danish cartoon, 102, 173–174, 181, 189, 198; Tafawa Balewa, 81, 116, 119, 149, 157, 195; urban, 17

Roca, Julio Argentino, 32

Roma people. *See* Gypsies

Rome Statute of the International Criminal Court, 29, 191

Roosevelt, Theodore, 32

Runciman, Walter, 91

Russia, 42, 47; German murders in, 52; purges under Stalin, 54; response to Biafra Nigeria War, 128, 129

Russians, demonization of, 53

Rwanda, 27, 29, 30, 44, 49, 52, 54, 57, 59, 61, 62, 67, 68–69, 228; genocide in, 21, 22, 23, 45, 52, 58, 89–90, 201

Rwandan International Criminal Tribunal, 29, 192

Sarduana of Sokoto. *See* Caliphate of Sokoto

scapegoating, 45

schools: Christian, 86, 95, 164; violence against, 86, 111, 112, 124, 126, 127, 162, 164, 174, 183, 186, 199

sect members, arrest and persecution of, 138, 152, 163, 179

security agents: as conflict party, 107, 110, 166, 182; as perpetrators of violence, 140, 155, 167, 183, 194, 198, 214; as victims, 111, 135, 136, 138, 142, 145, 156, 168, 176, 183, 194, 199

Serbia, 52, 66

settler colonialism, 28

settler/non-indigene issues, 10, 45, 75, 78, 103, 151, 161, 164, 178, 179, 209, 211, 216, 227

Seyawa Christians, 149, 195

Shagari, Shehu, 81, 133, 134

Sharia Enforcement Agency (HISBA), 164, 197

Sharia law: abuse of Christians due to, 85, 86, 104, 140, 164, 170–171, 203, 205, 211, 218, 219, 220; adoption of by Nigerian states, 16, 84; as basis for "othering", 218; and Boko Haram, 175, 187, 198; debates in the Constituent Assembly over, 137, 159–160; historic application of, 5, 6, 8, 8–9; institution in northern states, 75, 84, 85, 91, 104, 195, 208, 223; implementation of, 163, 164, 219, 223–224; in Katsina, 154; move to impose across Nigeria, 180, 187, 190, 191, 196–197, 200, 201, 208; imposition of, 193, 219, 223–224; and Islamization, 85, 96; in Nigeria, 137; non-Muslims' opposition to, 76–77, 85, 104, 160, 164, 180, 200; as relates to ethno-religious conflict, 86, 87, 103, 111, 154, 164, 169, 180, 185, 193; Sharia implementation program, 196; Sharia restoration campaign, 16; in Zamfara, 16, 84, 162, 196–197, 210

Shekarau, Ibrahim, 215

Shi'ite (Shiite) Muslims, 148, 149, 209

Shonekan, Ernest A.O., 147

shootings, 131, 185

slavery, 5, 6

social chaos, 112, 131, 145, 158, 171, 187

social class, and power, 81–84

social cubism, 71–80, 95

Social Democratic Party (SDP), 147

Social Identity Theory, 92–95, 95–96, 96, 211

social revolution, and genocide, 29
Sokoto, 3, 6, 7, 12; violence in, 185, 211, 215
Sokoto Caliphate, 5–6, 7, 12; center-periphery model, 3; ethnic groups in, 4. *See also* Caliphate of Sokoto
Songhai Empire, 5
Southern Nigeria: Igbos from, 131; North's fear of dominance by, 119, 120, 134, 190; as predominantly Christian, 75, 110, 120, 142, 164, 167, 183, 194, 200, 203, 211, 219, 223; protectorate of, 7; reprisals in, 91, 106, 107, 125, 141, 155, 165, 166, 167, 168, 181, 182, 197, 198; retaliatory attacks in, 174, 219
Soviet Union. *See* Russia
Soyinka, Wole, 128
Srebrenica catastrophe, 67
Stalin, Josef, 29, 42, 46, 54, 61
starvation, 15, 112, 118, 122, 123, 124, 125, 130, 190, 193, 202, 214, 218
state-building, and genocide, 29
stereotyping, 88, 94
sterilization, forced, 23, 60
strangers quarters, 94
Structural Adjustment Program (SAP), 148
Sudan, 45, 201, 228. *See also* Darfur
Sufi, tensions between brotherhoods, 6
suicide bombings, 104, 112, 176, 177, 178, 185, 212
Sultan of Sokoto. *See* Caliphate of Sokoto
Supreme Council for Islamic Affairs (SCIA), 148
Supreme Military Council (SMC), 117, 133

Tafawa Balewa riots, 81, 116, 119, 149, 157, 195
Tajfel, Henri, 92
Taliban, 103, 138
Taraba, violence in, 216, 219
Tarok Christians, 160, 163, 165, 196, 204
Tasmanians, annihilation of, 32
territorial nationalism, 27
terrorist activity, 26, 58, 106, 181
theocracy, Muslim demands for, 148

Thomson, George, 128
Tijaniyya brotherhood, 6, 11, 12, 136
Tiv/Jukun crisis, 153, 156, 157, 214, 216
Tojo, Hideki, 42
torture, 26, 27, 32, 124, 181
trade, trans-Saharan, 4–5, 7
traditionalists, 79
Tudjman, Franjo, 52
Turner, John, 92
Tutsi people, 21, 22, 44, 46, 52, 54, 57, 58, 59, 88, 90

Ukraine, mass murder in, 29
UNAMIR peacekeeping force, 69
unemployment, 78, 103, 120, 139, 153, 179, 190, 195, 216
United Nations: bombing of, 176, 199; military force of, 67; response to genocide by, 67
United States: ethnic diversity in, 36; narcissism in, 47; response to Biafra Nigeria War, 128, 129; westward expansion in, 32
UNPROFOR, 67
Upper Peru, genocide in, 62
uprisings, 138, 153, 155, 163, 179
urban riots, 17

Viet Nam, 62
Vietnamese minority (Cambodia), 24, 25, 58
violence: anti-Igbo, 78; attempts at intervention, 169; brutal, 200; continuing, 190–191; escalation of, 196; ethnic, 121, 140, 175, 196; excessive, 27; exterminatory, 31; inter-communal, 51; and the nation-state, 35; perpetrators of, 48, 55, 107, 112, 117, 126, 131, 142, 145, 155, 158, 166–167, 170, 182–183, 190, 191, 196, 215–216, 219; political, 26, 121, 165, 181; pre-meditated, 106, 121, 123, 125, 141, 154–155, 165, 181, 190, 195, 197, 200; against refineries, 124; religious, 48–49, 118, 134–135, 140, 152, 160, 163, 179, 216; sectarian, 92, 106, 140, 154, 165, 166, 181, 200, 215; tit-for-tat,. *See also* reprisal killings; retaliation; retribution 106, 111, 121,

143, 156, 165, 168, 184; urban riots, 17; assault; barbarism; beheadings; bloodbath; bodies mutilated or burned; bombs and bombings; carnage; churches and chapels, violence against; drive-by shootings; gun battles; hit and run shootings; killings; lynchings; maiming; mass killings; mass murders; massacres; mayhem; mosques, violence against; Muslim-Christian hostilities; mutilation; pogroms; rape; riots and rioting; shootings; torture

war, 23, 26; and genocide, 29; in pre-colonial Northern Nigeria, 5. *See also* Biafra Nigeria War
Warri, 123
Wase, violence in, 151, 163, 170, 203, 209
West African colonization, 7
Western philosophy opposition, 11, 86, 103, 121, 139, 164, 180, 190, 191, 197, 200
Why Men Rebel (Gurr), 90
women: as victims of violence, 24, 26, 33, 45, 124, 161, 162, 175, 198, 214; maltreatment of, 127; protection for, 23
World Muslim League, 13

Wusasa Christians, 139, 144, 194, 209, 213

xenophobia, 43. *See also* "other"; "othering"; "otherness"

Yakubu, Yahaya, 149
Yar'Adua, Umaru, 74, 173
Yelwa, violence in, 151, 160–161, 162, 165, 166, 167–168, 168–169, 170, 178, 182, 196, 204, 209–210, 214, 215, 216, 217, 219
Yobe, violence in, 17, 176, 198, 211, 215, 219
Yorubas : under colonialism, 11, 72, 73, 75, 76, 81; reaction to massacre of Igbos, 128; as victims, 139, 141, 167, 202, 208, 219
Yugoslavia, 42, 61, 66, 201
Yusuf, Mohammed, 176, 181

Zamfara, violence in, 162, 169, 171, 196–197, 210, 211, 215
Zangon Kataf, violence in, 76, 151–152, 153, 154, 155, 156, 209
Zaria, violence in, 76, 135, 137, 138, 139, 140, 141, 142, 144, 148, 152, 157, 178, 194, 209, 213, 215
Zimbardo experiments, 40
Zuru Christians, 76

About the Author

Grace Okoye is a conflict resolution practitioner from Nigeria, with interests in genocide intervention measures and developing non-violence means to peace settlement using dialogue, negotiation, and other alternative dispute resolution approaches. She holds a Master's degree in International Administration from the University of Miami, and a Doctorate in Conflict Analysis and Resolution from Nova Southeastern University. Dr. Okoye is married with five children.